C000148425

Born in Lancashire and educat[...] Anthony Holden was an award [...] prolific writer and broadcaster. [...] praise for his translations of Greek poetry and opera libretti as well as his definitive biographies via wide range of figures, both living and historical.

Best-known for his studies of Tchaikovsky, Laurence Olivier and the Prince of Wales, Holden has also written a history of the Hollywood Oscars and *Big Deal*, an account of a year as a professional poker-player which was praised by enthusiasts from Walter Matthau and David Mamet to Salman Rushdie. These were followed by *Bigger Deal: A Year on the New Poker Circuit* and *Holden on Hold'em: How to Play and Win at the Biggest Deal in Town*. He has published poetry, music and drama criticism, and polemical pamphlets advocating constitutional reform. He has recently co-edited the anthologies *Poems That Make Grown Men Cry* and *Poems That Make Grown Women Cry* with his son Ben Holden.

Anthony Holden has presented numerous TV documentaries, and continues to write regularly for a wide range of newspapers and periodicals on both sides of the Atlantic. He is a Fellow of the Centre of Scholars and Writers at the New York Public Library.

By Anthony Holden

The St Albans Poisoner

Charles, Prince of Wales

Olivier

Big Deal: A Year as a Professional Poker Player

Bigger Deal: A Year on the New Poker Circuit

Holden on Hold'em: How to Play and Win at the Biggest Deal in Town

The Oscars: The Secret History of Hollywood's Academy Awards

The Tarnished Crown: Crisis in the House of Windsor

Tchaikovsky

Diana: A Life, A Legacy

The Mind Has Mountains (co-ed.)

There Are Kermodians (co-ed.)

Charles at Fifty

William Shakespeare: His Life and Work

The Drama of Love, Life and Death in Shakespeare

William Shakespeare: An Illustrated Biography

The Wit in the Dungeon: A Life of Leigh Hunt

Lorenzo Da Ponte: The Man Who Wrote Mozart

Poems That Make Grown Men Cry (co-ed. with Ben Holden)

Poems That Make Grown Women Cry (co-ed. with Ben Holden)

JOURNALISM

Of Presidents, Prime Ministers and Princes

The Last Paragraph: The Journalism of David Blundy (ed.)

TRANSLATION

Aeschylus' Agamemnon

The Greek Anthology (contrib.)

Greek Pastoral Poetry

Mozart's Don Giovanni (with Amanda Holden)

The Wit in the Dungeon
A Life of Leigh Hunt

ANTHONY HOLDEN

ABACUS

First published in Great Britain in 2005 by Little, Brown

This paperback edition published in 2016 by Abacus

1 3 5 7 9 10 8 6 4 2

Copyright © 2005 Anthony Holden

The moral right of the author has been asserted.

A CIP catalogue record for this book
is available from the British Library.

ISBN 978-0-349-11770-6

Typeset in Perpetua by M Rules
Printed and bound in Great Britain by
Clays Ltd, St Ives plc

Papers used by Abacus are from well-managed forests
and other responsible sources.

Little, Brown
An imprint of
Little, Brown Book Group
Carmelite House
50 Victoria Embankment
London EC4Y 0DZ

An Hachette UK company
www.hachette.co.uk

www.littlebrown.co.uk

For Joe

'common stock in trouble as well as joy'

CONTENTS

You will see Hunt – one of those happy souls
Who are the salt of the earth, and without whom
This world would smell like what it is – a tomb;
Who is, what others seem; his room no doubt
Is still adorned with many a cast from Shout,
With graceful flowers tastefully placed about;
And coronals of bay from ribbons hung,
And brighter wreaths in neat disorder flung;
The gifts of the most learned among some dozens
Of female friends, sisters-in-law, and cousins.
And there is he with his eternal puns,
Which beat the dullest brain for smiles, like duns
Thundering for money at a poet's door;
Alas! it is no use to say, 'I'm poor!'
Or oft in graver mood, when he will look
Things wiser than were ever read in book,
Except in Shakespeare's wisest tenderness. –

Shelley, 'Letter to Maria Gisborne', 1 July 1820

Posthumous Poems, 1824

I now know that Keats was a boring, conceited, self-pitying, self-
indulgent silly little fool . . . as well as an incompetent,
uninteresting, affected, non-visualising, Royal-Academy-picture
salacious, mouthing poet. He's still better than Shelley, though.
Shelley didn't have Keats's excuse of not knowing any better. Leigh
Hunt was a better man and poet than either.

Kingsley Amis, letter to Philip Larkin, 4 August 1950

The Letters of Kingsley Amis, 2002

PROLOGUE

When Leigh Hunt died in the summer of 1859, even his local paper in west London expressed surprise that he had still been alive. Since the height of his fame forty years earlier, as a second-generation Romantic poet on a par with Keats and Shelley, and a political journalist jailed for his beliefs, the world had moved far on. Though respected in the Victorian era as an elder statesman of English letters, Hunt had long since lost his public.

In the first few years of the twenty-first century, as this book has been gestating, there have been signs of a revival of interest in Hunt unprecedented since his lifetime, perhaps even since his eventful youth. The publication in 2003 of a posthumous *Festschrift*, with the professed goal of restoring Hunt to his 'rightful prominence', proved but the prelude to a six-volume reissue of his *Selected Writings*, weighing in at 2784 pages and a purchase price of £495, which aspired to present Hunt as 'unmistakably, one of the leading writers of his age'.

Towards the end of 2003 this moved the *London Review of Books* to note the 'growing awareness of the significant contribution [Hunt] made to poetry and belles-lettres' amid 'a belated realization that . . . he was one of the most important radical journalists of the early nineteenth century'. Reviewing the same volumes in March 2004, the *Times Literary Supplement* finally acknowledged that Hunt 'embodied the spirit of his age as emphatically as any of his contemporaries', declaring him fit 'to stand alongside Hazlitt and Lamb' as 'a shrewder, more eloquent and more conscientiously consistent advocate for social and aesthetic reform than critics have previously appreciated'.

This was surely the most generous remark made about Hunt in the century-plus history of the *TLS*. During the twentieth century interest in Hunt all but evaporated; his name was kept fitfully alive only by a handful of disparate, often rather unlikely admirers, as if he were the obscure guru of some long-defunct cult. In her diary for 13 August 1921, Virginia Woolf hailed Hunt as 'our spiritual grandfather, a free man . . . a light man, I daresay, but civilized . . . These free, vigorous spirits advance the world.' Appearing on BBC Radio's *Desert Island Discs* in April 1975, the then Poet Laureate John Betjeman, asked which poets had most influenced him as a young man, replied: 'William Blake first. Nursery rhymes, then William Blake, then Keats, Leigh Hunt, and most of all Tennyson.'

Beyond these unlikely bedfellows – Woolf, Betjeman and Kingsley Amis (as biliously quoted on p. viii of this book) – posterity has been less kind to Hunt than his contemporaries, Romantic or Victorian. Immortalised in verse tributes by Keats and Shelley, admired (until they fell out) by Byron, praised by fellow writers from Hazlitt and Lamb, Carlyle and Macaulay to Elizabeth Barrett, Charlotte Brontë and Elizabeth Gaskell, Tennyson, Browning and Thackeray, even his eventual nemesis Dickens, Hunt proceeded to disappear almost without trace, except as a malign influence on Keats in the steady stream of studies of the prematurely deceased poet whose name so swiftly came to overshadow that of his mentor, champion and friend. The same was true of Hunt's closest friend, Shelley, even more so of Byron, and to some extent of Hazlitt, Lamb, Carlyle and others. Only as a walk-on cameo player in the biographies of others did Hunt live on, usually in disparaging terms, always as a lesser man.

Few have summed up the Hunt dilemma better than one of the first editors of a collection of his essays, Arthur Symons, thirty years after Hunt's death: 'The position of Leigh Hunt in our literature might easily be exaggerated, and still more easily underestimated.' By way of explanation, the editors of the recent *Selected Writings* point out that assessments of Hunt's position in English literature have been frustrated by the absence of 'anything resembling' a collected edition of his work. Definitive editions of De Quincey, Lamb and Hazlitt all appeared around the turn of the twentieth century, yet Smith and Elder's seven-volume set of Hunt's later work, published in the 1870s, remained unmatched until Pickering and Chatto's six-volume selection at the beginning of the twenty-first.

Even that exemplary edition, beyond the financial reach of all but libraries, does not entirely satisfy the complaint of Sir Edmund Gosse in 1923 that Hunt remained 'alone among the leading writers of his age' in that 'no definitive or even collected edition of his works has been forthcoming'. It would also have pleased the Victorian critic George Saintsbury, without fully answering his protest at the lack of a 'complete and uniform issue, the want of which . . . is never quite made up by a scratch company of volumes of all dates, sizes and prints'. Now even that 'scratch company' has long since been dispersed.

If the renewed interest at the start of the present century does prove to herald a renaissance in Leigh Hunt studies, it is woefully overdue. Since his death Hunt has had but few significant champions, primarily the First World War poet Edmund Blunden, whose critical study of 1930 was the only book in English before this one that could lay claim to being a full-length biography. During his long academic exile in Hong Kong, Blunden also enjoyed rare (and unlikely) access to a complete set of Hunt's journal *The Examiner*, which resulted in his *Leigh Hunt's 'Examiner' Examined* (1928); a fellow 'Bluecoat', or alumnus of Christ's Hospital, Blunden also paid surrogate homage to Hunt (as well as Coleridge and Lamb) in coediting a history of their alma mater, *The Christ's Hospital Book* (1953).

Sixty years after Hunt's death, Blunden rightly observed that 'a careful life of Leigh Hunt should have been written many years ago, when some who had known him were still alive, and when the documents were still mainly assembled'. Soon after Hunt's death, his son Thornton edited a new edition of his *Autobiography*, as well as his *Collected Poems* and a two-volume edition of his *Correspondence*. Otherwise the first attempt at a Life, by the poet Cosmo Monkhouse in 1893, represented little advance on Hunt's own rambling, self-indulgent, largely recycled autobiography (1850, revised 1860, republished in a single volume edited by the historian J.E. Morpurgo, then director-general of Britain's National Book League, in 1949; ten years later Stephen F. Fogle edited a slim but invaluable volume of the work's 'earliest sketches' for the University of Florida). In 1928 the American scholar George Stout published his Harvard doctoral thesis under the title *Studies Towards a Biography of Leigh Hunt*; and the British critic Reginald Brimley Johnson essayed a brief life in his 1896 appraisal of Hunt's writings – emulated the best part of a century later, in 1977, by James R. Thompson of the University of Michigan in Twayne's English Authors series. But it took a Frenchman, Louis Landré, to offer the most complete survey of Hunt's life and work yet attempted, when he converted his own doctoral thesis into the exhaustive two-volume, nine-hundred-page *Leigh Hunt: Contribution à l'histoire du Romantisme anglais* (1936), the first volume a *tour d'horizon* of Hunt's life and significance, the second a critical analysis of his writings – neither of which has ever been republished or translated into English.

Landré received invaluable assistance from the American collector Luther R. Brewer, whose *My Leigh Hunt Library: The First Editions* (1932) and *The Holograph Letters* (1938) spell out the Hunt letters in his unique collection, now in the library of the University of Iowa. The somewhat obsessive Brewer also used to publish each year a Christmas volume for his friends, usually concerning some arcane aspect of Huntiana, which also unveiled useful if random material. In the mid-twentieth century the American husband-and-wife team of Lawrence and Carolyn Houtchens edited ground-breaking anthologies of Hunt's political and occasional essays and dramatic criticism, while Theodore Fenner of the University of Michigan performed the same service for his musings on opera. Some of Hunt's reviews and contemporary reviews of his own work were also collected in Donald H. Reiman's nine-volume anthology *The Romantics Reviewed: Contemporary Reviews of British Romantic Writers* (1972).

As an essayist, Hunt was well served in anthologies edited by, among others, Arthur Symons (1888 and 1903), Brimley Johnson (1891) and J.B. Priestley (1925); Johnson also edited a collection of his prefaces (1927). Thereafter Hunt's many millions of words were allowed to drift out of print until Manchester's Carcanet Press published a slim selection of his writings in 1990, edited with a brief introduction by the former head of English at Christ's Hospital, David Jesson Dibley.

American academics and their university presses have sporadically come up with handy labours of love, such as a 1973 facsimile reprint of Alexander Mitchell's 1931 bibliography, which is supplemented by further bibliographies edited by David Bonnell Green and Edwin

Graves Wilson (Nebraska, 1964), Robert A. Hartley (Nebraska, 1978) and Timothy J. Lulofs and Hans Ostrom (Boston, 1985). But a 1970 reprint of Alexander Ireland's 1868 anthology of the writings of Hazlitt and Hunt was otherwise all that remained of him before Oxford published token samples in Michael O'Neill's *Literature of the Romantic Period: A Bibliographical Guide* and Duncan Wu's *Romanticism: An Anthology* (second edition), both in 1998. Facsimile editions of *Leigh Hunt's London Journal* and the *Companion* were published by AMS of New York in 1967 and 1976 respectively, and a fifteen-volume facsimile of the *Examiner* under his editorship (1808–22) by Pickering & Chatto of London in 1999.

Other recent, if shorter volumes have included Ann Blainey's *Immortal Boy* (1985) and Molly Tatchell's *Leigh Hunt and his Family in Hammersmith* (1969), the latter published by the Hammersmith Local History Group. The American academic David Cheney has long been at work on a complete edition of Hunt's correspondence; in the meantime, Eleanor M. Gates of Falls River, Connecticut, edited and published a meticulous if necessarily selective *Life in Letters* (1999), followed by a survey of Hunt's correspondence with Hazlitt (2000).

A slim volume of Huntiana edited by Robert A. McCown emerged from a symposium held on 13 April 1984, to celebrate the bicentenary of Hunt's birth, at the University of Iowa – now, thanks to the Brewer Collection, the incongruous world headquarters of Leigh Hunt studies. The other US-based treasure trove of Hunt documents is the Carl H. Pforzheimer Collection, housed in the New York Public Library since the Shelley connoisseur's death in 1957. Over thirty-five years this has now produced for Harvard University Press ten volumes of the monumental series *Shelley and his Circle*, the first four edited by Kenneth Neill Cameron, subsequent volumes by Donald H. Reiman and Doucet Devin Fischer. Volumes 9 and 10, which reach the end of 1820, appeared in the autumn of 2002. Their work continues.

Otherwise the twentieth century's disregard of Hunt continued through the New Historicists' domination of Romantic studies in the 1980s. But signs of a revival began during the Keats bicentenary of 1995, when Hunt figured prominently in several anthologies and critical works. The trend began with Rodney Stenning Edgecombe's *Leigh Hunt and the Poetry of Fancy* (1994) and continued with Jeffrey Cox's

Poetry and Politics in the Cockney School (1998), Richard Cronin's *The Politics of Romantic Poetry* (2000) and Ayumi Mizukoshi's *Keats, Hunt and the Aesthetics of Pleasure* (2001). But perhaps the most striking, if least academic and certainly least expected tribute to Hunt's dogged staying power came in the fifth year of the new millennium:

> And all the scene, in short – sky, earth and sea,
> Breathes like a bright-eyed face, that laughs out openly.

In 2004, one hundred and forty-five years after Hunt's death, this typically wide-eyed couplet was enjoying pride of place atop countless packets of Whole Earth organic cornflakes ('Nothing Artificial – Gluten Free'), available at most self-respecting supermarkets. How it got there is anyone's guess; either breakfast-cereal marketing is the highest an Eng. Lit. graduate can aspire to these days; or some bright advertising spark had been browsing through the third (1992) edition of the *Oxford Dictionary of Quotations*, where these undistinguished lines from the first Canto of Hunt's early poem *The Story of Rimini* appear as one of seventeen entries – an improvement, at least, on the mere seven he was granted in the second edition (1953), even if they had disappeared again by the fifth (1999).

What has Hunt's florid alexandrine to do with cornflakes, organic or otherwise? Let that pass. In its forlorn way this could be considered Leigh Hunt's finest literary hour; at last this long-suffering scribbler was reaching a far wider audience than he ever managed in his long lifetime – or indeed in the century and a half since his death, during which his name has sunk out of sight, crowded out by those of his more lasting contemporaries, from Keats, Shelley and Byron, Hazlitt and Lamb, to Carlyle and Thackeray, Tennyson and Dickens. The only pity is that he wasn't still around to pick up some much-needed royalties.

The present book could not have been written without the privilege of a Fellowship at the Dorothy and Lewis B. Cullman Center for Scholars and Writers at the New York Public Library in its inaugural year, 1999–2000, which enabled the author to mine the treasures of the above-mentioned Pforzheimer Collection and other departments of that great institution. He offers heartfelt thanks to the Center's founder, Dorothy Cullman, for adding the words 'and Writers' to its otherwise academic remit, without which he would never have gained admission; to the New York Public Library's president, Paul LeClerc, for his genial interest; to the Center's founder-director, Professor Peter Gay, for his unstinting advice, encouragement and friendship; to Pamela Leo, its assistant director, for her cheerful support; and, for one of the most enjoyable and productive years of my life, my fellow-Fellows Paul Berman, Sven Beckert, D. Graham Burnett, Kathleen Neale Cleaver, Pamela Clemit, Andrew Delbanco, Gregory Dreicer, Christian Fleck, Ada Louise Huxtable, Marion Kaplan, Allen Kurzweil, Howard Markel, Francine Prose and Harvey Sachs.

Also at the New York Public Library I must acknowledge the expertise and generosity of Stephen Wagner, curator of the Pforzheimer Collection, assisted by Laura O'Keefe, and their colleagues Doucet Devin Fischer, current co-editor of *Shelley and His Circle*, Daniel Dibbem and Elizabeth Denlinger; Virginia Bartow, curator of the NYPL's Rare Books department; Rodney Philips, then curator of the Berg Collection; Stewart Bodner of the Journals and Periodicals Collection; and Anne Skillion, editor of the house magazine, *Biblion*.

For further encouragement, friendship and hospitality during what turned out to be three years in New York, I also thank Tina Brown, Richard Cohen, Sharon and Denis Dalton, Sir Harold Evans, Everett Fahy, Sarah Giles, the late Walter Goodman, David Hershey, Christopher Hitchens, Nicholas von Hoffman, Susan Kamil, Stryker McGuire, David Plante, Peter Pringle, Eleanor Randolph, Kathy Robbins, Charles Simmons and friends, John Stravinsky and friends, Ed Vulliamy, Gully Wells, Catherine Williams and Maury Yeston.

Among Hunt scholars who have encouraged and advised me, I am especially grateful to Michael Eberle-Sinatra (formerly Michael Laplace-Sinatra) of the University of Montréal, and Robert Morrison of Queen's University, Kingston, Ontario, co-editors of the six-volume *Selected Writings*, both of whom were kind enough to read the book in manuscript and make many helpful suggestions. The same is true of my friend Charles Mahoney of the University of Connecticut, editor of Volume Four of the *Selected Writings*, and Professor John Barnard, formerly of Leeds University, a Keatsian kind enough to read the relevant chapters. For genial interest and support I am also grateful to David H.

Stam, director (now retired) of the Syracuse University Libraries, formerly Andrew W. Mellon Director of the Research Libraries, New York Public Libraries; Duncan Wu of St Catherine's College, Oxford, formerly of Glasgow University; and Dr Robert Woof, director of the Wordsworth Trust and resident curator of Dove Cottage, the Wordsworth home and museum in Grasmere.

The staff of the London Library were at least as helpful to me as they appear to have been to Hunt in the 1840s and beyond (see Chapter 12, pp. 289-90). He might have mourned the passing of the British Museum's reading room, but would have loved the sleek efficiency of the new British Library, whose staff were unfailingly obliging. I am grateful to James Powell of Pickering & Chatto for help in obtaining sets of the fifteen-volume reprint of the *Examiner* and six-volume *Selected Writings* which have recently given such a boost to Hunt studies. I have also received invaluable sustenance and support, through good times and bad, from several other writers and/or academics who also happen to be friends: Al Alvarez, Melvyn Bragg, Logan Browning, Marjorie Chadwick, John Hollander, John Jones, Sir Frank Kermode and John David Morley.

My late brother-in-law George Baty Blake generously gave me his first edition of the two-volume US edition of Hunt's *Men, Women and Books*; my friend Christian Digby-Firth undertook research from his and Hunt's alma mater, Christ's Hospital, to Hampstead's misnamed Vale of Health, and miraculously came up with that packet of organic cornflakes; Leigh Hunt's closest living descendant and dedicated 'keeper of the flame', Richard Russell CVO, former headmaster of St George's School, Windsor, offered hospitality, gifts of books and – an especial thrill – the inscription on the silver goblet presented to Hunt by the people of Plymouth in 1822 (p. 155), of which he is now custodian. He also compiled the family tree on p. 367.

My professional creditors are headed by my literary agent Gill Coleridge and her colleague Lucy Luck, and Time Warner's UK Publisher Ursula Mackenzie, with whose editorial skills I was reunited when she inherited a work originally commissioned by my friend Alan Samson, now Publisher of Weidenfeld & Nicolson. At Time Warner Books (UK) I am also very grateful to my desk editor, Stephen Guise; copy editor Richard Dawes; publicity director Rosalie Macfarlane and her colleague Tamsin Barrack; picture researcher Linda Silverman; and indexer Catherine Hookman. At Time Warner (US): my editor Asya Muchnick and publisher Michael Pietsch. All of the above were remarkably patient, beyond the call of duty, when my work ran into a prolonged if unexpected and unavoidable delay. Once I resumed my task, back home across the Atlantic, I was uniquely sustained by the interest and support of Jane Wellesley.

Even more than his elder and younger brothers, Sam and Ben, my son Joe Holden shared my mood swings throughout these five years, both in New York and London. Joe has richly deserved his dedication — even if neither this book nor its subject is or was as generous as he would see fit towards his literary hero, George Gordon, Lord Byron.

New York–London, 1999–2004.

'Fit for nothing but an author'

1784–1802

Leigh Hunt's grave in Kensal Green Cemetery, north-west London, is not easy to find. Though clearly marked on a helpful map for visitors – fork left past his friend Thackeray, straight on past Brunel, sharp right towards Trollope – monument number 13650 defies location as stubbornly as its coordinates, square 121, row 3.

The problem, for the visitor who knows the least about his quarry, is that Joseph Durham's distinctive bust of the 'immortal boy' would seem likely to stand out from a distance amid the otherwise featureless ranks of Victorian worthies and eccentrics peopling the now desolate deathscape that calls itself 'London's foremost necropolis'. Only after a despairing struggle through the winter mud, aghast at the cemetery's air of abandon, does the persistent pilgrim finally stumble upon Hunt's celebrated epitaph for Abou Ben Adhem – 'Write me as one that loves his fellow-men' – and thus upon the melancholy truth. Durham's handsome bust of Hunt, which took ten years to finance by public subscription after his death in 1859, has long since been lost to twentieth-century vandals.

It seems an aptly forlorn postscript to a long literary life in which so little went right, so much wrong, and such feverish energy was expended with such mixed results. There is now no surviving memorial to Hunt in the London he loved and so lavishly chronicled. Few, if any, of his more than eighty published works remain in print. He was poet, critic, editor, essayist, novelist and playwright, the mentor and friend of Keats and Shelley, colleague and sparring partner of Byron and Hazlitt, intimate of Lamb and Carlyle, Browning and Dickens. Alongside Wordsworth, who largely eschewed literary London, Hunt's was the longest nineteenth-century literary life, with the widest circle of acquaintance and as large a claim as any to the shaping of literary opinion.

The Victorian critic George Saintsbury granted Hunt 'almost the first place in a history of prosody'; a century later, in 1990, he was still regarded as having 'no rival in the history of English criticism' in Professor Ian Jack's Oxford survey of *English Literature 1815–1832*. Later writers have commended Hunt's gifts and his influence as an all-round man of letters, as friend and mentor to three remarkable generations of writers. Yet it was in none of these many roles, but in a court of law – as a journalist, a passionate advocate of radical reform – that James Henry Leigh Hunt first made his name.

On 10 December 1812, at the Court of the King's Bench, Westminster, a hand-picked jury of twelve loyal monarchists and true took ten minutes to agree that twenty-eight-year-old Leigh Hunt was guilty of what the supposedly impartial Lord Chief Justice called a 'foul, atrocious and malignant' libel against the Prince of Wales, also Prince Regent during the descent into madness of his father, King George III. For his outrage at the Prince's betrayal of the cause of Catholic emancipation in Ireland, Hunt was fined the huge sum of £500, required to come up with a further £500 as surety of his 'good behaviour' and jailed for two years.

Neither his health nor his finances would ever entirely recover. But this was the moment that made the name of a literary man, never primarily a political animal, who would outlive all his Romantic contemporaries to become an elder statesman of Victorian letters.

Hunt was born in the year Samuel Johnson died, and died in the year A.E. Housman, Conan Doyle and Jerome K. Jerome were born. The seventy-five years of his life uniquely span two distinct if interlinked eras of English life and literature, as the Romantic revolution was absorbed into the Victorian sensibility. On Wordsworth's death in

1850, the poet laureateship could have been Hunt's rather than Tennyson's, forty years after he had been the first to publish Keats and Shelley, had it not been for his youthful assault on royalty. Thirty-five years after his imprisonment, when his reputation stood high enough for Lord John Russell's government to award Hunt a state pension 'in consideration of his distinguished literary talents', the Prime Minister wrote personally 'to add that the severe treatment you formerly received, in times of unjust persecution of liberal writers, enhances the satisfaction with which I make this announcement'.

Hunt would live long enough for Dickens, born in the year of that libel trial, to look back on his imprisonment as 'a national disgrace'. At the time Keats wrote a sonnet protesting at the incarceration of Hunt – 'wrong'd Libertas' – 'for showing truth to flatter'd state'. And a high-spirited Lord Byron dashed off a verse invitation to his fellow poet Thomas Moore to join him in visiting Hunt in jail:

> Tomorrow, be with me, as soon as you can, sir,
> All ready and dress'd for proceeding to sponge on
> (According to compact) the wit in the dungeon . . .

Leigh Hunt's earliest memory was of a jail cell. 'The first room I have any recollection of is a prison,' he wrote late in life, no doubt intending a sly reference to that later imprisonment for his political beliefs which would serve as a lasting badge of honour. But this cell of his childhood memory was in a proto-Dickensian debtor's jail, where the large Hunt brood was confined because of the inability of its ageing paterfamilias, Isaac, to make ends meet. Like father, like son: the struggle to fend off debt would also be the undercurrent of Leigh Hunt's long and productive life – costing a gifted, industrious and virtuous, albeit eccentric and flawed man a higher place in literary history.

Hunt was always something of an alien presence in respectable English society, impervious to its rigid codes of conduct, not least because he was the child of American parents. His father was the son of another Isaac, rector of what was then the parish church of St Michael's (and is now the cathedral) in Bridgetown, Barbados. By Hunt's own account he was descended on his father's side from Tory cavaliers who 'fled to the West Indies from the ascendancy of

Cromwell', and on his mother's from 'a curious mixture of Quakers and soldiers' up to and including Irish kings (via the O'Briens or Bryans).

All his life Hunt, whose white skin was described by contemporaries as of unusually dark hue, laid exotic claim to a dash of 'creole' blood, hinting at miscegenation in his family's West Indian past. One friend would speak of his 'black eyes, and his mouth, which was expressive, but protruding: as is sometimes seen in half-caste Americans', another of his 'brisk and animated countenance, receiving its expression chiefly from dark and brilliant eyes, but supplying unequivocal evidence of that mixed blood which he derived from parent stock'; a third, alluding to his 'flow of animal spirits', observed that Hunt had 'tropical blood in his veins'.

On his Caribbean genes, in his brothers as well as himself, Hunt did not hesitate to blame 'a certain aversion from business'. As for his father, 'his West Indian temperament spoiled all'. Eschewing the family's ecclesiastical tradition, Isaac Hunt determined upon the law, persuading his indulgent parents to pay his way through college in Philadelphia and New York. He took his BA at the College of Philadelphia (now the University of Pennsylvania) in 1763 and his MA in 1771, moving on to another MA at King's College, New York (now Columbia University). A 'spoilt' son, according to his own, 'with plenty of money to spoil him more', the student Isaac became 'the scape-grace who smuggled in the wine, and bore the brunt of the tutors'.

On leaving Philadelphia, Isaac gave the farewell address at his graduation ceremony – during which, according to family lore, two young women present fell in love with him. Though much the same age, they were the daughter and sister of a wealthy local merchant named Stephen Shewell; either would have been quite a catch for the son of a colonial vicar. It was the daughter, Mary, whom the handsome, well-mannered Isaac chose to woo, reading her the classics of English poetry in his finely modulated voice – which seems also to have won over her mother, who persuaded her husband to abandon his plans for Mary to wed a wealthy neighbour's son. Instead she married Isaac Hunt in 1767, still 'against her father's pleasure'.

In the description of their grandson, Thornton Hunt, Isaac was 'a man rather under than above the middle stature, fair in complexion, smoothly handsome, so engaging in address as to be readily and undeservedly suspected of insincerity', while Mary was 'a tall, slender woman, with Quaker breeding, a dark thoughtful complexion, a heart tender beyond the wont of the world, and a conscience tenderer still'.

Tom Paine and Benjamin Franklin, whose offer of guitar lessons Mary shyly declined, were among visitors who gave some indication of the politics of the Shewell household. Come the revolution, by some accounts, the patriarch deemed it prudent to conceal the royalist sympathies he privately harboured; yet his son-in-law was openly and outspokenly of that persuasion – an active orator and pamphleteer, the future author of (among other such titles) *The Rights of Englishmen: An Antidote to the Poison now Vending by the Transatlantic Republican, Thomas Paine* (1791). Although mismatched from the start, in all but their capacity for mutual devotion through good times and bad, the Hunts had six children in eight years, four of whom survived infancy.

Then, in 1775, came the crisis which altered all their lives and, to some not inconsiderable extent, the course of nineteenth-century English literature. Renowned in those revolutionary days for his loyalty to the crown, in the detested shape of George III, Isaac Hunt was a sufficiently prominent dissident for a mob to descend on his house and drag him out, to be paraded in disgrace through the streets before being tarred and feathered. 'Conceive', as their (yet to be born) son shuddered fifty years later, 'the anxiety of his wife!'

But Isaac enjoyed a series of lucky escapes, the first due to a friendly officer who managed to overturn the barrel of tar standing ready to deprive Leigh Hunt's future father of any more children. Imprisoned overnight, he then managed to bribe a guard to help him escape. Finally, as doubly good fortune would have it, a merchant ship belonging to his father-in-law, Stephen Shewell, was departing that very night for his homeland, the West Indies. Isaac scrambled aboard to flee a certain death for his loyalist sympathies; after a brief, restorative sojourn with his family in Barbados, he finally took ship for England to begin a new life.

It was many months before his wife was able to catch up with him, all four sons in tow. The last time Mary Hunt had seen her

husband, he was 'a lawyer and a partisan, going out to meet an irritated populace'; on her arrival in England, she beheld him 'in a
pulpit, a clergyman, preaching tranquillity'. How deftly their
youngest son would capture, seventy-five years later, the dramatic
change in the Hunt family's fortunes; unable to continue as a lawyer,
which might have seen his family prosper as it had in America, Isaac
had eschewed the advice of some actors that he consider a career on
the stage and opted instead for a theatrical career in the church.
Ordained by the Bishop of London, he swiftly developed a reputation
as an inspirationally fiery preacher, to the point where he was
rebuked by his bishop for giving too many charity sermons – considered, because of the extensive advertising involved, ostentatious to a
point unbecoming his cloth.

But Isaac was essentially miscast as a clergyman; his faith was speculative and his way of life too convivial. Fond of claret and
conversation, he stinted himself in neither, to the point of falling out of
favour with the church authorities, if not his congregations. Carriages
crowded the doors of the churches where he preached, and one ardent
female fan even left him a handy legacy of £500. But Isaac, in his son's
estimation, was by nature 'a true exotic' who 'should have been kept
at home in Barbados', where 'he might have preached, and quoted
Horace, and drunk his claret, and no harm done'. His career as a
Universalist cleric in respectable London society was too cavalier to
thrive for long.

Isaac's sermons, delivered from the pulpit of Bentinck Chapel in
Lisson Green, Paddington, were elegant but empty, suggesting that
most of their appeal lay in the panache with which they were delivered.
Their appearance in print was vanity publishing, at his own expense,
and thus that of his parish landlord, who soon despaired of his rent and
evicted the maverick vicar. The four boys were farmed out to schools
or friends, while their parents gratefully accepted the hospitality of the
American painter Benjamin West, who had married Mary Shewell's
aunt – that other young woman who had so admired Isaac's farewell
address at Philadelphia.

Born in Pennsylvania, West had prospered since arriving in England
from Italy in 1763; a protégé of Joshua Reynolds, he enjoyed the admiration and patronage of the King, with whom he formed a friendship

unshaken even by his patriotic sympathy for the colonists during the American revolution. As George III's illness saw him withdraw from the public stage, after West had succeeded Reynolds as president of the Royal Academy, West's fortunes would falter; but that still lay some years ahead as this modest, good-hearted man took it upon himself to look out for his less fortunate relatives, offering them shelter in his comfortable home in Newman Street.

It was not too long before the Hunts, with West's assistance, found another home of their own in the rural village of Hampstead, four miles to the north-west of London, where Isaac enjoyed one more stroke of luck before finally landing his family in that debtor's jail. As a regular preacher in nearby Southgate, he won the admiration of the local squire, the Duke of Chandos – 'the grandson of Pope's and Swift's Duke of Chandos', as literary Leigh would proudly recall – who offered him the post of tutor to his son, James Henry Leigh. So it was while installed on the Duke's estate in a house named Eagle Hall that Isaac and Mary found she had conceived their seventh child. When a son was born on 19 October 1784, they paid Isaac's employer the gracious, if self-interested compliment of seeking his permission, which he was pleased to grant, to name the boy after his father's pupil: James Henry Leigh Hunt.

With yet another mouth to feed, the indigent preacher clung to two last hopes of advancement. A tutorship in a noble household could often prove a stepping stone to a bishopric; and his patron, the Duke, was a state officer (Master of the Horse) and a favourite of the King. So, too, was his kinsman West, who also petitioned the monarch on Isaac's behalf. But Isaac's outspokenness, not least against the recent conduct of His Majesty's government, proved his undoing. Even the King could not sway the bishops. All that could be secured on Isaac's behalf was a pension of a meagre £100 a year for his services to the loyalist cause. Had he stayed in America, he reflected, he would have been worth seven or eight times as much, while still pursuing a prosperous career in the law; as it was, this seemed poor reward for sacrificing that life (in, moreover, a 'cheaper' country) for his royalist beliefs – and not enough, as it proved, to keep him out of jail. 'My poor father!' sighed Leigh. 'He grew deeply acquainted with prisons.'

His mother, meanwhile, had not recovered (and never would) from the trauma of seeing her husband dragged out of their home, apparently to a grisly death, by that mob in Philadelphia. Her aversion to violence of any kind was so acute that she would avoid the park when walking her children, for fear of encountering a platoon of soldiers. She even went through great agonies when her youngest son played with a toy drum and sword; looking back, the elderly Hunt still seems surprised she permitted him to have such toys. 'Why? Because, if the sad necessity were to come, it would be her son's duty to war against war itself – to fight against those who oppressed the anti-fighters.' The seeds of his crusading, pacifist spirit were sown early.

A sickly, stuttering child, who had inherited from his mother a tendency to jaundice, and seemed to work his way through every childhood ailment known to medical science, the young Hunt meanwhile derived from his father a remarkable capacity to remain cheerful in adversity, showing the world a bright, optimistic face amid the direst of difficulties. Cruelly teased by his 'unimaginative' brothers, he inherited his mother's 'anxious, speculative' temperament. 'As I do not remember to have ever seen my mother smile, except in sorrowful tenderness,' he wrote late in life, 'so my father's shouts of laughter are now ringing in my ears.' This and their shared love of literature seem to have been the saving of his parents' marriage. Isaac's acutely long-suffering wife could apparently endure constant sickness, his frequent and sudden arrest for debt ('frightful knocks at the door') and all manner of domestic calamity for the sound of that well-modulated voice calmly reading to her each evening.

Although 'socially' inclined, according to Thornton Hunt, Leigh's father read 'eloquently and critically', his mother 'earnestly, piously, and charitably'. In their youngest son, soon joined by a baby sister, Mary, this rare parental panacea appears to have bred, from a very early age, an intense, almost animal affection for books and their contents. At the age of six the wordsmith-in-the-making was precocious enough to write to his aunt Lydia in Philadelphia: 'It is with pleasure I inform you that I have recovered my health, and can devote myself to my studies which consist at present in learning the Latin Nomenclature of which I can perfectly repeat 2,063 words. Writing also fills up some of my time. Books of amusement I read at my leisure . . .'

In later life this lover of words would suggest it was no coincidence that his father's name, Isaac, derived from the Hebrew for 'mirth' and his mother's, Mary, from that for 'melancholy'. The combination of the two would colour more than merely his early years. If, at his impressionable age, the youngest Hunt boy sensed in literature some sort of refuge from harsh reality, the same does not seem to have been true of his elder brothers, one of whom went to sea (a 'great blow' to his mother), the others being articled or apprenticed to a lawyer, an engraver and a printer respectively. Amid all his own vicissitudes, Isaac Hunt went to some lengths to see all his sons set up in promising careers. His own fortunes would eventually improve considerably, thanks to a legacy from a West Indian aunt, before his death in 1809 at the age of fifty-seven.

In 1791 all Isaac could do for his youngest son was throw himself on the mercy of the governors of a school with a nobly charitable tradition, Christ's Hospital, pleading a wife and five children, and 'humbly beseech your Worships, in your usual Pity and Charity to distressed Men, poor Widows and Fatherless Children, to grant the Admission of his said Child into Christ's-Hospital, named James Henry Leigh Hunt, of the Age of Seven Years & upwards, there to be Educated and brought up among other poor Children'.

Beyond the humiliation of producing evidence of his 'honest origins' and current poverty, Hunt's father was also obliged to consign his son's fate 'to the Disposal of the Governors of the said Hospital, to bind him an Apprentice to such Trade or Calling, whether for Land or Sea Employments, as they shall judge the said Child most fit and proper for' – by the age of fifteen at the latest.

Isaac's application proved successful. All that remained was to fulfil the school's requirement that his son be baptised – a surprising omission for an ordained minister, perhaps occasioned by his regular incarcerations – before, on 23 November 1791, handing over seven-year-old Leigh to be clad in the school's 'Bluecoat' uniform and removed from his parents' care to join six hundred other boys in a monastic cloister then in Newgate Street, in the shadow of St Paul's Cathedral. (Not until the early twentieth century was the school transplanted to its current site near Horsham, West Sussex.)

Founded by Edward VI in 1553, with the object of 'reducing the vagabondage and destitution which disgraced London in the sixteenth century', Christ's Hospital had swiftly grown into a high-class breeding ground for the professions, the Church and the services. Thanks to its charitable charter, it was unlike most English public schools in drawing pupils from all social classes, rarely from the nobility. A touching symbol of the school's comparative classlessness proved one of Hunt's lasting memories: 'In my time there were two boys, one of whom went up into the drawing-room to his father, the master of the house; and the other down into the kitchen to his father, the coachman.' Early products of Christ's Hospital had included two very different contemporaries of Shakespeare, the poet-playwright George Peele and the Catholic martyr Edmund Campion. As Hunt arrived 250 years later, recently departed alumni included such writers as George Dyer, Samuel Taylor Coleridge and Charles Lamb – the first to become a casual acquaintance, the second a distant hero, the third a lifelong friend.

A timid boy cursed with a nervous stammer, bred with his father's sense of duty to others but his mother's horror of violence of any kind, the young Hunt was required to make some fundamental psychological adjustments to survive the school's rigid disciplinary regime. Even the unwonted sight of boys fighting at first frightened him as 'something devilish'; to the end of his life he could recall the name of one of the first boys he saw condemned to corporal punishment, the very thought of which reduced him to tears. Even at so tender an age, however, Hunt carried in him considerable moral courage combined with a strong sense of right and wrong. He developed a reputation for standing up to bullies, whatever the consequences; and he endured daily beatings on the hand with a knotted handkerchief rather than agree to become an older boy's 'fag' (or lackey performing menial chores). The combination of his parents and his schooling was teaching him 'the power of making sacrifices for the sake of a principle'.

In later years, however speciously, Hunt would blame his ineptitude with figures – and thus with money – on the decision of the elders of Christ's Hospital to consign him to its Grammar rather than its Mathematics School. In truth, it was the making of him. The young Hunt didn't much care for Homer, Demosthenes and Cicero, but close study of Greek and Latin would bequeath him that natural ability to

shape stylish English sentences which is the good fortune of all writers
bred on the classics. This he soon began to practise in exercises such as
essays on 'Ambition' or 'The Love of Money' or the making of précis
of articles in the *Spectator*. Already he was teased by school-fellows as 'a
fool for refining' – which his son Thornton later defined as 'a hair-
splitting anxiety to be precise', which remained a 'leading foible'
throughout his life.

Like all such schools, Christ's Hospital had its share of distinctive
staff who would leave a lifelong impression on their pupils. In Hunt's
day there was William Wales, the mathematics master, every schoolboy's hero because he had sailed round the world with Captain Cook.
There was Matthias Hathaway, the Steward, whom the boys called 'the
Yeoman' in well-educated reference to Shakespeare's father-in-law. In
the lower school he enjoyed the kindly but lax supervision of the
Reverend Matthew Field, a good-natured but ineffective man who
'carried his cane like a lily' and daydreamed almost as much as his
pupils.

On graduating to the Upper School, however, Hunt could apparently do nothing to please its formidable senior master, the Reverend
James Boyer, generally accounted an inspirational teacher, but a stern
disciplinarian who took an instant dislike to this nervous, sickly, dark-
skinned waif with a hint about him of the rebellious colonies of his
parentage. Boyer had a habit of pinching his pupils under the chin, and
on the earlobes, until they bled. On one occasion, infuriated by Hunt's
stammering (which of course made it all the worse), he knocked out
one of the boy's teeth with a well-aimed volume of Homer.

But it was not for that reason that Hunt regarded Homer 'with
horror'. Resisting whatever he was force-fed, like so many school-
boys with a true, innate feel for literature, he revelled in those English
writers absent from the school syllabus, notably Spenser, Collins and
Gray. In retrospect it may have been a blessing that he was so at odds
with his teacher. Coleridge spoke of the 'inestimable advantage' of
having been taught literature by Boyer, 'a very sensible, though at the
same time a very severe master'. But Coleridge had been one of the
favoured whose essays were occasionally chosen – four times, in his
case – for inclusion in the sacred 'Book', or Liber Aureus, in which
pupils were invited to enter an essay or poem which had especially

pleased Boyer. Even Lamb, who left Christ's Hospital early, made it once into The Book.

But the record shows no entry by Leigh Hunt in Boyer's 'Book'; his essays were more often scrumpled up before the class and thrown to his fellow pupils, as to dogs, with a 'Here, children, there is something to amuse you.' Refugee-like, Hunt felt driven to seek his literary pleasures elsewhere, beyond the school bounds – at the circulating library in Leadenhall Street, for instance, or among the bookshops of Paternoster Row, where he 'doted on' the sixpenny editions of the English poets and became a 'glutton of novels'. Confined to the school infirmary after scalding his legs in a schoolboy prank, Hunt devoured Samuel Butler's *Hudibras* 'at one desperate plunge'.

In the infirmary, where he developed a schoolboy crush on his nurse's daughter, Hunt formed two lifelong habits: flirting and playing the invalid. More importantly, the combination of schoolboy bullying and magisterial tyranny bred a deep-seated resentment of injustice which would lead him to take bold, independent stands throughout his long life. 'Hunt's opposition to this system of "wanton school tyranny"', as the scholar Nicholas Roe observes of his objections to fagging, 'caught the revolutionary spirit of the 1790s, and marked the beginning of his career as an enemy to oppression.' With the consequences of the French Revolution swirling on the school's very doorstep, in the rush of radical pamphlets crowding the stalls of the booksellers in St Paul's Churchyard, Hunt himself was already aware that he 'unquestionably felt inclined to be an innovator; to redress wrongs; and to reconcile discords . . .'

More than most such schools, nonetheless, Christ's Hospital is recalled with rose-tinted affection by those alumni eminent enough to publish accounts of their early days. Hunt's own memories of the place (and its 'sacred cloister'd walks / That saw my early days pass quiet on') are no exception, not least because his formative years there seem to have nurtured the gift for friendship which would become as much a mainstay as a hallmark of his long life. By surrounding himself with a coterie of like-minded people, he derived the strength to take his own independent stands, the ability to separate 'my own sense of personal antagonism' from 'something at stake which, by concerning others, gave me a sense of support, and so pieced out my want with their abundance'.

Lasting friends from Christ's Hospital included the Le Grice brothers, Charles and Samuel, the elder of whom was described by Lamb as 'full of puns and jokes, very genial', the younger by Hunt as 'the maddest of all the great boys in my time: clever, full of address, and not hampered by modesty'. There was John Rogers Pitman, who would become an admired preacher and learned author; such writers-in-the-making as Barron Field and Thomas Mitchell, translator of Aristophanes and influential critic for the *Quarterly Review*; and Thomas Barnes, all-round athlete and scholar whose wit, courage and intellect would see him become one of the legendary editors of *The Times*. Barnes and Hunt liked to escape the school to go bathing and boating on the Thames. A typical vignette of their literary childhoods is Hunt's delighted memory of their learning Italian together, with anyone within earshot surely thinking them 'mad' as they 'went shouting the beginning of Metastasio's *Ode to Venus*, as loud as we could bawl, over the Hornsey fields'.

Christ's Hospital, as Hunt himself later noted, 'sent out more living writers, in its proportion, than any other school'. The teenage Hunt was soon remarkably well-read for his age. His enthusiasms already ranged eclectically, if far and wide, from Chaucer to the *Arabian Nights*, though his future hero Milton as yet remained more of a duty than a pleasure. For a great essayist in the making, his heart does not at this stage seem to have been in the writing of prose, or even the dread Boyer might have encouraged the boy, as he did with volumes of Pope and Johnson when Hunt showed more of a penchant for verse. The first poem he wrote consisted of lines in honour of the Duke of York's apparent 'victory' at Dunkirk (which, to his 'great mortification', turned out to be a defeat).

As he immersed himself in poetry, Hunt did not distinguish himself at Christ's Hospital. His shade would be as astonished as Boyer's to know that a royal visit in October 2003 saw Queen Elizabeth II look on as the school's president, the Duke of Gloucester, formally opened a newly refurbished boarding house called Leigh Hunt. By the time he left in 1799, at the age of fifteen, this 'Bluecoat Boy' had made it to the rank of 'first Deputy Grecian' but not, to his dismay, to the rarefied heights of 'Grecian' – those senior boys selected to go on to university. He had, however, accumulated enough polished poems to earn a much more unusual, if premature, distinction.

* * *

'In affectionate recollections of the place where he was bred up, in hearty recognitions of old schoolfellows met with again after a lapse of years, or in foreign countries, the Christ's Hospital boy yields to none,' wrote Charles Lamb. 'I might almost say, he goes beyond other boys.'

So it was with Leigh Hunt. For all his mixed feelings about his schooldays, later converted into undiluted gratitude for the excellent literary grounding he received, fifteen-year-old Hunt felt somewhat lost on leaving Christ's Hospital in November 1799. 'For some time after I left school,' he recalled, 'I did nothing but visit my schoolfellows, haunt the bookstalls, and write verses.' Many was the day he spent at the British Museum, being fed fowl and literature by the librarian Thomas Maurice, an old Bluecoat poet who had been a protégé of Dr Johnson. But most afternoons Hunt would end up hanging around the school gates, waiting to spend a few hours in the company of friends still there, missing 'the regularity and restriction' of the daily schedule to the point where he even felt 'the pressure of my hat, like a headache'.

'At the age of fifteen,' according to his son Thornton, 'he threw off his blue coat, a tall stripling, with West Indian blood, a Quaker conscience, and a fancy excited rather than disciplined by his scholastic studies.' By the end of his 'long semi-monastic confinement' at Christ's Hospital, the young Hunt took much more after his mother than his father. Where Isaac was 'in most things utterly unlike his son', Mary's 'thoughtful' and 'tender' nature 'contributed more than the father to mould the habits and feelings of the son. School and books did the rest.'

'A man is but his parents . . . drawn out,' mused Hunt towards the end of his life. But the young Leigh was 'little of a Hunt', according to Thornton, save in his 'gaiety' and avowed love of 'the pleasurable'. His 'natural energy, which showed itself in a robust frame, a powerful voice, a great capacity for endurance, and a strong will, seems to have been inherited from Stephen Shewell, the stern, headstrong and implacable . . . His mother transmitted her own material tendency to an over-conscientious, reflective, hesitating temperament, which drew back from any action not manifestly and imperatively dictated by duty. The son showed all these contradictory traits even in his aspect and bearing.'

Young Leigh was tall, all but six feet, with his height concentrated in his trunk rather than his legs; throughout his life, until stooped by old age, he was typically described as 'remarkably straight and upright in his carriage, with a short, firm step, and a cheerful, almost dashing approach – smiling, breathing, and making his voice heard in little inarticulate ejaculations.' He had straight black hair, parted in the centre, with black eyebrows beneath a 'singularly upright, flat, white forehead'. His brown eyes 'beamed . . . dark, brilliant, reflecting, gay and kind, with a certain look of observant humour', his mouth 'large and hard in the flesh' with a long upper lip, his chin 'retreating and gentle like a woman's', his sloping shoulders 'not very wide', his chest of 'ample' proportions . . . of a compass not every pair of arms could span'. In short, the young Hunt looked like 'a man cut out for action – a soldier'; but he 'shrank from physical contest, telling you that his sight was short, and that he was "timid"'.

With the family fortunes as parlous as ever, Isaac was impatient for his youngest son to find work. Insisting that he was 'fit for nothing but an author', Leigh proved his point by winning a literary competition in a magazine called the *Monthly Preceptor*, to which he had submitted a translation of Horace (beating into third place another young aspirant named Thomas De Quincey). So Hunt's proud father decided to show off his son's precocious talents to the world by publishing them as a not-so-slim volume, under the title of *Juvenilia*, financed by subscription.

'I was as proud, perhaps, of the book at the time as I am ashamed of it now,' Hunt would say in later years, declaring his teenage self's out-pourings 'a heap of imitations, all but absolutely worthless'. At the time it earned the young poetaster premature plaudits which showed no signs, as yet, of proving a mixed blessing.

His father's industry played as big a role as his connections in securing a remarkable list of names on both sides of the Atlantic willing to subsidise the promising but immature, derivative verse of sixteen-year-old Leigh Hunt. The roll-call of names thanked in the book's list of subscribers included an impressive array of aristocrats, churchmen (including the Archbishop of Canterbury), statesmen (including Henry Addington, George Canning, Charles James Fox and William Wilberforce) and lawyers – among them Lord Ellenborough, the future Lord Chief Justice who would a dozen years later preside over the boy poet's libel trial, and Sir Simon le

Blanc, who would pronounce the resulting jail sentence. A long list of artists, including Royal Academicians from Fuseli to Stubbs, were corralled by the ever-helpful Benjamin West, while Isaac himself rounded up an equally eminent array of religious and medical men. Literary subscribers were led by the Poet Laureate, H.J. Pye, the playwright Richard Brinsley Sheridan and the radical reformer John Horne Tooke. The names of several good-hearted Christ's Hospital masters were on the list, but not that of the Reverend James Boyer. One other notable subscriber was a kindly doctor named Batty, who gave the young poet a lock of Milton's hair, launching a collection which would become a lifelong obsession for Hunt, eventually covering the history of English literature from Milton, Swift and Johnson to the Romantic poets and beyond, not to mention Napoleon, George Washington and Lucrezia Borgia.

Dedicated to his noble namesake, the Hon. James Henry Leigh, on 17 May 1800, Leigh Hunt's *Juvenilia; or, A Collection of Poems Written between the ages of Twelve and Sixteen by J.H.L. Hunt, Late of the Grammar School of Christ's Hospital* proved successful (or voguish) enough to enjoy three more editions over as many years. By the fourth edition, of 1804, the list of subscribers included none other than Lord Nelson. But it is scant surprise that none of these adolescent effusions survived into the poet's later collections.

Even the adolescent Hunt felt obliged to warn the reader 'how much superior some of the following poems are to the others . . . written at a very early age'. The opening ode on *Macbeth* ('or The Ill Effects of Ambition') is declared, as if by way of apology for its orotund emptiness, to have been written at the age of twelve. Even so, it shows a remarkably precocious technique, as do the marginally more mature teenager's fluent if florid pastiches of Spenser and Pope, Dryden and Gay, Thomson and Johnson, even Akenside and Ossian; but the guiding spirit of the collection is the recently deceased William Collins, then as fashionable as now he is neglected. The young Hunt's eye for the visual arts is already evident in a Collins-esque ode, 'The Progress of Painting', acknowledging a touching debt to his kindly uncle West ('Britain's fav'rite') for introducing him to the delights of 'expressive Raphael . . . strict Correggio . . . Titian's glowing hand . . . Fus'li's gigantic fancy'.

All too typical was the clear echo of Coleridge's recently published 'Frost at Midnight':

> Reared
> In the great city, pent 'mid cloisters dim
> And saw nought lovely but the sky and stars.

in the young Hunt's 'Remembered Friendship':

> before the gentle sweets
> Of sleep had clos'd our eyes, how oft we lay
> Admiring thro' the casement open'd wide
> The spangled glories of the sky . . .

It says something for the paucity of the literary moment that the *Monthly Mirror* avowed that Hunt's *Juvenilia* contained 'proofs of poetic genius, and literary ability, which reflect great credit on the youthful author, and will justify the most sanguine expectations of his future reputation'. Singled out for attention as 'a specimen of the abilities of the juvenile bard' was his pedestrian 'Ode to Genius'. The child prodigy sent the editors a fulsome letter of thanks for 'your flattering critique on my juvenile trifles', enclosing further poems for potential publication. 'Song in Imitation of the Scotch manner' duly appeared in the *Mirror* of July 1801, and 'The Petition' in May 1802.

Suddenly young Hunt was the talk of the town, a 'young Roscius' lionised at literary salons and soirées. He had his portrait done by fashionable artists of the day, who captured the shy vulnerability in what was still the face of a child, for all its deep brow, resolute mouth, piercing brown eyes and newly grown beard. Proudly his father paraded him around town as 'the example of the young gentleman and the astonishment of the ladies'.

But Hunt's *Juvenilia* was to prove a deceptively false dawn, as Coleridge was one of the first to sense. 'Thank Heaven,' remarked Hunt's fellow Bluecoat, 'I was flogged rather than flattered! Thank Heaven, it was not the age nor the fashion of getting up prodigies! At twelve or fourteen I should have made as pretty a juvenile prodigy as was ever emasculated and ruined by fond and idle wonderment.'

How right he was. For the next four years Hunt would do little but write more derivative, unoriginal verse, still proclaiming to his family that he was 'fit for nothing but an author'. As his older self perceived, this early success had given him a false sense that he had 'attained an end, instead of not having reached even a commencement'.

2

'Needled & threaded out of my heart'

1802–9

On 8 March 1802, not for the first time, seventeen-year-old Leigh Hunt wrote an ornate letter to the editor of the *Poetical Register*, enclosing for his consideration some poems in the manner of Pindar. 'You will perceive, Sir, that I have sent you Ode, Epistle, Epitaph, Epigram, sentimental Song, Sonnet and Translation; to make this heterogeneous collection more complete, I would add a Pindaric, and an Anacreontic Song . . .'

The success of *Juvenilia* had added an unfortunately smug note to the young poet's voice. 'Believe me, Sir, it is not vanity which influences this second offer; but "si me tuis vatibus inseres," I think my Muse will not be a little proud of, Sir, your humble servant, J.H. Hunt.'

Three years earlier, while her son was still at Christ's Hospital, Mary Hunt had written to her father in Philadelphia that 'My boy Leigh is a steady, sensible, good boy.' Enclosing some of his poetic 'exercises' for his grandfather's perusal, she went on: 'They are serious and uncommon for his years. He is not yet fifteen.' Even now that his youngest grandson was a published poet, however, the stolid Stephen Shewell remained unimpressed by his literary success. If young Leigh would come to America, wrote his grandfather, he would 'make a man of him'. The proud young poet declined, boldly replying that 'Men grow in England as well as America' – an embryonic version of his later view that 'Americans are Englishmen with the poetry and romance taken out of them'.

The teenage Hunt's most striking characteristic, beyond literary precocity and a tendency to melancholy, was a restless, nervous energy which seemed to erupt spasmodically after long, sedentary sessions spent reading, reading, reading. Visiting his schoolfriend Papendieck in Oxford, Hunt was so absorbed in a novel that he almost drowned when their boat overturned; with another friend, John Robertson, he walked from Margate to Brighton, covering 112 miles in four days while 'chattering, laughing and eating prodigious breakfasts'. At 'squalid & clogged up' Sandwich, Hunt 'wondered how the Romans could come there for oysters'.

Large meals seem to have been the highlights of the excursion. If the travellers reached dinner-time without seeing an inn, they would boldly knock on the doors of farmhouses, and were always made welcome. At one such improvised meal they were waited on at table by the farmer's 'very pretty' daughter, moving a delighted Hunt to reflect that this was not the English fashion. 'No, God forbid,' he imagines some 'crabbed or debauched' reader of his reminiscences protesting. 'God forbid that it should be. My dear Sir, we will not trust you, depend on it: when we come to be farmers & have daughters.' Such readers were 'very unlike' those Hunt hoped to have.

But they may well have been right not to trust him with their daughters. Already, by his own account, Hunt had fallen in love several times, most recently with a 'hoyden' with 'laughing eyes' named Harriet, the daughter of an east London tradesman, who would nonchalantly leave the couple alone in his back parlour. While her suitor 'hung upon her face like a goddess's', Harriet would extol the 'delicacy' of his hands and the 'cunning' of his eyes before plunging her hair in a tub of water and shaking it in his face 'like a mop'. Hunt could 'make her cheeks glow' with his words, but the affair did not last; he was later saddened to hear that she married unhappily and died young. 'Poor soul!' he wrote fifty years later. 'I find it difficult, after all, to associate the idea of trouble with her velvet cheeks, & pretty little confident head & the name of Harriet is still the name with me for a careless beauty & a romp . . .'

Before that there had been the sister of a schoolfriend, his 'fair' cousin Fanny, and an 'enchanting' girl named Almeria. 'His severest trial,' wrote his son Thornton, 'arose from the vanities, rather than the vices to which such a youth would be exposed'; mercifully, in Thornton's view, the young Hunt was 'shielded from the worst seductions than can beset a youth'. And it was now, while still in his mid-teens, that he met the woman with whom he would share the many vicissitudes of his life.

It was through his friend Robertson that Hunt was first introduced, early in 1801, into the household in Little Titchfield Street, Marylebone, of the Kent family: Anne, a widowed dressmaker who had once been a milliner at court, and her three children, Mary Anne, Elizabeth and Thomas. Although barely eleven, the precocious Elizabeth Kent had admired some articles by Hunt in the *Monthly Preceptor*; when Robertson said he knew the author and offered to bring him calling, the bookish Elizabeth could not contain her excitement. Normally Hunt did not trust his friend's taste in the opposite sex – Robertson had a tendency to 'gift' any woman he chose with 'gratuitous perfections' – but on this occasion he permitted himself to be taken along. He was not to regret it.

Anne Kent's late husband had been a Brighton draper, a man of 'fast' ways (in Hunt's words) with 'more taste for pleasure than business'; after his premature death his widow had proved herself 'a woman of clear management and unflinching will' while resuming work as a seamstress to provide for her children. From seeing them so often in his mother's hands, Hunt had acquired what he called a 'reverence' for needles and threads, while agreeing with an early feminist (writing in the *London Magazine*) that sewing was 'little else but a waste of time & an excuse for not cultivating the mind'. Nonetheless, he now found himself 'needled & threaded out of my heart' by one of the Kent daughters, who would sew from morning till night, 'till she sometimes fainted on her chair'.

But it was not, surprisingly, the aspirant writer Elizabeth (or 'Bessy') whose admiration had brought Hunt calling in the first place – and which would never dim over the ensuing six decades. It was her fourteen-year-old sister Mary Anne (or Marian), whose dark hair and eyes and full figure combined with the 'filial excess of her industry, & the evident peril into which her health was brought by it', with whom the industrious, unhealthy, sixteen-year-old Hunt found himself smitten.

Marian Kent was 'not pretty, at least in the face'; she was 'something better', namely 'piquant and genial'. Her figure was 'allowed to be beautiful, being no less delicate in the waist than plump where it ought to be', with shoulders 'fit for one of Titian's portraits', and 'an ankle which bore it all, like roses on the stalk.' In short, she was 'a little brunette; not so little either, as to be too short for her sex; nor half so much so, as her slipper pretended'. Her nature, as Ann Blainey has observed, was a striking contrast to Hunt's: self-confident, pert, unanxious, even careless, and given to frequent tantrums. 'To someone shy and vulnerable, these qualities no doubt seemed attractive and comforting. She prattled on unselfconsciously and he was required to make little effort to get to know her. She for her part was undoubtedly flattered and pleased to have attracted so important a suitor; possibly even more so if she realized her sister, Bessy, also coveted him. Having little reserve, Marian showed her pleasure in his attentions, and Hunt was both reassured and enchanted.'

Hunt became a regular visitor to the Kent household, wooing Marian with an ardour that earned a reprimand from his friend Barron Field, who took him to task for being too physically demonstrative. 'He undertook to rate me in a very singular way,' Hunt told her. 'Upon my putting my arm now and then round your waist and taking your hand: he said that these kind of things were never done in company at all gen-teel and were a great mark of vulgarity.' An irritated Hunt chose to ignore Field's protests.

When he fell ill at the Kent house one day, Marian's mother put him to bed and summoned a doctor, who diagnosed a painful skin disorder called St Anthony's fire. To his mother's distress, and his father's (finan-cial) relief, Hunt chose to stay beneath the Kent roof for what turned out to be ten weeks of recovery and convalescence. So tender were Marian's ministrations that it was worth being ill. Once fully recov-ered, he could not bring himself to leave. Gratefully he accepted her mother's offer of two rooms in the house, and stayed on as a paying lodger.

It seemed like divine providence when, in December 1802, Marian's mother married a prosperous, well-connected bookseller of

Hunt's acquaintance, Rowland Hunter of St Paul's Churchyard. Hunt seized the opportunity to become a fixture in the expanded, now comfortably-off Marylebone household. He may no longer have been a lodger, but he remained a regular visitor, with Sunday lunch at the Hunter household the still centre of his turning world. Hunt would sit in silence holding his beloved's hand, in such peaceful contentment that 'the crackling of the fire was audible'; or he would read to her from his favourite books, stroking her hair with one hand while turning the pages with the other. 'I have made love', he recalled impishly, 'over the gravest pages.'

Hunt's 'warm West Indian blood' was up; sexual longings seethe through his daily letters to Marian, still only fifteen to his eighteen, and not yet able to reply in kind. Nor was she as regular in her replies, or as artful, as he would have wished. Hunt loved Marian desperately – the very 'idea' of her 'soothes my slumbers at night and wakes with me in the morning' – but he began to fret about her feelings for him. Through the mists of his infatuation, moreover, he realised with a start that she was barely literate. If she was to be his wife, he had one very specific role-model in mind: his beloved mother, an intelligent, cultured and very capable woman. 'The wish to excel in the eyes of those we love is the first step towards excellence . . . True regard may be defined to be a desire to make its object happy and to be rewarded by that object's good opinion,' he wrote firmly to Marian. Then he set about educating her, with a directness which evidently dismayed the poor teenager.

From the start there was in his letters a threatening note which did not bode well for the relationship: 'Beware, my dearest, dearest Marian, how you slide into that negligent state of affection, which thinks it has nothing more to do to preserve the love of another than to profess every now and then an unaltering affection, without taking care to alter what might be altered . . .' He expected her to share with him everything she did, even her innermost thoughts: 'Everything that concerns you.' While writing his own letters in an uncharacteristically copperplate hand, to set her the example to which he expected her to rise, he also demanded prompt responses. 'Do me the favour,' he wrote peremptorily, 'of sitting down to your pen and ink immediately you receive this epistle, and writing me a letter somewhat longer than your last.' He also set out to improve her spelling, and despaired when her letters were marred by ink blots. If Marian truly loved him, she would have to rise to the standards he expected of a potential wife, signalled for the moment by the promptness and care with which she answered his letters. She would have to rise, whether he himself realised it or not, to the exemplary standards set by his mother.

In the spring of 1803, for all this awkward start, Hunt won Marian's and her mother's permission to be regarded as her future husband; although she was still only fifteen, and he eighteen, they became engaged. 'Remember me in your prayers to that God who has made our hearts for each other,' he wrote to her from Oxford on 22 April. The letter reflects what Marian was up against. One minute her suitor is in sombre mood: 'I feel a sort of – not melancholy – but stillness and seriousness, a kind of gravity which I cannot account for and by no means wish to repress: a divine calmness of spirit, which must be nearer to the pure raptures of heaven than any enjoyment of which mortals are possessed.' The next he is playful: 'I peremptorily and absolutely forbid you to eat more than ten walnuts in one day; and if I find, when I return, that this my injunction has been neglected, take care of the look I shall give you: you see, I can threaten, after all . . .'

Most of the time he is simply devoted – but demanding: 'For the love of all the feelings of the soul, write to me immediately on the receipt of this letter.' Another letter from the same period apologises for the 'coarseness' of the paper on which it is written; yet another, confessing his love for 'a little black-eyed girl of fifteen, whom nobody knows, with my whole heart and soul', explains: 'You see lovers can no more help being poets, than poets can help being lovers.'

But there is a less lyrical recurring theme: 'I am always so delighted when I see a married couple, who are known to be fond of each other in private, behave with a polite attention to each other in public; and for the same cause, it always gives me a grateful sensation when I receive a letter from you carefully and neatly written.' Only Hunt's half of the correspondence survives; but it is clear from his continuing complaints that Marian was struggling to keep up with his demands of her. One letter of August 1803 makes a melodramatic meal of the fact that she briefly kept him waiting when he called at Little Titchfield

Street to say goodbye as she left for a week in Brighton with her mother. Evidently he had made his feelings plain (although 'one who, when he utters an unkind word to you, is putting a thousand daggers to his own breast'); he rehearses the entire incident with some feeling ('you might have come down before a *quarter to nine*, considering I was not to see you for a week'), then collapses with remorse: 'However, you are a dear affectionate girl . . . God bless you and yours: Heaven knows that every blessing it bestows on you is a tenfold blessing on your H.'

Marian's Henry (as she called him) was clearly becoming a bit of a trial. Within six months, by late 1803, she broke off their engagement. In the words of their son Thornton, after both were dead, 'The lover [Hunt] could not be content unless he urged the young lady to cultivate her faculties somewhat in his own conscientious and scholastic spirit . . . and on her side, although her affections were manifestly pledged, the young lady could not conceal a disposition to keep a reserve of independence, and to resent dictations which tended to put a bent upon her own personal feelings and turns of thought.'

The couple remained estranged for several months, through Christmas 1803 and beyond. In a long letter begging Marian's forgiveness, written late at night on 10 February 1804, Hunt goes down on his literary knees. Was this to be the last time he addressed her? Without her, his heart was like a desert without water. 'Dearest girl, refuse not what I ask: I would entreat you for the sake of our former love, had I not so miserably forfeited it . . . Dispel this cloud that hangs over me, and take once more to your bosom your again dear Henry, now no longer fretful and melancholy, but prepared to be happy himself and to do everything he can to make you happy too . . .' In a covering letter to her mother, meanwhile, Hunt calmly intimated that, if Marian proved obdurate, he would transfer his affections to her younger daughter, Bessy.

But forgive him Marian evidently did, for within two weeks he is again billing and cooing in high literary style, as if his life depended on it – which it may well have done. Hunt's health had collapsed under the strain of their separation; he had come close to some sort of breakdown. All too soon, with Marian's love restored to him, he was back in overly self-confident mode, making those 'dictations' she so clearly resented. It was to be some years yet before he could be sure of her heart.

From Marian's point of view, Hunt was not exactly a catch. He may have been tall, handsome, literary and ardent, but he was also broke. It was in that same covering letter to her mother, written in February 1804, that he confessed: 'I am afraid it is all over with our paper: one of the proprietors has withdrawn his assistance at the very moment when everything was ripe for publication. This was highly inconsiderate, and very much chagrins my brother John . . .' That very morning, he cannot resist adding, a footman had arrived from Buckingham House 'to desire the Editor to send the paper to Her Majesty'.

John Hunt had long nourished the ambition to progress from printer to publisher. Raised in a household of vigorous political views, the son of a pamphleteer father and an equally outspoken mother, he was a forthright moralist himself, eager to join in the revival of radical journalism inspired by the success of William Cobbett's *Political Register*. Undaunted by this first failure, John took little more than another year to realise his plans for an eight-page weekly paper called the *News*, launched in May 1805 and comprised of political, financial and international coverage as well as pages devoted to the arts and literature. His first recruit was his brother Leigh, to whom he gave the job of drama critic.

'How hard it goes with one who would like to have been known as a poet,' Hunt once confessed, 'to concede that he has more of a hand for prose.' The precocious poet had already made a start as a prose writer with a series of essays published in the *Traveller*, inspired by the elegant musings he had enjoyed in the lively pages of the *Connoisseur*. Like his early poetry, Hunt's prose at this stage was largely derivative; but he now began to develop his own voice, and to lay the foundations of a career that would establish him as one of the finest essayists in the language.

As yet, on these nursery slopes of his literary career, his pay was five or six copies of the newspaper – more, he said, than he had hoped for, but scarcely enough to offer any sort of future to a potential bride. There was an urgent need to earn a living of some sort. Already his father had been hard at work, at first apprenticing him in the same legal practice as his brother Stephen. But Leigh had not lasted long in 'that gloomiest of all "darkness palpable," a lawyer's office.' Then, in 1805, as John sought backing for *The News*, Hunt senior's connections brought a positive reply from a recent Prime Minister, no less, in Henry Addington. A job for young Leigh could be found as a lowly clerk in the War Office.

His only qualification for any such role, as Napoleon declared himself Emperor and threatened 'to come among us', was a brief spell as a volunteer in the St James regiment, based at Burlington House, Piccadilly. Hunt himself did not share the view that an invasion was at all likely – 'very strange it was to think that some fine morning I might actually find myself face to face with a parcel of Frenchmen in Kent or Sussex, instead of playing soldiers in Piccadilly' – but he braved his mother's fear of all things military by signing on for training which largely amounted to marching from Piccadilly via Acton to Ealing, and back again. The only action he saw became an anecdote of which he was almost too fond, when the regiment's self-important new colonel made a grand equestrian entrance into the courtyard of Burlington House, where his troops were drawn up to offer their formal greeting – only to suffer the indignity of being pitched over his horse's head on to the parade ground at their feet.

It was through the unlikely route of the army that Hunt first got involved in the theatre. Stage-struck since his brother Stephen had taken him to a comic opera called *Egyptian Festival* in 1800, he now made several actor friends among his fellow volunteers, one of whom introduced him to the celebrated Irish tenor Michael Kelly, who had known Mozart and twenty years before sung in the first performance of his *The Marriage of Figaro* in Vienna. Now reduced to running a music shop in Pall Mall, Kelly clearly took to the young poet, offering to see if he could find a management willing to stage a farce he had dashed off. The project came to nothing, but gave Hunt the notion of writing about, rather than for, the theatre.

Hunt's military career did not last long. Nor, as it turned out, would his desk job at the War Office. But it was paid work for a prematurely published poet at last being forced by his family to realise that he had to earn his own keep. Brother John was willing to house him, as well as to employ him; so the next few years of his pursuit of Marian were spent reluctantly clerking at the War Office by day and writing drama reviews by night. As ill-cast and ineffective as Hunt was in the one role, so he excelled at the other. He did not much enjoy it; the more he attended the theatre with notebook in hand, the more he longed for the days of 'unembarrassed delight' when playgoing was less a duty than a pleasure, when he went 'only to laugh or be moved'. But it brought out the best in him, steeled by John's fierce spirit of independence.

As theatre critic for the *News*, Hunt pioneered the art of objective, disinterested theatre criticism as we now (for the most part) know it. Before this independent-minded young upstart arrived on the scene via his brother's paper, theatrical reviewing amounted to little more than advertising – 'as short and favourable a paragraph on the new piece as could be' – in exchange for free tickets, from writers who thrilled to the company of the actors they chronicled and were only too pleased to accept their hospitality. 'Puffing and plenty of tickets were the system of the day,' as Hunt put it. 'It was an interchange of amenities over the dinner table; a flattery of power on the one side, and puns on the other; and what the public took for criticism on a play was a draft on the box-office, or reminiscences of last Thursday's salmon and lobster sauce.'

Hunt would 'as lief have taken poison' as accepted a free ticket. Getting to know the actors he wrote about, let alone dining or becoming friends with them, was to him 'a vice not to be thought of'. The first decade of the nineteenth century may not have been one of the richest periods of British playwriting; its star practitioners were Andrew Cherry, Thomas Dibdin and Frederick Reynolds, all of whom the brash twenty-year-old critic attacked for their 'miserable productions'. But the London stage boasted its familiar quota of bravura performers, led by John Philip Kemble, whose affected pronunciation, or 'vicious oetheopy', Hunt delighted in satirising. While he hailed Kemble's noble Roman profile and allowed that he excelled in soliloquies and 'stage artifice' generally, especially when conveying 'the more majestic passions', a simple interjection like 'Oh!' could become 'an eternal groan . . . as if he were determined to shew that his misery had not affected his lungs'. Instead of 'To err is human', Kemble would say, 'To *air* is human.' In Kemble's mouth, 'earth' became '*airth*', aches '*aitches*', beard '*bird*', 'fair' '*fay-er-r-r*', 'sovereign' '*suvran*', 'virtue' '*varchue*'; and he was liable to 'bring off such a line as "*Ojus, insijus, hijus,* and *perfijus*"'. Kemble was eventually moved to dismiss his nemesis as 'that damned boy'.

Hunt's dramatic notices may have been overwritten, full of his still youthful literary pretension, but at least they were – for the first time in theatrical history – honest, impartial reviews of the performers and productions, offering the reading public an entertaining consumer guide to the constantly changing crop of theatrical offerings. 'Nothing seemed to escape his eye or ear,' write the editors of a latter-day collection of Hunt's theatrical criticism. 'The faulty articulations of a rising young actress, the fitness of her movements and gestures to her part, an actor's artificiality and bombast, an author's wordy, stagnant dullness – all are accurately noted and sharply held up for attention.' To another scholar of the period, moreover, Hunt's reviews of the London stage – of which he would eventually write more than six hundred – 'opened the way for theatrical criticism by Coleridge, Hazlitt and Lamb'.

There was many a complaint to the *News*, much to brother John's delight, from performers and stage managers alike. Hunt's 'castigations', according to Thornton, 'made actors wince and playwrights launch prologues at him'. His outspokenly independent approach to his work soon saw him hailed by the writers James and Horace Smith as 'the Jove of the modern critical Olympus, Lord Mayor of the theatric sky'. His praise became rare enough to be especially prized; Mrs Charles Mathews felt moved to note that an appreciative review of her husband's Sir Fretful Plagiary came from 'the greatest dramatic critic of that day, Mr Leigh Hunt, whose judgement was universally sought and received as infallible by all actors and lovers of the drama'.

By the end of 1807 John Hunt saw fit to capitalise on his brother's growing renown by publishing a collection of his reviews from the *News* in book form, under the title *Critical Essays on the Performers of the London Theatres, including General Observations on the Practice and Genius of the Stage*. Leigh repaid the compliment by dedicating the volume to his brother. If Leigh had cause to be grateful to John, John had an equal debt to acknowledge to Leigh, whose pugnacious work had become the mainstay of the *News*'s rising circulation. As always, the measure of this was the volume of readers' letters, both excited and outraged, which

Leigh Hunt's unprecedented approach to theatre criticism provoked.

In an appendix entitled 'Rules for the Theatrical Critic of a Newspaper', the cocky young critic underlined his rewriting of the theatrical rules with some none too gentle mockery of his rivals, in the shape of a glossary explaining the truth of some terms in common usage:

A crowded house – a theatre on the night of a performance when all the back seats and upper boxes are empty.

An amusing author – an author whose very seriousness makes us laugh in spite of himself.

A successful author – an author who has been damned only four times out of five.

A good author – the general term for an author who gives good dinners.

A respectable actor – an insipid actor; one who in general is neither hissed nor applauded.

A fine actor – one who makes a great noise; a tatter-demalion of passions; a clap-trapper; one intended by nature for a town-crier.

A good actor – the general term for an actor who gives good dinners.

A charming play – a play full of dancing, music and scenery; a play in which the less the author has to do, the better.

Great applause – applause mixed with hisses of the gallery and pit.

Unbounded and universal applause – applause mixed with the hisses of the pit only.

So well did the *News* prosper that John soon launched a companion publication, a Whig-supported evening paper called the *Statesman*, also using his brother's drama criticism as one of its major selling points. In 1806–7 he persuaded Leigh to edit, and their artist brother Robert to illustrate, a five-volume anthology of eighteenth-century stories entitled *Classic Tales, Serious and Lively*. Drawing on the work of such writers as Henry Brooke and Henry Mackenzie, as well as his beloved Voltaire and Samuel Johnson's *Rasselas* (which 'for a model of grave and majestic language will claim perhaps the first place in English composition'), the collection is notable for Hunt's essay on Goldsmith, whose *Enquiry into the State of Polite Learning in 1759* he adapted to his own age.

The young Hunt's confident judgements already show the sharp critical eye and ornate language which would come to characterise his mature work. But it is interesting to note at this early stage that he hails Cowper and Southey as the outstanding poets of the moment, with proto-feminist nods to other contemporaries such as the sonneteer Charlotte Smith and the tragedian Joanna Baillie, without even mentioning the work of Blake or Lamb, Moore or Crabbe, Landor or Godwin, let alone Wordsworth or Coleridge, whose *Lyrical Ballads* had been in print almost ten years.

If, like so much of Hunt's work, the marginal musings in *Classic Tales* show signs of haste, cobbled together by day as he dashed off theatre reviews by night, it may be because he was still engulfed in his long, turbulent courtship of Marian Kent. Throughout 1805, moreover, there was no time for poetry, with little for more than occasional prose, as Hunt's pursuit of his personal muse was dogged by the painful knowledge that his mother was dying.

Stricken with rheumatism and liver failure, Mary Hunt had taken to gazing at the sunset and beyond, to the Heaven in which she devoutly believed, and a serene vision of her family reunited there in death. For all his oft-stated devotion to her, the hard-working Leigh was the least diligent of visitors during this painful period. As Ann Blainey, chief psychologist of the Hunt family, has put it, 'Sweet-natured, homely Robert visited her constantly; indolent, generous Stephen less often; busy, dutiful John when he could; and Leigh much less often than he ought.' These last, confessional words were his own. 'I was as giddy as I was young,' he recalled by way of excuse – inadequate excuse for a man sentimental enough to write more than twenty years later: 'My mother . . . I can never write those words without emotion.'

After her death in November 1805, at the age of fifty-three, Mary Hunt's grave in Hampstead churchyard became a place of regular pilgrimage for a son who, preoccupied as he was by his work and his courting, perhaps lacked the courage to pay regular visits to the deathbed of the woman he idolised (and idealised). Only recently freed from her dominant influence, finally beginning to carve out his own distinctive niche in the world, Hunt may have feared a relapse into the dependence on his mother of which he speaks throughout his work.

If 'any circumstance of my life could give me cause for boasting,' he wrote towards its end, 'it would be of having such a mother.' Her last two letters to him, written with 'failing eyes, a trembling hand, and an aching heart', he kept lovingly beside him all his days. 'Knowing what she was . . . I now feel her memory as a serene and inspiring influence, that comes over my social moments only to temper cheerfulness, and over my reflecting ones to animate me in the love of truth.'

Such tranquil remembrances were as yet years off. At the time, early in 1806, Hunt finally suffered the breakdown which seemed to have been waiting some time to happen. In retrospect he did not associate it with the recent loss of his mother, or his continuing vicissitudes with Marian, but blamed it on 'living too well' and obstinately refusing to consult a doctor, for fear of what he might discover.

The first symptoms were palpitations of the heart, which he dealt with by riding at speed on horseback. 'The more I rode, and (I used to think) the harder I rode, the less the palpitation became.' As long as these and other symptoms persisted – nausea, giddiness, blurred vision – he slept sitting up, for fear of dying if he lay down. He also tried a vegetarian diet, which made him so weak and faint that he could not walk down a street without clinging to the railings. It was all, he later decided, quite avoidable.

Throughout his life, which would see him succumb to at least three prolonged such attacks, Hunt's dogged determination to overcome them without professional help or the support of friends caused him untold and wholly unnecessary suffering. Instead of taking medical advice, which would have remedied his condition in months rather than years, he tried to think his way out of it, plaguing himself with mental exertions 'which are the pastimes of better states of health, and the pursuits of philosophers'.

Hunt always considered his nervous attacks the result of poor physical health, rather than the other way around. So he countered them with a variety of eccentric physical regimes which no doubt made them worse. After the failure of the vegetarian diet, he tried a milk-only regime, which 'did nothing but jaundice my complexion'. Then he tried 'a modicum of meat, one glass of wine, no milk except in tea, and no vegetables at all'. Though this produced a marked physical improvement, it did nothing to calm his mental distress. He would try freezing-cold baths in winter, scorching-hot ones in summer, and seem surprised that they did little for his mental stability.

His friends could see that he was unwell, but he prided himself in keeping the true depths of his despair to himself. Seeking his solace in work, he kept up a feverish regime of reading, reviewing and essay writing, taking out his woes on those closest to him – notably, after his mother's death, the long-suffering Marian. 'There is nothing which my mother has left behind her,' he told his betrothed, 'to which you are not the proper heiress in the truest sense of the word.' His depression, anxiety, insecurity and lack of confidence again soured to irritability in his letters to her. 'Now cannot you sit down on Sunday, my sweet girl,' he wrote to her in February 1806, 'and write me a fair, even-minded honest hand, unvexed with desperate blots and skulking interlineations?'

Hunt was writing from Lincolnshire, where he had been sent to recuperate as the guest of John Robertson's artist brother Charles. His letters to Marian reflect his violent mood swings, from more irritable complaints about the inadequacy of her replies to manic elation about the blissful prospect of their future together. 'I am naturally a man of violent passions,' he declares, 'but your affection has taught me to subdue them.'

At moments like this he encloses long verse epistles declaring his undying love. If only she could have replied in kind; that is clearly what he would have wished, a wife-to-be of some artistic accomplishments, as he encourages her to enclose drawings with her own letters, even dreams of her sketching roses for him. But all such lyrical moments are inevitably undone by more harsh words about her failure to reply in the same style he lavished on her. 'As you have done so much for me in correcting the errors of my head, you will not feel very unpleasant when I venture to correct the errors of your hand . . .'

Hunt was, of course, deluding himself. Having nearly lost Marian once, he was in truth terrified that she might desert him again; this was the subtext of all his cajoling, complaining, criticising. But if Hunt wanted to bind Marian to him with hoops of steel, he was going about it entirely the wrong way. The vicissitudes of his own life he took out on her, growing especially tetchy during another supposedly recuperative trip out of London – to the home in Barnes of his schoolfriend Papendieck, whose parents were courtiers, 'completely German in their habits', with an unquestioning reverence for royalty. Their independent-minded young house guest was dismayed that this indiscriminate respect for rank seemed to have infected their son. Hunt could not contain his scorn, which swiftly curtailed the visit. But it was Marian who took the brunt of his irritability, to the point where her own health began to falter.

In March 1807 her mother dispatched Marian to her uncle's seaside home in Brighton, where she lingered for most of the year. By July, Hunt was feeling neglected. Suspecting his beloved's motives in staying away from him so long, he took his own summer break in Margate, whence a patronising note in one letter earned an angry response. 'Your last letter is so good that I expect the next one to be without any wrong spelling, and interlineations, and deficiencies of words,' he wrote on 21 July, only to be fulminating six days later:

I requested, with a manner that shewed my confidence in your love, that you would write me a <u>careful</u> letter, and you know that all I wanted, or all that I expected from you, was <u>carefulness</u>, a talent which everybody may attain who wishes. Yet you send me, still send me, a hasty, careless letter, in which you have not even attended to the little but earnest request I made respecting scratching out. You talk of having a few minutes only, before the post sets out. Is this because the post surprises you by being uncommonly early, or because you delay your letter till the last moment? I answer your letters almost the instant I receive them . . .

On <u>Tuesday</u> I wrote [you] a long, an affectionate letter; on <u>Sunday</u> I receive a very short, a very careless, and therefore, it pains me to say, a most unaffectionate one.

Oh Marian, I did not think you would suffer yourself, at such a moment, to be led into this afflicting indolence, into this neglect of my highest wishes in the most easy matters. Is it to punish me for my own former neglect? Alas, or rather God be thanked, you have not the misfortune to weigh you down that I had. But you know what I lost by <u>want</u> of exertion, you know what I have since gained by exertion: – we all lose & gain by the same means.

I have no heart to write any more . . .

Rather than visit Marian in Brighton, Hunt meant to taunt her by going to Margate with his War Office boss, a man named Stuart, and his unmarried sister, evidently an attractive and accomplished woman whose praises he sang with obvious, none too subtle intent. 'You need not be jealous of Miss S.,' he reassures Marian with clearly mixed motives, 'or of any other girl upon earth, while you try to improve yourself . . .'

At the same time his letters to Marian's mother and her husband sent out contrasting, carefree signals. That same month the pleasures of a bath are compared in a letter to the Hunters with the sensuous delights of 'those luxurious fellows, the Turks: the bath wanted nothing but three or four sofas with silken-skinned damsels, drinking coffee on their elbow or tying up their long tresses with taper fingers; that is, you know, for the effect – the mere effect – not that I mean &c. &c.'.

This pattern continued another year or more, through trips by each outside London for their health, as Hunt succumbed to bilious attacks, giddiness, palpitations and headaches, while Marian endured all sorts of nervous upsets, from backache to depression. For a while in mid-1808 there was a rare oasis of calm as he praised her attempts to learn sculpture while regaling her with his adventures on a journalistic assignment to Nottingham. By that summer, however, the unusually hot weather was taking its toll on them both. As Marian's mother packed her off hither and thither for the benefit of her health, Hunt began to suspect a plot to part them – perhaps with reason, for Mrs Hunter was all too aware of the demands he was making of her daughter, as well as the unconventional religious views with which he was bombarding her. The lyrical love letters of the previous summer turned sour again until the approach of his twenty-fourth birthday, in the autumn of 1808, when he wrote to Marian: 'I hope to God I shall never see another birthday without you, without my wife. Everything I do, and almost everything of which I think, looks towards that time.'

In Hunt's own head, at least, their agreement to marry seems to have survived his own erratic, importunate posturings, Marian's regular (and no doubt consequent) collapses and her mother's growing

impatience with the remorseless siege laid to her daughter by this idio-
syncratic, highly strung, worryingly unorthodox literary man, with
little money to his name and equally scant prospects. But there is no
doubt that Hunt loved Marian passionately, whatever misgivings his
constant demands and expectations may have sowed in her young mind.
The fact that she was not yet quite twenty-one (there was some doubt
over her date of birth, given on her tombstone as 28 September 1787)
further complicated his attempts to agree a date for the wedding, while
he expected his potential stepfather-in-law, Hunter, to see to all such
tedious necessities as obtaining a licence and liaising with the vicar.

So there were to be more disappointments for Hunt – his hopes of
a wedding on 12 June failed to materialise – before they were finally
married on 3 July 1809 at St Clement Danes in the Strand. After
dining with her family, the newly-weds walked to their new home in
the Strand, 15 Beaufort Buildings, where there were dwelling units as
well as his brother's offices. In effect, their married life would begin as
John's lodgers. 'Thereafter,' in the (overly charitable) words of their
oldest son, Thornton, 'the vicissitudes of his life, save in the inevitable
vicissitudes of mortality, were professional rather than personal;
though he always threw his personality into his profession.'

To Marianne (as he now chose to style her), who had been staying
with friends in High Wycombe, Hunt had written a last premarital
letter almost inarticulate with joy: 'I am not exactly agitated, but I have
feelings that I hardly know how to define except that I seem as if I were
going to be very happy. As if! – do I say? I am sure I shall be happy as
happy, I trust, as you will make me. I bless myself every day that I *know*
you so truly. You are a lesson, which I have studied six years & got
soundly by heart . . .'

On the subject of money, he invoked the sacred memory of his
mother to make (in one interminably long sentence) a pledge which,
however well meant, merely underscores the lack of self-knowledge
with which his wife would have to cope:

'I can anticipate what your love might prompt you to say – that we
could live on little – but I have seen so much of the irritabilities, or
rather the miseries arising from want of a suitable income, and the best
woman of her time was so worried, and finally worn out with the
early negligence of others in this respect, that if ever I was determined

in anything, it is to be perfectly clear of the world, and ready to meet the exigencies of a married life before I do marry, for I will not see a wife, who loves me and is the comfort of my existence, afraid to speak to me of money matters; she shall never tremble to hear a knock at the door, or to meet a quarter-day; she will tremble, I hope, with nothing but love and joy in the arms of her husband.'

Money – its elusiveness, his carelessness with it, his dependence on the assistance and generosity of others – was to become a corrosive constant of Leigh Hunt's life, and of his long, sometimes turbulent marriage to Marianne. As yet, however, he could afford to point to his parents' example as a cautionary tale, to be learnt from and avoided. For the other reason that he and Marianne were finally able to marry was the unwonted fact that Hunt was now gainfully employed, in a fraternal project of a year's standing which was showing every sign of lucrative success.

At the back of Leigh Hunt's *Critical Essays* a notice had announced two forthcoming publications from the same press, his brother John's: a volume of translations of Horace by the same author; and a prospectus for the *Examiner*, a new weekly paper 'upon Politics, Domestic Economy and Theatricals'. The first seems never to have materialised, but the second would earn both Hunt brothers a lasting place in the history of journalism and free speech.

3

'The Prince on St Patrick's Day'

1807–12

Other friends and colleagues may have left behind more famous names, but none played as significant a role in the early life of Leigh Hunt as his estimable brother John. A reformist as radical as any but more modest than most, John preferred the less conspicuous if no less courageous roles of printer and publisher to those of writer or editor.

'As noble a specimen of a human being as ever I met in my life,' was the painter Benjamin Haydon's verdict on Leigh Hunt's American-born brother. 'I have never seen in anyone else so perfect an outward symbol or visible setting forth of the English character, in its most peculiar and distinguishing features, but also in its best and brightest aspect,' wrote his friend and colleague P.G. Patmore (father of Coventry). 'A figure tall, robust, and perfectly well-formed; a carriage commanding and even dignified; without the slightest apparent effort or consciousness of being so; a head and set of features on a large scale, but cast in a perfectly regular mould; handsome; open, and full of intelligence . . .' Dedicating his *Political Essays* to John Hunt in 1819, William Hazlitt – not a writer from whose pen compliments flowed easily – praised him as 'the tried, steady, zealous and conscientious advocate of the liberty of his country, and the rights of mankind'.

All that lay in the future as John Hunt decided to take a mighty commercial and ideological risk, doubling the stakes by trusting his younger brother to play the major part in pulling it off. In twenty-three-year-old Leigh, nine years his junior, John sensed the perfect partner for the mighty enterprise he had conceived: the launch of a weekly paper to take a defiantly independent, reformist line on the great issues of the day.

As Napoleon marched across Europe, apparently threatening England with the same fate as Austria and Prussia, Lord Portland's weak Tory government was signally failing to confront the long-term consequences of the industrial revolution: the rise of the urban middle class, a growing divide between rich and poor, increasing unemployment and a depressed farming industry. The two great statesmen of the day, William Pitt and Charles James Fox, had both died the previous year, ending forty-three years of Whig administration and leaving a legacy of political turmoil and economic crisis in which combative journalism thrived. Both Hunt brothers believed passionately in such causes as parliamentary reform and the emancipation of Irish Catholics. Leigh had made a name as a stylish, outspoken theatre critic, immune to vested interests, linking the decline in theatrical values and riots among audiences to the social and political conditions of the day, as covered on the adjacent pages. He had also begun a campaign against the ruthless exploitation of child actors. What if they applied the same principle – fearless independence – to politics?

John Hunt knew a good commercial idea when he heard one. In the autumn of 1807 the brothers published a prospectus for a new weekly paper, the *Examiner*, of which John would be publisher and Leigh editor and chief contributor. To be published on Sundays, it would consist of a sixteen-page, two-column quarto costing 7½d. 'Party is the madness of the many for the gain of the few' was the paper's slogan, taken from Pope (although at first wrongly attributed to Swift), which adorned the outspoken front-page political leader as of the first issue, published on 3 January 1808. Wrote Hunt anonymously on its front page, signed merely with the Indicator symbol ☞ which was to become his trademark:

The great error of politicians is that old fancy of Solon, who insisted that it was infamous for a citizen to be of no party, and endeavoured by a law to make the Athenians hypocrites. This conceit not only destroys every idea of mediation between two parties, but does not even suppose that both may be wrong. Yet all history may convince us that he who resolutely professes himself attached to any party, is in danger of yielding to every extreme for the mere reputation of his opinion; he will argue for the most manifest errors of this or that statesman, because he has hitherto agreed with him – an obstinacy as stupid as if a pedestrian were to expose his satisfaction with a tempest at night, because he had enjoyed sunshine in the morning . . .

A wise man knows no party abstracted from its utility, or existing, like a shadow, merely from the opposition of some body. Yet in the present day, we are all so erroneously sociable that every man, as well as every journal, must belong to some class of politicians; he is either a Pittite or a Foxite, Windhamite, Wilberforceite, or Burdettite, though at the same time two thirds of these disturbers of coffee-houses might with as much reason call themselves Hivites, or Shunamites, or perhaps Bedlamites.

The pattern was for Hunt's editorial to be followed by foreign and domestic news, state papers and parliamentary reports, more editorial comment written by Hunt and signed with his Indicator hand; and more news. The back half was opened by the 'Theatrical Examiner', also signed with Hunt's Indicator symbol, followed by 'Miscellaneous Sketches', law reports and a final page of 'Police News', bankruptcy announcements and other miscellanea. No advertisements were accepted, for fear of compromising the journal's independence.

Bankruptcies were there not just to fill space; their growing number was an indication of the dire economic state of the nation, thanks to the combined effects of the war with France, the Luddite riots and three years of poor harvests amid mass enclosures in an attempt to feed both army and populace. As the *Examiner*'s editor would sum up in 1810:

State of the nation . . . Bankruptcies, unprecedented in number, occasioned by a ruined commerce – a depreciated paper currency, and the disappearance of precious metals – a national expenditure which Mr Huskisson, the friend of Mr Pitt, says cannot much longer be supported – an enormous taxation, which Mr Huskisson says cannot be encreased – an army in Portugal, which everybody says can do no good – an imperfect representation, which the House of Commons say shall not be reformed – his Majesty incapacitated – Mr Perceval his minister – Mr Yorke at the head of the Admiralty – and Bonaparte at the head of the French nation – these are a few of 'the evils which surround and oppress us'.

The tone for the paper was set by Hunt's front-page editorial, which was almost recklessly outspoken from the outset. After the declaration of political independence in the first issue, the second was led by a denunciation of the slave trade in the West Indies, attacking the opposition of Jamaican planters to its abolition as 'one of the most lamentable instances of the selfishness of human nature' and aligning the paper with William Wilberforce in concluding that 'it will be more glory to England to have abolished the Slave Trade' (as was to happen within the year) 'than if she had conquered the universe'.

Not that Hunt wanted England to do that. By the fourth issue he was dissenting from Pitt's system of continental subsidies, and opposing the war with Napoleon, by suggesting that 'England has ever sacrificed her best interests to her allies' while condemning the 'eternal war which she injudiciously began and which she now finds it necessary to protract', ending: 'Let us be wise, and leave the continent to itself.'

There followed assaults upon the government's relaxation of inheritance tax, and all aspects of fiscal policy designed to perpetuate the rule of an elite oligarchy and hamstring the middle and lower classes. Hunt declared the *Examiner* strongly opposed to the indiscriminate use of the death penalty and in passionate favour of civil rights for Irish Catholics. But one theme above all others became the focal point for these and countless other passing issues: reform of a parliament still corrupted by the feudal system of rotten and pocket boroughs. On 30 October 1808, linking military to political corruption, Hunt put the *Examiner* squarely in the vanguard of the liberal agenda: 'A reform in parliament will purify the whole constitution.' He was equally unflinching on all the other major issues of the day, at home and abroad, from Napoleon's imperial ambitions to liberation movements in South Africa.

There was a huge audience for reformist propaganda, and the *Examiner* flourished. By November, eleven months after its launch, weekly sales were 2200, rising to a target of 3000 by Christmas, and complete sets were highly prized, with individual issues changing hands for as much as five or six shillings.

Hunt's youthful outspokenness may have been good for sales, but it was almost wilfully asking for trouble. Apprehensive about what it believed to be subversive elements, Portland's nervous government had recently given itself special powers to curb the influence of an increasingly unruly press. New legislation now gave the Attorney-General the power to lay an 'ex-officio information' against a paper for libel, thus bypassing the traditional need to appear before a grand jury before bringing its editor and publisher to trial. In practice, laying the information often proved deterrent enough; the law gave the government scope to keep the charge hanging over an editor's head pending better behaviour, with the threat of eventual trial menacing his paper indefinitely. During the years 1808–11 the government set in motion forty-two prosecutions for libel, of which only twenty-six were brought to trial.

The other weapon at the government's command was the introduction of a 'special' jury, drawn from the ranks of its supporters ('an esquire or person of higher degree', bankers and merchants) for trials in cases 'of too great nicety for the discussion of ordinary freeholders'. In 1809 Jeremy Bentham wrote an angry polemic against 'jury-packing' – 'as applied to Special Juries, particularly in cases of Libel Law'. But even Bentham lacked the courage to publish it for another twelve years – too late, as it transpired, to save Leigh and John Hunt.

In the *Examiner* of 9 October 1808, incensed by the 'disgrace' of the Convention of Cintra – in which two British officers made undue concessions to the French after their defeat in Portugal by Sir Arthur Wellesley, the future Duke of Wellington – Hunt boldly questioned the competence of the King's second son, Frederick, Duke of York, as commander-in-chief of the Peninsular campaign. This alone would have given the government the chance it was looking for to prosecute him for libel, had he not returned to the subject in even stronger terms two weeks later, following the publication of a pamphlet by an Irish major named Hogan entitled *Appeal to the Public, and a Farewell Address to the Army*.

Hogan had resigned his commission in disgust that July, having been denied the promotion which was his due (as testified by some of his superior officers) after fourteen years' service, nine of them as a captain. During the period in which he had made repeated applications to the Duke, who had replied merely that Hogan 'had been noted for promotion and would be duly considered', no fewer than forty officers junior to him had been awarded the advancement he sought. Why? The promotion could have been his, Hogan revealed, had he been prepared to pay a bribe of £600. He had, of course, indignantly declined, considering it inconsistent with his honour 'to owe the King's commission to low intrigue or petticoat influence' – a reference to one of the Duke's many mistresses, Mrs Mary Ann Clarke, who openly took advantage of her position to sell military commissions and other royal perks such as the privilege of preaching before the King.

Under the headline 'Military Depravity', Hunt weighed into the system of military promotion as 'a perfect Falstaff, a dastardly carcass of corruption, full of sottishness and selfishness, preying upon the hard labour of honest men, and never to be moved but by its lust for women or its lust for money . . . The time has at length arrived when either the vices of one man must be sacrificed to the military honour of the country, or the military honour of the country must be sacrificed to the vices of one man – an alternative truly monstrous and detestable.' He then proceeded, amid a spirited defence of Hogan, to name the Duke of York as 'the promoter and foster-father, if not the begetter, of these corruptions'.

The Duke immediately ordered a prosecution for libel to be mounted against the *Examiner*. But the Hunt brothers had scarcely had time to decline the offer of a public subscription, to cover the costs of their inevitable trial, when the suit was sidelined by an upright MP named Gwyllym Lloyd Wardle, who persuaded the Commons to vote in favour of a parliamentary investigation into the Duke of York's conduct 'with regard to promotions, exchanges and appointments to commissions in the army'. Mrs Clarke's outspoken appearance before the House caused so lurid a scandal that the Duke, though his name was effectively cleared by the abandonment of the investigation, felt obliged to resign his command. The case against the Hunt brothers never came to court.

This exposure of widespread corruption in high places, and the squalid political infighting which had sought to conceal it, gave a new lease of life to Hunt's denunciations of the Tories and his zeal for parliamentary reform. As the government sought a second chance to silence him, it took the political chaos of October 1809 for Hunt again to overstep the mark. The political disagreements of the War minister Castlereagh and the Foreign Affairs minister Canning had escalated to the point of a duel on Putney Heath, resulting in a flesh wound to Canning, the resignation of both ministers and the collapse of Portland's government. The machinations of the Prince of Wales, seeking to divide the Whig Lords Grey and Grenville, had led both to refuse to join a coalition.

During the interregnum, before a compromise Tory government was formed under Spencer Perceval, Hunt seized the moment to return to his passionate support of the rights of Irish Catholics. 'The subject of Ireland, next to the difficulty of a coalition, is no doubt the great trouble in the election of His Majesty's servants,' he wrote under the heading 'Change of Government' in the *Examiner* of 1 October. Knowing that justice would never be done in Ireland under the present regime, Hunt risked a slur on the king's mental health – rumoured to be in decline again after twenty years of instability – by welcoming the prospect of his son George, Prince of Wales, as Prince Regent. 'What a crowd of blessings rush upon one's mind, that might be bestowed upon the country in the event of such a change! Of all the monarchs indeed since the Revolution, the successor of George the Third will have the finest opportunity of becoming nobly popular.'

Hunt's enthusiasm for a regency (soon to be dispelled) was based on the Prince's long-standing closeness to the late Fox and other Whig leaders in open opposition to his royal father's instinctive Tory sympathies. This brash insult to them both – appearing to welcome the King's descent into madness, and suggesting it would be equally welcome to his son and heir – was gleefully reprinted by the Whig daily, the *Morning Chronicle*, whose Tory rival, the *Morning Post*, promptly hit back: 'Never, surely, was anything more calculated to insult the good sense, or horrify the pure and amiable nature of His Royal Highness; nor was ever anything more calculated to call forth the indignation and execration of a loyal and admiring people, upon the wretch who is capable of broaching an idea at once so repugnant to the feelings of the illustrious heir apparent and to the ardent wishes of every good and (also) virtuous subject.'

Libel charges were swiftly brought against both the *Examiner* and the *Morning Chronicle*. Bizarrely, in the view of many contemporary observers, the case against the copiers of the libel, the *Chronicle*, was to be heard before that against its instigators, the *Examiner*. Hunt's own explanation, having retained his eloquent Whig friend Henry Brougham as his counsel, was that the Attorney-General, Sir Vicary Gibbs, saw easier meat in the shape of James Perry, proprietor of the *Chronicle*, who had decided to save legal fees by pleading his own case.

Even Perry himself confessed that he had 'suffered no ordinary ridicule, even in the streets, from strangers as well as from friends', since his determination had 'spread abroad'. Come his day in court, however, Perry was triumphantly vindicated. For all its amateurish long-windedness, his defence of the right to free speech won the day when the jury took only two minutes to return a verdict of 'Not guilty'. As an irritated Lord Ellenborough called the next case, The King v John and Leigh Hunt, Sir Vicary had no option but to rise and declare: 'My Lord, I withdraw that.'

Denounced in the *Edinburgh Review* as a republican, Hunt poured out a series of articles in the *Examiner* – which he took the trouble to reprint as a pamphlet – strenuously denying the charge and arguing that his chief objective, devoid of party leanings, was the elimination of corruption and the wholesale reform of parliament. Among those unconvinced, and made all the more determined by this latest failure to silence the Hunts once and for all, were Ellenborough and Gibbs. Given the recklessness of Hunt's editorial decisions in pursuit of his ideals, their next opportunity to go after him was not long coming.

Outraged by institutional abuse of any kind, Hunt took as his next *cause de guerre* – amid continuing assaults on King, Prince and Government – the then widespread practice of military flogging. On 2 September, after the *Stamford News* chronicled a lurid example under the headline 'One Thousand Lashes', Hunt reprinted it in the *Examiner*. Well aware of the legal risk he was taking, he added a commentary conceding that discipline was of course necessary to the proper maintenance of any army, but that flogging was a 'particularly revolting' form of 'degradation'. As if to incite the government's wrath, he further observed that he did not necessarily mean to endorse Bonapartism by noting that his 'refractory' troops did not have to endure any such ordeal: '*His* soldiers have never yet been drawn up to view one of their comrades stripped naked, his limbs tied with rope to a triangular machine, his back torn to the bones by the merciless cutting whipcord, applied by persons who relieve each other at short intervals, that they may bring the full unexhausted strength of a man to the work of scourging . . .' Nor had they 'with tingling ears listened to the piercing screams of a man so tortured; they have never seen the blood oozing from his rent flesh; they have never beheld a surgeon, with dubious look, pressing the agonized victim's pulse and calmly calculating, to an odd blow, how far suffering may be extended, until in its extremity it encroach upon life itself . . .'

This was enough for the Attorney-General to raise the stakes to a charge of 'seditious' libel, on the grounds that Hunt's words might not only 'excite the disaffection of the soldiery' and 'deter the other liege subjects from entering the said army' but further 'represent the treatment of Bonaparte's troops . . . as infinitely preferable to the system employed in Great Britain'.

Hauled before the Court of King's Bench on 22 February 1811, Lord Ellenborough again presiding, the Hunt brothers listened with mounting pessimism as the prosecutor reminded the court that, only the previous summer, William Cobbett had been found guilty of libel on a similar charge. The comparison of the British army to Bonaparte's was 'mischievous' and 'seditious'. Brougham countered that the comparison had been 'so qualified as to make it perfectly fair'; that many respected military men themselves disapproved of the barbarous practice of flogging; and that this trial was really about an Englishman's right to 'free discussion'. Did he not still have 'the privilege of expressing himself as his feelings and his opinions dictate' on the most 'important and interesting' subjects of the day? Summing up, Ellenborough made his own view perfectly plain: this was an 'inflammatory' libel. An hour after retiring, the jury requested a copy of the paper containing the article in question. Less than an hour later it returned a verdict of 'Not guilty'.

The Hunts were as astonished by the acquittal as was Brougham, who had warned them to expect the worst. Their counsel's eloquent defence of the brothers, calling on the jury to rule 'whether an Englishman still enjoys the privilege of freely discussing public measures', was to prove his making as the darling of radical Whig reformers, eventually to become Lord Chancellor in Earl Grey's great reformist administration of 1830. And the case brought into Leigh Hunt's life a young man whose friendship would sustain him through the coming, even more turbulent decade.

'Permit me, although a stranger, to offer my sincerest congratulations on the occasion of that triumph so highly to be prized by men of liberality,' began a letter to Hunt dated 2 March 1811 from Percy Bysshe Shelley, then a nineteen-year-old Oxford undergraduate. Shelley went on to submit for Hunt's consideration, 'as one of the most fearless enlighteners of the public mind at the present time', a scheme 'of mutual safety and mutual indemnification for men of public spirit and principle'. He enclosed his manifesto for the formation of 'a methodical society, which should be organized so as to resist the coalition of the enemies of liberty, which at present renders any expression of opinion on matters of policy dangerous to individuals . . .'

Hunt's young admirer ended by informing him that 'My father is in parliament, and on attaining twenty-one I shall probably take his seat.' As Hunt later wrote: 'He had only to become a yea and nay man in the House of Commons, to be one of the richest men in Sussex. He declined it, and lived upon a comparative pittance. Even the fortune that he would ultimately have inherited, as secured to his person, was petty in the comparison.'

A haunted, questioning youth since childhood, the eldest son and heir of Sir Timothy Shelley Bt. of Castle Goring, Sussex, Shelley had been expelled from Eton for such unruly behaviour as setting trees on fire, and was soon to be sent down from University College, Oxford, for publication of a pamphlet advocating atheism. 'His way of proceeding,' as Hunt put it, 'was entirely after the fashion of those guileless, but vehement hearts, which not being well replied to by their teachers, and finding them hostile to inquiry, add to a natural love of truth all the passionate ardour of a generous and devoted protection of it.' Shelley's other hero of the hour was William Godwin, eventually to become his father-in-law; Godwin's *Enquiry Concerning Political Justice*

(1793), he wrote to its author early in 1812, 'opened to my mind fresh and more extensive views. It materially influenced my character, and I rose from its perusal a wiser and a better man.'

Hunt does not seem to have taken up young Shelley's suggestion of a 'methodical society'; but the two were soon to meet via the good offices of Hunt's father-in-law, Rowland Hunter. When Shelley arrived at his publishing house with some samples of his poetry, Hunter sent him round to see the political campaigner he so admired, also a poet, and editor of a journal which might print his work. They met on Sunday, 5 May 1811, when Hunt felt obliged to dissuade Shelley from publishing his early effusions – advice Shelley appears to have accepted with good grace. 'He is a man of cultivated mind, and certainly exalted notions,' Shelley wrote of Hunt to his friend Thomas Jefferson Hogg (soon to be sent down from Oxford with him for co-publishing the atheist tract). There was little sign of the momentous friendship ahead as Shelley paid Hunt a few more short visits, which 'did not produce intimacy. He was then a youth, not yet come to his full growth; very gentlemanly, earnestly gazing at every object that interested him, and quoting the Greek dramatists'.

If Shelley would not be a major player in Hunt's life for a while yet, his eventual publisher already was. Charles Ollier, a clerk at Coutts bank who would soon start a publishing imprint with his younger brother, was one of Hunt's growing circle of literary acquaintance contributing to the *Reflector*, a quarterly launched by Leigh and John in 1810. Designed to complement the *Examiner*, whose launch it followed hard upon, the *Reflector* aspired to be an improvement upon its many contemporaries in the coverage of politics, the fine arts 'and all subjects relative to Wit, Morals and a true Refinement'. Declared Hunt: 'Reform of periodical writing is as much wanted in Magazines, as it formerly was in Reviews, and still is in Newspapers.' What he did not spell out publicly was that this new journal also gave its editor, now known as a strange combination of drama critic and fearless political polemicist, the chance to re-emerge as a poet.

Since his *Juvenilia* Hunt had written little poetry and published less; after some lyrics set to music by John Whitaker, occasional contributions to the *Poetical Register* and a handful more in the *Examiner*, he now published his first substantial work in the *Reflector* under the title

'Politics and Poetics'. Subtitled 'The Desperate Situation of a Journalist Unhappily Smitten with the Love of Rhyme', it takes the form of highly personal, autobiographical musings upon the role of poetry as an escape route from the workaday worlds of politics and publishing. There are references to the failed prosecutions against the *Examiner*, and apparent intimations of forthcoming events, as well as fierce *ad hominem* attacks on political writers not to his taste: Canning and Gifford, Scott and Sheridan. These he toned down in later versions, eventually deleting them altogether. But it remains a lively, vigorous piece, freighted with signs of what the mature Hunt would be capable of, in verse as in prose.

To him, the launch of the *Examiner* had 'found literature, poetry especially, sunk to the feeblest, tamest and most artificial of graces – the reaction upon the long-felt influence left by the debauchery of the Stuarts and the vulgarer coarseness of the early Georges . . .' Hunt found the 'mild' William Hayley and the 'mechanical' Erasmus Darwin 'occupying the field', with Pope 'the accredited model'. He 'revolted against copybook versification, the complacent subserviency and mean moralities of the muse in possession'. The *Reflector* was designed to supplement the *Examiner* in setting all this to rights. 'Leigh Hunt,' as his son Thornton put it, 'had not the sustained melody and pulpit morals of the Lake School; but he gave the example and encouragement to writers of still greater force and beauty.'

When the first issue of the *Reflector* appeared in January 1811, it was one of at least thirty such magazines being published in London, despite the government's attempts to control the press by means of stamped paper. This was the year that saw Cobbett jailed for criticising the Cabinet, his *Weekly Register* as influential as Francis Jeffrey's *Edinburgh Review* and William Gifford's *Quarterly Review*. Also predominant were the *Gentleman's Magazine* and the *European Magazine*, which both dated well back into the previous century. Hunt immediately made powerful enemies by declaring that some of the *Reflector*'s rivals were 'in their dotage', while most of the new arrivals 'have returned to the infancy of their species – to pattern-drawing, doll-dressing, and a song about Phillis'.

The *Reflector* was to prove as short-lived as many of its fellows; but its four issues over fifteen months were to make a lasting impact by relaunching the art of the 'occasional essay', as developed by Hunt and refined by his fellow Bluecoat, Charles Lamb. Acknowledging a debt to Addison and Steele, Hunt took Dr Johnson's moralistic view of the essay form, that it should 'inculcate wisdom and piety'. The personal element was also part of the fabric of the 'familiar' essay, as in Hunt's celebrated exercise in making something out of nothing, 'A Day by the Fire'. In the judgement of posterity, more than one critic has rated Hunt the 'greatest' of English essayists, rivalled only by his friends Lamb and Hazlitt. The Victorian critic George Saintsbury testified that Hunt 'transformed the 18th Century magazine essay', the American scholar Kenneth Neil Cameron that 'the ancestry of the magazine article of today can be traced more readily to Hunt than to any other writer' and the British historian E.P. Thompson that 'The *Examiner* served with brilliance as the weekly of the Radical intelligentsia.'

Hunt's own contributions to the *Reflector*, while also its editor and part-owner, ranged from political and theatrical musings to poetry, satire and essays. Still only twenty-six, he was already approaching the height of his powers, soon to be dented by his own penchant for out-spokenness; as editor of the *Examiner* he was an influential figure, content to make enemies in high places and among his rival editors. Both would return to haunt him. But the *Reflector* also saw the first flourishings of Hunt's gifts as a friend; he was what would nowadays be called a 'networker', or (more accurately) an 'enabler', the focal point of a diverse group of cultured men often more gifted than himself, their promoter and champion, but also the driving force behind their mutual influence and productivity.

Prominent among them was to become Charles Lamb, some of whose finest early work appeared in the *Reflector*. Now thirty-five (ten years older than Hunt), and earning his living as a clerk at East India House, Lamb was also guardian to his sister Mary, who suffered peri-odic attacks of insanity, during one of which she had attacked their parents with a knife, wounding their father and killing their mother. To spare his sister permanent incarceration in an asylum, Lamb had taken her into his own home in 1799. Amid further bouts of insanity on Mary's part, they had nevertheless managed to collaborate on several books for children, most famously *Tales from Shakespeare* (1807). All his life Lamb chose to wear long clerical gaiters, knee-breeches and tail-coat, all long out of fashion; his many friends remarked on 'the special sweetness of his expression', Hunt describing his features as 'strong yet delicately cut in a face that carried great marks of feeling and thought'.

Also a playwright, Lamb published his *Specimens of English Dramatic Poets* in 1808 and became a regular contributor of poems and essays to both the *Examiner* and now the *Reflector* – fourteen in its first year alone, ranging from his celebrated essays on Shakespeare, Hogarth and Garrick to his famous 'Farewell to Tobacco' and another which would eventually become one of his *Essays of Elia* (1823), 'A Bachelor's Complaint of the Behaviour of Married People'. How Hunt and Lamb were brought together at this time is disputed – they had been aware of each other's existence since childhood but had not yet become friends – but Lamb was henceforth to be a mainstay of Hunt's life, both social and professional.

It was Lamb who introduced Hunt to Hazlitt, whom he had first known as a portrait painter in the early 1800s. Having abandoned fine art for polemical journalism, the belligerent radical had already fallen under the tutelage of Coleridge and published several philosophical and literary works as well as contributing to Cobbett's *Political Register* and working as a parliamentary reporter on Perry's *Morning Chronicle*. Hazlitt and Hunt shared ecclesiastical parentage with New World connections; theirs was to prove a long, momentous partnership, not without its difficulties.

By the time Marianne had given birth to their first child, a son named Thornton, in 1810, the Hunts had moved out of John's lodgings to Beckenham, Kent, where their home became the centre of lively evenings of debate – literary, political and philosophical – among a vivid, wide-ranging circle of highly individual talents, fuelling their own pens while filling the pages of Hunt's various publications. Whatever lesser claim he may have to literary immortality, it is this gift of friendship which distinguishes Hunt from so many of his contemporaries and became the hallmark of a life much longer than many of them were to enjoy.

'Friendship,' as he himself put it, 'was a romantic passion with me . . . I call friendship the most spiritual of the affections.' The literary circle in which he moved was developing a weekly routine around individual homes, including Hunt's; the group has been described as 'inbred' and 'the same set of acquaintances moving from one drawing-room to the next' but also, more justly, as 'a loose grouping of minds who, finding each other's company stimulating, framed the week in order to enjoy it'.

Sunday lunch was taken at the home of the painter Haydon; on Tuesdays, 'at home' for music and whist, was Thomas Alsager, Thomas Barnes's assistant at *The Times*, to Hunt 'the kindest of neighbours, a man of business who contrived to be a scholar and a musician'. Music was also on the menu at the home of the composer Vincent Novello, along with cheese and beer. But the highlight of the week was generally regarded as Thursday evening *chez* Lamb – suppers which were 'feasts less for the palate than the mind and soul', involving other regulars such as Hazlitt and the lawyer-diarist Henry Crabb Robinson.

'What I would not give for another Thursday evening!' sighed Hunt on Friday mornings. 'How often did we cut into the haunch of letters, while we discussed the haunch of mutton on the table!' laughed Hazlitt. 'How we skimmed the cream of criticism! How we got into the heart of controversy! How we picked out the marrow of authors!' Lamb's puns and witticisms had 'a smack in them, like a roughness on the tongue'.

The circle's court jester was not Lamb himself, nor Hazlitt or Hunt, but the poet and radical George Dyer, an absent-minded eccentric who had been known to mistake a coal-scuttle for his hat, and once arrived home after dinner at Hunt's before realising that he had left one of his shoes under his host's table. The great punster Lamb was also the resident drunkard; Hunt was soon to note with surprise, after dining with Lamb and his sister, that he was 'very temperate and pleasant – poor fellow! He has every excuse for being otherwise, and therefore twenty times the usual credit for self-restraint.' (In 1812 Lamb published a remarkably candid essay under the title 'Confessions of a Drunkard'.)

The Lambs' circle also came to include Wordsworth and Coleridge, William Godwin, Thomas De Quincey and Robert Southey, all of whom would remain outside Hunt's regular coterie. Crabb Robinson, indeed, reports Lamb ('in his droll and extravagant way') rebuking Hunt for calling their schoolfellow Coleridge a bad writer. In time,

Hunt would become the focal point of a group boasting even more lustrous names as friends and colleagues. For now, Christ's Hospital alone provided such *Reflector* contributors as Lamb, Barnes, Dyer, James Scholefield and Thomas Mitchell; others included Ollier, Barron Field (now of *The Times*), the artist Henry Fuseli, the Irish poet Thomas Moore and Hunt's painter-uncle, Benjamin West. The *Reflector* would see the first publication of Hunt's verse survey of classic and contemporary poetry, *The Feast of the Poets*, which would undergo numerous revisions (over almost half a century) as his views evolved. This and other of his erudite effusions, from translations to Latin epigrams and sundry ornate asides, had never really been at home in The *Examiner*, which suggests that the *Reflector* was launched to suit Hunt rather than its readership, for all the commercial instincts of his brother John.

Hunt himself wrote nine articles in the first issue, amounting to 108 pages and constituting forty-three per cent of the content; but all his ornate contributions, which diminished over subsequent numbers, were overshadowed by the effortlessly elegant contributions of Lamb – on topics from hissing at theatres to burial societies.

By the time the fourth issue appeared in March 1812 the *Reflector* was improving with each edition, but its financial fortunes were flagging. Despite a rising circulation, the 'radical reformers' who amounted to its core subscribers were not 'sufficiently rich or numerous to support such a publication'. The depression of 1810–12 was certainly a factor in the suspension of publication for what Hunt, in later years, described simply as 'want of funds'. The optimistic word 'suspension' implies that this worthy enterprise might have resumed in happier times. But even the possibility was to be forestalled by the next momentous event in the life of Leigh Hunt, which was to be the making of his name but also, perhaps, the catalyst for a long-term reversal of his fortunes.

In the autumn of 1810, while celebrating fifty years on the throne, King George III had begun to show signs of sliding back into the mental illness which had periodically afflicted him for thirty years. George was 'an old, mad, blind, despised and dying king', as Shelley put it, his reign 'virtually over'.

The King was seventy-two years old, all but blind, and deeply dismayed by decades of conflict with his dissolute, debt-ridden son and heir George Augustus Frederick, Prince of Wales. Back in 1788, when the first onset of the King's illness had forced William Pitt's government to draw up contingency plans for a regency, albeit a restricted one, Pitt had prudently employed delaying tactics in hope of the King's recovery, fearing the consequences for his own government of the Prince's long-standing close ties to the Whig leadership. After some anxious weeks Pitt had been vindicated. The King did indeed regain his wits sufficiently for a regency to be deemed unnecessary; after months of political jockeying the dismayed Prince and would-be Regent had been left no option but to retreat and lick his wounds.

Now another Tory Prime Minister, Perceval, found himself engulfed in a replay of Pitt's dilemma. As medical men gave evidence on the King's condition to parliamentary committees, most of them motivated as much by their political leanings as their Hippocratic oath, furious lobbying in political and royal circles marked the drafting of another regency bill – again, to the Prince's dismay, denying him those of the sovereign's powers (such as the right to appoint peers) which would enable him to control the balance of power in parliament and thus shape the government.

This time the King did not recover, but the Prince's bargaining position had been weakened by the open secret of his illegal marriage to his Catholic mistress, Mrs Maria Fitzherbert, the scandals surrounding his subsequent, disastrous marriage to Princess Caroline of Brunswick and his continued accumulation of vast debts with which only the government could assist him. His own robust political views, moreover, had severely stretched his Whig sympathies. He was more in the Tory camp in favouring vigorous continuation of the war with Napoleon and vehemently opposing the emancipation of Irish Catholics.

In February 1811 George, Prince of Wales was duly sworn in as Prince Regent, unable to avoid accepting certain restrictions on his quasi-regal powers. Enraged by his retention of the Tory government, and yet more by his betrayal of Catholic emancipation, Hunt launched a series of scathing attacks on the Prince which soon found a focus bound to attract huge popular support.

One of the new Regent's first moves was to press for the reinstatement of his brother Frederick, Duke of York, as commander-in-chief of the armed forces. On 19 May the *Examiner*'s editorial mused that the Prince, for all 'his follies and his vices', had never, like the Duke, 'publicly degraded himself'. Two weeks later, when the Duke was indeed restored to his command, Hunt raged that the King's insanity must be hereditary, for only 'a native imbecility – an inborn ricketiness of mind' could have persuaded the Regent to reappoint 'one of the most imbecile persons existing'.

While allowing his anger to get the better of his prose style, Hunt did indeed find public opinion on his side. So unpopular was the Duke's reappointment that the government reluctantly stayed its hand against the *Examiner* – then at the peak of its popularity and influence, with a weekly sale of seven thousand copies – read 'especially', according to Jeremy Bentham, 'among the high political men'. But its editor was now hell-bent on a collision course with the Prince Regent that could only end in court. On the front page of the issue of 8 March 1812, under the heading 'Princely Qualities', Hunt tried in vain to come up with a single act of 'generosity', 'patriotism' or 'magnanimity' on the Prince's part, proceeding to put himself in the royal shoes and spend an average day doing the rounds of his cronies and mistresses, boldly identified by their initials: 'I was at Mrs R's, Mrs C's and Mrs F's, at my Lady J's and my Lady H's.'

Finally he imagines the Prince's conscience challenging him to explain why he had 'turned out of doors' the Whigs, to which Hunt's Prince responds: 'I referred him for a convincing argument in my favour to a particular "Book" in my library, with another – an account-book – by the side of it.' If the latter was a clear reference to the Prince Regent's debts, the first 'Book' referred to could only be the 'Delicate Investigation' by Perceval, when Attorney-General, of the Prince's charges of adultery against his wife, Caroline. When his attempt to divorce her had failed, this black propaganda 'Book' had been suppressed and all copies supposedly tracked down and withdrawn from circulation. Hunt appeared to be taunting both Prince and government that a copy had come his way.

If this was a veiled threat, his sustained anger against the Prince was inspired above all by rage at his betrayal of Ireland's Catholics. Suddenly, in the early months of 1812, the *Examiner* was full of all

manner of squibs, taunts and thinly disguised satires ridiculing the
Prince and his circle. On 15 March Hunt published Lamb's anonymous
poem 'The Triumph of the Whale'. With his sister Mary in confinement, Lamb 'threw caution to the winds' in writing 'The Whale'
(believed by some to have been the work of Byron). Not really a political animal, Lamb seized his chance to reply to attacks from Gifford in
the *Quarterly Review* while his 'voice of reason' – who might normally
have 'checked his pen' – lay 'raving in a madhouse'.

Typical of the poem's fifty-two stinging lines mocking the 'finny
people's King' was:

> Not a fatter fish than he
> Flounders round the polar sea.
> See his blubbers – at his gills
> What a world of drink he swills,
> From his trunk as from a spout
> Which, next moment he pours out,
> Such his person – next declare,
> Muse, who his companions are.
> Every fish of generous kind
> Scuds aside or shrinks behind;
> But about his presence keep
> All the monsters of the deep;
> Mermaids with their tails and singing
> His delighted fancy stinging . . .
> Name or title, what has he?
> Is he Regent of the Sea?
> . . . With his wondrous attributes
> Say what appellation suits?
> By his bulk and by his size,
> By his oily qualities,
> This (or else my eyesight fails),
> This should be the Prince of Whales.

That month the annual celebrations of St Patrick's Day in London
happened to coincide with the approach of the Prince Regent's fiftieth
birthday. At the Freemasons Tavern, with many senior public figures

present, the King's health was drunk with 'enthusiastic and rapturous applause'. When the Marquis of Lansdowne proposed that of the Prince of Wales, however, there were 'loud and reiterated hisses'; when the playwright Richard Brinsley Sheridan, a close friend of the Prince, tried to speak up for him, he was 'coughed down'. Outraged by reports of the event, the Tory *Morning Post* chose to mark the Prince's half-century with a verse tribute extolling him as the 'Glory of the People . . . the Protector of the Arts . . . the Maecenas of the Age'. It continued: 'Wherever you appear, you *conquer all hearts*, wipe away tears, excite *desire and love*, and win *beauty* towards you . . . You breathe *eloquence* – You inspire the Graces – You are an *Adonis in Loveliness*!' As if this were not enough, subsequent adjectives included 'delightful', 'blissful', 'wise', 'pleasurable', 'honourable', 'virtuous', 'true' and 'immortal'.

That weekend, on 22 March, Leigh Hunt published a long, vigorous riposte in the *Examiner* under the heading 'The Prince on St Patrick's Day':

> What person, unacquainted with the true state of the case, would imagine, in reading these astounding eulogies, that this *Glory of the People* was the subject of millions of shrugs and reproaches! That this *Protector of the Arts* had named a wretched Foreigner his Historical Painter in disparagement or in ignorance of the merits of his own countrymen! That this *Maecenas of the Age* patronized not a single deserving writer! That this *Breather of Eloquence* could not say a few decent extempore words – if we are to judge at least from what he said to his regiment on its embarkation for Portugal! That this *Conqueror of Hearts* was the disappointer of hopes!

> As for the *exciter of Desire*, well, 'bravo, Messieurs of the *Post*!' Far from being an '*Adonis in Loveliness*', Hunt's furious polemic concluded, this princely betrayer of Catholic emancipation was a 'corpulent gentleman of fifty . . . a violator of his word, a libertine over head and ears in debt and disgrace, a despiser of domestic ties, the companion of gamblers and demireps, a man who has just closed half a century without one single claim on the gratitude of his country or the respect of posterity'.

This time, even his friends agreed, Hunt had finally gone too far. He might well have argued that his remarks about the Prince were true and justified; but that was no defence, as well he knew, against the legal measure of their tendency to bring the Regent into 'public hatred, contempt or ridicule'. A lawsuit seemed inevitable. 'Everything is a libel, as the law is now declared,' Hunt shrugged to his friends, 'and our security lies only in their shame.' Undeterred, he maintained the bombardment in the following issue, whose editorial 'Proceedings of the Regency' ended with heavy irony: 'The rest of this week [the Prince] spent, of course, in the usual manner, with the usual society; and tomorrow he goes to St James's Chapel *to receive the sacrament!*'

On 20 April the Hunt brothers, as editor and publisher, were formally notified that an 'information for libel' had been laid against them, to be heard in court on 27 June. That weekend Hunt dared the legal establishment to 'Do your worst!' in a leader fearlessly discussing the 'Charge of Libel for Explaining the True Character of His Royal Highness the Prince Regent'. Even the headline was inflammatory; that defiant 'True Character' amounted to a repetition of the libel. The trial was set for July, and the brothers retained their friend Brougham for the defence.

Come the appointed day, the court was extremely crowded 'in expectation' (in the words of the official report) 'of hearing this important case'. But, the report goes on: 'When the names of the special jurors were called, out of twenty-four who had been, or ought to have been, summoned, only six answered; and the Crown not being willing to make up the other six from the Common Jurors in attendance (Householders of Westminster), Mr Garrow [the Solicitor-General] announced that the trial must be postponed . . . The cause therefore stands over till next term.'

Garrow was relieved to postpone, as he had been appointed to his high office only that day and thus had had no time to prepare. But the Crown had also learnt, from those previous debacles involving the Hunts among others, not to entrust important verdicts like this to 'common' jurors. The delay would give the prosecution the chance to stack the jury.

Some of the *Examiner*'s supporters, including the editor himself, at first regarded the postponement as a sign of weakness on the Crown's part. Hunt returned to his studies with 'the same quietness and serenity that had accompanied me through this and a similar suspense formerly'. But it soon became clear that the opposite was true; the delay would serve merely to strengthen the prosecution's hand. 'I feel somewhat anxious about the verdict,' Brougham wrote to Earl Grey, 'but am full of confidence as to the defence and its effects all over the country; it will be a thousand times more unpleasant than the libel.'

As they soberly prepared for jail, the uncomfortable waiting period for the Hunts and their families extended into all of six months. Nothing daunted, Hunt maintained his tireless public fusillade against the Prince, climaxing in November with a long Open Letter in the 'Political Examiner', which referred to several meetings in Downing Street and the royal palaces about the wisdom of proceeding with the suit, and assured him: 'Sir, you have most unaccountably mistaken your men, if . . . you conclude that any one thing upon earth, short of your own amendment, can alter our opinion of your proceedings, or our determination to express it to the very utmost that English freedom will allow.' It continued:

> The question is not between a Prince and a mere libel; it is not between the sovereign dignity and a popular piece of presumption; it is, as I have already stated, between the Licentious Example of a Court and the Voice of Public Virtue; it is a question of how far those vices, which do not come under the cognizance of the laws, are to be subject to the control of the public spirit . . .
>
> It is a question, in short, how far the petty comfort of one man is to be preferred to the vital interests of millions, and to the last security of national existence.

Jailing his critics, Hunt warned the Prince, would succeed only in 'mending the nib of an editor's pen, and in only making it sharper by reducing it of its bluntness'. The Prince should ask his friend Sheridan, the playwright, about rhetoric. 'Rhetoric has weapons, which nothing can either escape or arrest. A prison will only give us double leisure to polish them.'

For all his braggadocio and the apparent defiance with which he awaited his fate, Hunt suffered mightily during the lengthy postponement of his trial. For the first six months of 1812 his health had been unusually sound; by July, after the case was put back, he was again subject to the familiar palpitations, dizziness, spots before the eyes and sleepless nights. His weekly work for the *Examiner* began to flag accordingly.

With Marianne heavily pregnant again, John's plans to send Leigh to recover with relatives in Somerset had to be put on hold. Not until she had given birth to their second child, John Horatio Leigh, in early August was he dispatched to the country. But his letters home showed no sign of improvement; he tells Marianne of lurid nightmares amid forlorn longings for her and their children.

By August Hunt was so ill that he had to decline a coveted invitation to dinner with Jeremy Bentham, whose praises he had been singing in the *Examiner*. Obsessed as ever with exercise and diet, he grew wary of the simplest foods. 'My disorder has been a bilious one, of a most annoying and hypochondriac description,' he wrote to Tom Moore in September. 'A potato or a glass of milk would cause me more trouble than all the princes and attorney-generals put together.' He was also worried, very worried, about money.

In a desperate letter to his brother dated 14 July, Hunt confesses to staggering debts and requests John's help with them. 'I have made the requisite summaries out of Mrs Hunt's account-books, and I have been truly dismayed at finding the difference between the total sums which tens, fifteens & twenties make in the mind, & what they produce upon paper . . . The whole of what I owe amounts to £550 & a few shillings. This is every tittle – but you will think it enough to frighten both you & myself . . .'

An interim banker's loan of £50 seems to have eased his immediate worries; his voice grows calmer in the letter forwarding the money to Marianne, whose own letters no longer give him cause for complaint. 'The roles in their relationship had reversed, and she had grown stronger, he weaker,' as Blainey divined. 'She was no longer his wayward pupil, but rather his protector and mother.'

By early September Hunt could no longer bear the country exile which seemed to be doing him so little good. 'Do not be alarmed at finding me very thin,' he warned Marianne before embarking on the journey home from Taunton. He arrived back in London 'reduced to skin-and-bone'. The immediate solution, pending the trial, seemed to be a move out of town to the rural village of Hampstead, where the Hunts took a cottage in West End Lane.

'There is a green about it,' he wrote to Brougham, 'and a little garden with laurel.' It was a bona fide cottage, 'with most humble ceilings and unsophisticated staircases'. He soon felt the better for filling his room with his 'little library of poets', hanging his beloved portrait of Milton in pride of place, and preparing once again to entertain as he regained strength 'by small degrees and small portions of exercise'.

Within days, however, young Thornton was taken ill after a country walk in 'shoes too thin for the country ground after these rains'; and his father's health re-collapsed in sympathy, as if looking for an excuse to avoid society under the strain of the impending trial.

But Brougham was an unavoidably frequent – and welcome – visitor, as they prepared the case together over 'a plain joint and a pudding' and many a glass of fine wine. The frequent correspondence between them at this time speaks as much of poetry and the theatre as of freedom of speech, but the strain on Hunt remained evident. Amid his continuing money worries, it was also Brougham who relayed what appeared to be another message from nervous royal circles.

'We were given to understand . . . in a manner emphatically serious and potential, that if we would abstain in future from commenting upon the actions of the royal personage, means would be found to prevent us going to prison.'

Calling it what it was – 'an attempt to bribe us' – Hunt noted merely: 'I need not add that we declined.'

4

'The wit in the dungeon'

1812–15

The case of The King v John and Leigh Hunt finally opened at the Court of King's Bench on 9 December 1812, nine months after publication of the offending article, in front of the Lord Chief Justice, Lord Ellenborough. Some ten thousand supporters of the Hunts' cause crowded against the court doors, temporarily preventing them from being opened. When order was eventually restored, the charge against the brothers, framed by the previous Attorney-General, Sir Vicary Gibbs, was formally read: 'Publication of a libel tending to traduce and vilify the Prince of Wales, Regent of these realms, and to bring him into contempt and disgrace.' The defendants pleaded not guilty.

After the offending passage had been read to the court, the Solicitor-General, Sir William Garrow, rose to suggest to the jury that this 'bare' reading of Hunt's 'malignant' words should be enough to convict the defendants. 'Every dispassionate, cool-thinking, reasonable man must be satisfied that the publication . . . was a libel', the whole point of which was 'to reduce the Prince Regent to the lowest point of derogation'.

Sir William granted that 'subtlety of reasoning or vehemence of argument' might sometimes plead in mitigation of 'warmth' of language, but in this case there was no such excuse. He was 'utterly at a loss' as to conceive what arguments the learned counsel for the defence would use; he would listen to those arguments carefully, of course, but thought it highly unlikely that he himself would have to trouble the jury again. A guilty verdict would 'transmit [their] names to posterity' as 'men of fidelity, of integrity, and of courage, and as men who had done nothing beyond their strict line of duty'.

Brougham began by reassuring the jury that it would not be necessary, as he made the case for the defence, 'to violate the purity of the court' by attacking 'those exalted persons around whom the constitution had thrown a shield', and for whom he entertained a 'most sincere' respect. He knew a much better way to a verdict of acquittal: the case for free speech. He pointed out that his clients had twice stood before the same court on similar charges which had eventually been dropped for that very reason. As Brougham began to go into detail, Garrow felt moved to intervene, swiftly supported by Ellenborough, to warn him to stick to the case at hand. Courteous to a fault, Brougham acquiesced.

But he had a strategy, on which Ellenborough was keeping an eagle eye. Brougham was not going to attempt, he told the jury, to demonstrate that the remarks about the Prince were true, merely that they were justified. In so doing he managed to produce enough evidence to suggest that the supposed libels were in fact true as well as justified. Alas, his ingenuity was to be wasted on a hand-picked jury and a hostile judge.

Leigh Hunt, Brougham argued, had written the article in question without 'any personal feelings of animosity towards the Prince, nor any wish to vilify or traduce his private character'. His words arose from 'the bitterness of disappointment at the hopes which he had entertained of the emancipation of the Catholics when the Prince Regent came into power'. The observations Hunt had made about the Prince were not from any knowledge of his private character. Hunt himself was a young man, under thirty, unacquainted with law courts and their ways, of studious and retiring habits, whose companions were 'books rather than men'. Politics certainly came 'within his range', but his chief preoccupations were literary criticism, history, poetry and 'other topics connected with the passing occurrences of the day', from the African slave trade to the governance of Ireland.

Hunt was a man of opinions, continued Brougham, who might be accused of being wrong, or of taking those opinions too far; but he was surely, as 'a free subject of these realms', entitled to those opinions. They were the result of 'deep-thinking'; and 'a person of ardent mind, who writes upon any subject to which he has given his attention, generally thinks he is right, and that he has justice on his side'. When the powers of the Prince of Wales had been advanced, when he had taken upon himself the administration of the government, Hunt was among those who had reason to expect him to maintain his previous position concerning the emancipation of Irish Catholics. So he was surely entitled to express disappointment and dissent when those hopes were cheated, when what he had considered 'almost within [his] grasp' was 'turned loose and astray, and not within the reach of realization'.

Brougham reminded the jury of the meeting at which there had been 'expressions of discontent' and 'marks of disapprobation' when the name of 'a certain person' was mentioned. Those sentiments may not have been justifiable, but was it so extraordinary that 'one at a distance should view their feelings with an eye of approbation, should enter into the spirit of those feelings, and comment upon the conduct of those who produced the sentiment therein expressed'? Combined with the 'gross and ridiculous' flattery of the Prince Regent in 'another publication', was it any wonder that Hunt saw this as an opportunity for observation and comment? The very men who used such flattery were 'giving up their prince to the power of his enemies'; the 'gross despiser of truths' was to be considered as the worst of the enemies of a prince. 'He who by his insidious arts seduced to vice, and then to continue the seduced in his error, covered him by gross praise, was indeed a detestable enemy. But to show that he was right in this statement, he had proofs to adduce that . . .'

At this point, just as Brougham was getting up a head of steam about the Prince, Ellenborough intervened to urge caution. Liberty of speech was given to court advocates, but must not be abused beyond the bounds of moderation. What proofs the learned counsel could adduce His Lordship knew not, in a case where the libel was 'so manifest'.

Any attempt to produce 'proofs' of the supposed libel were just what court and government dreaded. As Brougham tried to proceed, Garrow joined the Lord Chief Justice in protesting against the production of such 'proofs', to the point where Ellenborough felt moved to observe that 'to offer proofs in vindication of a manifest libel cannot be received'. There ensued heated debate between the three, which the Lord Chief Justice closed by forbidding 'any further observations as in justification of the libel'.

So Brougham again changed tack, attempting to demonstrate that Hunt was commenting not on the Prince himself, but on the 'dangerous' doggerel about him in the *Morning Post*, which threatened 'that most exalted and illustrious person with the grossest and most abominable ridicule'. It was true, of course, that HRH was 'too exalted to be affected by it'; that 'his high and illustrious station made him superior to the shafts of such evil-disposed persons'. It would take an 'inferior' person – himself, for instance, or, come to that, any member of the jury – to be sunk into ridicule and contempt by such 'trash'.

Indeed, an apology was required even for repeating such gross flatteries – which Brougham proceeded to do, purely to demonstrate that Hunt had been doing no more than examining with a 'just and critical eye' remarks which were 'a disgrace to the age'. He wrote merely 'with a view to publish and expose the absurdity of them'. If, in the process, he had succumbed to 'heat of irritation and feeling', then his own remarks should be seen in the context of those which had provoked them.

With Ellenborough waiting to pounce again, Brougham embarked on a lengthy diversion about Edmund Burke, who had denounced an act of parliament as an instance of 'great cruelty and injustice' if it had been passed in any other legislature. Elsewhere this 'person of loyalty and genius' had observed that 'kings are naturally the lovers of low company; that they are rather apt to hate rather than love their nobility', many of whom are themselves 'apt to act the part of parasites, of flatterers, and of pimps, and of buffoons, possessing more the qualities or lurking remains of Italian eunuchs'. Did Burke, asked Brougham, entertain a contempt for the monarchy when he wrote this? Did he not, on the contrary, exhibit a love for the monarchical part of the constitution; and did he not 'support it . . . to the last moment of his life'?

So it was with the defendant. If an 'incautious' word had escaped him in a moment of enquiry, should he any more than Burke be held up as worthy of punishment, as 'a person dangerous to the constitutional existence of the realms'? Anyone who so believed must 'give up the reins of free enquiry, denounce the observations of individuals upon public topics, and give a licence to persecution whenever it came'.

Leigh Hunt's counsel confessed that he wished his client's remarks had not 'escaped his pen', but stressed they had done so 'in the heat of deliberation' as 'nothing more than the effect of serious thinking, of due deliberation upon the ridiculous matter originally ushered to the public in the *Morning Post*'. To have suggested, for instance, that the Prince might have violated his word was not meant for a moment to vilify or traduce his character. 'God forbid that such motives could be ascribed to the defendants.' No, it was simply an allusion to the 'pledges and promises' which the Regent had formerly been 'supposed' to have given in respect to the Catholic cause. They were meant only to remind HRH of the bitter disappointment to which those Catholics had been subjected.

As to the suggestion that the Prince was 'in debt and disgrace', this did not, of course, apply to him as an individual. It was well known that the Prince had been heavily in debt; once he had been advanced to the office of Regent, the country had become liable for his debts, and had indeed paid them. To say, therefore, that he had run into debt, was in fact to say that 'one branch of the revenue was in arrears to the head of the government'.

Much the same, Brougham attempted to argue, applied to the 'delicate' and 'disagreeable' suggestion that the Prince was a 'despiser of domestic ties'. Again it was not a reference to private matters. It was a 'notorious fact', and so had become a matter of legitimate public interest to taxpayers. This was a question so delicate that Brougham 'trembled' as he approached it; he was relieved to move on to one where he found 'better footing' – the charge that HRH was 'the companion of gamblers and demireps'. This, too, was a 'notorious' matter of public knowledge. An Irish jury had recently convicted a member of the royal household of adultery, as duly reported in the *London Gazette*. The 'studious' Hunt, most of whose time was passed in solitude, was given to 'puritanical' notions about public virtue, and took as a 'grievous calamity' what more worldly men might see as nothing more than a 'light matter'. Those who chose to take up public life, those such as this courtier (whom he would not name in court), must pay the consequences. They were not entitled to have 'all their little merits basking in the sunshine, and all their great failings hid in the shade'. If such men chose to 'forsake the crook of the shepherd and to rest upon the kingly sceptre', they must 'accept the consequences of their temerity'.

To sum up: 'To repress the power of committing the opinions of individuals to writing' was 'a dangerous experiment'. There was nothing to fear from public discussion, much to fear from the repression of it. 'To stifle discussion is to nip the bud of freedom, to stop the genuine and legitimate plant in its growth . . . The weeds of disaffection might grow in its place . . .' During his father's unfortunate 'affliction', the present head of the executive government was surrounded by a court 'which in point of eastern magnificence might vie with any the most splendid' – a court against which any attack, however violent, could not succeed. But the jury were being asked 'to dread a line or two in a Sunday newspaper'.

Citing Cromwell and Milton as examples of great men immune to mere 'paper-shot', Brougham challenged the prosecution to demonstrate the public danger which could possibly arise from his clients' acquittal. Distant ages would look with a 'scrutinizing' eye upon this jury's verdict. When it came to the issue of free speech in a healthy society, his clients had not committed a crime but performed a public duty.

Were the jury prepared to let open the floodgates of immorality – to usher to the eyes of later ages a verdict which struck at the very existence of public and free discussion? If so, they would 'let loose a reign which, compared with that of Charles I, would show the latter reign as a wise one, and that of Charles II, gay, licentious and wicked as it was, a virtuous, honourable and upright one'. Posterity would 'reap the fruits' of an acquittal. Brougham knew that he and his clients were safe in the hands of this jury, for 'truth and justice must prevail'.

Noting the 'vehement' tone of his learned friend's remarks, the Solicitor-General proceeded to counter that the jury was faced with a duty which was growing more important by the day: to protect 'a foundation built by our ancestors', nothing less than the British constitution itself.

He, Garrow, was not acquainted with the ways of men 'in the newspaper line', but he questioned the 'warmth' in the style of a writer at work three days after the appearance of the article he was disposed to attack. He suggested that the Prince Regent had not 'changed his mind' about Ireland, merely continued to implement the policy of a royal father whose speedy recovery was prayed for throughout the nation. 'Shall it be said,' asked Garrow in the Prince's name, 'that when my afflicted parent was reclining on the pillow of affliction, I eagerly and greedily seized upon that power for the purpose of introducing new counsellors, so that when he returned to health, he might find to his regret his old advisers had been disregarded and dismissed?' Nothing suggested by his learned friend could justify the assertion that His Royal Highness was a 'violator of his word', and therefore to be held up to detestation. If Mr Hunt had discussed the policy and necessity of Catholic emancipation in a reasoning manner, then no possible objection could be raised. But he did not. There could be no excuse for the publication of his libels.

Garrow deplored a recent spate of libel cases, about some of which he went into detail – with no interference, this time, from the Lord Chief Justice. Skimming over the details of Brougham's defence, and speculating that Burke would be sorry that such a remark about royalty and the company it keeps had 'escaped' him, he put it to the jury that Hunt's article was written 'deliberately for the purpose of writing down the character of the Prince Regent, and so bring him into contempt'. Its publication was a 'gross, wicked and diabolical' libel.

Summing up, the Lord Chief Justice said the question before the jury was 'whether we should live under the dominion of libellers, such as the defendants, or whether we should seek the protection, and live under the control of, the law'. Hunt – the 'present libeller' – had 'put on a bold front', suggesting that anyone who inherits lofty rank by definition renounces the protection of the law. If men in elevated positions were to be subject to attacks of this kind, without the possibility of punishing the authors, what man possessing 'the least sensibility' would ever 'accept station or rank in this country'? If this spirit of libelling was not checked, it would in time produce the 'most fatal' effects: 'the destruction of those sensibilities, which were the strongest excitements to virtue, which were in truth the fosterers and protectors of all public virtue'.

As for the Prince Regent: the security of the empire, nothing less, might in great measure depend on the estimation in which he was held. If the public were brought to believe that he was one of the basest of mankind, could the exercise of the functions of sovereign authority be safely performed? Could anything be more 'calamitous' than the charges made by the defendant? Was it to be endured that HRH be held up to the subjects of this country as a person who, in the course of half a century, had done nothing – nothing – to entitle him to the gratitude of that country?

'To represent him as a person worthless for the past, and hopeless for the future!' concluded Ellenborough indignantly. 'I state to you that it is a foul, malignant and atrocious libel. If you are of that opinion, say so by your verdict.'

It took the jury all of ten minutes to decide that they agreed with His Lordship and return a verdict of guilty against both defendants.

Imprisonment seemed inevitable, as did some sort of fine. But how draconian would the sentence be? The brothers would have to wait six weeks to learn their fate. Hunt appears to have spent the unwelcome interval showing considerable grace under pressure. He declined an offer from Perry, the editor of the *Morning Chronicle*, to threaten publication of the 'Book' so dreaded by the Prince. 'Knowing that what it is very proper sometimes, and handsome for persons to offer, it may not be equally so for other persons to accept, and not liking to owe our deliverance to a threat or a *ruse de guerre*, we were "romantic" and declined the favour.'

In the *Examiner* Hunt brazenly continued to attack the Prince Regent and the 'vices' of his court, while boldly and indignantly arguing that Ellenborough, as a frequent visitor to the Prince Regent's homes in London and Brighton, had been unfit to try the case. At home he underwent another period of uncertain health and violent mood swings. After visiting him in Hampstead on 29 January, four days before sentence was due to be passed, his painter friend Haydon noted in his diary that they had 'walked out and in furiously' after dinner. 'Leigh Hunt's society is always delightful: I do not know a purer, a more virtuous character, or a more witty, funny, or enlivening man.'

At the time Hunt was encouraging Haydon to air his grievances against the Royal Academy in the *Examiner*. 'Hunt gets his living by such things,' Haydon was told by their mutual friend, the Scottish painter

David Wilkie, in an attempt to dissuade him. 'You will lose all chance of it. It is all very fine to be a reformer; but be one with your pencil, not with your pen.' Although as deeply in debt as Haydon, in one of his own many moments of crisis Hunt 'behaved nobly. He offered me always a plate at his table.' Hunt's own debts of £550 arose from expenditure of £871 the previous year, including the huge sum of £50 on that portrait of Milton. ('It was madness, I allow.') Already he was increasingly showing the signs of recklessness with money – and imperviousness to an extravagant wife, Marianne having run up an upholsterer's bill for £340 – which would cumulatively cost him dear. With it came a lifelong capacity for self-deception. 'I am quite aware I can have no command of my happiness,' he had told John, 'until I reduce my expenses to obedience.' He never would.

It was Wilkie who had first introduced Haydon to Hunt; both artists had been fans of his 'remarkably clever' theatre reviews in the *News*, and set out to make his acquaintance, even betting on who would meet him first. 'We liked each other so much that we soon became intimate,' wrote Haydon, after Wilkie had won the bet. In their first five minutes of conversation, even though Hunt 'held forth' while Haydon merely 'talked', Hunt had shown a 'frankness' that appealed to Haydon; as they grew to know each other, Haydon thought of Hunt, 'with his black bushy hair, black eyes, pale face and "nose of taste", as fine a specimen of a London editor as could be imagined'.

Three years older than Haydon, Hunt was 'assuming yet moderate, sarcastic yet genial, with a smattering of everything and mastery of nothing; affecting the dictator, the poet, the politician, the critic and the sceptic, whichever would at the moment give him the air to inferior minds of being a very superior man'. While disliking what he saw as Hunt's 'effeminacy' and other 'peculiarities', Haydon admired 'the fearless honesty of his opinions, the unscrupulous sacrifice of his own interests, the unselfish perseverance of his attacks on all abuses, whether royal or religious, noble or democratic, ancient or modern' – to the point where he 'suffered this singular young man to gain an ascendancy in my heart' and 'swore eternal friendship'.

Hunt's mind, to Haydon, was 'poetical in a high degree'; perhaps it facilitated friendship with so volatile a painter that Hunt, in Haydon's

view, 'relished and felt Art without knowing anything of its technicalities'. In 1809, while Haydon was painting his mighty canvas, 'The
Assassination of Dentatus', Hunt took a close interest, calling the finished picture 'a bit of old embodied lightning'. Haydon's account of
Hunt helping him carry it down to the Royal Academy could be a
scene from Puccini's *La Bohème*. 'Full of his fun', according to Haydon,
Hunt kept 'torturing' him the whole way, saying, 'Wouldn't it be a
delicious thing now for a lamp-lighter to come round the corner and
put the two ends of his ladder right into Dentatus's eye? Or suppose we
meet a couple of dray-horses playing tricks with a barrel of beer,
knocking your men down and trampling your poor Dentatus to a
mummy!' Hunt made Haydon 'so nervous with this villainous torture
that in my anxiety to see all clear I tripped up a corner man and as near
as possible sent Dentatus into the gutter'. Hunt had 'an open, affectionate manner which was most engaging' and 'a literary, lounging
laziness of poetical gossip which to an artist's eye was very improving'.
Whether in private or in public, alone or surrounded by friends, 'in
honesty of principle and unfailing love of truth, in wit and fun, quotation and impromptu, one of the most delightful beings I ever knew'.

As these two friends now talked of Hunt's forthcoming imprisonment, Hunt said it would be 'a great pleasure' to him if he were to be
sent to Newgate, because it was so near his old school. He would be
among friends. He and Haydon both 'laughed heartily at the idea of his
being in the midst of his friends at Newgate, and his being reduced to
say it would be a great pleasure to be sent there'.

John Hunt was painted by West at this time in the guise of a Roman
centurion. His less phlegmatic brother approached their day of judgement in more playful mood, heading back to court on 2 February
1813 in a new hat and gloves specially bought for the occasion and
clutching a copy of a favourite work, the 'Comus' of a Dutch poet,
Erycius Putaneus.

After they had entered the dock together, Leigh anxious to hide his
emotions for the sake of his 'excellent' brother, they listened to the
rereading of the libel, and of an affidavit in which they argued that they
had been actuated by no personal malice, or purpose of slander, and
were 'conscious of no motives which were not honourable'.

The sentencing judge was Mr Justice Le Blanc. Under the watchful

eye of Lord Ellenborough, he begged leave to differ with the defendants' estimate of themselves and their actions. They had been
convicted of printing and publishing a 'scandalous and defamatory'
libel on the Prince Regent. It was impossible for anyone to doubt that
its publication was a 'mischievous and daring' attack on 'a person who
was to be looked upon as filling the first situation in the government of
the country'.

For what purposes this libel was published, if not for those of slander or personal malice, it was impossible for the court to conceive.
Perhaps the defendants' motive was to gratify 'mischievous curiosity',
to 'minister to that diseased taste of the public, which was greedy to
catch at every attempt to pull down exalted characters to the lowest
level'. It was the court's duty to protect the government from those
who acted on such motives and opinions.

'In order to deter others from committing a like offence, by the
example of the present punishment', the defendants were each sentenced to two years' imprisonment, John Hunt in Coldbath Fields
prison, Clerkenwell, and Leigh Hunt in His Majesty's jail for the
County of Surrey, in Horsemonger Lane, Southwark. Each was also to
pay the King a fine of £500, along with a further £500 surety for good
behaviour over the next five years.

The Hunt brothers had been expecting prison – but together, not
apart. This was a huge psychological blow. As they were condemned
to two years in separate jails, the brothers 'pressed each other's
arms'. Neither had anything more to say to the court; Leigh felt that
John was looking to him, as the writer, to come up with a few appropriate and dignified words; but he was overcome by the fear that he
would start stammering, as always at his most nervous moments. It
was a risk he could not take, so the brothers accepted their punishment in silence.

They had not expected sentences as long as two years; and they had
anticipated being imprisoned side by side, on hand to help each other
through the ordeal of so long a separation from their wives and children. By parting them, the authorities were no doubt intent on making
it as difficult as possible, if not impossible, for the Hunts to continue
editing and publishing the *Examiner* from their respective prison cells.
Without even being allowed to speak to each other, they were taken

from the dock and 'torn asunder', escorted in different directions to different jails. 'It was,' recalled Leigh, 'a heavy blow.'

A Cruikshank cartoon depicting Hunt in chains as 'A Free Born Englishman! The Pride of the World!' was little consolation to him as he was taken by hackney coach, escorted by a tipstaff and his friend Barron Field, directly from the court to the Surrey jail. His first sight of its fearsome gate and high walls abruptly drove home the enormity of what had happened to him, bringing wistfully to mind his hopes of riding on Brighton Downs; but he took solace in considering himself one of the few inmates to arrive there with a clear conscience.

And he soon found unexpected entertainment in the shape of his jailer, a man named Ives, of whom he later painted a word portrait worthy of Dickens. Having been kept waiting in the prison yard 'as long as if it had been the anteroom of a minister', Hunt was eventually led into the presence of 'the great man', who rose from a bowl of broth to greet him with due solemnity. 'He had a white night-cap on, as if he was going to be hanged, and a great red face, as if he had been hanged already.'

Ives, it seems, was far from well. Under doctor's orders not to speak above a whisper, he confided to Hunt: 'I'd ha' given a matter of a hundred pounds that you had not come to this place – a hundred pounds!' Ives wondered what the government meant by entrusting such a gentleman as Hunt to his care; this was 'not a prison fit for a gentleman'.

Both his own gallows humour and his jailer's obsession with money were to return to plague Hunt. As in his childhood, he would be unnerved by some of the sights and sounds only to be expected in a jail; and he would have to bribe his way towards a degree of comfort and civilised living which might not. The process began that very evening, with Ives painting a grim portrait of life in the prison's regular cells, while suggesting that quarters befitting a gentleman like Hunt might be available in his own house – at a price.

When none of the prices suggested by Hunt seemed to reach his expectations, Ives agreed to house him for now in an empty garret, pending the arrival of his bed from home and the glazing of its barred and shuttered windows. The immediate price Hunt paid was a dispiriting evening of polite conversation with his jailer, who fancied himself, if not a literary man (he was dazzled by Hunt's bewildering copy of Pindar), a fit dinner companion for a gentleman.

In sharp contrast was the under-jailer named Cave, whose fearsome exterior belied a kind heart, and whose wife had the thoughtfulness to turn the key in the lock of Hunt's temporary cell at night so quietly that he was unaware of it. Later, however, as he heard less considerate staff slamming and locking the dozen or so gates between him and the world beyond the prison walls, Hunt slumped into a deep depression: 'The weaker part of my heart died within me. Every fresh turning of the key seemed a malignant insult to my love of liberty.' To fend off the nervous fits which always accompanied any blow to his fragile morale, he paced up and down his cell for three hours before climbing into bed and falling into a dreamless sleep.

At the age of twenty-nine, Hunt had not slept away from home 'above a dozen weeks in my life'. Intensely lonely, he shared his doubts and fears with his extended family of *Examiner* readers. In the issue of 7 February 1813, four days after his sentence had begun, he confided to them how much he missed his brother:

> Why separate two persons who are brothers still more by affection than by blood! A mere imprisonment, it may be answered, we could have borne with patience: – so we could; but is bearing with patience bearing with pleasure?
>
> And is the loss of liberty itself not enough punishment for inhabitants of this free country in our circumstances? But the law must make an example of us. Be it so, but let the example be according to the nature of the 'offence'. What feelings of brotherhood have we violated? What domestic ties have we torn asunder? What contempt exhibited for virtuous attachment and the charities of relationship! But let this subject pass. The thing is done, and we must submit to it.

Marianne was allowed to visit – but not yet, as both wished, to move in with him. 'I have the delight of knowing that she is a true Englishwoman both in spirit and tenderness,' he wrote in that same issue of the *Examiner*, 'and that as a palace itself would be a prison to me where my family are not, so the worst of prisons, where I was, would be a palace to them.'

The truth was that the less stoical Marianne was in danger of cracking under the pressure. 'I am almost envious when I see women going along arm in arm with their husbands,' she wrote, recovering sufficiently to adopt tones ironic enough to reassure him: 'It is for the public good, my dear love, therefore we must bear it with composure.'

On 5 February, three days after his incarceration, Hunt had submitted petitions to the prison governor and local magistrates pleading illness – 'violent attacks . . . accompanied with palpitations of the heart and other nervous afflictions' – as reason enough for his wife and children to be allowed to join him, and friends to pay him visits by day. Brougham proved a strong and supportive ally, calling regularly to see what he could do to improve Hunt's conditions, as did Field, still an apprentice lawyer, but eager to help in the drafting of petitions and other legal documents. Ironically, Hunt's doctor, Sir William Knighton, was also personal physician to the Prince Regent, so excused himself from any involvement; but the prison doctor, Robert Gooch, gave the evidence needed to support Hunt's cause, and suggested to the governor that the prisoner might be moved to a suite of two empty rooms on the south side of the prison infirmary.

As malevolent bureaucracy kept him waiting, Hunt complained to *Examiner* readers that he was 'cut off from all other, and locked up at six. From seven o'clock in the morning to five in the evening the chains of felons are clanking in my ears; my windows are too high to afford me any look out as I stand, and if I were to get upon a table for that purpose, I should only have the additional affliction of seeing what I hear . . .'

A Tory MP, Holme Sumner, was meanwhile telling the House of Commons that Hunt's room had a view over the Surrey hills, with which he was 'very well content'. Hunt's especial scorn was reserved for this particular visitor, who, arriving one day to inspect his conditions, bowed to the visiting Marianne, pinched the cheek of the infant Hunt in her arms and then 'went down and did all he could to prevent our being comfortably situated'.

By mid-March, however, Hunt's argument that he was a political prisoner, and so entitled to certain privileges, combined with influential Whig voices in the world at large to win the concessions he craved.

First, thanks to a kindly newcomer to the magistrates' bench, Lord Leslie (later Earl of Rothes), Marianne was allowed to move in, bringing the infant John with her, Thornton having been deemed too sickly and lodged with friends. Then the family were told they would soon be allowed to move to the infirmary wing, where a painter and carpenter were laid on to decorate the two rooms to Hunt's specification. Elated by news that brother John was receiving equally preferential treatment, and had been joined by his own family in 'comfortable' rooms at Coldbath Fields, Hunt could not wait to escape the noise of the chains.

By the time the Hunt family moved in on 16 March, its paterfamilias had created a room which would soon house a salon unique in either literary or penal history. Its walls were papered with a trellis of roses, its ceiling painted as a cloud-speckled sky and the barred windows hidden behind Venetian blinds. While the carpenter built him some bookshelves, in came as much of his furniture as the larger of the two rooms would accommodate, plus a piano, a lute and busts of the great poets.

His portrait of Milton hung on one wall, another of brother John in pride of place above the fireplace. There was 'not a handsomer room on that side of the water', declared Hunt himself, while one of his first and most constant visitors, Charles Lamb, mused that 'there was no other such room except in a fairy tale'.

The small prison yard outside Hunt meanwhile converted into a pastoral bower, shut in with green palings, his own prison version of his Arcadian Hampstead. This time the trellised plants, flowers and small trees were real, as were a neatly manicured lawn and an apple tree which eventually provided enough fruit for an apple tart, served by the maid also allowed to complement the Hunt ménage. By May 'the yellow globes were out and full, the Persian lilac hung with delicate bunches of blue, the daisies stood up quite swelling and proud, the broom shot out a profusion of snowy blossoms along its rods, and the left-hand rhododendrons threw up the promise of a splendid flower.'

In this garden Hunt would write as much as he read over the two summers of his imprisonment. Beyond its wicket-gate lay a larger prison yard sewn with blossoming cherry trees, which his imagination converted into Hampstead Heath. He would make a point of 'dressing myself as if for a long walk; and then, putting on my gloves, and taking my book under my arm, stepped forth, requesting my wife not to wait dinner'.

When, after a few weeks, Thornton joined them, he would often take his elder son along as his companion, and they would play 'all sorts of juvenile games' together. The poignancy of a small boy confined to jail was not lost on the childless Lamb, who felt moved to write a verse letter to young Thornton, whom he addressed as 'My Favourite Child':

> Gates that shut with iron roar
> Have been to thee thy nursery door;
> Chains that clank in cheerless cells
> Have been thy rattle and thy bells;
> Walls contrived for giant sin
> Have hemmed thy faultless weakness in;
> Near thy sinless bed black Guilt
> Her discordant house has built
> And filled it with her monstrous brood –
> Sights, by thee not understood,
> Sights of fear, and of distress,
> That pass a harmless infant's guess.

Lamb seems to have noticed the physical and psychological toll prison life was taking not just on Hunt, but on his two-year-old son, who went into so sharp a decline that it was reluctantly decided in April that Marianne should take the children to Brighton for a few weeks, leaving her sister Bessy in her place to look after her fragile husband.

When the weeks stretched into three months, not least because young Thornton proved as sickly a child as his father, the stream of letters between the couple could not conceal their sexual longings for each other. 'Pray do not repress your dear, dear feelings,' Leigh instructed his wife; and Marianne did not, responding with remarkable candour as to how she missed the union of their bodies as much as their hearts: 'You know what I mean . . . I must not think about it.' Replied Hunt: 'We shall mingle into one another and be inseparable.'

Separation from his family apart, Hunt admitted that after a while he began almost to enjoy jail, but only because he himself had converted his confinement into an alternative version of home – a literary salon which it soon became fashionable to visit. The easing of his conditions was due in large part to public indignation at his imprisonment, led by a sizeable contingent of political and literary sympathisers. Prominent among them was the Irish poet Thomas Moore, who anonymously published some verse attacks on the government under the title 'Intercepted Letters'. One, published in the *Examiner* of 2 May 1813, purported to speak in the voice of the Prince Regent, gloating over his opponent's discomfiture:

> The dinner, you know, was in gay celebration
> Of my brilliant triumph and H——t's condemnation;
> A compliment too to his Lordship the J——e
> For his Speech to the J——y – And zounds! who would grudge
> Turtle-soup, though it came to five guineas a bowl,
> To reward such a loyal and complaisant soul?
> We were all in high gig – Roman Punch and Tokay
> Travell'd round, till our heads travell'd just the same way;
> And we car'd not for Juries or Libels – no – damme! nor
> Ev'n for the threats of last Sunday's Examiner!

Moore, who had known Hunt since 1811, admired the 'manly' spirit with which he had undergone his trial and imprisonment. Despite a brief skirmish over whether Hunt was responsible for revealing Moore's identity as the author of the anonymous verses – which Hunt emphatically denied – Moore was sufficiently impressed by his first visit to the jailed editor to promise to return with his friend Lord Byron.

Byron, also of Whig sympathies, had been intrigued by Moore's description of Hunt's life in prison – his 'luxurious comforts . . . trellised flower-garden without, and his books, busts, pictures and pianoforte within' – and shared Moore's indignation over the brothers' treatment. Although himself on nodding terms with the Prince Regent, Byron expressed 'a strong wish to pay a similar tribute of respect', i.e. visit the incarcerated poet, laying plans to do so in a verse letter to Moore dated 19 May 1813:

But now to my letter – to yours 'tis an answer –
Tomorrow be with me, as soon as you can, Sir,
All ready and dress'd for proceeding to spunge on
(According to compact) the wit in the dungeon –
Pray Phoebus at length our political malice
May not get us lodgings within the same palace!
I suppose that tonight you're engaged with some codgers,
And for Sotheby's Blues have deserted Sam Rogers;
And I, though with cold I have nearly my death got,
Must put on my breeches, and wait on the Heathcote;
But tomorrow, at four, we will both play the Scurra,
And you'll be Catullus, the Regent Mamurra.

It was four years since Hunt had first set eyes on Byron, swimming in the Thames 'under the auspices of Mr Jackson, the prizefighter'. But he had then felt no urge to introduce himself; to Hunt, back in 1809, Byron had been simply 'a young man who, like myself, had written a bad volume of poems' (although Hunt's indefatigable champion Edmund Blunden has argued that reading Hunt's *Juvenilia* as a Harrow schoolboy had 'pointed the way' to Byron's *Hours of Idleness*). The publication of *Childe Harold* in March 1812 – the month of Hunt's attack on the Prince Regent – had since changed all that; at twenty-four, five years younger than Hunt, Byron had made his reputation. In the first version of Hunt's *The Feast of the Poets*, which he was now revising in jail, Byron merits only a note – but a note describing him as a poet 'of great promise'. By the 1815 version, Hunt's Apollo would be showering Byron with praise while lamenting his penchant for 'misanthropy'. Byron in turn would be sending Hunt a copy of his *English Bards and Scotch Reviewers*, suppressed at the time, with a note explaining that it was 'a thing whose greatest value is its present rarity'.

That lay two years in the future when Byron came to pay his respects to the 'wit in the dungeon' on 20 May 1813. The afternoon passed in 'the most easy and discoursing manner', ending with an invitation from Hunt to return another evening for dinner. This Byron did, again with Moore, the following month; according to Moore, the evening was 'if not agreeable, at least novel and odd'. Having requested that no one else be present, apart from the inevitable members of the Hunt family, Moore was put out that they were joined by Hunt's friend Thomas Mitchell, the 'ingenious' translator of Aristophanes. Soon after dinner, furthermore, 'there dropped in some of our host's literary friends, who, being utter strangers to Lord Byron and myself, rather disturbed the ease into which we were all settling'. Moore's hindsight may have been clouded by the fact that one of them was the writer John Scott, subsequently author of some 'severe' attacks on his beloved Byron.

From Byron's point of view, the visit evidently went well enough for him to return alone a few days later, bearing a gift of books — 'with the air', as Hunt wrote to Marianne in Brighton, 'of one who did not seem to think of himself as conferring the least obligation'. Hunt was trying to win over his wife to Byron, about whom he knew she nursed doubts. But he was not to be deterred. 'It strikes me that he and I shall become *friends*, literally and cordially speaking; there is something in the texture of his mind and feelings that seems to resemble mine to a thread; I think we are cut out of the same piece, only a different wear may have altered our respective naps a little.'

More visits ensued, with Byron bringing Hunt Italian sourcebooks for his poetic work-in-progress, *The Story of Rimini*, a marathon update of Dante as experimental in form as *The Feast of the Poets*. The younger poet appeared to be developing a high regard for this literary man jailed for his political views, who cut such a beguiling figure in his prison salon. On 1 December 1813 Byron wrote in his journal: 'Hunt is an extraordinary character, and not exactly of the present age. He reminds me more of the Pym and Hampden times – much talent, great independence of spirit, and an austere, yet not repulsive, aspect. If he goes on *qualis ab incepto*, I know few men who will deserve more praise or obtain it. I must go and see him again.'

Byron regretted that 'the rapid succession of adventure, since last summer, added to some serious uneasiness, and business' had interrupted his acquaintanceship with Hunt. 'But he is a man worth knowing; and though, for his own sake, I wish him out of prison, I like to study character in such situations. He has been unshaken, and will continue so. I don't think him deeply versed in life; he is the bigot of virtue (not religion), and enamoured of the beauty of that "empty name", as the last breath of Brutus pronounced, and every day proves it.

'He is, perhaps, a little opinionated, as all men are who are the centre of circles, wide or narrow – the Sir Oracles, in whose name two or three are gathered together – must be, and as even Johnson was; but, withal, a valuable man, and less vain than success and even the consciousness of preferring "the right to the expedient" might excuse.' The following day Byron wrote to Hunt suggesting another visit: 'It is my wish that our acquaintance or, if you please to accept it, friendship, may be permanent.'

The scheme for *The Story of Rimini* had first occurred to Hunt on a holiday at Hastings with Marianne and Thornton; so uncomplicatedly happy had it been, and so wary was Hunt of the end of such happiness, that he returned to the celebrated section in the fifth Canto of Dante's *Inferno* where the dangers of such intimations are immortalised via the incestuous love story of Paolo and Francesca. Hunt's intent was 'to break the set cadence for which Pope was the professed authority, as he broke through the set morals which had followed in reaction upon the licence of many reigns'. He would 'shock the world with colloquialisms in the heroic measure, and with extenuations of the fault committed by the two lovers against the law matrimonial'. Both style and content, then, were wilfully controversial, with Hunt as intent to correct Pope's error in mistaking 'mere smoothness for harmony' as to develop his own new brand of couplet, largely dispensing with the customary end-stops and caesuras by scattering his metrical breaks throughout his lines, occasionally varying them with alexandrines and triplets.

Byron was to argue with Hunt about the 'system' behind the poem, which he expounded at length in a belligerent preface. He was also among the first to discern Hunt's failings: his worldly innocence ('not deeply versed in life'), his sometimes arrogant presumption, especially on matters poetical, and his pained sense of martyrdom. As yet, however, Byron was prepared to give this essentially 'good' man the benefit of doubts not yet confirmed; and he was also among those to discern with unqualified admiration what this supposed innocent was up to.

While continuing to lambast the Prince Regent and the judge who jailed him in vigorous fusillades in the *Examiner*, Hunt was craftily turning his imprisonment into a sustained and potent, if unspoken, attack on the government by maintaining 'a kind of prison salon of Whigs and reformers'. Among others who came to express a curious combination of sympathy and homage were his old friends Field and Mitchell, the philosopher and political journalist James Mill, the banker-poet Samuel Rogers, the novelist Maria Edgeworth and Hunt's patron (and kinsman) Sir John Swinburne, the wealthy, radical parliamentarian to whom he would later dedicate his poem *Foliage* with the words: 'You who visit the sick and the prisoner.'

Haydon felt 'the pride of a fellow-rebel' when visiting John Hunt as well as Leigh: 'I used to visit him and breakfast with him very often, and have spent many evenings very happily in his prison, and have gone away through the clanking of chains and the crashing of bolts to the splendid evenings at the British Gallery, and thought of my poor noble-hearted friend locked up for an imprudent ebullition of his brother's on a debauched prince who at that time amply deserved it.'

Hunt's earliest visitors also proved the most constant. Apart from Byron, Lamb and his wayward sister Mary 'came to comfort me in all weathers, hail or sunshine, in daylight and in darkness, even in the dreadful frost and snow' at the beginning of 1814. The Lambs felt 'an enormous debt of loyalty' to Hunt, who was in turn 'always afraid of talking about them, lest my tropical temperament should seem to render me too florid.' Hunt wrote a poem, 'To C.L.', in appreciation of these visits, and his welcome knock at the door. 'Then the lantern, the laugh, and the "Well, how d'ye do!"'

As well as paying regular visits, Hunt's literary friend Charles Cowden Clarke sent a hamper of fresh vegetables every Saturday: 'My father so entirely sympathized with my devoted admiration of Leigh Hunt,' Clarke recalled, 'that . . . I was seconded in my wish to send the captive liberal a breath of open air, and a reminder of the country pleasures he so well loved and could so well describe, by my father's allowing me to dispatch a weekly basket of fresh flowers, fruit and vegetables from our garden at Enfield.'

Clarke's father John was headmaster of the school near Enfield, ten miles north of London, where the young John Keats had been a pupil. Clarke himself, who had also taught Keats, had befriended Hunt the previous year in a circle built around the Olliers, four more brothers named Gattie, and Henry Robertson, brother of the John Robertson who had introduced Hunt to the Kent household and thus to Marianne. To receive a letter from Hunt, Clarke testified, 'was a pleasure that rendered the day brighter and cheerier . . . The very sight of his well-known hand-writing, with its delicate characters of elegant and upright slenderness, sent the spirits on tip-toe with expectation at what was in store.' Clarke spoke of Hunt's manner as 'fascinating, animated, full of cordial amenity, and winning to a degree which I have never seen the parallel'. It 'drew me to him at once, and I fell as pronely in love with him as any girl in her teens falls in love with her first-seen Romeo'.

Typical of Hunt's social arrangements in the Surrey jail was a jaunty letter to Clarke, acknowledging his regular hamper, on 13 July 1813: 'Dear Sir, I shall be truly happy to see yourself and your friend to dinner next Thursday, and can answer for the mutton, if not for the "cordials" of which you speak. However, when you and I are together, there can be no want, I trust, of cordial hearts, and those are much better. Remember we dine at 3. Mrs Hunt begs her respects, but will hear of no introduction, as she has reckoned you an old acquaintance ever since you made your appearance before us by proxy in a basket.' Hunt's letters from jail were sealed with an inscription reading '*E solo libero*' – 'And I alone am free'.

This rare prisoner's days were soon full of 'bustling talk and merriment' with 'music in the evenings, which always does me service', the table full and the conversation ranging around 'all sorts of subjects – politics, histories, poets, orators, languages, music, painting'. It was not long before his jailers were in some awe of the celebrated poet-prisoner and his succession of august visitors, who were allowed to stay as late as 10 p.m., when the under-turnkey would come with his lantern to escort them out. Hunt remembered him as 'a young man with . . . much ambitious gentility of deportment', who combined with the good manners of his friends to scatter 'an urbanity about the prison, until then unknown'.

That man of the people William Hazlitt, the passionate political and literary essayist whom Hunt had met through Haydon, felt obliged to linger on the threshold to exchange civilities with the young jailer, to the point where Hunt had 'great difficulty' in parting them. 'I know not which kept his hat off with the greater pertinacity of deference, I to the diffident cutter-up of Tory dukes and kings, or he to the amazing

prisoner and invalid who issued out of a bower of roses.' As if in a show
of solidarity – and admiration, though theirs was to prove a turbulent
partnership – Hazlitt soon became a valued contributor to the *Examiner*.

When Jeremy Bentham visited the Surrey jail, Hunt was playing
battledore (a forerunner of badminton). Upon joining in, the philosopher, 'with his usual eye towards improvement', suggested 'an
amendment in the constitution of shuttlecocks'. An elephant's trunk,
he explained to Hunt, could lift a pin or twelve hundredweight; the
same principle should be applied to the handle of shuttlecocks.
'Extraordinary mind!' exclaimed Hunt. 'Extraordinary!' echoed
Haydon, when he told him the story. Thrilled to receive so august a visitor, the prison governor marvelled at Bentham's 'local knowledge
and vivacity', remarking to Hunt: 'Why, Mister, his eye is everywhere
at once!'

Dubbing Hunt 'the Vates', Byron sent pheasants as well as books;
Field brought his sisters; Barnes of *The Times* brought his colleague
Alsager, music and financial critic, who soon became a firm family
friend. 'What a man he is!' purred Marianne with evident longing.
Now and then Haydon 'blew in', declaring himself 'ravenously hungry'
and demanding eggs, which Bessy duly cooked. The impoverished
painter even borrowed money from the impoverished prisoner, who
did not have the sense to accept it back when offered. When Haydon
finished his vast painting *The Judgment of Solomon*, he had the twelve-foot
canvas bought into the jail for Hunt's inspection.

For all these diversions, Hunt's first year in prison was 'a long pull
uphill': 'All these comforts were embittered by unceasing ill-health,
and by certain melancholy reveries, which the nature of the place did
not help to diminish.' In his infirmary suite, although he had escaped
the dread sound of the clanking of chains, he was regularly confronted
by the sight and sound of gallows being erected in the neighbouring
prison yard.

On one occasion the prison keeper took Hunt up on the roof, supposedly to show him the view of the countryside. In fact all he saw was
a sight he would never forget: 'a stout country girl, sitting in an
absorbed manner, her eyes fixed on the fire. She was handsome, and
had a little hectic spot in either cheek, the effect of some gnawing
emotion.' The keeper told Hunt she was in jail for the murder of her

illegitimate child. 'I could have knocked the fellow down for his unfeel-
ingness in making a show of her.' She was headed for the gallows.

After a joyous September reunion, Marianne was forced to leave again
within the month, taking a sickly John to the fresh air of Sydenham and
leaving Thornton alone with his father in jail, where they delighted in
each other's company. Bessy moved back in; and even John's sons,
Marriott and Henry, came to stay. Hunt's dependence on Marianne was
increasingly evident in the distress of his letters longing for her return;
after the turbulence of their courtship she was now more than ever the
dominant partner in the marriage. 'He needed her more than she
needed him,' as Blainey has observed. During her absences from her
imprisoned husband's side, Marianne 'began . . . to realize that the
marital power was hers'.

Certainly, Marianne's absence always brought out Hunt's depressive
streak, with which he could cope only by hurling himself into his work.
As well as his editorial duties, which proceeded with 'steadiness and
gratification', to the point where the compositors of the *Examiner* were
'petrified' by the 'volume and punctuality' of his output, he was also
pouring out sheet after sheet of florid, highly perishable verse.

The halfway point of Hunt's imprisonment was marked by the publication of the revised version of his verse satire *The Feast of the Poets*.
First published in the fourth issue of the *Reflector*, in March 1812, this
much-enlarged version was complemented by voluminous notes containing some of his most acute literary criticism. Although the work
would undergo numerous further revisions until the year of his death,
this first full version sets out Hunt's stall by borrowing a device from
Sir John Suckling (and ultimately, as Hunt owned, from the Italian
school) in setting Apollo in judgement upon the poets of the day, com-
paring and contrasting them with the classical masters. In this first full
version, only Thomas Campbell, Walter Scott, Robert Southey and
Thomas Moore are welcomed, amid some reservations, to Apollo's
table; George Crabbe is left waiting in an antechamber while
Wordsworth and Coleridge are rudely excluded and Gifford storms
out in a huff.

Perhaps prudently dedicated to his schoolfriend Thomas Mitchell,
who would soon become one of the first to lose patience with his

highly wrought style, Hunt's assessment of his contemporaries is chiefly interesting for his candour about Byron, whom he already seems to be treating in rather cavalier fashion, as if some sort of pro-tégé. 'I feel a more than ordinary interest in his fame,' wrote Hunt in the notes, 'and have had some chords about me so touched by his poetry, as to speak whether I will or not.' He intended, in other words, to offer the younger poet a few home truths. Hunt wished, for instance,

that, in the first place, he would habituate his thoughts as much as possible to the company of those recorded spirits and lofty counte-nances of public virtue, which elevate an Englishman's recollections, and are the true household deities of his country – or to descend from my epithets, that he would study politics more and appear oftener in Parliament; – secondly, that he would study society, not only in its existing brilliance or its departed grandeur, but in those middle walks of life, where he may find the cordial sum of its hap-piness, as well as the soundest concentration of its intelligence; – and thirdly, that though he has done a good deal already, he would consider it as little until he could fully satisfy himself – or if this could be difficult, perhaps impossible – that he would consider what he has done as too full of promise to warrant his resorting at any time to a common property in style, or his use of such ordinary expedients in composition, as a diligent student of our great poets will be too proud to adopt.

Byron seemed to take all this in remarkably good part. Thanking Hunt for a copy, in a letter of 9 February 1814 His Lordship expressed gratitude for his 'very handsome note . . . Of myself, you speak only too highly – and you must think me strangely spoiled, or perversely peevish, even to suspect that any remarks of yours, in the spirit of candid criticism, could possibly prove unpalatable.'

Is there a note of irony in this? It seems not – not yet, anyway – as the correspondent addressed as 'Dear Byron' ignores Hunt's saucy informality, and closes: 'I shall break in upon you in a day or two – dis-tance has hitherto detained me; and I hope to find you well and myself welcome.'

Drowning in debt, Hunt maintained an astonishing literary output amid all his incarcerated journalism and socialising. Soon he was to dedicate his next work, *The Descent of Liberty: A Mask*, to another schoolfriend, Thomas Barnes. 'I dedicated the first poetical attempt of my maturer years to a man of wit and scholarship, who stood the next above me at school: — allow me to present the second to another, who stood the next below. How far he was my superior in general knowledge, and the anticipation of a manly judgment, I well remember.' A vision of post-Napoleonic Europe, written by one political prisoner contemplating the exile of another, the mask was an enlargement of Hunt's 'Ode for the Spring of 1814', published in the *Examiner* of 17 April.

'Who, that has any fancy at all, does not feel that he can raise much better pictures in his own mind than he finds in the theatre?' asked the former drama critic in a preface explaining why he had chosen to revive the moribund genre of the Elizabethan masque, while intending his work to live in the reader's imagination rather than onstage. A meditation on his love–hate attitude towards Napoleon, whose armies Hunt depicts soaring above the stage on clouds, *The Descent of Liberty* has been called 'the principal poetic vision of Napoleonic Europe before Hardy's *Dynasts*'; certainly it was well received at the time, swiftly reprinting, and earning its author a long congratulatory letter from Henry Robertson, Ollier and others: 'In our admiration of its abundant beauties we were unanimous, whether we viewed it for its fancy, for the fine human feelings that it excites, or for the grand abstractions that abound particularly towards the close of the poem. Our hearts and imaginations were alike delighted, and we found the true ends of poetry answered . . .'

Hunt's hopes that the abdication of Napoleon, 'the great Apostate from Liberty', would lead to a change in 'the social atmosphere of the world' were to prove, of course, as utopian as his vision. The work was to be republished once, in 1819, before sinking into oblivion during Hunt's lifetime. But it has enjoyed something of a revival with recent critics, not least for its artful blending of 'high' and 'low' culture, with 'one foot in the aristocratic and high cultural heritage of the Stuart courtly masque and another in the popular culture of the masquerades'.

All this time Hunt continued to edit and contribute prolifically to the *Examiner*, while working on his romance *The Story of Rimini* amid these two other hastily produced works. As before and for long after, his prison years were immensely productive; for all his ill-health, a flow of letters also continued amid all the journalism, verse and conversation.

Throughout his first year in prison, 'all the prospect was that of the one coming'; during the second, 'the days began to be scored off, like those of children at school preparing for a holiday.' As this second year wore on, Hunt began to develop a kinship with his fellow inmates, who seemed to him remarkably cheerful in their adversity. 'Poor ignorant wretches, sir,' Cave remarked to him one day as they watched another new batch arriving. Although ahead of his time in linking a penchant for petty crime to the social conditions of the offenders, Hunt found himself more interested in the display of the human spirit; in the evenings, when they went to bed, he would stand in the prison garden listening to 'the cheerful songs with which the felons entertained one another'. Even the debtors, whom he came to pity more than the criminals, had their 'gay parties and jolly songs'. To Hunt, who had good cause for fellow feeling, there was an 'obstreperousness' in the debtors' mirth, which 'looked more melancholy than the thoughtlessness of the lighter-feeding felons'.

When Marianne again took the children to Brighton for their health in the summer of 1814, Hunt felt 'ready to dash my head against the wall' that he could not join them. 'I would sometimes sit in my chair with this thought upon me, till the agony of my impatience burst out at every pore.' He learnt to prevent it by 'violent' exercise, becoming an early evangelist for preventive (and genetic) medicine: 'All fits of nervousness ought to be anticipated as much as possible with exercise. Indeed, a proper healthy mode of life would save most people from these effeminate ills, and most likely cure even their inheritors.'

But Hunt believed in nurture as much as nature. To three-year-old Thornton in Brighton he wrote: 'Pray tell me what is the Greek for a horse, and a man, and a woman; a boy, a girl, the moon, and a flower; and as many of your fifty words as mamma chooses to ask you. You ought now to learn the Greek for the sea, as you are in the habit of seeing it; it is *thalassa*, and *kuma* is a wave – a ship you know already.'

By now the precocious young Thornton and his brother John had a sister, Mary – born in the Surrey jail in 1814, and delivered by her father: 'I was obliged to play the physician myself, the hour having taken us by surprise.' Hunt was almost as pleased to hear from his brother John that he, too, was still being decently treated at Coldbath Fields by 'a host who deserved that name as much as a gaoler could'. Amid the continuing stream of visits and letters – including one that November answering Cowden Clarke's request for a list of the finest arias of Mozart, of whom Hunt was an early champion – Brougham regularly sent material for Hunt's continuing harangues in the *Examiner* against the Prince Regent, enabling its imprisoned editor to write of 'the hissing, groaning, &c., with which the Prince is received wherever he goes', even of 'fright and signs of capitulation in Carlton House'.

On 21 September 1814, as Hunt entered the last months of his captivity, the lawyer relayed even more valuable – and extraordinary – news from a member of the jury which had convicted the brothers. This 'honest and amiable' man had, it seems, 'never ceased since the trial to lament his joining in the verdict' and was anxious to appease his guilty conscience by paying the brothers' fines. The offer had first been made soon after sentence had been passed, but Brougham had waited till now to relay it, while working – in vain, as it had transpired – for remission of their sentences.

So he had recently reopened negotiations with this 'excellent' man, whose offer still stood – 'a feeling', as Brougham put it, 'the more honourable because its duration clearly shows it not to be momentary ebullition, or the result of what might be termed a compunctious visiting, but a sense of duty and principle'. Naturally, Brougham urged Hunt to accept, after consulting with his brother and his wife. Equally naturally, Hunt declined, 'with proper thanks' – 'and it became us to do so'.

Shelley, too, had written with a 'princely' offer to launch a public subscription to pay off the brothers' fines – 'which at the time I stood in no need of', Hunt typically deceived himself. Shelley himself had little money at the time, but still sent £20 'by way of stimulant to the public'. Hunt himself was well embarked upon his lifelong disregard for the meaning of money; whatever the cost of the refurbishment of his rooms in the prison infirmary, and of laying on meals for his legion of visitors, he was by his own confession 'destitute, at that time, of even a proper instinct with regard to money' and was 'forced to call upon friendship for its assistance'. With £250 surety to be paid upon his release, Hunt was obliged – by no means for the first or the last time in his life – to borrow from his publishers against the sales of two more books, thus landing himself with the prospect of yet more work on top of his already demanding commitments.

As the date of his release finally approached, Hunt was unsurprised to find himself as wary of the outside world as he had been upon leaving school. 'It was thought that I should dart out of my cage like a bird, and feel no end in the delight of ranging.' Not so. In this, as in so much else in his life, Leigh Hunt would once again prove himself *sui generis*, defying convention as much as expectations.

5

'A new school of poetry'

1815–17

Liberty did little to lift Hunt's spirits. Released from jail on 3 February 1815, he found he could not bear to keep his eyes on the tide of humanity swirling to and fro as his coach passed along the Strand: 'The whole business of life seemed a hideous impertinence.' Reflecting upon 'the iron that enters into the soul of the captive', the habituated inmate found himself prone to an acute, unwonted form of agoraphobia; dependent as he was on friendship, yet so accustomed to confinement within a fixed space, he fretted about offending his many friends by declining their invitations out, begging them rather to come to him. Even Byron's offer of free seats at Drury Lane, where he was on the board of governors, could not tempt Hunt to venture forth from this continuing, self-imposed brand of incarceration. Besides, he had his pride in his critical independence to maintain. Even Lord Byron would have to visit him.

Unable to afford the kind of house befitting his station, which he had taken as his due in more prosperous days, Hunt at first took lodgings in Maida Vale to be near his brother John, his reunion with whom was predictably joyful. 'When we met, we rushed into each other's arms, and tears of manhood bedewed our cheeks.' At the *Examiner* they continued their unabashed assaults on the Prince Regent, but it soon became clear that prison had altered Hunt's critical priorities.

Continuing political outspokenness may have been expected of him by his loyal legion of admirers, to whom his imprisonment would always make him a martyr to the cause of reform; but the tide of European politics was not drifting his way, and his love of literature had returned to challenge, as much as complement, his political zeal.

Napoleon had regained his freedom at much the same time as Hunt, whose head may have raged at a government still resisting Catholic emancipation and parliamentary reform, but whose heart had been recaptured by the poetry which beguiled his imprisonment. England had been at war with the United States when he entered prison; now the Congress of Vienna was negotiating Europe's future in the wake of the Peace of Ghent. Hunt's fierce *Examiner* editorials continued to champion the liberal ideals which had made his name as a political prisoner; but his campaigning energies were henceforth driven by literary and philosophical as much as political concerns. The thirty-year-old Hunt who emerged from the Surrey jail in 1815 was less the hot-headed young polemicist whose courage had landed him there two long years earlier than the all-round man of letters he had always been by inclination and education, and would now always remain.

Combining the two imperatives would henceforth become Hunt's trademark. Now more than ever the *Examiner* would seek 'to revive', in the words of his original manifesto, 'an universal and decent philosophy, with truth for its sole object' and 'to improve the style of what is called fugitive writing, by setting an example of, at least, a diligent respect for the opinion of literary readers'. Hunt's aspiration, as editor and writer, has been aptly summarised in a recent edition of his works as 'a merger between political analysis, philosophical reflection, and a writerly style . . .

'If the political scene seemed grim, one could still fight the good fight through a process of cultural education: one might not be able to change the government in the next election but one could educate the next generation to a broader, more liberal view . . .' Hunt 'continued to insist that the poetical is the political, that good literature and good government flow from the same font of inspiration, that in the cultural as well as social realms one must speak truth to power and keep hope alive'.

Playing 'Addison to Hazlitt's Steele', then, Hunt contributed articles on Chaucer and 'the Poetical Character', while launching a lifelong interest in the quotidian with an essay 'On Maidservants'; Hazlitt, meanwhile, mused on subjects from 'Classical Education' to 'The Causes of Methodism'. In time the essays from this period would form the nucleus of their joint production *The Round Table*, compiled by Hazlitt in 1817 and so titled to suggest the 'convivial intellectual adventure' on which this first circle of writers to gather around Hunt was embarked. Hunt's dozen contributions already show his distinctive hallmark of throwaway references to Shakespeare and Homer, Plato and Dante, Pope, Dryden and Johnson, the classical, French and Italian poets, regardless of the matter at hand.

It was the poet as much as the political activist whom an intrigued and admiring Byron took to visiting regularly in his ornate little study looking out from Edgware Road across the fields towards rural Westbourne, for all the world a re-creation of his prison 'salon' apart from the lilies which now took the place of those decorative roses. To Hunt, as awed by his visitor's rank as his genius, Byron's appearance at that time was 'the finest I ever saw it', most like the celebrated Phillips portrait he considered far the best that had appeared: 'I mean, the best of him at his best time of life.' Although 'fatter than before his marriage', Hunt's Byron was 'only just enough so as to complete the elegance of his person'; and 'the turn of his head and countenance had a spirit and elevation in it which, though not unmixed with disquiet, gave him altogether a very noble look'. The 'succinctness and gentlemanliness of his appearance' was enhanced by his dress, which was 'black with white trousers, and which he wore closely buttoned over the body'.

On one occasion Byron and Hunt sat talking so long that Byron's wife, left outside in their carriage after buying plants at a nearby nursery, twice sent word to remind her husband that she was waiting. Seeing the rocking horse at the end of the garden, a gift from a friend to the Hunt children, Byron could not resist dashing outside to ride it. There was during this period a carefree note in the growing friendship between the two poets, a bond of mutual literary respect, which could not anticipate the stormier passages ahead. Even their differences of opinion were genial; if the revisionist Hunt had now (in the latest version of his *Feast of the Poets*) changed his mind about Wordsworth, dubbing him the 'prince of bards of his time', Byron grinned and bore it, venturing only the caveat: 'Who can understand him?'

At the time Hunt's praise of Wordsworth in his revised *Feast* earned him a visit from the great man himself, dispensing his opinions on their fellow poets of the day in the same little study frequented by Byron. When Hunt tells us how pleased Wordsworth was to see his own works given pride of place alongside Milton on his bookshelf, it is hard not to wonder if they had been placed there especially for the occasion. In that very week's issue of the *Examiner*, Hazlitt had laid into Wordsworth with a will ('Had he lived in any other period of the world, he would never have been heard of'); but Hunt's visitor apparently chose to overlook the slur in gratitude for (as Hunt saw it) 'the zeal I had shown in advocating the cause of his genius'.

Even that was a revision of his earlier views. The younger Hunt had expressed reservations about the Wordsworth of the *Lyrical Ballads*, listing a tendency to 'morbidity' and an 'over-contemplative' nature among the 'defects of a great poet' which 'turn our thoughts away from society and men altogether'. His revisions in the second edition of *The Feast of the Poets* retained these strictures while also pointing to the poet's strengths; now he was 'the most prominent ornament' of the first wave of Romantic poets. To one twenty-first-century critic, Hunt 'took the lead in identifying the beauties and explaining the defects of Wordsworth's poetry, thereby initiating the critical reassessment which would establish Wordsworth's reputation for the nineteenth and twentieth centuries'.

It was mid-June 1815, the week of the Battle of Waterloo, and the visiting Wordsworth put Hunt in mind of Napoleon, with his habit of keeping his left hand in the bosom of his waistcoat, extracting it only to pluck book after book from Hunt's shelves as he pronounced solemn judgement on his contemporaries in his 'deep and roguish but not unpleasing voice' with its 'exalted mode of speaking'. Thirty years later, at the height of his distinction, the same lofty eminence would remind Hunt of the Duke of Wellington, his 'gallant bearing' by then 'greatly superior', being 'quite natural and noble, with a cheerful air of animal as well as spiritual confidence'.

As yet, however, that famously noble brow could even stoop to levity, as when a cart happened to pass by the window while Hunt was asking whether he would care for any refreshment. 'Anything which is *going forward*,' replied Wordsworth in his 'lofty' voice – a pun that Hunt seemed to think worthy of his fun-loving friend Lamb; 'whatever is going forward' became a favourite phrase for the rest of his life. But Wordsworth's visit had Hunt in awestruck mode, suppressing the temptation to reply in kind on the grounds that levity would have been 'inappropriate after so short an acquaintance'. Instead, they discussed Milton – and Wordsworth's eyes burnt 'like fires'. They were such eyes as Ezekiel or Isaiah might have had, 'half burning, half smouldering, with a sort of acrid fixture of regard, and seated at the further end of two caverns'.

For all these passing excitements, Hunt remained far from well, both physically and psychologically. Always a great believer in the mental benefits of physical exercise – a perennial champion of Juvenal's 'mens sana in corpore sano' – he found himself unable to leave home without a 'morbid' wish to return at once, for fear of a fit, even 'sudden death', in the streets. Well aware that he was to some degree a hypochondriac, he nevertheless found himself unable to concentrate in conversation with friends, few of whom were made privy to his inner troubles, whatever his outward appearance. 'When they thought I was simply jaundiced, I was puzzling myself with the cosmogony. When they fancied me wholly occupied in some conversation on a poem or a pot of flowers, I would be haunted with the question respecting the origin of evil.' The agonies he suffered in the wake of his release from jail, the 'horrible struggles between wonder and patience', could be relieved only by moving to his beloved Hampstead, whither he repaired 'for the benefit of the air, and for my old field walks' in the spring of 1816.

Four miles north of London, approached from the east via the villages of Kentish Town and Islington, from the west via those of Kilburn and Paddington, Hampstead was then a rural retreat from the metropolis renowned for its leafy walks, its sylvan glades, its profusion of wild flowers and birds, notably nightingales. From Hunt's point of view, London was within easy reach as he went about his continuing business for the *Examiner*. For all the travelling to and fro, Hampstead's rustic charms seemed to offer a contrast as beneficial for his health as his poetry:

> A steeple issuing from a leafy rise,
> With farmy fields in front, and sloping green,
> Dear Hampstead, is thy southern face serene,

Silently smiling on approaching eyes.
Within, thine ever-shifting looks surprise –
Streets, hills, and dells, trees overhead now seen,
Now down below, with smoking roofs between –
A village, revelling in varieties.
The northward what a range, with heath and pond,
Nature's own ground; woods that let mansions through,
And cottaged vales with pillowy field beyond,
And clump of darkening pines, and prospects blue,
And that clear path through all, where daily meet
Cool cheeks, and brilliant eyes, and morn-elastic feet.

Subsidised by his father-in-law, Hunter, he took a cottage in a
hollow on the edge of Hampstead Heath then as now called the Vale
of Health – a picturesque cluster of cottages sunk in a nether world of
its own, at the time one of Hampstead's less gentrified areas, surrounded by clay pits and scrub amid patches of undrained marshland
to the east of Whitestone Pond. In fact, as Nikolaus Pevsner reports,
the Vale's name (first recorded in 1801) 'may have been ironic,
for . . . the remote area attracted anti-social activities such as tan pits
and a varnish factory'. Certainly, Hunt and his family – and at least
one of their notable guests – were to enjoy less than perfect health
there.

For now, at least, Hunt was in his own earthly version of Paradise.
Here in the Vale of Health, as if to confirm it, the Hunts' fourth child
(and third son), Swinburne, was born in 1816. Hunt was so pleased to
be back in Hampstead that he expressed his devotion in another sonnet:

As one who after long and far-spent years
Comes on his mistress in an hour of sleep,
And half-surprised that he can silence keep,
Stands smiling o'er her through a flash of tears,
To see how sweet and self-same she appears;
Till at his touch, with little moving creep
Of joy, she wakes from out her calmness deep,
And then his heart finds voice, and dances round her ears –

So I, first coming on my haunts again,
In pause and stillness of the early prime,
Stood thinking of the past and present time,
With earnest eyesight, scarcely crossed with pain;
Till the fresh moving leaves, and startling birds,
Loosened my long-suspended breath in words.

From Hampstead he ventured back into London's theatre-land, where he was one of the first to divine the talent of a rising star who had made his stage debut the year before, during Hunt's imprisonment: Edmund Kean. Of Kean's Richard III, Hunt professed himself 'perplexed' at first by the actor's 'stagy' manner and energetic delivery; but soon he found himself warming to the gestures and 'turns of countenance' which, he wrote, had a naturalness exhibiting 'the great desideratum': the capacity 'to unite common life with tragedy'. To Kean's first biographer, Hunt's 'important' return to drama criticism saw him exhibit 'a tasteful sensibility to those exquisite touches in Kean's acting which in the very midst of tragedy introduced a noble and natural familiarity . . . He regarded him to be equal at all times to the best actors in vogue, and to going far beyond them in particular passages.'

At home in Hampstead, yet another ailment for young Thornton moved Hunt to one of his most touching occasional verses, 'To T.L.H. six years old, during an illness':

Sleep breathes at last from out of thee,
My little, patient boy;
And balmy rest about thee
Smooths off the day's annoy.
I sit me down and think
Of all thy winning ways;
Yet almost wish, with sudden shrink
That I had less to praise.

Thy sidelong pillowed meekness,
Thy thanks to all that aid,
Thy heart, in pain and weakness,

Of fancied faults afraid;
The little trembling hand
That wipes thy quiet tears,
These, these are things that may demand
Dread memories for years.

Sorrows I've had, severe ones,
I will not think of now;
And calmly, midst my dear ones,
Have wasted with dry brow;
But when thy fingers press
And pat my stooping head,
I cannot bear the gentleness —
The tears are in their bed.

Ah, first-born of thy mother,
When life and hope were new,
Kind playmate of thy brother,
Thy sister, father too;
My light, where'er I go,
My bird, when prison-bound,
My hand in hand companion — no,
My prayers shall hold thee round.

To say 'He has departed' —
'His voice' — 'his face' — 'is gone';
To feel impatient-hearted,
Yet feel we must bear on;
Ah, I could not endure,
To whisper of such woe,
Unless I felt this sleep ensure
That it will not be so.

Yes, still he's fixed, and sleeping!
This silence too the while —
Its very hush and creeping
Seem whispering us a smile:

> Something divine and dim
> Seems going by one's ear,
> Like parting wings of Cherubim,
> Who say 'We've finished here.'

Hunt also wrote a verse fairy tale for four-year-old John ('Ah, little ranting Johnny') amid a sudden burst of verse in the *Examiner*, including a verse epistle to Byron on his imminent departure for Greece and a series of letters in verse to Moore, Hazlitt, Lamb and Field under the satirical nom de plume 'Harry Brown'. At the same time he was putting the finishing touches to his romance *The Story of Rimini*, begun in happier times before his imprisonment, while heavily under the influence of Dryden, but largely written as an involuntary guest of His Majesty.

Byron seems to have been pleased to reply to Hunt's request for criticism of *Rimini*. For all the poem's excellence and originality, he wrote – while scattering such comments in the margins as 'Very, very good', 'The whole passage is fine and original', even 'Superlative!' – Hunt was guilty of 'occasional quaintness and obscurity' and 'a kind of a harsh and yet colloquial compounding of epithets'. To his friend Moore, Byron privately enthused that 'Leigh Hunt has written a really good and very original poem, which I think will be a great hit. You can have no notion how very well it is written . . .' An excited Hunt wrote to Brougham: 'You will be pleased to hear that Lord Byron thinks my poem is original & that he has made several pencil-marks in it extremely flattering to me, though I differ with him in one or two points, & wish it to be still more original than he thinks I ought to be, principally in the use of a common, idiomatic style.'

In later editions of the poem Hunt would find himself accepting Byron's strictures to the point of removing some of its more unorthodox mannerisms. At the time, while consenting to make some amendments but insisting on retaining the spirit of the original – 'in vindication of a theory . . . by which [it] must stand or fall' – he made so bold as to ask His Lordship if he would speak to his publisher, John Murray, about the work. Again Byron appears to have been content to assist, telling Murray that Hunt's poem was 'the safest thing you ever engaged in. I speak to you as a man of business; were I to talk to you as a reader or a critic, I should say it was a very wonderful and beautiful performance, with just enough of a fault to make its beauties more remarked and remarkable.'

Soon Byron was able to inform Hunt of Murray's willingness to negotiate with him. With due thanks, Hunt offered Murray the poem for £450. Murray haggled, arguing that such a price would necessitate the sale of at least ten thousand copies; he offered to publish it at his own risk, with a print run of 500–750 copies, and pay Hunt half the profits, plus the copyright of any subsequent editions. Hunt had no option but to accept, and *Rimini* was duly published early in 1816. By March, after earning £45, Hunt tried to persuade Murray to buy out the copyright. Insufficiently impressed by the poem's prospects, Murray declined, causing a breach between them which would never heal. When Byron heard about it, he wrote sadly to Murray from Venice: 'You and Leigh Hunt have quarrelled then, it seems? I introduced him and his poem to you, in the hope that (*malgré* politics) the union would be beneficial to both, and the end is eternal enmity; and yet I did this with the best intentions . . .'

Hunt had good reason to be grateful to Byron, to whom he dedicated *Rimini*. 'My dear Byron,' he joked, 'you see what you have brought yourself to by liking my verses.' The familiarity of address would later become a bone of contention between them; for now, Byron seems to have taken it all in good part, and offered the poem his significant public support. Privately, he was still trying to persuade Moore of its virtues: 'Leigh Hunt's poem is a devilish good one – quaint, here and there, but with the substratum of originality, and with poetry about it, that will stand the test. I do not say this because he has inscribed it to me, which I am sorry for, as I should otherwise have begged you to review it in the *Edinburgh*. It is really deserving of much praise, and a favourable critique in the *E.R.* would do it justice, and set it up before the public eye, where it ought to be.'

Byron was proved right; the *Edinburgh Review* did indeed hail *Rimini* as a 'gem of great grace and spirit, and in many passages and in many particulars, of infinite beauty and delicacy'. Even when Hunt's poem was scorned in the *Quarterly Review*, Byron only slightly backtracked: 'I thought, and think very highly of his poem; but I warned him of the row his favourite antique phraseology would bring him into.' But Moore was not to be persuaded. 'With respect to Hunt's poem,' he replied, 'though it is, I own, full of beauties, and though I like himself sincerely, I really could not undertake to praise it seriously. There is so much of the quizzible in all he writes, that I never can put on the proper pathetic face in reading him.'

Hazlitt, meanwhile, wrote to Hunt: 'I have read the story of Rimini with extreme satisfaction. It is full of beautiful & affecting passages. You have, I think, perfectly succeeded. I like the description of the death of Francesca better than any. *This will do.* You are very metaphysical in the character & passion, but we will not say a word of this to the ladies . . .' Reviewing the poem (as Byron hoped) in the *Edinburgh Review*, Hazlitt praised Hunt's mix of 'tears with smiles, the dancing of the spirits with sad forebodings, the intoxication of hope with bitter disappointment, youth with age, life and death together . . . the voluptuous pathos of Boccaccio with Ariosto's laughing graces'.

Byron's differences with Moore over Hunt would never be resolved. The following year, writing from Venice, he asked Moore to 'present my remembrances' to 'our republican friend Leigh Hunt', only to learn that they had fallen out. After starting as an almost obsequious admirer of Hunt's, initiating a correspondence which grew into a friendship as he hankered for the praise of the *Examiner*'s influential editor, Moore had only recently revised his opinions. 'I wish I could send you Hunt's *The Feast of the Poets*, just republished,' he had written to his mother in 1814, 'where I am one of the *four* admitted to dine with Apollo; the other three, Scott, Campbell and Southey. Rogers, very unfairly, is only "asked to tea".' Moore confessed himself 'particularly flattered by praise from Hunt, because he is one of the most honest and candid men I know'.

Now, three years later, he was stung by an aside in Hunt's review of Byron's *Monody on the Death of Sheridan*, in which he described Moore as a 'refined Bacchanalian' poet who could never be 'a very grave one'. Moore would soon be writing in his diary: 'I had much rather Hunt would *let me alone.*' To Hunt himself he wrote: 'You . . . are always right in *politics* – &, if you would but keep your theories of religion & morality a little more to yourself . . . you would gain influence over many minds that you now unnecessarily shock and alienate.' Much the same,

Moore was heavily hinting, applied to Hunt's views on the work of other poets.

At the time, the dedication of *Rimini* moved the *Quarterly Review* to opine: 'We never, in so few lines, saw so many clear marks of the vulgar impatience of a low man, conscious and ashamed of his wretched vanity, and labouring, with coarse flippancy, to scramble over the bounds of birth and education, and fidget himself into the stout-heartedness of being familiar with a Lord.'

Cowden Clarke leapt to Hunt's defence, publishing a pamphlet rebutting the *Quarterly*'s 'surprisingly offensive' strictures; but this proved a mere foretaste of worse, much worse, to come. For all Byron's distinguished patronage, *Rimini* would soon make Hunt the target of ferocious attacks on his political and social attitudes as much as his literary skills. In the circle gradually forming around him, to the distaste (and concern) of Tory traditionalists, these two sides of Hunt and his coterie of fellow writers fed hungrily upon each other.

All that still lay in wait as Hunt seized the chance to offer Byron public support of his own, in a very different arena. Amid rumours of difficulties in Byron's marriage, which were causing great consternation in Tory circles, Hunt paid his first return visit on the man who had so often called on him in jail and Maida Vale – only to find him unwell, 'his face jaundiced with bile'. They were on terms intimate enough, it seems, for Hunt to enquire as to the truth of the scandal-sheet reports, to which Byron replied candidly. 'Of the "fifty reports", it follows that forty-nine must have more or less error or exaggeration,' Hunt reported Byron as replying. 'But I am sorry to say that, on the main and essential point of an intended, and it may be, an inevitable separation, I can contradict none.'

In the *Examiner* of 21 April 1816, Hunt wrote under the heading 'Distressing Circumstances in High Life': 'We have the honour of knowing the Noble Poet . . . Knowing him as we do, one fact at least we are acquainted with; and that is that these reckless calumniators know nothing about the matter; and we know further, that there have been the vilest exaggerations about it; and that our Noble Friend with all his faults, which he is the last man upon earth to deny, possesses qualities which ought to crumble the consciousness of these men to dust.'

Four days later Byron left England for Italy. Some time later he told his confidant Thomas Medwin: 'When party feeling ran high against me, Hunt was the only editor of a paper, the only literary man, who dared say a word in my justification. I shall always be grateful to him for the part he took on that occasion.'

In his front-page editorial for the 25 August 1816 issue of the *Examiner*, Hunt worked himself into a fine fury about the latest iniquities of the 'sinecurists' (among whom Moore would soon number himself); in the literary pages he penned a long verse epistle to his old friend Lamb, lamenting his recent absence from his fireside, where their conversation had ranged so far and wide, from Shakespeare and Marvell to 'Chapman, whose Homer's a fine, rough old wine'.

Hunt's friend Thomas Alsager, financial and musical editor of *The Times*, was the proud possessor of a 1616 folio edition of George Chapman's translation of Homer, which he lent that same summer to Cowden Clarke. When Keats visited Clarke in London that October, they sat up all night reading Chapman together. So enraptured was Keats that a sonnet began taking shape in his head as he walked home to his lodgings in Dean Street at 6 a.m.; within four hours 'On First Looking into Chapman's Homer' had been delivered to Clarke's breakfast table.

A surgeon's apprentice at the time, Keats was not yet confident of his poetic vocation. Clarke had already shared some of his early poems with Hunt, who had published 'To Solitude' as an *Examiner* page-filler on 5 May, crammed beneath a round-up of foreign news and signed simply 'J.K.'. Now, nearly six months later, it was with a wild surmise of his own that the young medical student finally approached his first meeting with the man he had so long admired from a distance, and described in a sonnet to Haydon ('Great spirits now on earth are sojourning') as:

> He of the rose, the violet, the spring,
> The social smile, the chain for Freedom's sake . . .

''Twill be an era in my existence,' Keats wrote to Clarke, who himself called it a 'red-letter day' as he accompanied his young friend on the walk north to Hunt's home:

'The character and expression of Keats's features would arrest even the casual passenger in the street; and now they were wrought to a tone of animation that I could not but watch with interest, knowing what was in store for him from the bland encouragement, and Spartan deference in attention, with fascinating conversational eloquence, that he was to encounter and receive. As we approached the Heath, there was the rising and accelerated step, with the general subsidence of all talk.'

Keats had been reading the *Examiner* since his orphaned schooldays under Clarke's father. Clarke tells us that his father had taken the paper since its inception, and that father and son 'revelled' week after week 'in the liberty-loving, liberty-advocating, liberty-eloquent articles of the young editor'. That Keats, too, had long been an admirer of Hunt, as much for his political convictions as his poetic style, is evident from a sonnet he had handed Clarke nearly two years earlier, 'On the Day that Mr Leigh Hunt Left Prison'. To his schoolmaster and friend, it stood as 'the first proof . . . of his having committed himself in verse'.

> What though, for showing truth to flattered state,
> Kind Hunt was shut in prison, yet has he,
> In his immortal spirit, been as free
> As the sky-searching lark, and as elate.
> Minion of grandeur! think you he did wait?
> Think you he naught but prison walls did see,
> Till, so unwilling, thou unturned'st the key?
> Ah, no! far happier, nobler was his fate!
> In Spenser's halls he strayed, and bowers fair,
> Culling enchanted flowers; and he flew
> With daring Milton through the fields of air:
> To regions of his own his genius true
> Took happy flights. Who shall his fame impair
> When thou art dead, and all thy wretched crew?

Hunt could not have been aware of this, nor that Keats (in a letter to his brother George in 1816) had also dubbed him 'wrong'd Libertas'. But Clarke had been encouraged to bring him round since showing Hunt some of Keats's first poems a few weeks earlier. Now he arrived clutching a 'sheaf' of recent work – 'the promise of which', to Hunt, 'was seconded by the fine fervid countenance of the writer. We became intimate on the spot, and I found the young poet's heart as warm as his imagination.'

They read together, took long rural walks and swiftly became kindred spirits. 'No imaginative pleasure was left unnoticed by us, or unenjoyed, from the recollection of the bards and patriots of old to the luxury of a summer rain at our window, or the clicking of coal in the winter-time.' Soon Hunt was showing Keats's poems to anyone who came calling, not least Godwin and Hazlitt, to find them adjudged 'as extraordinary as I thought them'. To Hunt, Keats was capable of passages 'for which Persian kings would have filled a poet's mouth with gold'.

Keats found his tall, slender new friend 'dark and vivid with the exotic flavour of Creole descent' and 'remarkably straight and upright in his carriage with a short, firm step and a cheerful, almost dashing approach – smiling, breathing, and making his voice heard in articulate ejaculations'. Another description of Hunt at this time has his black hair falling 'thickly from a central parting to frame his large but delicately featured face and short-sighted eyes'; his mouth was large and 'hard in the flesh' with 'a long upper lip'; and his forehead was 'singularly upright, flat and white'. Some friends considered Hunt rather feminine in both appearance and manner; although 'dandified', even 'lack-adaisical', however, he was usually bursting with infectious enthusiasm: 'brilliant, reflecting, gay, and kind, with a certain look of observant humour, that suggested an idea of what is called shyness when it is applied to children or to a girl'.

Hunt, in turn, would later record a vivid thumbnail sketch of the young Keats he first met that day: 'Under the middle height; and his lower limbs were small in comparison with the upper, but neat and well turned. His shoulders were very broad for his size: he had a face in which energy and sensibility were remarkably mixed up; an eager power, checked and made patient by ill-health. Every feature was at once strongly cut, and delicately alive. If there was any fault of expression, it was in the mouth, which was not without something of the character of pugnacity. His face was rather long than otherwise; the upper lip projected a little over the under; the chin was bold, the cheeks sunken; the eyes mellow and glowing; large, dark and sensitive.'

Anticipating Hunt's kindly approval and encouragement for the work of 'a youth under age', even Clarke's 'partial spirit' was not prepared for the 'unhesitating and prompt admiration' which 'broke forth before he had read twenty lines of the first poem'. As this first visit stretched into three morning calls, punctuated by walks around nearby Caen (now Ken) Wood, Keats's delight in finding himself so warmly welcomed, and so swiftly made 'a familiar of the household', moved him to a sonnet declaring himself 'brimful of the friendliness / That in a little cottage I have found' – and soon another, upon being compelled to 'Leave Friends at an Early Hour'. The long walk back to London from Hunt's home inspired yet another, much in the manner of Wordsworth:

> Keen, fitful gusts are whisp'ring here and there
> Among the bushes, half leafless, and dry;
> The stars look very cold about the sky,
> And I have many miles on foot to fare . . .

In the autumn of 1816, their shared enthusiasm for all matters classical, not least Lemprière's *Classical Dictionary*, made Keats especially responsive to Hunt's appraisal of Wordsworth's *The Excursion*, specifically Book IV ('Despondency Corrected'), whose praise of Greek pantheism discernibly influenced the next section of his own work-in-progress, *Endymion*. Hunt and Keats soon recognised another central characteristic they shared: each 'sympathised with the lowest commonplace'. To Hunt, he and Keats 'might have been taken for friends of the old stamp, between whom there was no such thing even as obligation, except the pleasure of it . . . I could not love him as deeply as I did Shelley. That was impossible. But my affection [for Keats] was second only to the one I entertained for that heart of hearts.'

The feeling, in that case, was mutual. Shelley re-entered Hunt's life at the beginning of December 1816, in the wake of his *Examiner* essay 'Young Poets', in which Hunt became the first to commend to the world the work of 'a new school of poetry': Keats, Shelley and another of his young disciples, John Hamilton Reynolds. Reynolds's reputation may have fared less well with posterity, but he was then regarded as equally promising, and became another habitué of Hunt's Hampstead salon – despite, to Keats's disapproval, combining poetry with training for the law, so he could afford to marry. The opening of Reynolds's 'Naiad' made its debut in print within Hunt's article, as did Keats's sonnet on reading Chapman's Homer: 'Much have I travel'd in the realms of gold . . .'

Hunt's subsequently celebrated article hailed Keats for his 'ardent grappling with nature', Shelley as a 'very striking and original thinker', citing his 'Alastor, or The Spirit of Solitude', while engagingly admitting that his commendation was based on other poems 'no sooner sent us than we unfortunately mislaid them'. Apparently undismayed that Hunt had lost the manuscript of his 'Hymn to Intellectual Beauty', Shelley was quick to write him a long, confessional note of thanks for this unexpected recognition, which had 'undeceived' him in the belief that 'I have powers deeply to interest, or substantially to improve mankind'. The praise of so 'gentle and sincere' an editor made a happy contrast to the fact that 'all else abhor and avoid me'; between them, Shelley's unconventional private life and unorthodox public pronouncements had hitherto rendered him 'an outcast from human society'.

From Marlow, where he was staying with his friend and fellow poet Thomas Love Peacock while house-hunting, Shelley came to London to meet Hunt, to whom he also appears to have made the first of many financial donations. No sooner had he returned to Bath, where he was living with Mary Godwin, daughter of William Godwin and Mary Wollstonecraft, than a dramatic letter from his former publisher, Thomas Hookham, brought him racing back to London to take up open-ended residence as Hunt's guest in dire circumstances.

The previous November, Shelley had casually asked Hookham to make enquiries as to the whereabouts of his estranged wife Harriet, and their two children, whom he had abandoned for Mary four years earlier. Hookham's news was grim. Harriet had last been seen in September, when she had left the children with her parents in Chapel Street, before taking up lodgings in Chelsea, near the barracks, under the assumed name of Smith. On 9 November, according to her landlady, she had disappeared. A body fished out of the Serpentine on 10 December, that of a heavily pregnant woman, was identified as hers. Harriet had killed herself.

Given the mysterious circumstances, the coroner's jury had returned the gently ambiguous verdict of 'found drowned'. But *The Times* of 12 December went much further, reporting that 'a respectable female, far advanced in pregnancy, was taken out of the Serpentine River, and brought home to her residence in Queen Street, Brompton, having been missed for nearly six weeks. She had a valuable ring on her finger. A want of honour in her own conduct is supposed to have led to this fatal catastrophe, her husband being abroad.'

Much partisan dispute still surrounds the poignant, premature demise of Harriet Westbrook Shelley, whom the poet had married in Scotland in August 1811, when he was nineteen and she sixteen, after they eloped from London. Within months of remarrying her under English law in March 1814, to render their two children legitimate, he had absconded with Mary ('in the spirit', as Hunt put it, 'of Milton's doctrines'). But Harriet was still his legal wife; the potential for scandal, to the errant son of a prominent baronet, transfixed even the wilfully unconventional Shelley. By whom was Harriet pregnant? There were suggestions, on which he swiftly fastened, that she had 'descended' into prostitution; that she had been multiply 'unfaithful' to him; that the child's father was an officer from the nearby barracks named Smith – if not her 'husband', as reported by *The Times*, currently posted 'abroad'. Just as plausible is the theory that Shelley himself was the father of the child poor Harriet was carrying; the proponent of free love had visited his wife in London before leaving for Geneva with Mary early that year. Did he, as one recent biographer has asked, 'seeking to comfort Harriet at a time when he was leaving the country for an undetermined period, make love to her'?

On 16 December Shelley wrote to Mary: 'Leigh Hunt has been with me all day, and his delicate and tender attentions to me, his kind speeches of you, have sustained me against the weight of the horror of this event.' With 'unfailing sympathy and kindness', Hunt housed Shelley, consoled him and supported him, both privately and publicly, during what one of his many biographers has called 'one of the most severe emotional crises of his life'. As Shelley fought a bitter legal battle with Harriet's family for custody of their two children – to whom, it must be said, he had not hitherto been the most attentive of fathers – Hunt rose to the occasion in the *Examiner*, excoriating a legal system whose disapproval of Shelley's morals finally consigned his off-spring to foster-parents:

> In this country of England, so justly called free on many accounts, and so proud of its 'Englishman's castle' – of the house which noth-ing can violate – a man's offspring can be taken from him tomorrow, who holds a different opinion from the Lord Chancellor in faith and morals. Hume's, if he had any, might have been taken. Gibbon's might have been taken. The virtuous Condorcet, if he had been an Englishman and a father, would have stood no chance. Plato, for his *Republic*, would have stood as little; and Mademoiselle de Gournay might have been torn from the arms of her adopting father, Montaigne, convicted beyond redemption of seeing farther than the walls of the Court of Chancery.

It was this degree of support, plus a thousand other kindnesses, that would lead Shelley to say of Hunt: 'One more gentle, honourable, innocent and brave; one of more exalted toleration for all who do and think evil, and yet himself more free from evil . . . one of simpler, and, in the highest sense of the word, of purer life and manners, I never knew.' Interestingly, Hunt himself makes no mention in his autobiog-raphy of his hospitality to Shelley at this time, preferring to dwell on Shelley's generosity to others, not least himself – once (in January 1818) his beneficiary to the extraordinary tune of £1400, to 'extricate' him from a debt. 'I was not extricated, for I had not yet learned to be careful: but the shame of not being so, after such generosity, and the pain which my friend afterwards underwent when I was in trouble and he was helpless, were the first causes of my thinking of money mat-ters to any purpose.'

Hunt and Shelley shared an unconventional (to say the least) attitude to money, which was to cause both lifelong difficulties of differing scale and degree. Their mutual version of the redistribution of wealth was to share money when it was in plentiful enough supply, with mutual feelings of gratitude rather than obligation. In later life this syn-drome would hound Hunt towards his grave; for now, as he developed a (well-deserved) reputation for incompetence with money and con-stant solicitation of gifts or loans, Shelley's 'last sixpence was ever at my service, had I chosen to share it'. All Hunt could offer in return, as throughout his life, was a public platform for Shelley's work and a prominent voice to champion it, not to mention friendship and hospitality. 'He was so kind as to listen to the story of persecution which I am now enduring from a libidinous and vindictive woman,' Shelley wrote to Byron of Hunt, 'and to stand by me as yet by his counsel, and by his personal attention to me.' Byron, too, would soon be learning more, much more, about Hunt and money – not least from Shelley.

In the meantime, Shelley's frequent visits to the Hunt home would sometimes last several days. 'He delighted in the natural, broken ground, and in the fresh air of the place, especially when the wind set in from the north-west, which used to give him an intoxication of animal spirits.' Here Shelley would 'swim' his paper boats on the ponds and play with Hunt's children – 'particularly with my eldest boy, the seriousness of whose imagination, and his susceptibility of a "grim" impression (a favourite epithet of Shelley's) highly interested him.' Shelley would play a game he called 'frightful creatures' with Thornton, whom it filled with such a 'fearful joy' that he would beg Shelley not to 'do the horn' – a way he had of 'screwing up his hair in front, to imitate a weapon of that sort'.

As a further example of Shelley's playfulness – 'when in good spirits' – Hunt loved to recall the occasion on which they were riding to town together on the Hampstead stage, accompanied only by an old lady who sat 'silent and still, after the English fashion'. Sensing disapproval of his ebullience in her silence, eyes steadfastly averted, Shelley provoked her to a satisfying look of 'the most ludicrous astonishment' by regaling his friend with a favourite line of Shakespeare. 'Hunt', he exclaimed,

> For Heaven's sake! Let us sit upon the ground.
> And tell sad stories of the death of kings.

The old lady, Hunt recalled, duly looked down at the floor of the coach, 'as if expecting us to take our seats accordingly'.

On other occasions a more sombre Shelley would forever impress upon Hunt his constant anxiety 'for the good of mankind in general'. Hunt soon found that when Shelley entered his house, he could not

Leigh Hunt aged seven, in his mid-twenties and in his mid-thirties (from a drawing by Joseph Severn).

Previous page: Hunt at fifty by Daniel Maclise.

Christ's Hospital in Hunt's day.

Hunt in his early thirties (top left), when Shelley (top right) and Keats (bottom left) frequented his house (opposite, top) on Hampstead Heath (opposite, bottom).

Mary Shelley (top left),
Thomas Moore (top
right) and Byron.

Hunt fills all available space in a letter to the Shelleys (see pp. 141–2).

Louis Edouard Fournier's *The Cremation of Shelley* (1889) shows a bereft Hunt (foreground) and Byron watching the flames consume their friend's miraculously pristine corpse.

know whether to expect a Greek quotation or a question about public affairs. Wringing his hands, settling down by the fire knee to knee, and pausing gravely as if about to embark on a question of some domestic delicacy, Shelley one day asked Hunt the precise amount of the national debt.

The poem Hunt had once lost, 'Hymn to Intellectual Beauty', Shelley had first sent to him over the signature 'Elfin-Knight' (one of Mary's pet names for him); and this was the attribution given on the poem's first publication in the *Examiner* of 6 October 1816: 'The Elfin-Knight, the first opportunity'. The sequel was printed in the *Examiner* of 18 January 1817, signed Percy B. Shelley, with a notice proclaiming: 'The following Ode, originally announced under the signature of the Elfin Knight, we have since found to be from the pen of the author whose name was mentioned among others a week or two back in an article entitled "Young Poets". The readers will think with us, that it is also sufficient to justify what was there observed.' Other Shelley poems, such as 'Ozymandias', also made their first appearance in the *Examiner* (11 January 1818).

Together, over the coming few years, the two friends were to share what Hunt would call their 'common stock in trouble as well as joy'.

It was under Hunt's roof in the Vale of Health, in the first week of December 1816, that Shelley first met Keats. According to their host, 'Keats did not take to Shelley as kindly as Shelley did to him.' Conscious of his humble origins, Keats 'felt inclined to see in every man of birth a sort of natural enemy'. But this was written with the benefit of hindsight. Although favoured by Hunt with an affectionate nickname mocking his uncultured accent – 'Junkets' – Keats may in truth have been jealous of the visibly closer bond between his host and Shelley.

Whatever tensions would gradually arise between them, Hunt and Keats at this stage forged a triumvirate with Shelley which lay at the heart of the Hunt salon at its zenith. Along with Reynolds and other 'new' poets whose work Hunt championed, both young men seemed content – as yet, in Keats's case – to give Hunt the pleasure of thinking they formed the nucleus of the 'school' of poets he had dreamed of in that influential article – 'a new generation of poets' (as the present Poet Laureate has put it) 'that shared and validated his own beliefs'.

For most of Keats's biographers, Hunt's article had been the making of him: 'This confirmation of his powers, when he most needed it, swept all Keats's doubts away.' Unlike Reynolds, Keats was not going to let poetry come second to his day-job, medicine. He showed Hunt's article to a friend named Henry Stephens, a fellow medical student, who vividly remembered the effect it had upon him: 'This sealed his fate.' From that moment, thanks to Hunt, 'Keats's apprentice years were over'.

Soon Keats had contentedly become part of the growing group which met and dined, argued and philosophised at Hunt's Hampstead home. There was Barnes, editor of *The Times*, and John Scott, the liberal jour-nalist who had visited Hunt in jail and would later edit the *London Magazine*; there was Godwin, Lamb, Clarke, Ollier, the musician Novello – and, above all for Keats, Benjamin Haydon. 'Very glad I am,' wrote Keats to Cowden Clarke, 'at the thoughts of seeing so soon this glorious Haydon and all his creation'; Haydon, for his part, was equally grateful to Hunt for introducing him to Keats's 'prematurity of intellect and poetical power'. As he listened to conversation ranging from 'Wordsworth's merit to the principles of punning, from the life of Petrarch to the latest *Political Register*', hearing Hunt 'read' his prints of Claude and Poussin, Keats was entranced. Though naturally 'shy and embarrassed, as of one unused to society', he was soon, in his friend Joseph Severn's words, 'intoxicated . . . with an excess of enthusiasm'.

The Hampstead house was often filled with music, Hunt being a proficient pianist and possessing a 'sweet, small baritone voice'. An early and passionate champion of Mozart, he was especially fond of singing Don Ottavio's arias from *Don Giovanni* as his contribution to reg-ular musical evenings here or at the Novellos. 'Nature had gifted him with an intense dramatic perception, an exquisite ear for music, and a voice of extraordinary compass, power, flexibility and beauty,' recalled Thornton. 'It extended from the C below the line to the F sharp above: there were no passages that he could not execute; the quality was sweet, clear and ringing.' Thornton's father was not above resorting to falsetto, he adds, for the 'tender treble' of the Countess in *Figaro* or Polly in *The Beggar's Opera*. 'He was passionately fond of music.'

Another fixture on the Hampstead routine was an occasional *jeu d'esprit* in the form of a competition to write a sonnet in fifteen minutes. On 30 December 1816, with Cowden Clarke as timekeeper, Hunt proposed to Keats as their subject 'On the Grasshopper and the Cricket'.

Keats :

The poetry of earth is never dead:
When all the birds are faint with the hot sun,
And hide in cooling trees, a voice will run
From hedge to hedge about the new-mown mead;
That is the Grasshopper's, – he takes the lead
In summer luxury, – he has never done
With his delights, for when tired out with fun
He rests at ease beneath some pleasant weed.
The poetry of earth is ceasing never;
On a lone winter evening, when the frost
Has wrought a silence; from the stove there thrills
The cricket's song, in warmth increasing ever,
And seems to one in drowsiness half lost,
The Grasshopper's among some grassy hills.

Hunt :

Green little vaulter in the summer grass
Catching your heart up at the feel of June,
Sole voice that's heard amidst the lazy noon,
When ev'n the bees lag at the summoning brass;
And you, warm little housekeeper, who class
With those who think the candles come too soon,
Loving the fire, and with your tricksome tune,
Nick the glad silent moments as they pass:
Oh sweet and tiny cousins, that belong,
One to the fields, the other to the hearth,
Both have your sunshine; both though small are strong
At your clear hearts; and both were sent on earth
To sing in thoughtful ears this natural song –
In doors and out, Summer and Winter, Mirth !

Hunt especially admired Keats's first line – 'Such a prosperous

opening!' – and his 'Wordsworthian' tenth and eleventh lines: 'Ah!
That's perfect! Bravo, Keats!' On their walk home, however, Keats
told Cowden Clarke he thought Hunt's sonnet the finer. Shelley could
not be present, nor take part in the contest, because this was the day he
took advantage of Harriet's death to marry Mary Godwin. It was his
best chance, so he (wrongly) thought, of gaining custody of his children, to add to the son he already had by Mary.

From Keats's point of view, Shelley was 'everywhere . . . He dashed
from Hunt to his lawyers, to Mary's stepmother and back again to Hunt.'
Shelley sought Hunt's agreement to take in his children, if necessary; and
readily obtained it, which moved him to write to Mary that Hunt's support sustained him against the 'weight and horror' of losing them.

With Shelley so distracted, Keats spent much time at Hunt's home over
the coming months, the rapt if least vigorous contributor to fierce discussions involving Hunt, Haydon, Cowden Clarke and their circle that
ranged from poetry and politics to astronomy and religion. Shelley flitted
in and out, according to the progress of his custody suit, leaning on Hunt
for hospitality as much as Keats, whose seminal poem *Sleep and Poetry*
emerged from a few nights spent on the sofa in Hunt's library, surrounded
by 'The glorious features of the bards who sung / In other ages . . .'

The record shows that both Hunt and Keats were present, along
with Godwin, Hazlitt, Hogg and Walter Coulson, at a typical Vale of
Health dinner presided over by Hunt on 26 January 1817. Hazlitt
could find Hunt irritating, especially when 'harping' upon his pet
theories about sexual politics: 'Damn him. It's always coming out like
a rash. Why doesn't he write a book about it, and get rid of it!' Hunt's
friendship with Hogg, to whom he was introduced by Shelley, was
also to turn sour; at the time, however, he accepted his offer of a loan
of £20, which he took several years to repay. Hogg also presented
Hunt with some ceremonial vases, in celebration of their friendship.

Keats was so happy in Hunt's circle that he identified him, along with
Wordsworth and Haydon, as 'great spirits' in a sonnet he sent Haydon
the following autumn, suggesting that Hunt was right to think of them
all combining to launch a new era, both literary and philosophical:

> And other spirits there are standing apart
> Upon the forehead of the age to come;

These, these will give the world another heart,
And other pulses. Hear ye not the hum
Of mighty workings in a distant Mart? –
Listen awhile ye nations, and be dumb.

Hunt, too, had addressed a sonnet to Haydon, written in a blank leaf of his copy of Vasari's *Lives of the Painters*, and published in the *Examiner* of 20 October 1816:

Haydon, whom now the conquered toil confesses
Painter indeed, gifted, laborious, true,
Fit to be numbered in succession due
With MICHAEL, whose idea austerely presses,
And sweet-souled RAPHAEL, with his amorous tresses;
Well hast thou urged thy radiant passages through
A host of clouds; and he who with thee grew.
The bard and friend, congratulates and blesses.
'Tis glorious thus to have one's own proud will,
And see the crown acknowledged that we earn;
But nobler still, and nearer to the skies,
To feel one's-self, in hours serene and still,
One of the spirits chosen by heaven to turn
The sunny side of things to human eyes.

But Haydon was suspicious of Hunt's influence on Keats, and was already trying to extract him from the Vale of Health's charmed circle. 'He was fond of being the idol of a circle,' muttered Haydon of Hunt. 'Content if the members of it adored, he shut his eyes on his faults himself and believed them unseen by others.' While jealous of his young friend's attachment to another mentor, Haydon also feared that Hunt's florid ways would contaminate Keats's style; he needed to find a voice of his own, not an echo of Hunt's. Beyond poetry, Haydon was also suspicious of Hunt's politics, if not his patriotism; during a conversation eighteen months earlier, after the Battle of Waterloo had finally brought about the fall of Napoleon, Haydon had found Hunt quiet and despondent. 'Terrible battle this, Haydon,' said Hunt. 'A glorious one, Hunt,' replied Haydon. 'Oh, yes, certainly,' came the reply, and 'to it we went'.

At least Hunt took 'a just and liberal view' of Napoleon's defeat; Hazlitt, by contrast, was distraught: 'He seemed prostrated in mind and body, he walked about unwashed, unshaved, hardly sober by day, and always intoxicated by night, literally, without exaggeration, for weeks; until at length wakening as it were from his stupor, he at once left off all stimulating liquors, and never touched them after.' Despite such disagreements with Hunt, Haydon was capable of thinking him 'one of the most delightful companions on earth – full of poetry & wit & amiable humour . . . We argue with full hearts on everything but religion and Bonaparte, and we resolved after a little never to talk of them.' Haydon's ambivalence about Hunt would continue for the rest of both their lives, finally resolving itself, after a long estrangement, in elderly amity; in his hot-blooded youth, however, he wanted to be the centre of attention just as much as he believed Hunt did.

As Haydon painted what he considered his masterpiece, *Christ's Entry into Jerusalem*, including the faces of several contemporaries alongside those of Newton and Voltaire – but only if they were devout believers, such as Keats, Hazlitt and Wordsworth – he began to think that the Hunt coterie was wilfully mocking his Christianity. After dining at Hunt's one evening, he thought he had been deliberately placed opposite a combative Shelley, who opened the conversation 'in a most feminine and gentle voice', by saying: 'As to that detestable religion, the Christian . . .' Astounded, in his own word, Haydon looked round the table for moral support, only to see by Hunt's amused expression of ecstasy that 'I was to be set at that evening *vi et armis.*' He waited until the servant had gone, and then 'we went like fiends. I felt exactly like a stag at bay and resolved to gore without mercy . . . We said unpleasant things to each other, and when I retired to the other room for a moment I overheard them say, 'Haydon is fierce.' 'Yes,' said Hunt, 'the question always irritates him.'

On these and other grounds, literary and religious, there ensued a coolness between Hunt and Haydon, which Hunt's sunny personality could always defuse at will. 'Accidentally meeting him at a friend's,' Haydon conceded, 'he was so exceedingly delightful I could not resist the dog. We forgot our quarrels and walked away together, quoting, and joking and laughing as if nothing had happened.'

Keats himself remained sensible, as yet, of the debt he owed his admirer and promoter, who published his poems in the *Examiner* as fast as he could write them. When Ollier determined to publish Keats's first volume of poetry in March 1817, he was still a regular visitor to the Vale of Health, where the last proofs were delivered one evening with a note requesting that, if the book were to have a dedication, it be sent to the printer as soon as possible. With no hesitation, according to those present, Keats 'drew to a side-table and, in the buzz of a mixed conversation', dashed off a sonnet dedicating his first published collection 'To Leigh Hunt Esq.':

> Glory and loveliness have pass'd away;
> For if we wander out in early morn,
> No wreathed incense do we see upborne
> Into the east, to meet the smiling day:
> No crowd of nymphs soft voic'd and young, and gay,
> In woven baskets bringing ears of corn,
> Roses, and pinks, and violets, to adorn
> The shrine of Flora in her early May.
> But there are left delights as high as these,
> And I shall ever bless my destiny,
> That in a time, when under pleasant trees
> Pan is no longer sought, I feel a free,
> A leafy luxury, seeing I could please
> With these poor offerings, a man like thee.

This momentous event in their friendship soon led to a curious incident which also, perhaps, marked the beginning of its long-drawn-out end.

With the publication of his poems, Keats had achieved the 'flowering laurel' predicted for him by Hunt; and, that very evening, he was to receive it all too literally. On Saturday 1 March, amid unseasonably fine weather, Keats walked to Hampstead clutching an advance copy of his volume – delivered to him only that morning – to present to its dedicatee. As he turned from Pond Street up Millfield Lane, heading up the hill towards the Vale of Health, he met Hunt coming the other way – a coincidence both naturally deemed propitious. Together, in the highest spirits, they roved the Heath before heading back to Hunt's for dinner.

This evidently convivial evening continued in Hunt's garden, where the two poets sat under the stars, their postprandial mode ebullient; with no Shelley on hand to shift the conversation on to a more abstruse plane, they waxed poetic, responding like urban bards to the poetry in the air of the balmy spring evening. Both, in one description of what followed, 'may have felt the necessary luxury of being a little silly'. It was an instance of what Haydon described as 'the excessive mad anticks of people of real genius when they meet after hard thinking'.

Having promised Keats a metaphorical laurel, Hunt now proceeded to celebrate the publication of his first volume of poems with a literal one, picking and entwining a laurel wreath and placing it on his young friend's brow. Out of courtesy, no doubt, as much as respect, Keats proceeded to repay the compliment, weaving a chaplet of ivy and placing it on Hunt's forehead. Inevitably, Hunt then suggested commemorating the moment with a sonnet – another competition, with a fifteen-minute time limit. While Keats hesitated, managing only to fashion a stumbling verse concocted from lines (some his own, some of others) already swimming around his head, Hunt dashed off two in the allotted time. Reads one:

> It is a lofty feeling, yet a kind,
> Thus to be topped with leaves; – to have a sense
> Of honour-shaded thought, – an influence
> As from great nature's fingers, and be twined
> With her old, sacred, verdurous ivy-bind,
> As though she hallowed with that sylvan fence
> A head that bows to her benevolence,
> Midst pomp of fancied trumpets in the wind.
> 'Tis what's within us crowned. And kind and great
> Are all the conquering wishes it inspires,
> Love of things lasting, love of the tall woods,
> Love of love's self, and ardour for a state
> Of natural good befitting such desires,
> Towns without gain, and hunted solitudes.

At which moment, to their mutual mortification, unexpected visitors arrived – usually identified as Reynolds's sisters. Not wishing to look ridiculous, especially in front of women, Hunt removed his laurel wreath before receiving the new arrivals. Keats, 'in a kind of obstinate self-justification', decided to keep his on throughout their stay, after which he proceeded to write yet another sonnet, 'even weaker': 'To the Ladies Who Saw Me Crown'd'.

It was the kind of episode we remember, on the sober morrow, either with affectionate pleasure or acute embarrassment. The different ways in which the two men behaved in its aftermath symbolise the difference between them, and seem to have been the beginning of what would soon become – on Keats's part – disenchantment. While he acknowledged the 'silliness' of the occasion, and the inadequacy of his sonnet – showing it only to Reynolds, because it involved his sisters – Hunt proudly showed off both sonnets to all-comers, and, to Keats's evident mortification, even published his own in the *Examiner*.

To one Keatsian, his 'instinct that he had betrayed the sacred trust of Apollo by indulging in such a mockery was not a reaction as unreal as the occasion that provoked it; it was literally and almost tragically true'. Keats had 'written himself down' – and betrayed the trust of his published volume – as one to whom verse was 'a mere pastime, the total opposite of the dedicated vessel of the lines in his own *Sleep and Poetry*'. Hunt's publication of such doggerel was to provide further ammunition for the critical onslaught which was soon to befall them both.

Keats expressed his frustration in a letter to his friend Benjamin Bailey:

There's Hunt infatuated – there's Haydon's picture [*Christ's Entry into Jerusalem*] *in statu quo*. There's Hunt walks up and down his painting room criticizing every head most unmercifully – There's Horace Smith tired of Hunt . . . I am quite disgusted with literary men and will never know another except Wordsworth – no, not even Byron . . . Here is an instance of the friendships of such – Haydon and Hunt have known each other many years – now they live *pour ainsi dire* jealous neighbours. Haydon says to me Keats don't show your lines to Hunt on any account or he will have done half for you – so it appears Hunt wishes to be thought.

In the summer of 1817 money worries forced Hunt to leave
Hampstead for Paddington, where he took lodgings at 13 Lisson Grove
North, just down the road from Haydon, who lived at 22. Keats had
mysteriously vanished – 'What has become of Junkets I know not,'
Hunt wrote to Clarke, 'I suppose Queen Mab has eaten him' – but
Shelley was soon visiting, and trying to raise money to keep Hunt
afloat. The following January he was able to advance Hunt the huge
sum of £1400, which he had in turn borrowed from his father-in-law,
Godwin. 'I walk out quite a buck again, with my blue frock coat and
new hat,' Hunt wrote to the Shelleys in Italy that April. By July he had
moved his family to a larger house in nearby York Buildings, New
Road (now Bayswater Road). But his ebullient mood was about to be
shattered.

6

The 'Cockney' School

1818–21

> Our talk shall be (a theme we never tire on)
> Of Chaucer, Spenser, Shakespeare, Milton, Byron,
> (Our England's Dante) – Wordsworth – HUNT, and KEATS,
> The Muses' son of promise; and of what feats
> He yet may do . . .

Those capital letters didn't help. These lines from a sonnet by Hunt's friend Cornelius Webb were a gift of an epigraph to John Gibson Lockhart, assistant editor of the high Tory *Blackwood's Edinburgh Magazine*, briefed by his eponymous editor to sharpen his pen after the magazine had suffered a lacklustre launch the previous year.

The scion of an ancient Lanarkshire family, educated at Oxford and briefly in Goethe's circle in Weimar, Lockhart needed little encouragement from William Blackwood to attack the reformist Whig principles espoused by the magazine's rivals, Francis Jeffrey's *Edinburgh Review* and Archibald Constable's *Scots Magazine*. A protégé of Scotland's most celebrated Tory, Sir Walter Scott, and soon to become his son-in-law, Lockhart was only too happy to make his name in 'the Maga' (as *Blackwood's* came to be known) with a fiercely conservative counterblast to these upstart metropolitan Whigs.

Writing anonymously as 'Z', Lockhart chose Hunt and his coterie as his first victims, launching a scathing attack on them as the 'Cockney' school of poets – vulgar amateurs with ideas above their station. His launch pad was mere snobbery: 'All the great poets of our country have been men of some rank in society, and there is no vulgarity in any of their writings; but Mr Hunt cannot utter a dedication, or even a note, without betraying the Shibboleth of low birth and low habits.' But his ends were ideological, outraged as he was at what he saw as the blasphemy and aberrant sexual content of the group's poetry as much as its ornate style.

Fuelled by mutterings (then as now) that Hunt's florid ways were the ruination of Keats, even Byron, Lockhart could not tolerate such a coarse, suburban 'group' or 'circle' wielding as much influence as it appeared to, in so many liberal causes he so vigorously opposed. Why, if Hunt's poetry was as ineffective and insignificant as he sneered, expend so much energy and ink attacking it, thus advertising it to a much wider audience? This was a question Lockhart was too focused to address as he railed against the 'chief Doctor and Professor' of the Cockney School and his disciples. His chosen way of pillorying them was to use a review of Hunt's *The Story of Rimini* to mock their poetry as well as the profuse mutual esteem in which they appeared to hold each other.

Although only twenty-three, Lockhart proved capable of invective and satire as potent as any in the language, not hesitating to distort the facts of the case if it suited his argument. In the October 1817 issue of *Blackwood's*, having launched his 'Cockney' theme, he employs his trademark sarcasm to pretend to rebuke the *Quarterly Review* for a 'very illiberal attack on *Rimini* ' before proceeding to offer his own opinion of Hunt's work:

> One feels the same disgust at the idea of opening Rimini, that impresses itself on the mind of a man of fashion, when he is invited to enter, for a second time, the gilded drawing-room of a little mincing boarding-school mistress, who would fain have an *At Home* in her house. Everything is pretence, affectation, finery and gaudiness. The beaux are attorneys' apprentices, with chapeau bras and Limerick gloves – fiddlers, harp teachers, and clerks of genius; the belles are faded fan-twinkling spinsters, prurient vulgar misses from school, and enormous citizens' wives. The company are entertained

with lukewarm negus, and the sounds of a paltry pianoforte . . .

The extreme moral depravity of the Cockney School is another thing which is for ever thrusting itself upon the public attention, and convincing every man of sense who looks into their productions, that they who sport with such sentiments can never be great poets. How could any man of high original genius ever stoop publicly, at the present day, to dip his fingers in the least of those glittering and rancid obscenities which float on the surface of Mr Hunt's Hippocrene? His poetry resembles that of a man who has kept company with kept-mistresses. His muse talks indelicately like a tea-sipping milliner girl. Some excuse for her there might have been, had she been hurried away by imagination or passion; but with her, indecency seems a disease, she appears to speak unclean things from perfect inanition.

This, moreover, was a toned-down version of Lockhart's original polemic. The eponymous Mr Blackwood had taken it upon himself to edit out the worst excesses of 'Z', thinking it 'proper to soften some expressions'. But Hunt was not spared such passages as: 'The very concubine of so impure a wretch as Leigh Hunt would be to be pitied, but alas for the wife of such a husband! For him there is no charm in simple seduction; and he gloats over it only when accompanied with adultery and incest.'

In a frenzied prose style bordering on the obsessive, 'Z' was intent on deluding his readers into accepting that Hunt's own sexual habits were no different from those of the incestuous characters in his (or Dante's) poem – thus, as one critic has observed, making 'Hunt far more compelling than he would otherwise have been'. Nor did he shrink from character assassination of a wholly speculative breed: 'The poetry of this man is always on the stretch to be grand. He has been allowed to look for a moment from the antechamber into the saloon, and mistaken the waving of feathers and the painted floor for the *sine qua non*'s of elegant society. He would fain be always tripping and waltzing, and is sorry that he cannot be allowed to walk about in the morning with yellow breeches and flesh-coloured silk-stockings. He sticks an artificial rosebud into his button hole in the middle of winter. He wears no neckcloth, and curls his hair in imitation of the prints of Petrarch.'

Then he began the insidious task – in which he would enjoy some success – of trying to break up the 'Cockney School' by making its other members embarrassed to count Hunt as a friend, let alone their 'leader':

The founder of the Cockney School would fain claim poetical kin-dred with Lord Byron and Thomas Moore. Such a connexion would be as unsuitable for them as for William Wordsworth. The days of Mr Moore's follies are long since over; and, as he is a thor-ough gentleman, he must necessarily entertain the greatest contempt for such an underbred person as Mr Leigh Hunt. But Lord Byron! How must the haughty spirit of Lara and Harold con-temn the subaltern sneaking of our modern tuft-hunter. The insult which he offered to Lord Byron in the dedication of Rimini, in which he, a paltry Cockney newspaper scribbler, had the assurance to address one of the most nobly-born of English patricians, and one of the first geniuses whom the world ever produced, as 'My dear Byron', although it may have been forgotten and despised by the illustrious person whom it most nearly concerned, excited a feeling of utter loathing and disgust in the public mind, which will always be remembered whenever the name of Leigh Hunt is mentioned.

The 'incestuous' element of Hunt's poem was, of course, merely a retelling of Dante. But the charge soon gave rise to scandalous rumours of a liaison between Hunt and his sister-in-law, Bessy, who was living with the Hunts at the time but now felt obliged to move out. Hunt's protestations of innocence were not helped by common knowledge of a drama reported by Keats to Haydon in which Bessy, 'who, is in love with Hunt, tried to drown herself [in Hampstead pond] . . . being pulled out by two labourers!' Haydon, who was jealous of Hunt's effortless appeal to women, bridled at his 'smuggering fondness' for Bessy, accusing him of 'torturing' Marianne with it; but even he con-ceded that Hunt, whatever Shelley-inspired views he may have held on free love, was incapable of 'the resolution or the desire to go to the full extent of a manly passion, however wicked'.

The Hunt brothers promptly demanded in the *Examiner* that 'Z' reveal his true identity. Not merely did Lockhart refuse to do so; he sent Hunt a confessional letter signed John Graham Dalyell – the name, in truth, of a prominent Edinburgh Whig known for his fervid opposition to *Blackwood's*. 'Oh, the villainy of these fellows!' protested Dalyell.

Far from revealing himself, 'Z' was just warming to his theme. In the November issue of *Blackwood's* he addressed himself directly to Byron, acidly offering a direct comparison of the 'incest' in his *Parisina* and Hunt's *Rimini*, and threatening to expose His Lordship as just another 'Cockney' unless he were swiftly to mend his ways.

Then in January 1818 'Z' published an open 'Letter to Leigh Hunt, King of the Cockneys', purporting to be the maligned victim of a defamatory riposte from Hunt – who had, as yet, to make any public response. 'A lover of virtue,' railed 'Z', 'has poured out his bitter indignation against the husband and the father who has dared to be the apologist of adultery and incest.' There followed a list of charges. 'I mean to handle each of these topics in turn, and now and then to relieve my main attack upon you, by a diversion against some of your younger and less important auxiliaries, the Keatses, the Shellys [sic], and the Webbes [sic].' The next attack saw 'Z' overreaching himself, with talk of 'the leprous crust of self-conceit with which [Hunt]'s whole moral being is indurated' and 'the odious and unnatural harlotry of his polluted muse'.

By August 'Z' had turned his venom on Keats and Hazlitt. Keats, like Hunt, rolled with the punches; 'I never read anything so virulent,' he mused, while adding, none too convincingly, 'I don't mind the thing much.' 'Pimpled' Hazlitt, 'the Cockney Aristotle', sued – successfully, receiving an out-of-court payment. Although his assaults continued for some time yet, Lockhart slowly began to defuse them; but Gifford's *Quarterly* maintained the broadsides which had started it all.

The previous spring, the *Quarterly's* anonymous reviewer – later found not to be Gifford himself, as Hunt believed, but one of his colleagues, probably John Wilson Croker – had dismissed *The Round Table* as a gallimaufry of 'vulgar descriptions, silly paradoxes, flat truisms, misty sophistry, broken English, ill humour and rancorous abuse'. Now *Endymion* was 'cut up', showing Keats to be a mere 'copyist of Mr

Hunt', offering 'the most incongruous ideas in the most uncouth language'. Hunt himself displayed 'the vulgar impatience of a low man', guilty in *Rimini* of 'inaccurate, negligent and harsh versification' and 'ungrammatical, unauthorized, chaotic jargon'. His new collection, *Foliage*, was 'just what might have been expected from a pert, forward boarding-school girl in her seventh or eighth year'. Hunt was a man of a 'namby-pamby' disposition, who would 'live and die unhonoured in his own generation, and, for his own sake it is to be hoped, moulder unknown in those which are to follow'.

Gifford had nursed a grudge since Hunt had first mocked him in *The Feast of the Poets*; Hunt had then further alienated him by leaping to the (posthumous) defence of the poet Mary Robinson (even though she had been yet another mistress of his reviled Prince Regent) against Gifford's onslaughts. That particular feud would run and run, enabling Hunt to hit back by proxy while boasting in a letter to Shelley that 'I made no answer to Gifford myself, partly out of contempt, partly (I must really say) out of something bordering on a loathing kind of pity, & partly for the sake of setting an example always praised but seldom or never practiced.'

To his dying day Hunt believed, with good reason, that the attacks in both *Blackwood's* and the *Quarterly* were motivated by political more than literary animus; invited by Murray to contribute to the journal when it was founded, back in 1809, he had very publicly declined for fear of compromising his political independence. When the attacks began, in a magazine owned by the poet's own publisher, he had tartly noted that Murray was 'indifferent to the *politics* of those who came to his house'. Now, to his relief, the Tory fusillade soon became so indiscriminate that metropolitan London rallied to the Cockneys' defence, leaving Murray, Lockhart and Gifford out on a limb as the *Pamphleteer* and the *Critic* defended Hunt and his circle against charges of illiteracy and perversion.

The feud was to simmer on for a year or two more, until John Scott put an interim end to it in a series of articles in the *London Magazine* in 1820–1, replying in kind by renaming *Blackwood's* 'Reekie' magazine – Reekie being 'an expressive Scotch word for SMOKED. It also means the capital of Scotland.' This and other doughty defences of Hunt led to the most tragic consequence of the entire episode: a friend of

Lockhart's named Jonathan Henry Christie challenged Scott to a duel, in which Scott fell mortally wounded.

Lockhart's attacks, which continued for six articles over two years (before resurfacing in December 1822 and August 1825), have often been used to portray Hunt as a malign influence on early Keats, and to a lesser extent Shelley and Byron. But a recent, historicist school of thought takes them rather to confirm Hunt's role at the centre of a literary and political group so ambitious and effective that conservative forces could not let it go unchallenged. The high priest of this view is the American scholar Jeffrey N. Cox of the University of Colorado, who sees Hunt as the founding father of a 'visionary company . . . working to reform culture and society', with a membership including Shelley, Byron, Keats, Reynolds, Hazlitt and others. 'This gathering of writers and artists who at times imagine themselves the "unacknowledged legislators of the world" echoes the dream of a "republic of letters" that moved many in early-modern Europe.'

At the time Lockhart's invective may have helped distance Keats from Hunt, though it served only to tighten his bond with Shelley and others. But Keats had already begun to grow disenchanted with Hunt, largely under Haydon's influence, as can be seen from a series of letters starting as early as 11 May 1817, within months of the dedication of his poems to his sometime mentor, and continuing with increasing vehemence until the end of the following year. 'It is a great pity that people should by associating themselves with the finest things, spoil them,' Keats wrote to Haydon on 14 March 1818. 'Hunt has damned Hampstead and masques and sonnets and Italian tales . . .'

In April 1817 Hunt and Keats had temporarily gone their separate ways – Hunt for a long stay with the Shelleys at Marlow (where Mary was finishing her novel *Frankenstein*), Keats for an extended trip to the south coast and beyond. They spent a day together in Hampstead before Keats left for Southampton on 14 April. It was during this period that Hunt wrote to Clarke of Junket's mysterious disappearance: 'I have no doubt that he will appear before long very penitent & poetical, & really sorry. He wants a little more adversity, perhaps, to make him attend to others as much in reality as he wishes to do in theory; & all that we can hope at present is that a youth of his ardour may not bring too much upon him too soon.'

To Keats at this time, Hunt was a 'Selfdeluder' vain enough to flatter himself 'into an idea of being a great Poet'. Regardless of his growing disillusion with Hunt, to which Hunt was oblivious, Keats was anyway in the mood to put some distance between himself and literary London. Keats would not see even his closest friend, Cowden Clarke, for nearly two years, until they met at Charles Brown's home in Hampstead in February 1819, on the evening Keats read his 'Eve of St Agnes'.

Hunt must have been mortified not to have been invited to the celebrated dinner given by Haydon on 28 December 1817 to introduce Keats to Wordsworth; despite the presence of their mutual friend Lamb (who got entertainingly drunk) amid a curious assortment of guests at what Haydon himself called the 'immortal dinner', Hunt was excluded – supposedly because Marianne had borrowed some of Haydon's much-prized silverware and failed to return it.

We do know of a handful of encounters with Hunt in the interim – including tea with Reynolds at Hunt's home that October and a series of meals during Lockhart's attacks – when Keats, whatever his private feelings, proved man enough to rally round Hunt in his hour of need. But a sonnet from Hunt to Reynolds ('On His Lines upon The Story of Rimini') perhaps shows why Reynolds soon joined Keats in keeping his distance.

> Reynolds, whose Muse, from out thy gentle embraces
> Holding a little crisp and dewy flower,
> Came to me in my close-entwined bower,
> Where many fine-eyed Friendships and glad Graces,
> Parting the boughs, have looked in with like faces,
> And thanked the song which had sufficient power
> With Phoebus to bring back a warmer hour,
> And turn his southern eye to our green places:
> Not for this only, but that thou dost long
> For all men's welfare, may there be a throng
> Of kind regards, wherever thou appearest;
> And in thy home, firm-handed Health, a song
> Girt with rich-hearted friends, and she the nearest
> To whom the warble of thy lip is dearest.

To read this sonnet, in the judgment of one commentator, is 'to understand why . . . Reynolds was not out of place in warning Keats not to submit his poetry for Hunt's approval'. At a reunion *chez* Hunt on 4 February 1818, in the midst of 'Z''s tirades, Keats nonetheless seems content to have let himself be dragged into another sonnet-writing contest – this time with Shelley present. The subject on this occasion was 'The Nile'. Hunt's:

> It flows through old hushed Egypt and its sands,
> Like some grave mighty thought threading a dream,
> And times and things, as in that vision, seem
> Keeping along it their eternal stands,–
> Caves, pillars, pyramids, the shepherd bands
> That roamed through the young world, the glory extreme
> Of high Sesostris, and that southern beam,
> The laughing queen that caught the world's great hands.
> Then comes a mightier silence, stern and strong,
> As of a world left empty of its throng,
> And the void weighs on us; and then we wake,
> And hear the fruitful stream lapsing along
> 'Twixt villages, and think how we shall take
> Our own calm journey on for human sake.

Many Keatsians mutter disapproval about this practice of 'reducing poetry to a parlour-game'; but these frolics seem harmless enough. On this occasion the time limit appears to have been suspended, as Hunt stayed up all night to complete his sonnet, which even Robert Gittings (a fierce critic of Hunt on Keats's behalf) concedes to be 'the best of the three'. Keats, who had already written his Shakespearean sonnet 'Time's Sea' that same day, produced 'a poor effort' in the Miltonic form he had all but discarded – 'a mechanical throwback'.

By nightfall Keats had left Hunt and Shelley to it, seeking out Reynolds for more elevated companionship. He was stung, if truth be told, by Hunt's reaction to the opening section of his *Endymion*, which Hunt had read through hastily, criticising its overwrought language (as compared, believed Keats, with his own *Rimini*) and saying of the scenes between Endymion and Peona that 'it should be simple forgetting, do ye mind, that they are both overshadowed by a super-natural power'. Hiding his anger, as yet, from Hunt, Keats shared it with his brothers. Soon he was turning for advice to Hazlitt rather than Hunt.

When Hunt included two of his sonnets in his *Literary Pocket-Book*, an amalgam of verse, prose, almanac and travel guide, Keats wrote to his brother George that it was 'full of the most sickening stuff you can imagine'. Despite the names of Lamb, Shelley, Ollier and Cowden Clarke alongside his as willing contributors, Keats goes on to profess himself 'completely tired' of Hunt. 'He understands many a beautiful thing; but then, instead of giving other minds credit for the same degree of perception as he himself possesses – he begins an explanation in such a curious manner that our taste and self-love is offended con-tinually. Hunt does one harm by making fine things petty and beautiful things hateful . . . Through him I am indifferent to Mozart, I care not for white busts – and many a glorious thing when associated with him becomes a nothing – This distorts one's mind – makes one's thoughts bizarre – perplexes one in the standard of beauty.'

Hunt was too busy to notice, as he pleaded in a letter of apology to Clarke for failing to acknowledge receipt of some of his work. 'I have been very busy – so busy, both summer and winter, that summer has scarcely been any to me; and my head at times has almost grown benumbed over my writing . . . I have written prose, I have written poetry, I have written levities and gravities, I have written two acts of a Tragedy and (*Oh Diva pecunia*) I have written a Pocket-Book! . . .' At this time, ironically, Hunt was feeling about Clarke much the same as he did not realise Keats was feeling about him – that Clarke's impor-tunity was rather too persistent and fawning, and that his verse was decidedly mediocre.

Obsessed with the continuing assaults of Gifford, about whom he was now embarking upon a satire entitled *Ultra-Crepidarius*, Hunt remained unaware of Keats's growing reaction against him. This was perhaps because Keats, while coming to terms with Hunt's inferiority as a poet, frequently softens his criticism with humour or a casual, throwaway air, as if guilt-stricken because of Hunt's unremitting kind-ness toward him. After all, as another Keatsian concedes, 'Hunt had given Keats a great deal.' Or, as yet another puts it, Keats's poetry 'would probably never have been reviewed by major periodicals if Keats had not been associated with Leigh Hunt'.

Even after extracting himself from Hunt's sphere of influence, Keats remained capable of quoting him approvingly, as in a letter praising his *Examiner* review of Hazlitt's withering riposte to the *Quarterly*'s assaults, 'A Letter to William Gifford' (in which Hunt wrote that Hazlitt had got Gifford 'fast by the ribs, forcing him, with various ingenuity of grip, to display unwillingly all the deformities of his moral structure'). Keats's growing disenchantment with Hunt's literary influence never blinded the younger poet to his discarded patron's many personal and professional kindnesses.

As late as 1820, a year before he was to die in Italy, Keats was again to be found accepting Hunt's material help and hospitality. Each admitted to finding himself in financial difficulties; Hunt explained that he had had to give up the lease on York Buildings and move to Kentish Town, where he had found cheaper lodgings at 13 Mortimer Terrace. Perhaps Keats would like to move nearby? He could call on the Hunts as often as he liked, and they would both be within a mile of their beloved Hampstead.

Within the month Keats had indeed moved to cheaper lodgings just a few doors from Hunt, in Wesleyan Place, and their friendship was resumed. Keats again became a regular visitor to the Hunt salon, for all its brood of unruly children and its paterfamilias's perennial concerns about money and his wife's health as he struggled to edit two papers and continue his own voluminous work. Keats no longer required Hunt's literary counsel; but he was content to accept the unstinting hospitality of a man whose finances remained as precarious as his own. After a haemorrhage on 22 June, with no one else to turn to, he spent seven weeks in the Hunts' 'little cage' of a house – receiving as much tender care and affectionate moral support as had Shelley in his own hour of need.

It was during this stay that Keats turned to his host one day, 'his eyes swimming with tears', and told him that his unrequited love for Fanny Brawne had him dying of a broken heart. There followed an unfortunate episode when a disgruntled servant left without, as instructed, delivering one of Fanny's letters to Keats; only a few days later did it finally reach him, its seal broken, via the grubby hands of one of the

Hunt children. After quitting the house in a rage, and crawling 'half-dead' towards Hampstead, Keats later sent Hunt a note recognising his innocence in the matter and thanking him for his 'patience at my lunes'. Hunt had behaved 'very kindly to me', he acknowledged in a letter that August.

Although they never met again, it seems that Keats finally accepted the truth vouchsafed by his trusty friend Cowden Clarke: however he had treated Hunt, the warmth of Hunt's feelings 'never varied towards Keats'. As for the now discredited view that Keats wrote his finest poetry only after escaping Hunt's influence, John Bayley ushered in a whole new school of thought when he declared in 1962 that Hunt's influence on Keats was 'almost wholly benign'.

Within the year Keats would travel to Italy for the sake of his health, never to return. Two years before, in March 1818, Shelley had made the same journey – with, as fate would eventually have it, the same result – but not before trying to ensure the material welfare of his friend Hunt. As long ago as mid-1817 Shelley had been writing to Byron that 'Hunt has been here with me, and we have often spoken of you . . . Hunt is an excellent man, and has a great regard for you.' The subtext of these letters soon became money. 'I cannot doubt that [Byron] would hesitate in contributing at least £100 towards extricating one whom he regards so highly from a state of embarrassment,' Shelley had written to Hunt as early as December 1816, in the very early days of their friendship.

By the time Shelley, too, left for Italy, the bond between them had indeed become deep. When the Hunts' fifth child, another boy, was born that year, he was christened Percy Bysshe Shelley Hunt. 'When shall I see you again? O that it might be in Italy,' Shelley wrote from Lyons on 22 March 1818. Chiding Hunt for not waking him to say goodbye before he left England – 'I take this as rather an unkind piece of kindness in you' – Shelley adds: 'I confess that the thought of how long we may be divided makes me very melancholy.'

The same letter offers guarded praise for Hunt's poem The Nymphs, published in Foliage, offering a gentle warning against introducing low diction into an 'idealized' poem. 'What a delightful poem The Nymphs is – especially the second part! It is truly poetical, in the intense and emphatic sense of the word. If six hundred miles were not between us, I should say what pity that *glib* was not omitted, and that the poem is not as faultless as it is beautiful . . .'

Shelley was right, of course. In the poem Hunt writes of the 'rounder murmur, glib and flush' of a stream, but is soon adding 'glib' flakes of water and 'glib' sea flowers. These repetitions smack more of haste than infelicity, but that is no excuse. Overproductivity, usually to meet hopeless debts, would lead Hunt into many such lapses throughout his writing life. But they weren't without their uses. By at least one view, Shelley's reading of Hunt's *Nymphs* 'taught [him] something, for it is in the mythmaking mode that he was to use with great effect in such poems as *Prometheus Unbound* and *The Witch of Atlas*'.

'By far the most interesting of his volumes', in the view of one contemporary scholar, Hunt's *Foliage (or Poems Original and Translated)* contained works both already published and fresh-minted: an occasional verse marking Marianne's birthday and those poems to Thornton and 'little ranting Johnny' as well as the 'Harry Brown' epistles to Byron, Moore, Lamb, Hazlitt and Barron Field, with sonnets for Keats, Shelley, Reynolds, Haydon and Horace Smith. Lines addressed to Novello, Henry Robertson and John Gattie celebrated their mutual love of music. Even his mother-in-law and sister-in-law received verse salutations. There were translations from Latin and Greek poets, and a summary in his introduction of the literary revolution inaugurated twenty years earlier by Wordsworth and Coleridge: 'A sensitiveness to the beauty of the external world, to the unsophisticated impulses of our nature, and above all, imagination, or the power to see, with verisimilitude, what others do not – these are the properties of poetry.'

It was 'high time' for all of them – Wordsworth, Byron, Moore and indeed himself – 'to look after health and sociability . . . We should consider ourselves as we really are – creatures made to enjoy more than to know, to know infinitely nevertheless in proportion as we enjoy kindly, and finally, to put our own shoulders to the wheel and get out of the mud upon the sward again, like the waggoner whom Jupiter admonishes in the fable.' Hunt himself did not write 'for the sake of a moral only nor even for that purpose principally: – I write to enjoy myself; but I have learnt in the course of it to write for others only; and my poetical tendencies luckily fall in with my moral theories. The main features of the book are a love of sociability, of the country, and of the fine imagination of the Greeks.'

Perhaps the most characteristically guileless of Hunt's collections, in the sheer innocence of its celebration of the joys of life and all things natural, *Foliage* also contained 'The Nile' and other products of his sonnet-writing competitions. Byron's sneer to Moore perhaps expended more verbal energy than Hunt's harmless little volume deserved: 'Of all the ineffable Centaurs that were ever begotten by Self-love upon a Nightmare, I think this monstrous Sagittary the most prodigious.'

By November 1818 Hunt was compiling another *Pocket-Book*. 'The booksellers tell me it will do exceedingly well; and Shelley will be at once pleased and surprised to hear that it is my own property.' As well as miscellaneous poetry and prose, these handy little volumes costing a half-crown also contained practical advice for the literary-minded traveller: the addresses of authors and scholars, libraries and bookshops, art galleries and concert halls. Hunt produced five such volumes between 1819 and 1823, their contents including his verse cycle *The Months*, published separately by Ollier in 1823. In July 1819 Ollier bought the copyright to the series from Hunt for £200, while continuing to pay him a modest fee as editor and contributor.

Hunt's literary ubiquity at this time, and his ability to endear himself even to his detractors, may be gleaned from a vignette in the memoirs of Henry Crabb Robinson, far from his biggest admirer. In April 1818 their paths crossed at Lamb's; Robinson found the socially gauche Marianne 'a very disgusting woman', but for once managed to find something positive to say about her husband: 'He, though a man I very much dislike, did not displease me this evening. He has improved in manliness and healthfulness since I saw him last, some years ago. There was a glee about him which evinced high spirits, if not perfect health, and I envied his vivacity . . .

'[The poet T.N.] Talfourd was there, and injudiciously loquacious . . . Hunt, who did not sympathize with Talfourd, opposed him playfully, and that I liked him for.'

Robinson also liked Hunt's impersonations, as we know from his report of another evening at Lamb's: 'Hunt imitated Hazlitt capitally, Wordsworth not so well.' Hunt's social life was as lively as ever, with newcomers such as the 'walking Encyclopaedia' Walter Coulson, a protégé of Bentham's, joining his regular reports to the Shelleys in Italy. 'I see a good deal of Lamb, Hazlitt, Coulson, the Novellos &c, but as much at their own houses as at mine, or rather more just now.' According to another new arrival in the circle, a young lawyer named Bryan Waller Procter, who published light verse under the nom de plume Barry Cornwall, 'Hunt never gave dinners, but his suppers of cold meat and salad were cheerful and pleasant; sometimes the cheerfulness (after a "wassail bowl") soared into noisy merriment. I remember one Christmas or New Year's evening when we sat there till two or three o'clock in the morning, and when the jokes and stories and imitations so overcame me that I was nearly falling off my chair with laughter.' Procter became as 'pleasant' a member of his circle, Hunt told the Shelleys, as such other old friends as Hogg and Peacock.

Between March 1818 and end of 1819 the Shelleys wrote the Hunts nineteen letters from Italy, and received twelve in return. Hunt's other preoccupations often conspired to make him a tardy correspondent. By the time he mailed his first letter to the travelling Shelleys, dated 24 April 1818 (but written over four days), he had received Shelley's third; the post between England and Italy then taking some two weeks, and the Shelleys making rapid progress from Milan via Pisa to Livorno and Bagni di Lucca, the couple had invariably moved on before Hunt's letters arrived. When eventually they did, they contained a welcome mixture of chatty news and literary observations, as in this first, which opens: 'Well, dear & illustrious vagabonds, and how do you find yourselves? We are all well here, and as musical and flowery as ever . . .'

Hunt goes on: 'It is delightful to hear of Shelley's improving health. The nearer he gets to the sun, the better he will be, I doubt not; but don't let him be too much out in it & burn his wings.' There follows much badinage, descriptions of his new bower ('filled with geraniums, myrtle and daisies, heartsease and a vase full of gay flowers'); more sightings of friends from Hogg and Peacock to Lamb (whose latest book is being published, thanks to Hunt, by Ollier); a meditation on Michelangelo; requests for long descriptions of Italy, especially Venice ('as I am writing a comedy, mixed with quieter matter, the scene of which is laid there'); and the usual family gossip. At one point Hunt signs off, preparing to hand the rest of the paper to Marianne; but

then he relents, saying she will write separately, and fills every corner
with random scribblings so as to save money by cramming as much as
possible on to a single sheet.

That November another belated letter from Hunt ('So Shelley has
been hanging his head, I fear, and saying: "Hunt is <u>too</u> careless"')
moved Shelley to reply: 'A letter from you is always so pleasant that
one never feels less inclined to complain of the long absence of such a
pleasure than at the moment when it is conferred.' March 1819 saw
Hunt telling Shelley: 'Hogg and Peacock generally live here over
Sunday, when the former is not on the circuit; and we pass very pleasant afternoons, talking of mythology, and the Greeks, and our old
friends.' Now more than ever he needed Shelley's friends around him,
as his brother John had retired to Somerset, so that his younger sons
'might be better furnished with means for entering into life', leaving
his eldest son, Henry (not to be confused with the contemporaneous
Henry 'Orator' Hunt), in charge of the business side of the *Examiner*.
This entailed Leigh's spending more time than ever at the office, so he
could not, as Shelley hoped, come to Italy. 'I cannot come; I wish to
God I could . . . There is not a day passes over my head, I assure you,
but what I think of Italy . . .'

Henry Sylvan Hunt, his fifth son and sixth child, now arrived to
swell the family and its budget. That July, still overproducing to fend
off debt, Hunt submitted a play to Covent Garden, only to have 'the
honour to be rejected', as he put it to Shelley in a letter on 8 July 1819.
'You will see in the *Examiner* what I have said about your lovely poem
of *Rosalind and Helen*, which is a great favourite of mine. I was rejoiced
to find also that Charles Lamb was full of it. Your reputation is certainly
rising greatly in your native country, in spite of its Promethean chains;
and I have no doubt it will be universally recognized on its proper
eminence . . .'

Hunt's poetry in the *Examiner* during the second half of 1819 was
filled with political anger, directed primarily at the government's and
the Prince Regent's continuing indifference to his advice. But his new
volume of poems was closer in spirit to the 'sociability' recommended
in the preface to *Foliage*; among reprints of *Rimini* and *The Descent of
Liberty* it contained his *Hero and Leander*, *Bacchus and Ariadne* and *The
Panther*, all works on mythological subjects which he also promised to

send the Shelleys. But the main burden of his letter was sympathy upon the loss of their son William in a malaria epidemic sweeping Rome: 'He was a fine little fellow, was William; & for my part, I cannot conceive that the young intellectual spirit which sat thinking out of his eye, & seemed to comprehend so much in his smile, can perish like the house it inhabited.'

The next paragraph illustrates the quasi-religious lines along which Hunt was beginning to think, eventually to form the nucleus of a meditation on the subject in book form. 'I do not know that a soul is born with us; but we seem, to me, to *attain* to a soul, some later, some earlier; and when we have got that, there is a look in our eye, a sympathy in our cheerfulness, and a yearning and grave beauty in our thoughtfulness that seems to say, "Our mortal dress may fall off when it will; our trunk and our leaves may go; we have shot up our blossom into an immortal air . . ."'

Although the letter began with the usual apologies for delay, explaining that he had been 'laid prostrate by a bilious fever', 1819 saw Hunt in generally better health, physically and spiritually, as can be told from the cheerful tones of his letters to Shelley and others. The one constant theme of Shelley's letters back had long been his increasingly insistent wish that the Hunts should come to join him and Mary in Italy. Soon he was associating Byron with this invitation. On 22 December 1818 Shelley had reported that Byron had offered to lend Hunt 'four or five hundred pounds' because he, too, wished to see Hunt in Italy. The offer was 'very frankly made, and it would not only give him great pleasure, but might do him service, to have your society . . . Pray could you not make it in some way profitable to visit this astonishing country?'

Shelley also wrote to their mutual friend Peacock, urging him to make up Hunt's mind for him. Peacock twice visited Hunt, then wrote to Shelley that a visit to Italy would 'ruin' him, 'for what in the interval would become of his paper?' In March 1819 Hunt confirmed Peacock's message in a long letter apologising that 'doubts and difficulties' had prevented a more prompt response. '"But what, Hunt, of Italy?" Oh, you see, I delay speaking of Italy. I cannot come; I wish to God I could.'

But Shelley would not give up. In May 1819, writing from Rome, he dedicated his verse drama *The Cenci* to Hunt:

MY DEAR FRIEND,

I inscribe with your name, from a distant country, and after an
absence whose months have seemed years, this the latest of my literary efforts. Those writings which I have hitherto published have
been little else than visions which impersonate my own apprehensions of the beautiful and the just. I can also perceive in them the
literary defects incidental to youth and impatience; they are dreams
of what ought to be or may be. The drama which I now present to
you is a sad reality. I lay aside the presumptuous attitude of an
instructor and am content to paint, with such colors as my own
heart furnishes, that which has been.

Had I known a person more highly endowed than yourself with all
that it becomes a man to possess, I had solicited for this work the
ornament of his name. One more gentle, honourable, innocent and
brave; one of more exalted toleration for all who do and think evil,
and yet himself more free from evil; one who knows better how to
receive and how to confer a benefit, though he must ever confer far
more than he can receive; one of simpler, and, in the highest sense
of the word, of purer life and manners, I never knew; and I had
already been fortunate in friendships when your name was added to
the list.

In that patient and irreconcilable enmity with domestic and political tyranny and imposture which the tenor of your life has
illustrated, and which, had I health and talents, should illustrate
mine, let us, comforting each other in our task, live and die. All happiness attend you!
Your affectionate friend,

PERCY B. SHELLEY.
ROME, 29 May 1819.

A few months later, in September, another letter from Shelley again
invites Hunt to meet up with him in Florence, where 'we would try to
muster up a "lieta brigata", which, leaving behind them the pestilence
of remembered misfortunes, might act over again the pleasures of the
Interlocutors in Boccaccio'. There is a touchingly plaintive note in
Hunt's frustrated reply, marooned as he was in London by debts and

Examiner duties: 'But Chaucer, as well as Milton, paid a visit to Italy; so did Gray, so did Drummond, Donne and the Earl of Surrey . . .'

All this was taking place against a backdrop of intense national unrest which saw supposedly literary Hunt back on the political barricades with a vengeance. 'This is the commencement, if we are not much mistaken, of one of the most important years that have been seen for a long while yet,' he wrote in the first issue of the *Examiner* for 1819. 'It is quiet; it seems peaceable to us here in Europe; it may even continue so, as far as any great warfare is concerned; but a spirit is abroad, stronger than kings, or armies, or all the most predominant shapes of prejudice and force . . .'

This was to prove a remarkably prophetic paragraph. Eighteen nineteen was a momentously double-edged year, aptly described as 'the *annus mirabilis* for many English writers and the *annus terribilis* of the political world'. In the eight years since the start of the Regency in 1811, and the four since Waterloo, the intransigence of monarchy and government on the causes Hunt had always championed – freedom of speech, parliamentary reform, Catholic emancipation – now combined with increased censorship of the press and fierce suppression of protest movements around the country to render some violent climax inevitable. It came in Manchester on 16 August, when armed troops charged into a sixty-thousand-strong protest meeting in St Peter's Fields, killing eleven people and wounding four hundred. The 'Peterloo massacre' moved Hunt to a rare but impassioned defence of his namesake and rival, Henry 'Orator' Hunt, with whom he had had his differences in reformist circles, but who had been addressing the meeting at the time of the attack. It also led to a rare and uncharacteristic lapse on Hunt's part with regard to his beloved Shelley.

'You do not tell me whether you have received my lines on the Manchester affair,' wrote Shelley to Hunt from Florence four months later. As soon as news of Peterloo reached him in Italy, Shelley had written *The Mask of Anarchy* in white heat; frustrated at his geographical detachment from political events in his homeland, he saw poetry as his only means of continued participation. And he relied on Hunt as his outlet to the world.

But answer came there none. For the next several months Hunt's

letters carried the usual literary chit-chat, gossip about mutual friends
and continued complaints at not being able to leave England. But he
never even acknowledged receipt of *The Mask of Anarchy*; nor, the following spring, of Shelley's satire on Wordsworth, 'Peter Bell the
Third', and an impassioned defence of the radical journalist and publisher Richard Carlile; nor, in May 1820, of his 'A Philosophical View
of Reform'.

In the wake of Peterloo, Hunt's friend Thomas Barnes had swung
The Times against the government. While Hunt's own *Examiner* editorials also railed against these 'Men in the Brazen Masks', however, he
otherwise felt moved to enter a rare period of editorial caution. So hostile did the climate between government and press become, and so
grave the danger of prosecution, that Hunt felt obliged for the only
time in his life to exercise a degree of self-censorship in his struggle to
keep the *Examiner* independent of party. His sole defence is that
Shelley's wildly angry poem, with its exhortation to the mob to rise up
against its masters, conflicted with his own belief in peaceful protest;
not until ten years after Shelley's death, when the climate had been rad-
ically altered by the Reform Bill of 1832, did he feel able to share with
the public 'the sincerity and kind-heartedness of the spirit that walked
in this flaming robe of verse' by editing and publishing an edition of *The
Mask of Anarchy*.

Irate though they wax over the episode, wishing Hunt had published one of Shelley's finest poems 'while the blood was still fresh on
the government's hands', even the most passionate Shelleyans find it in
their hearts to forgive Hunt. At least, as the late Paul Foot concedes,
'Hunt was in England publishing. Every issue of the *Examiner*, however
castrated, was liable to prosecution. Shelley risked nothing. He was
basking in the sunshine of Livorno or gazing at pictures in the
Florentine galleries or taking part in shooting competitions with Byron
at Pisa . . . It was his own decision, freely taken, to abandon the seat of
politics which interested him for "a poet's life". And so, by his own
admission in the very first line of "The Mask of Anarchy", he "lay asleep
in Italy" . . .'

Hunt's discomfort at suppressing such powerful political writing, as
evidenced in his evasions to his friend, is almost palpable throughout
the year. The contrast between the political fervour in his public jour-

nalism, itself somewhat muted, and the jaunty small talk in his private letters is never again so marked. By the autumn, it seems, his spine had again begun to stiffen, as the public appetite for his particular combination of prose polemic and poetical taste led him to launch a new journal, named the *Indicator* after the trademark ☞ with which he signed his otherwise anonymous *Examiner* articles. For a while 'the Indicator' had become Hunt's nickname among his friends. 'It is the object of this periodical work to notice any subjects whatsoever within the range of the editor's knowledge or reading,' he announced in the first issue, dated 13 October 1819. 'He will take them up, as they happen to suggest themselves; and endeavour to point out their essence to the reader, so as at once to be brief and satisfactory. The subjects will chiefly consist of curious recollections of biography; short disquisitions on men and things; the most interesting stories in history or fiction told over again, with an eye to their proper appreciation by unvulgar minds; and now and then a few original verses . . .' To friends and fellow contributors, Hunt summed up his latest journal's contents as 'honey from the old woods'.

Like so many of Hunt's publishing enterprises, the *Indicator* was to prove short-lived; but its seventy-six weeks of publication, eight pages for twopence every Wednesday, were to be marked by some memorable contributions. Designed as a counterweight to the *Examiner*, which had grown as brittle and agitated as the times, the *Indicator* (like the *Reflector* before it) gave Hunt an outlet for his literary enthusiasms while he let off feverish political steam elsewhere. If, in his own words, the *Examiner* was 'a room in a public tavern', the *Indicator* was a 'private room . . . a retreat from public cares'. But they were also complementary, feeding off each other in politico-literary vein, as when the *Indicator*'s review of Keats's *Hyperion* (2 August 1820) celebrates the resurgence of liberal thought at a time when the stagnation and indeed corruption of reactionary politics was vividly portrayed in the *Examiner*'s report of Queen Caroline's trial (20 August). This long-running saga was also the prime subject of Hunt's few satirical verses for the paper that year.

'Lucrezia Borgia was hardly worse, according to their account,' he scowls in a graphic account of Caroline's tormentors to Shelley in Livorno that week. Responding to Mary's complaint that he never sends political news, he discusses the revolutions in Spain and Naples, the Emperor of Russia and the Queen's trial (but still omits to mention Peterloo) on the first page of the letter whose reverse is reproduced in this book's picture section. 'How you delight me with what you say of the Indicator!' he continues there; 'I hope you will like the succeeding papers as well . . .' before moving on to gossip of their mutual friends the Gisbornes, John and Maria, with whom he is about to take tea. 'Keats, who is better, [is sens]ible of your kindness, & has sent you a letter & a fine v[olume of] poetry by the Gisbornes,' Hunt scribbles on the back of the envelope. 'He is advised to go to Rome, but will call on you at all events in the Spring.'

On the opposite side, in spidery writing, he scrawls: 'I have just seen the *Prometheus*. What noble, elemental things in it! What grand lines & affectionate thoughts! But it is liable to some of the objections against the Rev. of Islam.' Underneath, typically filling every nook and cranny of the single sheet, to save precious money, Hunt adds: 'You must not wonder at the state of the seal; for when I gave the letter to an acquaintance to put in the post, I forgot to <?> the payment.'

With Keats and Shelley, Hazlitt and Lamb all among its contributors, the *Indicator* would have earned its place in literary history solely for the first appearance of the original version of Keats's 'La Belle Dame Sans Merci'. But Hunt himself can, for once, lay claim to work as substantial as that of names better known to posterity; it was in the *Indicator* that he attempted to revive the essay style of the 'old' *Spectator* and *Tatler*, to 'perfect the art of the occasional essay first attempted in the *Reflector*'. It was not without reason that Hunt told friends he considered his *Indicator* essays were the best writing he had ever done. They are typical of the personal essays he poured out over almost half a century, relaxed and companionable, across an infinite range of topics from dancing to pig driving, people real and imaginary, everyday life and places from Pisa to St Paul's. Best of all, perhaps, were his meditations upon nature – hot days, cold days, rainy days, May days – and literature, combining close social observation with unusually astute self-revelation. While self-deprecating about his personal qualities, he established a natural rapport with his readers, vividly encouraging them to share his experiences.

Among the best known, 'On the Household Gods of the Ancients'

(10 November 1819) draws on his love of classical literature; 'Far Countries' (8 December 1819) milks the fashionable disdain for the French in remarking that 'the greatest height they go is in a balloon'; 'Coaches and Their Horses' (23 and 30 August 1820) explores every conceivable aspect of its subject, analysing the various types of coaches and horses to the point of examining different ways of entering, riding in and dismounting from a coach.

So well received were Hunt's musings upon 'fireside' matters that, in later life, he permitted himself to indulge in some vain recollection of his friends' favourites – 'for they liked it enough to have favourite papers' – among his own contributions. Hazlitt's was that on 'Sleep', Lamb's were 'Coaches', 'Deaths of Little Children' and 'Thoughts and Guesses on Human Nature', Shelley's 'Fair Revenge' and Keats's the witty series entitled 'A Now' (one of which they wrote together, belying subsequent suggestions of a terminal falling-out). Even the crusty Crabb Robinson enjoyed Hunt's contributions, noting how he seems, in stark contrast to Hazlitt, 'to love everything. He catches the sunny side of everything, and excepting a few polemical antipathies finds everything beautiful.'

The favourite of Mary Shelley, who had recently lost two infant children in Italy, was Hunt's poignant meditation on the 'Deaths of Little Children', written after visiting the grave of his mother:

We are writing, at this moment, just opposite a spot which contains the grave of one inexpressibly dear to us. We see from our window the trees about it, and the church-spire. The green fields lie around. The clouds are travelling overhead, alternately taking away the sunshine and restoring it. The vernal winds, piping of the flowery summer-time, are nevertheless calling to mind the far distant and dangerous ocean, which the heart that lies in the grave had many reasons to think of. So far from it, it is the existence of that grave which doubles every charm of the spot; which links the pleasures of our childhood and manhood together; which puts a hushing tenderness in the winds, and a patient joy upon the landscape; which seems to unite heaven and earth, mortality and immortality, the grass of the tomb and the grass of the green field, and gives a more maternal aspect to the whole kindness of nature.

Hunt also functioned as literary critic, reviewing Shelley's *The Cenci* and Keats's *Lamia*. But the *Indicator* was primarily a platform for his essays – which the other master of that art, Lamb, celebrated in verse:

> Your easy Essays indicate a flow,
> Dear Friend, of brain, which we may elsewhere seek;
> And to their pages I, and hundreds, owe,
> That Wednesday is the sweetest of the week.
> Wit, poet, prose-man, party-man, translator –
> H——, your best title yet is INDICATOR.

The first issue of the *Indicator* quickly went through four editions, and the entire collection of some six hundred pages was published in one volume after the journal's closure in 1822. Hunt himself reprinted many of his *Indicator* essays in his own collections, such as *The Indicator; and The Companion; A Miscellany for the Fireside* (1834) and *Essays by Leigh Hunt: The Indicator, The Seer* (1841). It closed on 21 March 1821.

By mid-1820 Shelley had clearly forgiven Hunt for failing to print his most outspoken political verse and prose; for it was during this period, still impatient for Hunt to join him in Italy, that he left his indelible portrait of his friend in his verse *Letter to Maria Gisborne*, dated 1 July 1820:

> You will see Hunt – one of those happy souls
> Who are the salt of the earth, and without whom
> This world would smell like what it is – a tomb;
> Who is, what others seem; his room no doubt
> Is still adorned with many a cast from Shout,
> With graceful flowers tastefully placed about;
> And coronals of bay from ribbons hung,
> And brighter wreaths in neat disorder flung;
> The gifts of the most learned among some dozens
> Of female friends, sisters-in-law, and cousins.
> And there is he with his eternal puns,
> Which beat the dullest brain for smiles, like duns
> Thundering for money at a poet's door;

Alas! it is no use to say, 'I'm poor!'
Or oft in graver mood, when he will look
Things wiser than were ever read in book,
Except in Shakespeare's wisest tenderness.

Much as he still longed to accept Shelley's invitation to Italy, Hunt's practical difficulties were soon compounded by illness. 'I would come to you instantly,' he wrote in August 1821, 'and I do not say that I shall not come to you before long; but there are obstacles . . .' Italy, for now, remained a 'beautiful impossibility'. During the winter of 1821–2, amid all her own perpetual ailments, Marianne wrote to Mary Shelley that her husband's condition saw him 'irritable beyond anything you ever saw in him, and nervous to a most fearful extent'. Suddenly, in the case of both Hunts, a trip to the Italian sun became desirable for health reasons. 'Ask Mr Shelley, my dear Mr Shelley, to *urge it to him*,' Marianne begged Mary. By March 1821 Hunt himself was conceding to Shelley: 'I have indeed had a hard bout of it this time; and if the portrait you have with you sympathized with my appearance, the patience you found in it ought to look twice as great, and the cheeks twice as small.'

That month Hunt also wrote to Joseph Severn in Rome, picking his way delicately around the fact that Keats had told him that 'in his sick moments, he never wished to receive another letter, or even see another face, however friendly'. Hunt, he told Severn, had recently been almost at death's door himself: 'Judge how often I thought of Keats, and with what feelings.'

If he can bear to hear of us, pray tell him – but he knows it already, and can put it into better language than any man. I hear that he does not like to be told that he may get better; nor is it to be wondered at, considering his firm persuasion that he shall not recover. He can only regard it as a puerile thing, and an insinuation that he cannot bear to think he shall die. But if his persuasion should happen to be no longer so strong upon him, or if he can now put up with such attempts to console him, tell him of what I have said a thousand times, and what I still (upon my honour, Severn) think always, that I have seen too many instances of recovery from apparently desperate cases of consumption not to be in hope to the very last. If he cannot bear this, tell him — tell that great poet and noble-hearted man — that we shall all bear his memory in the most precious part of our hearts, and that the world shall bow their heads to it, as our loves do. Or if this, again, will trouble his spirit, tell him that we shall never cease to remember and love him; and that the most sceptical of us has faith enough in the high things that nature puts into our heads to think all who are of one accord in mind or heart are journeying to one and the same place, and shall unite somewhere or other again, face to face, mutually conscious, mutually delighted. Tell him he is only before us on the road, as he was in everything else; or whether you tell him the latter or no, tell him the former, and add that we shall never forget that he was so, and we are coming after him. The tears are again in my eyes, and I must not afford to shed them . . .

Hunt's letter was dated 8 March 1821. Keats had died on 23 February.

Of Keats's death, Byron would famously write (in *Don Juan*) of the 'fiery particle' that was 'snuffed out by an article'. Shelley, too, thought that Keats had been done to death by his critics. But his friend Hunt, he wrote in his preface to his lament for Keats, *Adonais*, 'has a very hard skull to crack, and will take a great deal of killing'.

Hunt's critics may have laid off for a while, but his life was otherwise in its usual turmoil. Just as he finally seemed ready to make up his mind for Italy, right down to discussing with Marianne the sale of the furniture to pay their fares, events were again complicated by the law. The previous year John Hunt, now back at the helm of the *Examiner*, had again been jailed for an attack on the unreformed House of Commons in the issue of 23 July 1820. After another twelve months in Coldbath Fields, again liable for sureties of subsequent good behaviour totalling £1000, John suggested to Leigh that he withdraw from the proprietorship of the paper, to protect himself against further such prosecutions. 'I consented at last with the less scruple,' wrote Hunt to Shelley, 'not only because my health was the more precarious, but because my brother's name is obliged to be at the bottom of the paper as printer, and printers though not editors, are indictable, like proprietors.'

Eventually, this would lead to difficulties between the brothers; at the time, what seemed like another setback gradually turned into a blessing in disguise. During its editor's illness, when he ceased to appear in the pages of the *Examiner*, sales had declined to a low point of barely three thousand; now, as Leigh Hunt took up his pen again, the circulation began to recover. Suddenly hopes were revived that he might be able to write for the paper from Italy, thus financing his trip and paying his family's living costs while abroad. Letters between Hunt and Shelley on this subject crossed in the European mail; but Shelley, then visiting Byron in Ravenna, was well aware of Hunt's continuing financial problems and pleased to seek any solution to them which would involve his friend joining him in Italy. Now he had found a solution involving Byron – a man of considerable means.

On 1 June 1818 Byron had written of Hunt in a letter to Moore from Venice: 'He is a good man, with some poetical elements in his chaos; but spoilt by Christ-Church Hospital and a Sunday newspaper – to say nothing of the Surrey gaol, which conceited him into a martyr. But he is a good man. When I saw *Rimini* in ms., I told him that I deemed it good poetry at bottom, disfigured only by a strange style. His answer was, that his style was a system, or *upon system*, or some such cant; and, when man talks of system, his case is hopeless; so I said no more to him, and very little to anyone else . . . He believes his trash of vulgar phrases tortured into compound barbarisms to be old English . . .'

There follow sundry ruminations about the 'honest charlatan' Hunt – not least his 'skimble-skamble' views on Wordsworth's 'soi-disant poetry' – before Byron repeats: 'But Leigh Hunt is a good man, and a good father – see his Odes to the Masters Hunt; – a good husband – see his Sonnet to Mrs Hunt; – a good friend – see his Epistles to different people; – and a great coxcomb and a very vulgar person in every thing about him. But that's not his fault, but of circumstances . . .'

Over the ensuing three years Shelley had been working on Byron's personal affection for Hunt, whatever his reservations about his poetry, to find a way of bringing his friend out to Italy, and so solving his financial as much as his medical problems. Now, on 26 August 1821, Shelley again wrote from Pisa insisting that the Hunts join him and

Mary in 'these regions mild of calm and serene air'. This time he was able to add that Byron, whom Shelley had just visited in Ravenna, had apparently proposed that Hunt 'should come out and go shares with him and me in a periodical work, to be conducted here; in which each of the contracting parties should publish all their original compositions, and share the profits'.

Shelley said little of his own personal difficulties with Byron, which had been considerable (as depicted in his 'Julian and Maddalo'). He seems to have internalised them; while their rivalry had moved him to some of his finest work, Byron's company also cramped his style. Given Shelley's ill-disguised aspirations to be known as the poet of his age, Byron appeared to have snatched the crown from him. No vignette is more telling than the day Shelley spent hours trying to remove the name 'Don Juan' from the mainsail of the schooner delivered to Lerici for him by Byron's crony Edward John Trelawny; after failing to erase the large black lettering, he resorted to cutting out the name and patching up the sail. Shelley 'absolutely refused', as Richard Holmes puts it, 'to sail under the title of Byron's greatest work'.

Now, demoting himself merely to 'a sort of connecting link' between Hunt and Byron, Shelley insisted that he would forgo his share of the profits in the journal, let alone 'the borrowed splendour of such a partnership'. He asked Hunt to let this remain their secret from Byron – who, he reassured his friend, was now a 'reformed' character. 'You and he, in different manners, would be equal,' Shelley told Hunt, 'and would bring, in a different manner, but in the same proportion, equal stock of reputation and success. Do not let my frankness with you, nor my belief that you deserve it more than Lord Byron, have the effect of deterring you from assuming a station in modern literature, which the universal voice of my contemporaries forbids me either to stoop to or aspire to. I am, and I desire to be, nothing.'

Literary historians have disagreed along partisan lines as to who was the prime mover in the project that became the *Liberal*. Byron had previously suggested to Moore that they launch some sort of journal together – 'a newspaper – nothing more nor less, weekly or so' containing 'a piece of poesy from one or other of us two, leaving room, however, for such dilettanti rhymers as may be deemed worthy of appearing in the same column'. Knowing his friend's whimsical, at times capricious ways, Moore had firmly declined. Now Byron had fallen out with his publisher, John Murray, and suddenly saw some self-interest in a partnership with Hunt; he and his brother could serve as a route to publication of future works, in both periodical and book form, on his own terms. If the germ of the idea was Byron's, it was more for his own sake than Hunt's. Shelley, meanwhile, was simply missing his friend's company, and still looking out for his financial interests. 'Put your music and your books on board a vessel,' he insisted, 'and you will have no more trouble.'

Initially, for all Shelley's flattery, Hunt was still beset by problems, both professional and personal, which left him reluctantly hesitant. 'That ever the time should come, when I had such an offer to visit the country of Petrarch and Boccaccio, and think of refusing it!' he sighed in early September. But consultations with John now reassured him that his eagerness to join Shelley in Italy, so long frustrated by health and money worries, could be linked with the interests of the ailing *Examiner*. Now, at last, John encouraged his brother to go, suggesting that he himself undertake the 'struggle' to 'reanimate' the paper in England, while Leigh made a simultaneous effort in Italy 'to secure new aid to our prospects, and new friends to the cause of liberty'.

A fortnight later, on 21 September 1821, filled with 'strange new thoughts and feelings', Hunt was at last able to write to the Shelleys: 'We are coming.'

7

'I never beheld him more'

1821–2

On 16 November 1821, having borrowed the fare from his brother, Hunt led his wife, six children and a goat aboard a small brig named the *Jane*, which set off for Italy from Blackwall the next morning – carrying, to the Hunts' alarm, a cargo of gunpowder. For the sake of Hunt's health, Shelley had advocated a sea voyage rather than the arduous overland route. Hunt was by now so anxious to join his friend that 'if he had recommended a balloon, I should have been inclined to try it'. Marianne's doctor had also urged an ocean trip as 'the best thing in the world' for what appeared to be her advanced state of consumption. Alas, they had chosen the wrong winter.

If few of Hunt's enterprises ever ran smoothly, this one adventure abroad was to prove jinxed from the start. As luck would have it, he had chosen a season which would prove memorable in the annals of shipping for the 'continuity and vehemence' of its wild weather. As Shelley busied himself about Byron's instructions to rent the best unfurnished villa in Pisa, furnishing its ground floor for the Hunt family while anticipating their arrival 'anxiously and daily', the *Jane* had barely cleared the Thames before it was overtaken by fierce storms.

The tiny cabin in which the entire family (and the goat) were confined, with Hunt and Marianne obliged to sleep on the floor after cramming their six children into the scant available bunk space, put

Hunt in mind of 'the little back-parlour of one of the shops in Fleet Street, or the Strand, attached or let into a great moving vehicle, and tumbling about the waves from side to side, now sending all the things that are loose this way, now that'. It was as much of a relief as an anti-climax when, after only five days at sea, the captain felt impelled to take shelter in Ramsgate.

Obliged to disembark, the family took modest rooms while awaiting an improvement in the weather. Hunt killed the time by reading the Marquis de Condorcet's *View of the Progress of Society* (with 'a transport of gratitude to the author, though it had not entered so deeply into the matter as I supposed') and meeting up with Cowden Clarke and his father. On 11 December there was another false start; this time the *Jane* managed all of eleven tempest-tossed days at sea – looking like 'a wash-house in a fit' – and twice braved the Atlantic before being beaten back. It failed even to dock at Falmouth before finally finding safe haven at Dartmouth on 22 December. By 4 January, when the captain was ready to try again, Marianne was 'so ill that it was quite impossi-ble to move her'. So the *Jane* set sail without the Hunts, who duly forfeited their fare.

While his wife remained bedridden, losing worrying amounts of blood, Hunt felt that the sea air had done him good, and found himself able to write again, 'though by driblets'. His vivid journal of the aborted voyage, during which he helped avert a near collision with an Indiaman, during a fifty-six-hour gale that was the 'most tremendous' even the skipper had ever seen – and *his* hair was white from a ship-wreck – makes such sang-froid all the more remarkable:

The white clothes that hung up on pegs in the cabin took, in the gloomy light from above, an aspect like things of meaning; and the wind and rain together, as they ran blind and howling along by the vessel's side, when I was on deck, appeared like frantic spirits of the air, chasing and shrieking after one another, and tearing each other by the hair of their heads.

'The grandeur of the glooms' on the Atlantic was majestic indeed: the healthiest eye would have seen them with awe. The sun rose in the morning, at once fiery and sicklied over; a livid gleam played on the water, like the reflection of lead; then the storms would recommence; and during partial clearings of the clouds and fogs appeared standing in the sky, moulded into gigantic shapes, like antediluvian wonders, or visitants from the zodiac; mammoths, vaster than have yet been thought of; the first ungainly and stupendous ideas of bodies and legs, looking out upon an unfinished world.

Ever cheerful in the face of adversity, Hunt shifted his family to Plymouth, where he paid the master of a ship bound for Genoa a deposit of £30, promising the balance upon arrival. Having brought the family aboard, however, he began to doubt whether he could fulfil that obligation, and disembarked them again. Awaiting reassurance from Shelley that more funds would be forthcoming, and finally persuaded to ride out the dreadful weather on *terra firma*, they settled in the Stonehouse district of Plymouth for the winter. There were enough *Examiner* readers in the area for a ripple of excitement to greet the news of its editor's presence in their midst; he made lasting friends, among them the painter Philip Rogers and a teacher named Hine, then producing the first school edition of Wordsworth.

Still anxious about Byron's enthusiasm for the project with Shelley, not least for financial reasons, Hunt wrote him an exploratory letter from Plymouth in January: 'I was not sure whether it [the idea for the journal] was not a generous artifice of [Shelley's] own, and though I knew no reason why he should not be as plain with me on this as on all other occasions, I was additionally mystified by his giving me no answer to this question – perhaps an oversight of some important business.'

As if *en passant*, Hunt also asked Byron to advance him £250. Shelley had made it clear that he could no longer help financially, and was reluctant to put Hunt's case to Byron 'for fear of incurring an obligation'. But Hunt was desperate; he had built up debts to his brother approaching £2000. Inadequate record-keeping by all concerned, not least Hunt himself, leads to much confusion surrounding subsequent transactions; but it seems clear that Hunt again asked Shelley to intercede with Byron on his behalf, thus stretching their friendship to its limits. Himself in financial straits, Shelley had already sent Hunt £150, 'within 30 or 40 of what I had contrived to scrape together', but now agreed with ill-disguised unease to make a further approach to Byron. 'As it has come to this in spite of my exertions, I will not conceal from you the low ebb of my money-affairs in the present moment.'

Forwarding Hunt's letter to Byron, while conceding that it 'annoys me on more than one account', Shelley offered to stand as guarantor for any loan, candidly doubting that 'poor Hunt's promise to pay in given time is worth very much'. Hunt, a pained Shelley explained, had 'urged me more than once to ask you to lend him this money. My answer consisted in sending him all I could spare, which I have now literally done. Your kindness in fitting up a part of your own house for his accommodation I sensibly felt, and willingly accepted from you on his part; but, believe me, without the slightest intention of imposing, or, if I could help it, allowing to be imposed, any heavier task on your purse . . . I am so much annoyed by this subject that I hardly know what to write, and much less what to say; and I have need of all your indulgence in judging both my feelings and expressions.' Shelley's diplomacy seemed to do the trick. Byron consented 'with tolerable willingness' to part with £250 in Italian bills, which Shelley duly forwarded to Hunt in Plymouth. In the first few months of 1822, by one calculation of these labyrinthine dealings, Hunt received a total of £550: £400 from Byron and £150 from Shelley.

As concerns the journal, no reply from Byron to Hunt's letter is extant. But that same week, even while arranging Hunt's passage with Shelley, Byron was telling barefaced lies to his friend Moore: 'Be assured that there is no such coalition as you apprehend.' This was in reply to Moore's horror at hearing that Hunt was 'on his way to you, with all his family; and that the idea seems to be that you and Shelley and he are to conspire together in the *Examiner*. I cannot believe this, and deprecate such a plan with all my might.'

This was the first that Byron heard of anxieties among his friends and admirers in London about his stooping to partnership with the 'Cockney' Hunt and Shelley. 'Alone you may do any thing,' Moore continued, 'but partnerships in fame, like those in trade, make the strongest party answerable for the deficiencies or delinquencies of the rest, and I tremble even for you with such a bankrupt co . . . They are both clever fellows, and Shelley I look upon as a man of real genius; but I must again say that you could not give your enemies a greater triumph than by forming such an unequal and unholy alliance . . . You must

stand alone.' Before long, sensing that he could not talk Byron out of a
perceived loyalty to Hunt, Moore proceeded to concentrate his fire on
Shelley, arguing his potentially 'dangerous influence'; in vain did a
despairing Shelley write to Horace Smith, asking him to reassure
Moore (whom Shelley had never met, nor ever would) that 'I have not
the smallest influence over Lord Byron.'

Byron confided Moore's objections to his friend Thomas Medwin,
shrugging that he had 'pledged' himself, 'and besides, could not now,
if I had ever so great a disinclination for the scheme, disappoint all
Hunt's hopes'. Later, in Greece, he told another interested party that
his 'connection with these people [the Hunt brothers] originated from
humanity'; in a letter of 17 May 1823, again after the event, he
described the *Liberal* as 'a publication set up for the advantage of a per-
secuted author and a very worthy man'. Be that as it may, we do know
that this 'very worthy man' was then still fretting about the 'perse-
cuted' author's finances, and still trying to lend assistance at every
opportunity. When Moore sold the rights to Byron's letters and journals to Murray, Shelley wrote to his wife of his disappointment at not
having been 'in time to have interceded for a part of it for poor Hunt'.
He had raised Hunt's name with Byron, 'but not with a direct view of
demanding a contribution'.

Hunt could not know of that, nor judge anything of the prospects for
the journal, during almost six months marooned in Plymouth awaiting
favourable weather. It was all a source of some mirth to Hogg, who had
long since given up hope that Hunt would ever make it to Italy. 'I
would have written by Hunt,' he told Shelley, 'but I was unable to
muster up sufficient gravity to address a grey-haired, deaf, double,
tottering, spectacled old man, for such I was persuaded you would be
before he reached Pisa, if he is ever to reach it, and I was unwilling to
interrupt, by a recollection of "poor Hogg, who has been dead these
fifty years," the meeting of Old Shelley and Old Hunt, which might
possibly take place about the close of the nineteenth century.'

But the delay was no laughing matter to Shelley, who had written to
Hunt as long ago as January that 'the evils of your remaining in England
are inconceivably great if you ultimately determine upon Italy . . . the
best thing you can do is, without waiting for the spring, to set sail with
the very first ship you can'. There ensued reassurances about the rou-

tine nature of cargoes of gunpowder, and the prospect of a cook hired to await their arrival, along with warnings about Byron's vacillation over the journal: 'Many difficulties have presented themselves to the plan imagined by Lord B, which I depend on you for getting rid of.'

Having assigned and furnished for them a portion of his palace, 'Lord B' had further 'kindly insisted upon paying the upholsterer's bill, with that sort of unsuspecting goodness which makes it infinitely difficult to ask him for more'. Byron's patience appeared to be wearing thin. By March, Shelley quoted him expressing 'the greatest eagerness' about the journal, and 'forever dilating upon his impatience of your delay, and his disappointment at your not having already arrived'. Shelley worried a good deal about keeping Byron 'in heart with the project until your arrival . . . No feelings of my own shall injure or interfere with what is now nearest to them, your interest, and I will take care to preserve the little influence I may have over this Proteus in whom such strange extremes are reconciled until we meet – which we now must, at all events, soon do.'

Mary Shelley, meanwhile, dashed off similarly desperate letters to Marianne, regaling her with the delights of Italy, which 'each day becomes dearer and more delightful; the sun, the flowers, the air, all is more sweet and more balmy than in the Ultima Thule that you inhabit'.

But it was not until early May that the weather was finally declared fit for the voyage, and the Hunt family made ready for their third attempt to sail to Italy. On 6 May, a week before Hunt's scheduled departure, a delegation of Plymouth's 'lovers of free discussion on all subjects' presented him with a handsome silver goblet inscribed: 'To Leigh Hunt, Esq., In admiration of his long, continued & successful exertions in the cause of FREEDOM, TRUTH AND HUMANITY, his eminent talents and numerous virtues.' Then at last, on 13 May 1822, the Hunt family bade farewell to their new Plymouth brethren, apart from a local girl hired as their maid, and boarded the *David Walter* for Italy, with good weather finally in prospect.

Fascinated by all things maritime, Hunt left a vivid account of the seven-week voyage. Becalmed in the Bay of Biscay ('like repose in a boiling cauldron'), charmed by passing grampuses and sharks, he is to be found rapping himself stylistically over the knuckles while paying a compliment to Coleridge: 'The sea was swelling and foul with putrid substances, which made us think what it would be if a calm continued a month. Coleridge has touched upon that matter with the hand of a master, in his "Ancient Mariner". (Here are three words in one sentence beginning with *m* and ending with *r*, to the great regret of the fingers that cannot always stop to make corrections. But the compliment to Coleridge shall be the greater, since it is at my own expense.)'

For all his self-confessed haste, the voyage brought out some of Hunt's most vivid descriptive prose:

Then at night-time, there are those beautiful fires on the water. In a fine blue sea, the foam caused by the ship at night seems full of stars. The white fermentation, with golden sparkles in it, is beautiful beyond conception. You look over the side of the vessel, and devour with your eyes, as you would so much ethereal syllabub. Finally the stars in the firmament issue forth, and the moon; always the more lovely, the farther you get south. Or when there is no moon on the sea, the shadows at a little distance become grander and more solemn, and you watch for some huge fish to lift himself in the middle of them – a darker mass, breathing and spouting water.

The Atlantic put him in mind of his parents' America, 'and Columbus, and the chivalrous squadrons that set out from Lisbon, and the old Atlantis of Plato, formerly supposed to exist off the coast of Portugal . . .' One day the sea reminds him of the '*marmora pelagi*' of Catullus, another Africa speaks to him of Horace, who 'with a vigour beyond himself' called it the 'dry-nurse of lions'. As for the Mediterranean:

Countless generations of the human race, from three-quarters of the world, with all the religions, and the mythologies, and the genius, and the wonderful deeds, good and bad, that have occupied almost the whole attention of mankind, look you in the face from the galleries of that ocean-floor, rising one above another, till the tops are lost in heaven . . . There is Circe's island, and Calypso's, and the promontory of Plato, and Ulysses wandering, and Caymon and Miltiades fighting, and Regulus crossing the sea to Carthage . . .

He read *Don Quixote* while gazing at the Andalusian landscape, Ariosto and Berni ('for similar reasons, their heroes having to do with the coasts of France and Africa') and Bayle's 'admirable' *Essay on Comets* (in an attempt to dispense with all maritime superstitions). Onward Hunt enthused, quoting Marlowe on a majestic sunset over the Alps ('the first time I had seen mountains. They had a fine, sulky look . . .') until, at last, the Italy of his dreams hove into view; everything 'looked as Italian as possible'. Even the place names were alluring; up the Gulf of Genoa past Oneglia, Albenga, Savona (birthplace of the 'sprightly' poet Frugoni, 'whose works I was acquainted with') until finally the 'queen-like' city of Genoa appeared over the horizon, 'with white palaces, sat at the end of the Gulf, as if to receive us in state'.

As they entered the harbour Hunt heard his first words of Italian – a pilot saying, *'Va bene'. Va bene*, indeed, he thought: 'All goes well, truly.' He could not have been more wrong. As a violent thunderstorm escorted them north to Livorno, with perpendicular lightning treading the waves around their vessel 'like the legs of fiery spirits descending in wrath', Hunt still believed it impossible for the Mediterranean, 'that sunny and lucid basin', to play them 'any serious trick'. Within days, however, it was to prove the setting for 'a catastrophe . . . that should put an end to all sweet thoughts, both of the Mediterranean and of the south'.

'We have just arrived here,' Hunt announced to Shelley in a letter dated 15 June. In his autobiography Hunt gives 13 June as the date of his arrival in Genoa; but his journal of the voyage, published later, also notes: 'It was at 2 o'clock on the 15th of June that our vessel entered the harbour.'

'We felt as if the country Shelley was in embraced us for him,' he proclaimed, hiding his annoyance at a fortnight's stopover in Genoa, where he dashed off letters and spent the hot daytimes in churches for 'their quietness, their coolness and their richness'.

On 28 June they finally moved on towards Livorno, arriving after 'a long passage' on 1 July. Hunt had hoped that Shelley would be waiting for him when he finally disembarked his family for its long-anticipated Italian *vita nuova*, more than six months after first setting forth from

London. But Shelley's departure from Lerici had been delayed; Mary, apparently filled with foreboding, had begged him not to leave.

In an apologetic note to greet Hunt's arrival, Shelley urged him to visit Byron as soon as possible; thanks to Hunt's 'faculty of eliciting from any given person the greatest good they are capable of yielding . . . all will go well'. In a separate letter to Horace Smith in England, however, Shelley confessed to mounting doubts: 'Between ourselves, I greatly fear that this alliance will not succeed; for I, who could never have been regarded as more than the link of two thunderbolts, cannot now consent to be even that – and how long the alliance between the wren and the eagle may continue, I will not prophesy.'

In Shelley's place, Hunt was greeted in Livorno by Trelawny, Byron's swashbuckling, roguish 'jackal', standing aboard Byron's boat the *Bolivar* 'with his knight-errant aspect, dark, handsome, and moustachioed'. Byron had told Trelawny to expect 'a gentleman in dress and address', as first impressions indeed confirmed; Trelawny found Hunt 'that and something more; and with a quaint fancy and cultivated mind. He was in high spirits and disposed to be pleased with others. His anticipated literary projects in conjunction with Byron and Shelley were a source of great pleasure to him – so was the land of beauty and song . . . The pleasure that surpassed all the rest was the anticipation of seeing speedily his friend Shelley.'

But first, Byron – whom Hunt 'scarcely knew, he had grown so fat'. The great man was dressed in 'a loose nankin jacket and white trousers, his neck-cloth open, and his hair in thin ringlets about his throat', altogether presenting 'a very different aspect from the compact, energetic and curly-haired person whom I had known in England'.

Since those first few meetings in the Surrey jail and beyond – since the dedication of *The Story of Rimini* – Hunt and Byron had not stayed in regular touch. As Byron's reputation grew he retained a soft spot for the wayward bard of Hampstead, for all his increasing reservations about Hunt's work. The previous year, in March 1821, Byron had written to Murray about Hunt and the 'Cockneys' – in the wake of the *Blackwood's* attacks – in the warmest personal terms: 'The most rural of these gentlemen is my friend Leigh Hunt, who lives at Hampstead. I believe that I need not disclaim any personal or poetical hostility against that gentleman. A more amiable man in society I know not; nor (when he will allow his sense to prevail over his sectarian principles) a better writer. When he was writing his *Rimini*, I was not the last to discover its beauties, long before it was published.' But he had quibbles. 'Even then I remonstrated against its vulgarisms; which are the more extraordinary, because the author is anything but a vulgar man. Mr Hunt's answer was that he wrote them upon principle; they made part of his "system"! I then said no more. When a man talks of his system, it is like a woman's talk of her *virtue*. I let them talk on . . .'

Now that Hunt had finally arrived in Italy, the plan for the journal promised to build on the foundations of the private and professional rapport established before Byron left England. For his part, Byron remained all too aware of the growing unease among his friends, and abuse from his enemies, that the very notion of a partnership with Hunt was provoking back home. But he had not forgotten Hunt's public support during the scandal of his divorce. Writing to Sir Walter Scott from Pisa in January 1822, to thank him for some kind words about his *Childe Harold* in the *Quarterly Review*, Byron acknowledged that: 'You, and [Francis, Lord] Jeffrey, and Leigh Hunt were the only literary men, of numbers whom I know (and some of whom I had served), who dared venture even an anonymous word in my favour just then' – adding that Hunt had at the time been 'under no kind of obligation to me, whatever'.

Now Byron saw the Hunt brothers as a passport to publication of his work on his own terms. Murray had declined to publish his heretical satire *The Vision of Judgment*, which Byron now planned to hand to Hunt for the *Examiner*, if not for separate publication by John in its own right. Hunt, for his part, knew not what to expect beyond a joyous reunion with Shelley; but first he was obliged to pay his respects to the third party in their great enterprise. Hot and flustered after an arduous journey up to Villa Dupuy, the house at Monte Nero that Byron had rented for the summer, Hunt walked straight into a violent domestic fracas typical of the hot-blooded events which would soon force Byron to leave Tuscany.

As His Lordship introduced him to his resident mistress, Countess (Teresa) Guiccioli, Hunt found her in a state of great agitation. 'Her face was flushed, her eyes lit up, and her hair (which she wore hanging loose) streaming as if in disorder.' Upon the entrance of her brother,

Count Pietro, his arm in a sling, Hunt learnt that earlier that day the Count had been wounded while intervening in a quarrel among the servants; Pietro was 'very angry', Madame Guiccioli 'more so', not least because of the attitude of Byron, who was for 'making light of the matter'. Byron's Italian friends, by contrast, 'seemed to think the honour of their nation was at stake'.

By the time Byron set out for his evening drive, with Hunt in tow, the atmosphere was very tense, with the servant who had attacked Count Pietro waiting outside, 'glancing upwards like a tiger' and threatening to assault the first person to emerge. For Hunt, all this amounted to a 'curious' arrival in Italy: 'Everything was new, foreign and vehement.' Admiring Byron's sang-froid, while nervous at the Italians' ardour, he hid his own fear as the group set forth, 'all squeezing to have the honour of being first' – only to find the miscreant hurling himself on their mercy and bursting into tears. 'To crown all, he requested Lord Byron to kiss him' – an 'excess of charity' the noble Lord considered 'superfluous'. Byron pardoned the wretch – a figure, to Hunt, 'more squalid and miserable than an Englishman would conceive it possible to find in such an establishment' – and dismissed him.

Although this appeared to mollify the Countess and her brother, who were suddenly all smiles, the episode did not end there; having come to the attention of the Tuscan police, it contributed to the numbering of Byron's days in Tuscany. His continuing connections with the Gamba family, whose connections with the Carbonari made them a protoype of latter-day Mafiosi brigands, were already testing the authorities' patience with his outlandish lifestyle. He was now in Tuscany on sufferance, required by the Grand Duke's government to be 'discreet'; and this sort of incident was but the latest in a long line of indiscretions. Byron, for his part, was unwilling to bend his behaviour to any such grand-ducal diktat; soon after, having repaired to Pisa for a few months, he would remove himself to a different jurisdiction in Genoa.

So it was with some relief that Hunt retreated to the tranquillity of his inn at Livorno, where Shelley's arrival was eagerly anticipated. Nor did it disappoint. For Hunt, the emotion of the next day's reunion was too precious to share, even thirty years later: 'I will not dwell upon the moment.' But his son Thornton, then twelve, later recalled that Shelley 'rushed into my father's arms, which he did with an impetuousness and fervour scarcely to be imagined by anyone who did not know the intensity of his feelings and the deep nature of his affection for his friend'. Shelley was, he cried out, 'so *inexpressibly* delighted! – you cannot think how *inexpressibly* happy it makes me!' Sobered, perhaps, by hindsight, Hunt recalled merely that 'we talked of a thousand things, past, present and to come'. Shelley was 'the same as ever, with the exception of less hope'.

While awaiting Hunt's arrival, Shelley seems to have been content to act as Byron's acolyte, following his instructions to seek him out a grand Pisan palazzo, and sending wagons to Ravenna to collect His Lordship's worldly goods. While seeing himself as the inferior poet, Shelley often found himself disaffected by Byron's decadent lifestyle; over the years that both had spent in Italian exile, before Hunt's arrival, it was largely thanks to Shelley's indulgence of Byron's wayward ways that they had worked out a *modus vivendi*, involving frequent visits and much talk of literature and far-away England. If anything, Byron's company had exacerbated Shelley's anxiety for Hunt's. For more than four years now, Shelley had lived in hopes of this moment as high as Hunt's own.

The scheme for the *Liberal* 'could not have been contemplated', as Thornton Hunt later observed, unless Byron had 'risen in [Shelley]'s estimation'. At the time, as his father conversed excitedly with his friend, the young Thornton noted that 'a grand change had come over [Shelley's] appearance and condition. The southern climate had suited him . . . He had *grown* since he left England. For instance, in the interval since I had seen him his chest had manifestly become of a larger girth . . . His voice was stronger, his manner more confident and downright, and, although not less emphatic, yet decidedly less impulsively changeful.'

Ever sensible to the Hunts' impecunity, Shelley and his travelling companion, Edward Williams, escorted the family to Pisa, where he saw them installed in the ground-floor apartments of Byron's Villa Lanfranchi – 'assisting us', wrote Marianne, 'in any and every way, almost anticipating our wishes before we had formed them, with an instinct that nothing but an entire abandonment of self, and deep regard for others can give'.

Here the eminent physician André Berlinghieri Vacca was summoned to examine Hunt's wife, who was pronounced to be 'in
decline'; Marianne was unlikely, Vacca predicted, to live out the year.
(In fact she would outlive Vacca.) Byron was not sympathetic. 'Lord B's
reception of Mrs H was,' as Shelley put it to Williams, 'most shameful.
She came into his house sick and exhausted, and he scarcely deigned to
notice her; was silent, and scarcely bowed. This conduct cut H to the
soul . . .'

In his letter to Shelley of the previous September, finally agreeing to
come, Hunt had waxed optimistic about the prospects for co-operation
on the *Liberal*. 'Lord B . . . has it in his power, I believe, to set up not
only myself and family in our finances again, but one of the best-
hearted men in the world, my brother John and his.' Urging Shelley not
to be so modest, he had ended: 'What? Are there not three of us? And
ought we not to have as much strength and variety as possible? We will
divide the world between us, like the Triumvirate, and you shall be the
sleeping partner, if you will; only it shall be with a Cleopatra, and your
dreams shall be worth the giving of kingdoms.'

Now Shelley wrote to Mary of the Hunts: 'Lord Byron must of
course furnish the requisite funds at present, as I cannot; but he seems
inclined to depart without the necessary explanations and arrangements due to such a situation as Hunt's. These, in spite of delicacy, I
must procure . . .'

For five days discussion of the journal proceeded hand in hand with
that of the Hunt finances and furnishings. With a noble sigh, but mind-
ful of his own literary interests, Byron agreed to Shelley's request that
he take financial responsibility for the Hunts as recompense for the
energies Hunt would put into editing and contributing to the journal.
To both men's delight, Byron made over the copyright of *The Vision of
Judgment* for the first issue. 'This,' Shelley wrote to Mary, 'is more
than enough to set up the journal.' But the negotiations had taken their
toll. According to Trelawny, Shelley was in 'mournful' mood after his
meetings with Byron: 'Shelley found Byron so irritable, so shuffling and
equivocating, whilst talking with him on the fulfilment of his promises
with regard to Leigh Hunt – that, but for imperilling Hunt's prospects,
Shelley's intercourse with Byron would then have been abruptly ter-

minated.' Wrote Williams to his wife, to explain the delay in their return, 'I have been kept day after day, waiting for Shelley's definitive arrangements with Lord B. relative to poor Hunt, whom, in my opinion, he has treated vilely.'

On 8 July 1822, the day after Shelley's departure from Pisa, Byron wrote to Murray in London: 'I have consigned a letter to Mr John Hunt for the *Vision of Judgment*, which you will hand over to him . . . For Mr Leigh Hunt is arrived here, and thinks of commencing a periodical work, to which I shall contribute. I do not propose you to be the publisher, because you are unfriends . . .' Even to Moore, despite his continuing disapproval, Byron wrote that same week: 'Leigh Hunt is here, after a voyage of eight months, during which he has, I presume, made the Periplus of Hanno the Carthaginian, and with much the same speed. He is setting up a journal, to which I have promised to contribute; and in the first issue the "Vision of Judgment, by Quevedo Redivivus", will probably appear, with other articles. Can you give us anything? He seems sanguine about the matter, but (entre nous) I am not. I do not, however, like to put him out of spirits by saying so; for he is bilious and unwell. Do, pray, answer this letter immediately. Do send Hunt any thing in prose or verse of yours, to start him handsomely – anything lyrical, irical or what you please . . .'

So all, at last, appeared to bode well. His friends duly installed in the Villa Lanfranchi, and their great literary plans laid, Shelley was anxious to return to Lerici and his family. He and Hunt spent the afternoon of Sunday 7 July sightseeing in Pisa, wandering between the Leaning Tower, the art gallery and the cathedral in a state of 'Utopian delight' and vowing that they would not be parted for long. Hunt lent Shelley his copy of Keats's most recent volume of poetry, unobtainable in Italy, urging him to keep it until he could return it 'with his own hands'.

But there seemed something ominous in Shelley's parting words to Marianne: 'If I die tomorrow, I have lived to be older than my father; I am ninety years of age.' Waving Shelley and Williams off in the postchaise to Livorno, where Shelley's schooner awaited them, Hunt extracted a final promise that they would not sail if the weather turned ugly. He had seen the Mediterranean in its worst moods, and he knew the extreme fragility of Shelley's small craft. Shelley was not to 'give way to his daring spirit and venture to sea' unless conditions were favourable. 'He promised me he would not' – and the post-chaise departed.

Hunt 'never beheld him more'. It was ten days before Shelley's body was washed ashore near Viareggio, Hunt's volume of Keats still in his pocket, folded open at 'Lamia'. The precise sequence of events remains mysterious, and presumably always will. What is known is that Trelawny had planned to escort the *Don Juan* (which he had himself designed) back to Lerici aboard the *Bolivar*; but, at the last minute, he was prevented from leaving port as his clearance papers were not in order. Williams was as anxious to return to his wife as was Shelley; one of them – accounts vary – persuaded the other to set sail at once, without Trelawny, despite (or even because of) an unsettling change in the weather. With their boat boy, Charles Vivian, they sailed out of Lerici harbour around 2 p.m. on 8 July.

Trelawny watched them head out to sea through his spyglass. Another friend, Captain Roberts, took a telescope to the top of the lighthouse and anxiously watched the *Don Juan* disappear into a mist. Within a few hours it was overtaken by a violent storm. As all other craft headed for harbour, the *Don Juan* stayed stubbornly out at sea, in full sail. A local captain diverted to offer to take them on board, but a shrill voice, supposedly Shelley's, yelled 'No!' The captain urged them at least to reef their sails – 'or you are lost' – and watched in disbelief as Shelley seized Williams by the arm 'as if in anger' to stop him lowering them. The *Don Juan* soon sank into the Gulf of Spezia, some ten miles north-west of Viareggio, under full sail.

Back at the Byron villa, there was great anxiety about the violent storm which was seen to arise that evening; but Hunt could only hope that his friend had already successfully negotiated the fifty-mile, seven-hour voyage home. Not for a few days, until Trelawny arrived to tell Hunt and Byron that Shelley had gone missing, did they fear the worst.

Hunt then underwent 'one of the sensations we read of in books, but seldom experience: I was tongue-tied'. After a 'dreadful interval' of a week or more – during which Hunt wrote Shelley a letter 'terrible in its uninformed cheerfulness', reporting that plans for the *Liberal* 'go on remarkably well' – the news arrived that all three bodies had been washed ashore at various points between Massa and Viareggio. Shelley's corpse, whose exposed flesh had been eaten away, could be identified only by its clothing – and the copy of Keats found in his pocket. After a temporary burial in the sand, in compliance with the quarantine laws, Trelawny took the initiative in organising the funeral pyre which has passed into literary folklore. On 15 August Shelley's remains were burnt on the beach at Livorno, in the presence of Hunt, Byron and a few local fishermen. At Hunt's insistence, his copy of Keats – said to be the only one in Italy at the time – was cremated along with his and Keats's friend.

Hunt and Byron had reached the scene by carriage. 'Is that a human body?' asked Byron. 'Why, it's more like the carcass of a sheep, or any other animal, than a man: this is a satire on our pride and folly.' 'The lonely and grand scenery that surrounded us so exactly harmonized with Shelley's genius that I could imagine his spirit soaring over us,' recalled Trelawny, who consigned the poet's decomposing body to the flames. 'The heat from the sun and fire was so intense that the atmosphere was tremulous and wavy. The corpse fell open and the heart was laid bare. The frontal bone of the skull . . . fell off; and, as the back of the head rested on the red-hot bottom bars of the furnace, the brains literally seethed, bubbled and boiled as in a cauldron, for a very long time.'

Unable to watch, Byron walked away and began swimming out to the *Bolivar*. After throwing his own copy of Keats into the flames, Hunt chose to remain in the carriage, 'now looking on, now drawing back . . . with feelings that were not to be witnessed'. His own lyrical description has helped render the scene immortal :

The beauty of the flame arising from the funeral pile was extraordinary. The weather was beautifully fine. The Mediterranean, now soft and lucid, kissed the shore as if to make peace with it. The yellow sand and blue sky were intensely contrasted with one another: marble mountains touched the air with coolness; and the flame of the fire bore away towards heaven in vigorous amplitude, waving and quivering with a brightness of inconceivable beauty. It seemed as though it contained the glassy essence of vitality. You might have expected a seraphic countenance to look out of it, turning once more before it departed, to thank the friends that had done their duty.

That night Hunt and Byron got drunk together. On their way home through the forests of Pisa they 'sang' and 'laughed' and 'shouted' like men possessed, with 'a gaiety the more shocking, because it was real and a relief'. Making the scene the more gruesome, not least because it is a detail he fails to record, is the fact that Hunt was clutching Shelley's heart.

At the height of the makeshift cremation Trelawny noticed that while Shelley's flesh melted away, his heart remained strikingly intact in the centre of the flames, apparently refusing to yield to the forces of mere nature. With a typically theatrical flourish, he reached into the fire, badly burning his hand, and retrieved the poet's heart – presenting it, at his request, to Hunt.

There ensued an unbecoming disagreement with Mary, who not unnaturally claimed it for herself, enlisting Byron's support in her cause. For a while Hunt resisted, writing to Mary that it was not his 'self-love' that was at stake, but 'my love for my friend; and for this to make way for the claims of any other love, man's or woman's, I must have great reasons indeed brought me'. Knowing from Shelley himself that the couple had recently become estranged, Hunt repeated his need for 'great, unequivocal and undeniable' reasons why Shelley's widow had more claim to her late husband's heart than his best friend. 'In his case above all other human beings, no ordinary appearance of rights, even yours, can affect me.' Byron knew nothing of the matter until the heart was in Hunt's possession. 'He has no right to bestow the heart, and I am sure pretends to none. If he told you that you should have it, it could only have been from his thinking that I could more easily part with it than I can.'

Having unburdened himself of these remarkable sentiments, which may well be considered uncharitable, sentimental and ghoulish, Hunt eventually saw sense and handed the heart over to Mary Shelley, keeping for himself merely a portion of the poet's jawbone, which he had also filched from the ashes – and which remained on his desk for the rest of his life. This *memento mori* remained in the Hunt family until 1913, when his eldest grandson, Walter Leigh Hunt, gave it to the Keats–Shelley Memorial in Rome.

As for Hunt himself, his own heart 'died within me'. From that moment forth, Italy was 'a black place to me'. Shelley's memory would never dim. Nor could anyone, least of all Byron, take his place. 'What can fill up the place that such a man as S[helley] occupied in my heart?'

8

'The wren and the eagle'

1822–3

'Leontius!' As Hunt grieved for Shelley, Byron would mortify him each morning by hailing him with the nickname his dead friend had coined for him, a playful Roman version of 'Leigh Hunt'.

In the wake of Shelley's death, as plans to produce the *Liberal* proceeded in a numbed state of shock, Byron's daily routine could not have been more different from Hunt's. Having sat up late writing *Don Juan* ('which he did', according to Hunt, 'under the influence of gin and water'), His Lordship would rise late, breakfast, read, take his bath, dress and eventually emerge – often singing an air from Rossini (Hunt's least favourite composer, as he well knew) – into the courtyard of the Villa Lanfranchi, where his servants would place a group of chairs right outside Hunt's ground-floor study window.

'Leontius!' After rising early Hunt would by now have been writing for several hours. As irritated to be diverted from his labours as by Byron's hijack of Shelley's pet name for him, Hunt would feel obliged to set aside his pen and join Byron and his countess for conversation and light refreshment. Marianne's continuing ill-health prevented her joining in these proceedings, during which Hunt developed a love–hate relationship with Byron's mistress; while irritated by her languor and overly 'artful' appearance, he took an innocent delight in her Italianness. He had been told that she spoke a coarse Roman dialect, but 'to me, at that time, all Italian in a lady's mouth was Tuscan pearl; and she trolled it over her lip, pure or not, with that sort of conscious grace which seems to belong to the Italian language as a matter of right'.

In the cool of the evening Hunt would join Byron on his rides and drives into the country. 'Lord Byron requested me to look upon him as standing in Mr Shelley's place, and said that I should find him the same friend that the other had been.' But the loss of its moving spirit doomed what was left of the triumvirate. 'I made the proper acknowledgement; but I knew what he meant, and I more than doubted whether, even in that, the most trivial part of a friendship, he could resemble Mr Shelley.' By this, of course, Hunt meant his line of credit, leading Byron partisans to paint a mean-spirited portrait of their hero's new literary partner.

'Both men had suffered seriously from the shock of Shelley's death,' writes one such, 'and the effect on Hunt was to exaggerate some of his most unpleasing traits – to make him more than ever egotistical and vain and pettish. In his attitude to Byron there was neither measure nor dignity; and now he was so effusive and familiar as to overshoot the mark, now so distant and ceremonious as to appear absurd and stilted.'

In vain did Byron address him facetiously as 'Dear Lord Hunt', apparently hoping to limit the 'excessive frequency' of his 'Dear Lord Byron's'. Hunt 'posed and prated, was tart or sulky, but found it utterly impossible to achieve composure'. To Byron, Shelley had been 'the best and least selfish man I ever knew. I never knew one that was not a beast in comparison.' This seems in some degree to have been aimed at Hunt.

To be fair to Hunt, Byron seems to have enjoyed teasing him as an almost daily sport to offset his own idleness and boredom. The south may have begun to weigh heavily on the now reluctant exile, but the ways of his partner and patron were even more of a burden. Himself in poor health, frantic with worry about Marianne's, working as hard as ever each day, Hunt came to resent Byron's complacent ease, especially in matters where he considered himself his host's superior. 'Was it for this,' as one ironist asks, 'that he had affronted authority and suffered imprisonment?'

There was 'not a single subject', according to Trelawny, 'on which

Byron and Hunt could agree'. When Byron, for instance, one day mentioned that he had heard Hunt 'dabbling on the pianoforte' and proceeded to venture that musical gifts suggested effeminacy, Hunt snapped. 'He, the objector to effeminacy, was sitting in health and wealth, with rings on his fingers, and baby-work to his shirt; and he had just issued, like a sultan, out of his bath.' Hunt replied that, although a love of music might certainly be 'overdone', it would be 'difficult to persuade the world that Alfred and Epaminondas, and Martin Luther, and Frederick the Second, all eminent lovers of music, were effeminate men'. Byron did not deign to answer; less knowledgeable than Hunt in these matters, he 'retired from the unequal contest baffled and irritated'.

Amid these decidedly strained relations, plans for the *Liberal* continued sans Shelley. In August, less than three weeks after informing Moore of Shelley's death, Byron is again to be found attempting to overcome his old friend's opposition to his association with Hunt: 'Leigh Hunt is sweating articles for his new journal; and both he and I think it shabby in *you* not to contribute. Will you become one of the *properrioters*? . . . I recommend you to think twice before you reply in the negative.' Note that the *Liberal* was now, at least between Byron and Moore, 'his' (Hunt's) journal. To Moore and other London friends and associates, Byron was now dissociating himself personally from Hunt while continuing to cooperate with him professionally. 'I see somebody represents the Hunts and Mrs Shelley as living in my house,' he wrote to Murray the following month. 'It is a falsehood. They reside at some distance, and I do not see them twice in a month. I have not met Mr Hunt a dozen times since I came to Genoa, or near it.'

He hadn't been there that long. Byron's letter to Moore had been written from Pisa on 27 August; to Murray he wrote from Genoa less than a month later. In between, as Byron's dependants, Hunt and his family had been forced to leave the Pisa he loved (for all its poignant memories of Shelley) for Genoa – where the restless Byron could 'hover on the borders of his inclination for Greece'. Byron's party had travelled by 'caravan' on land, while Hunt chose to go by sea with his 'kraal'. En route they all met up at Lerici, where Hunt paced the empty rooms of Shelley's Villa Magni in disconsolate mood. 'The sea fawned upon the shore, as if it could do no harm,' he wrote to his sister-in-law Bessy. 'I have a few myrtle leaves for you, which I took from the garden of Shelley's house [where] I saw those melancholy rooms, to which he was returning, and did not return . . . I saw the waves foaming and roaring at the foot, and with an impatience which has seldom gone so far with me, could almost have blasphemously trampled at them and cried out.'

In the hill town of Albaro, above Genoa, the indulgent Mary Shelley had found Byron a handsome house befitting his station, the Casa Saluzzi, while taking the Hunts into her own, the forty-room, £20-a-year Casa Negrotto. It says much for Mary Shelley that she housed the Hunts. She had good reason to resent Leigh, if not Marianne; and she had endured a wretched year, of which she mused: 'What can I say of my present life?'

Shelley's death had come at the worst possible time for Mary, on whom he had blamed an unwonted spell of writer's block. After suffering a miscarriage she suddenly seemed to her husband to be exhibiting troubling signs of bourgeois conformity: 'Mary is under the dominion of the mythical monster "Everybody".'

By the time Shelley left her for his reunion with Hunt, the couple were estranged. Mary could not know how much Shelley had told Hunt of their difficulties; that he was privy to some of her husband's complaints she could judge by his cool conduct towards her, not least in the matter of the heart. Now, given her friendship with Marianne, she could only live in hope of a rapprochement with a man who had been devoted indeed to her husband and never known to harbour a grudge for long.

'The weather,' Mary's letter home continued, 'is bitterly cold with a sharp wind, very unlike dear, *carissima* Pisa; but soft airs and balmy gales are not the attributes of Genoa, which place I daily and duly join Marianne in detesting.' There was only one fireplace in the house, and the stove in Mary's room smoked too much to be lit in comfort. So she found herself obliged to spend most of her time in Hunt's sitting-room – 'which is, as you may guess, the annihilation of study, and even of pleasure to a great degree. For, after all, Hunt does not like me: it is both our faults, and I do not blame him, but so it is . . .'

For now Hunt remained cool towards Mary in the belief that she had made his friend's last months less than idyllic. In evidence, beyond

Shelley's own account, he now had a long letter from Jane Williams, widow of Shelley's friend who drowned with him; she had seen Bessy Kent on her return to London, whence she wrote about their mutual problem with Mary: 'You, I imagine, as well as myself, had seen that the intercourse between Shelley and Mary was not as happy as it should have been; and I remember your telling me that our Shelley mentioned several circumstances on that subject that distressed you during the short time that you were together, and that you witnessed the pain he suffered in receiving a letter from Mary at that period . . .

'I differ from you *entirely* as to the necessity of my telling Mary her faults: for I feel convinced I should only make her unhappy while I should fail in producing the desired effect. That task I leave to you, my dear friend, who are so well able to correct human follies and to drop a tear of pity on human weaknesses.'

So Hunt believed he had cause to speak his mind. But it was also at this time that Byron confided in Mary his impatience with the Hunt children: 'I have a particular dislike of anything of Shelley's being within the same walls with Mrs Hunt's children. They are dirtier and more mischievous than Yahoos. What they can't destroy with their filth they will with their fingers . . . Poor Hunt with his six little blackguards . . . Was there ever such a kraal out of the Hottentot country?' But Mary knew that Marianne was pregnant again, and a due degree of female fellow-feeling seems to have cancelled out the testosterone factor.

Relations between Hunt and Byron meanwhile cooled yet further: 'I saw less of him than before; and, under all the circumstances, it was well: for though we had always been on what are called "good terms", the cordiality did not increase.' Hunt's days at Albaro were 'melancholy', spent 'walking about the stone alleys and thinking of Mr Shelley'. And the more he missed Shelley, the more he resented Byron.

All too swiftly, it is clear, Byron in turn began to resent subsidising Hunt in the cause of a journal in which, after Shelley's death, he was fast losing interest: 'I am afraid the journal is a bad business, and won't do; but in it I am sacrificing myself for others,' he wrote to Murray from Genoa that October. 'I believe the Hunt brothers to be honest men; I am sure that they are poor ones; they have not a nap. They pressed me to engage in this work, and in an evil hour I consented. Still

I shall not repent, if I can do them the last service. I have done all I can for Leigh Hunt since he came here; but it is almost useless: his wife is ill, his six children not very tractable, and in the affairs of the world he himself is a child. The death of Shelley left them totally aground; and I could not see them in such a state without using the common feelings of humanity, and what means were in my power, to see them afloat again.'

For his part, Hunt reported that Byron had 'no real heart in the business, nor for anything else but a feverish notoriety'. Whatever he may have said or written to friends, Byron clearly begrudged what modest (by his standards) financial support he gave Hunt – an accomplished editor, after all, summoned from England to launch a magazine very much in His Lordship's interests – on top of his free accommodation. What little money he did part with was patronisingly and begrudgingly 'doled out' to Hunt by Byron's steward. Byron was 'seldom just and never generous', even Trelawny concedes. 'He was one of those that don't know how to give – except for ostentation.'

'Bitter indeed, for the first time in my life, was the taste I then had of obligation,' mused Hunt. He and Marianne now attempted to cut back their domestic budget, living in 'the most economical Italian manner', but he was still capable of alienating Byron with the clumsily jocular way in which he applied for funds. 'I must trouble you for another "cool hundred" of your crowns,' reads one such note from this period, which clearly did not amuse His Lordship. 'Sympathy,' as Hunt later noted of Byron, 'would probably have drawn upon you a discussion of matters too petty for your respect; and gaiety would have been treated to an assumption, necessary to be put down by sarcasms.'

To make matters worse, Hunt's wife was getting on even less well with Byron. 'What a pity it is,' Marianne wrote in her diary, 'the good actions of noblemen are not done in a noble manner! Aye, princely I would have them be.' When Byron remarked in jest that Trelawny had been impugning his morals, taunting her by asking 'What do you think of that?', Marianne replied: 'It is the first time I ever heard of them.' Byron, Hunt noted with satisfaction, was 'completely dashed, and reduced to silence'.

On another occasion, when Byron was contentedly speaking ill of various mutual acquaintances, Hunt asked him if he had heard what

Marianne told the Shelleys about the new, romantic portrait of him by G.H. Harlow: it put her in mind of 'a great schoolboy, who had a plain bun given him instead of a plum one'. This time, by Hunt's account, Byron failed to smile and 'looked as blank as possible'. But then Byron, as Marianne noted, had little experience of dealing with 'a woman of spirit'.

From one observer we have a somewhat different picture of Marianne Hunt at this time; to the Marchesa Iris Origo, friend of Byron's Countess Guiccioli, Marianne was 'one of the most uncompromisingly British matrons who ever set foot upon the Continent . . . as intransigent in her middle-class independence as in her moral outlook'. And from La Guiccioli herself we have an understandably partial view of Byron's dealings with Hunt: 'If Lord Byron appeared to be in good spirits, Hunt called him heartless; if he took a bath, a sybarite. If he tried to joke with him, he was guilty of the insufferable liberties that a great nobleman will allow himself with a poor man. If he presented Hunt with numerous copyrights, with the sole intention of helping him, it could only be because he lacked an editor. If he was charitable, it was out of ostentation.'

Wherever may lie the balance of truth, there can be no doubt that Hunt was deeply hurt by his host's conspicuous impatience with his loved ones. 'Can anything be more absurd than a peer of the realm — and a *poet* making such a fuss about three or four children disfiguring the walls of a few rooms?' complained Marianne to her diary. 'The very children would blush for him, fye Lord B. — fye!' To Byron, Hunt's children were 'little Cockneys'. To their father, they 'had lived in a natural, not an artificial state, and were equally sprightly, respectful, and possessed'. But Byron infuriated Hunt by stationing a fierce bulldog named Moretto on the palazzo's main staircase, to keep the 'Yahoos' and 'Hottentots' well away from his first-floor quarters. This same dog now savaged the Hunts' beloved goat, doughty survivor of that epic sea journey, biting off its ear before the long-suffering animal could be rescued.

Despite the sorry state of his relations with Byron, Hunt nevertheless pressed on with the original reason for his trip to Italy: the journal. Shelley's death had robbed his work of its pleasure, if not its purpose;

but the project originally to have been called the *Hesperides* was now renamed the *Liberal*, the first recorded example of that word's use as a noun. With the journal given the subtitle 'Verse and Prose from the South', work on its contents proceeded under Hunt's somewhat ill-tempered stewardship.

Here in Genoa, in September 1822, he received from his brother in England copies of the first issue. Dominating its pages, after Hunt's preface, was Byron's *The Vision of Judgment*, to even the jaundiced Hunt 'the best satire since the days of Pope', but rejected by Byron's London publishers on account of its 'fault-finding in Church and State'. Hazlitt contributed 'some of the most entertaining of his vigorous essays', while Shelley had bequeathed his 'masterly' translation of the *May Day Night* in Goethe's *Faust*.

But it was *The Vision of Judgment*, taking its title from Robert Southey's 1821 panegyric to George III, which caught the attention of the critical cynics back in London waiting for any opportunity to pounce on Byron or Hunt, or both.

> Saint Peter sat by the celestial gate,
> His keys were rusty and the lock was dull.

Its opening lines could not have offered more ammunition to the tormentors of the 'Cockney' school and its 'so much puffed and so long promised work'. Byron's attack on the Poet Laureate, 'apostate Jacobin' Southey, combined with his patronising portrait of the late king, moved Hunt to a definitive restatement of his creed about politics and literature: 'The object of our work is not political, except inasmuch as all writing nowadays must involve something to that effect, the connection between politics and all other subjects of interest to mankind having been discovered, never again to be done away.'

Back in London, those who knew the journal's provenance professed to have expected 'blasphemy and impurity of every kind to a certain extent, but we doubt that they can anticipate all the atrocity of the *Liberal*'. As for Byron's own contribution: 'Once the admirer of Milton, Dryden, Pope, he has become the associate of the Cockney Blue-stockings . . . he has sunk from the highest station of an English nobleman, and the highest place in English literature, to be the

colleague of Mr Leigh Hunt, the author of *Don Juan*, and a contributor
to the *Liberal*.'

To the *Literary Gazette,* Byron had contributed 'impiety, vulgarity,
inhumanity . . . Mr Shelley a burlesque upon Goethe; and Mr Leigh
Hunt conceit, trumpery, ignorance and wretched verses. The union of
wickedness, folly and imbecility is perfect.' By now many connois-
seurs of the literary scene had grown weary of the relentless attacks
from Lockhart and Gifford; the scandalous dimension to Byron's wilfully outrageous, anti-monarchical poem helped, if anything, to
increase sales. The first issue of the *Liberal* surprised all concerned by
making a profit of £377 16s, of which £291 15s went to Hunt.

Hunt himself had written more than half of it, as of all subsequent
issues of the *Liberal*, from essays and fables to a tourist guide to Pisa and
several translations from the Italian. The second issue, half again as long
as the first, was also opened by Byron, his 'Heaven and Earth' continuing to ruffle feathers back in London, as was Hunt's testy reply to his
detractors in a long satire in Byronic *ottava rima* entitled 'The Dogs',
inspired by the testimony of a soldier assigned to break biscuits for the
Duke of Wellington's hounds while himself starving ('I was very
hungry, and thought it a good job at the time, as we got our own fill
while we broke the biscuit – a thing I had not got for some days . . .').
Shelley's 'Song Written for an Indian Air' stood alongside his widow
Mary's 'A Tale of the Passions', with other contributions from Hazlitt
('On the Scotch Character'), Hogg and Charles Brown.

The third issue showed Byron's standards beginning to slip, with his
humdrum poem 'The Blues', but was distinguished by Hazlitt's immor-
tal essay 'My First Acquaintance with Poets'. Hunt contributed his
'Book of Beginnings' and another attack on Gifford in the shape of a
poem entitled 'To a Spider Running across a Room', while Horace
Smith excelled himself in a travel piece, 'A Sunday's Fête at St Cloud'.
In the fourth – and, as it transpired, final – issue, which appeared in
July 1823, Byron contributed merely a translation of 'Morgante,
Maggiore', while Hunt produced his elegant pastoral poem 'The
Choice' and his first verse venture into orientalism, 'Mahmoud'.
Hazlitt came up with two more powerful essays. Hunt's series of
'Letters from Abroad', a vivid travelogue containing some of his best
descriptive writing, ran through all four issues.

By the fourth issue of the *Liberal* Hunt was feeling betrayed. Byron had withdrawn his poems 'The Age of Bronze' and 'The Island' from the third, asking John Hunt to print them as separate works; reluctantly, John had little choice but to accede. While they sold well enough, the third and fourth issues of the *Liberal* flagged, to the point where Byron withdrew altogether, effectively closing down the journal. Although there was a sense of some disorder about the four issues, reflecting the chaotic conditions in which they were produced, and the fact that the mind of its presiding genius was largely elsewhere, the *Liberal* has deservedly earned a substantial niche in literary history, not least for the handful of lasting works which first saw the light of day there.

But one of the problems, as Hunt saw it, was Byron's insistence that articles appear pseudonymously – though discerning readers back in London were not slow to work out who wrote what. As for less well informed or discerning subscribers: 'The perplexity irritates them. They are forced to wait the judgments of others; and they willingly comfort the wound given to their self-love by abiding with such as are unfavourable, and pronouncing the articles to be of an undistinguishable mediocrity.'

Byron's interest in the project had quickly waned. For all the fact that he had been its prime mover, the loss of Shelley combined with his growing aversion to Hunt and his family, along with the negative press he was receiving back in London, to cause him to kill it off after only four months. 'The failure of the large profits . . . he had looked for,' as Hunt saw it, 'of the solid and splendid proofs of this new country which he should conquer in the regions of notoriety, to the dazzling of all men's eyes and his own – this it was, this was the bitter disappointment which made him determine to give way . . . From the moment he saw the modest profits of the *Liberal*, he resolved to have nothing farther to do with it in the way of real assistance. He made use of it only for the publication of some things which his Tory bookseller was afraid to put forth.'

By communicating his disenchantment to his friends back in England, not least to staunch their dismay with him, Byron meanwhile wilfully risked his views becoming public enough to hurt Hunt. '[Lord Byron] is sick and weary to death of the Hunts,' wrote Theodore Hook

in *John Bull* that October. 'He repents that he ever went into partnership with them in the money-making speculation of the magazine.' In
the back room of his publishing house, frequented by his literary
coterie, the disgruntled Murray had been sharing Byron's letters with
select friends likely to make them public. Byron, continued Hook,
'writes word that "Hunt is a bore; he is . . . a proser; Mrs Hunt is no
great things; and the six children perfectly untractable"'.

Hook could not resist adding: 'We should think the children must
have done the greatest part of the first number of the *Liberal*.' Later,
writing an anonymous 'Cockney's Letter' in *John Bull*, Hook imagined
himself alone in Byron's study, leafing through His Lordship's copy of
Hunt's *Rimini*; 'thinking to find it full of notes', he found instead that
it was 'not even half cut open', and on the last cut leaf appeared a
verse: 'O! Crimini, Crimini! / What a nimini pimini / Story of
Rimini.'

Murray's indiscretions were causing mayhem back in London, earning him a stern rebuke from Byron. As well as noising abroad his asides
about Hunt, Murray had passed on to John Hunt only the text of *The
Vision of Judgment*, minus its preface, as a result of which John now faced
prosecution as the poem's publisher; the preface, as an embittered
Murray well knew, would have afforded the work the context which
might have rendered its contents less actionable. 'If you have (as seems
apparently to be the case) purposely kept back the preface to the
Vision,' Byron wrote to Murray, 'I can only say that I know no words
strong enough to express my sense of such conduct.'

By now Byron's sneers had got back from London to Hunt in Italy,
as we know from another angry letter from Byron to Murray that same
month: 'My original motives I already explained (in the letter which
you thought it proper to show): they are the true ones, and I abide by
them, as I tell you, and I told Lh. Ht. when he questioned me on the
subject of that letter. He was violently hurt, and never will forgive me
at bottom; but I can't help that. I never meant to make a parade of it;
but if he chose to question me, I could only answer the plain truth: and
I confess I did not see anything in that letter to hurt him, unless I said
he was "a bore", which I don't remember.'

In a letter to Mary Shelley, Byron went on: 'Murray . . . seems to
stick at nothing in all that relates to Hunt and his family. As to any

expression in private letters about Hunt or others, I am not a cautious letter-writer and generally say what seems apparent at the moment . . . The whole thing has been a piece of officious malice on the part of [M] & not very discreet zeal on the part of Hunt's friends.' Hunt himself attempted to draw a line under the episode, however ill-humouredly, in a note to Byron that November: 'My "wife and six small" come rather hard upon me in the business – but a little reflection takes the heat out of my cheeks; and as to your "proser", God knows I should never think it worth a savager answer than to lay hold of one of my puns, and say you're a "worser".'

As Mary Shelley attempted to play peacemaker, Hunt made light of Byron's slights in a letter to his nephew Henry: 'He is but too likely to get into scrapes with saying one thing about persons at one time, & another at another; but I dare say this will be a lesson to him, how a mind like his condescends to such idling. Mrs Shelley tells me he says nothing of me to her but the handsomest things, & I can only say that from first to last it is he that has courted my society, not I his. But he is full & running over with the most extraordinary inconsistencies . . .'

Trying to run a business amid all this, John Hunt wrote to his brother on 25 February 1823: 'The sale has certainly not answered my expectations. Of the 1st. no. 7000 were printed, after I had obtained the best information I could of the probable sale of Lord B's perform-ances. Of that no. 4050 have been sold. Of the 2nd. 6000 were printed, but of that only 2700 have come off.' The first issue of the Liberal had made a profit of some £377, the second a loss of £41. Addressing Byron's opinion that the magazine should be abandoned, John advised Leigh: 'I would suggest to you the employment of your pen in a publication which might be made a companion to the Examiner, under the title the Literary Examiner. You might resume the Indicator in it.'

The Liberal had done well enough, but Byron had expected it to do better. Beyond his public bracketing with the 'Cockneys', his friends in London remained horrified at the alliance he had made with Hunt. We have Hazlitt's word for it that even allies as loyal as Moore and John Cam Hobhouse were 'thrown into almost hysterical agonies of well-bred horror at the coalition between their noble and ignoble acquaintance – between the patrician and the "newspaper-man"'. The

Tories were shocked that Byron should 'grace the popular side by his direct countenance and assistance', the Whigs that he should 'share his confidence and counsels with anyone who did not unite the double recommendations of birth and genius'. For all the caricature painted by Hazlitt, his friends' unease really troubled Byron. He seems to be blaming Hunt when, in the spring of 1823, he observes of himself that he had sunk 'as low in popularity and bookselling as any writer can be'.

In letters home he began busily – and brutally – dissociating himself from Hunt. 'Of Hunt I see little – once a month or so, and then on his own business, generally,' he wrote to Moore from Genoa in February 1823. 'You may easily suppose that I know too little of Hampstead and his satellites to have much communion with him. My whole present relation to him arose from Shelley's unexpected wreck. You would not have had me leave him in the street with his family, would you?

'Think a moment – he is perhaps the vainest man on earth, at least his own friends say so pretty loudly; and if he were in other circumstances I might be tempted to take him down a peg; but not now, – it would be cruel. It is a cursed business; but neither the motive nor the means rest upon my conscience, and it happens that he and his brother have so far benefited by the publication in a pecuniary point of view. His brother is a steady, bold fellow, such as Prynne, for example, and full of moral and, I hear, physical courage.'

After Byron's death Moore blamed this decline in his public esteem squarely on his 'unworthy' association with Hunt on the *Liberal*. Byron first got involved, by Moore's revisionist account, because of 'a wish to second the kind views of his friend Shelley in inviting Mr Hunt to join him in Italy; and . . . a desire to avail himself of the aid of one so experienced, as an editor, in the favourite project he had now so long contemplated, of a periodical work, in which all the various offspring of his genius might be received [as] fast as they sprung to light . . .'

It may have been characteristically generous of Byron to admit Hunt to his circle, argued Moore, but his opinions of Hunt's 'character and talents' fortunately restricted their association to 'a declared fellowship of fame and interest in the eyes of the world' rather than 'any degree of confidence or intimacy'. Even while Shelley lived, there had occurred 'some of those humiliating misunderstandings which money engenders – humiliating on both sides, as if from the very nature of the dross that gives rise to them'. But Shelley's death had proved the turning point; no longer could Byron take comfort in the 'suavity and good breeding of Shelley interposing a sort of softening medium in the way of those unpleasant collisions which afterwards took place' – equally trying to 'the patience of the patron and the vanity of the dependent'.

For Byron's enemies, the merest association with Hunt of 'Cockney School' fame was 'the signal for the bloodhounds to shake themselves clear and pursue, with the utmost speed, their victim'. Soon *Blackwood's* itself was seizing the chance to link Byron with the much-ridiculed 'Cockneys': 'You have perhaps heard of a journal which is to be written by him at Pisa, and sent over here for publication, in order that the balance of critical power may be restored, which has preponderated lately too much on the Tory side. In this great undertaking he has called to himself two allies, namely, Mr Bysshe Shelly [*sic*] and Mr Leigh Hunt, the latter of whom has abandoned his suburban villa (No. 13 Lisson Grove North), to brave with his wife and "Little Johnnys", a perilous ocean voyage on the now un-Cockney ocean. No one must twist him any more about "poplar rows" and "back gardens".'

In the anonymous shape, again, of John Gibson Lockhart, *Blackwood's* was highly amused by the thought of the aesthete Hunt in Italy: 'The pictures and statues will drive him clean out of his wits. He'll fall in love with some of them.' Lockhart also had fun with the thought of Hunt's influence over Byron: 'Now Leigh Hunt is about to join him, I'll lay a guinea to an apple-paring that his Lordship sets up an *Examiner*, or writes a Cockney poem, commencing,

> Lack-a-day! but I've grown wiser,
> Since Mister Hunt has come to Pisar.

The Pisan triumvirate was bound to disintegrate, Lockhart had predicted. 'Shelley will henceforth rave only to the moon; Hunt will sonneteer himself, and "urge tear on tear", in memory of Hampstead butter and Chelsea buns; and Byron, sick of his companions, and ashamed of his career, will at length ask his daemon, how it is that he has cast himself out of all the advantages that life lavished on him . . . Is an English nobleman to have no correspondent but his bookseller? No friends but a vulgar group, already shaken out of English society?

No objects but the paltry praises of temporizing reviews? And no studies but the shame and scorn of honourable literature?'

Even Wordsworth had privately expressed magisterial disapproval in a letter to Walter Savage Landor: 'Byron, Shelley, Moore, Leigh Hunt . . . are to lay their heads together in some town of Italy, for the purpose of conducting a journal to be directed against everything in religion, in morals and probably in government and literature which our forefathers have been accustomed to reverence.' The notion seemed 'very extravagant', but was 'perhaps the more likely to be realized on that account'. A contemporary biographer of Byron, John Watkins, further reported that he had convened a 'set of writers for the purpose of compiling a literary journal at Pisa', including the proprietor and editor of 'the most seditious paper in England' – a veritable 'academy of blasphemy' and 'poetical school of immorality and profaneness' which seemed likely to 'make a considerable noise in the world'.

All this was being noised abroad, both publicly and privately, while Hunt was still at sea. Byron and Shelley would, of course, have been more aware of it as the background against which the notion of their proposed journal was being received back home – and, in Byron's case, more concerned about it. Now that the venture had run its course, albeit without Shelley, Byron remained deeply unsettled by Hazlitt's amusement at Moore 'dart[ing] backwards and forwards from Coldbath-Fields Prison [where John Hunt languished until May 1822] to the *Examiner* office, from Mr Longman's to Mr Murray's shop to see what was done to prevent this degradation of the aristocracy of letters, this indecent encroachment of plebeian pretensions, this undue extension of patronage and compromise of privilege'. Finally, in Hunt's own amusing description, Byron's friend Hobhouse 'rushed over the Alps' to try to talk him out of the venture, 'not knowing which was the more awful, the mountains or the magazine'. Hobhouse had proved 'very polite and complimentary' to Hunt, but 'did all he could to destroy the connexion between us'.

Only success on an unexpected and unlikely scale could have saved or even prolonged a project in truth doomed from the day Shelley had set sail on his fatal voyage. Byron simply lost interest, and Hunt could but reflect upon another heroic failure. The episode ended in a poignant letter from Hunt to Byron dated 7 April 1823, apparently in reply to one from him. Significantly, he seems by this stage to have thought better of the familiar 'Dear Byron' in his mode of address:

Dear Lord Byron,

Among a variety of letters which Shelley wrote me from Italy, in several of which to the best of my recollection the proposal was mentioned, there is at all events one in my possession, in which he directly makes it to me as by your special request; and it was this letter which induced me to come over.

I do not wish to comment upon the manner in which the next sentence is worded. I must merely be allowed to say that I did *not* (at least not in the spirit which those strange words seem to imply) 'produce the very next day after my arrival at Pisa my brother's letter with a request for money to the amount of two hundred and fifty pounds.' Shelley saw me change countenance at a letter which I received by the post when he was with me; and learning the contents, he immediately with his usual kindness set about helping me the best way he could in a matter which he saw gave me grave anguish. I do not mean to say I should not have applied to you, had he been absent. I should. I should have overcome the pain of that abruptness by a greater. But I should have had no notion, at that time, that the application would ever have appeared to you in the light which I fear it seems to have done. When I arrived in Italy, it was with great surprise that I found there were some doubts of the proposed work taking place; and if I did not say any more upon that subject, it was certainly out of no want of delicacy . . . I will only remark for the present, that the failure of the *Liberal*, if it has failed, is no doubt partly owing to its having contained, from your pen, *none* but articles of a certain character, however meritorious in themselves, and to a certain want of superinduced cordiality towards it on your part, which you unfortunately allowed to escape to the public. Unquestionably, there was in other respects also a battle to fight; but in this, as in all other respects, fighting cordially and inflexibly is, I conceive, everything . . .

In a PS, Hunt added: 'I agree with you that there *appear* no reasons why the *Liberal* should be dropped. However injured, I do not know that it has failed altogether, although my brother seems to think your secession must be followed by its abandonment . . .'

Byron, for his part, was by now writing to Moore: 'You cannot imagine the despairing sensation of trying to do something for a man who seems incapable or unwilling to do anything further for himself – at least to the purpose. It is like pulling a man out of a river who directly throws himself in again.'

Byron had at least done the decent thing by John Hunt, paying the legal expenses arising from his prosecution as publisher of his *Vision of Judgment,* a fact duly acknowledged by his embattled brother: 'He felt very sensibly your kindness respecting the *Vision of Judgment.*' Tactfully, if not cravenly, Hunt omitted to mention the risk Byron had imposed on John by getting Murray to hand over his copy of the poem to him in London, so that it appeared in the *Liberal* before it had even been seen by its own editor; Byron had thus been far more aware than Hunt that the poem contained potentially actionable material.

Now, in the newly soured atmosphere, Byron became openly suspicious of John Hunt, resenting letters he had written to Leigh urging the continuation of the project on the strengths of his brother's own skills, even without Byron. The burden of Hunt's letter was primarily a defence of his brother against Byron's suspicions of his character, which succeeded rather in revealing further flaws in his own:

> With regard to my connection with my brother, it is no longer inextricable. I might dissolve it tomorrow, if I pleased. But unless his fortunes were changed, I should never think of doing so, because I plagued him a long time with my bad habits of business, and conceive I am bound to make up for them in every way I can. When that letter came to me at Pisa I was not only in debt to him myself, but he was bound to me for several petty creditors, whose claims altogether made up a large sum, for *us*; and when to these claims upon me is added his own illness at the time, just emerging from a second imprisonment, and the dangerous illness of his dearest and most useful son, who was all but given over, I am sure you will think not only that it was impossible for him to help writing, but that the subject of his letter was, after all, really an affair of my own.

As he continued to spar with Byron, another letter from this period shows that Hunt had at least managed to patch up relations with Mary Shelley. Planning to return to England, she applied to Byron for 'means', as he had promised. 'I waited in vain for these arrangements,' she wrote to Jane Williams. 'He chose to transact our negotiation through Hunt, and gave such an air of unwillingness and sense of the obligation he conferred, as at last provoked Hunt to say that there was no obligation, since he owed me £1,000 . . . Glad of a quarrel, straight I clap the door! Still keeping up an appearance of amity with Hunt, he [Byron] has written notes and letters so full of contempt against me and my lost Shelley that I could stand it no longer . . . His unconquerable avarice prevented his supplying me with money, and a remnant of shame caused him to avoid me . . .

'In the meantime Hunt is all kindness, consideration and friend-ship – all feeling of alienation towards me has disappeared down to its last dregs. He perfectly approves of what I have done.' Not long after, as she and Byron were both about to move on, Mary added: 'Hunt's kindness is now as active and warm as it was dormant before.'

Through it all, there were days on which Hunt and Byron somehow managed to maintain relatively civilised relations, talking of literature as they strolled the gardens of the Villa Saluzzi. To Hunt, Byron was at his 'pleasantest when he had got a little wine in his head . . . When in his cups, which was not often nor immoderately, he was inclined to be tender; but not weakly so, nor lachrymose.' In this mood Byron would beg Hunt not to leave – 'not yet' – and Hunt for his part would feel he was talking 'with the proper, natural Byron as he ought to have been . . . I used to think there was not a sacrifice which I could not have made to keep him in that temper, and see his friends love him as much as the world admired.'

But Hunt, for passing reasons he later regretted, was not capable of breaking the literary ice between them. 'It was not only an oversight in me,' he subsequently reproached himself. 'It was a want of friendship. Friendship ought to have made me discover what less cordial feelings had kept me blind to. Next morning, the happy moment was gone, and nothing remained but to despair and joke.'

Evidently, Byron was less candid with himself. He rejected Hunt's request for 'journey-money', promised to him as to Mary Shelley, and planned his own departure without troubling to inform the man he had brought out from England for the furtherance of his own interests. On 24 July 1823 Byron left Italy for Greece, without even bidding Hunt farewell. Their 'conversation', as Hunt succinctly put it, was 'at an end'.

9

'A hen under a penthouse'

1823–5

On 25 July, the day after Byron's departure for Greece, Mary Shelley left for England, with nothing but praise for her late husband's friend and his long-suffering wife: 'Just as I find a companion in [Hunt], I leave him. I leave him in all his difficulties, with his head throbbing with overwrought thoughts, and his frame sometimes sinking under his anxieties.'

Hunt escorted Mary the first twenty miles of her journey from Genoa: 'This was much, you will say, for Hunt,' she wrote to Jane Williams. 'But, thank heaven, we are now the best friends in the world. He set his heart on my quitting Italy with as comfortable feelings as possible . . .'

Jane knew of Mary's sufferings during the winter, when Hunt had turned away from her. 'He was displeased with me for many just reasons, but he found me willing to expiate, as far as I could, the evil I had done.' So they were reconciled: 'His heart was again warmed; and if, when I return, you find me more amiable, and more willing to suffer with patience than I was, it is to him that I owe this . . . You may judge if I ought not to be grateful to him.' Mary also spared a thought for 'poor Marianne', who had 'found good medicine, *facendo un bimbo*, and then nursing it, but she, with her female providence, is more bent by care than Hunt'.

There was yet another son, Vincent, to the Hunts' name by the time they left Genoa for Florence in 1823. Much as Hunt relished the romantic bustle of the historic port, Florence held more literature, more art, more history 'and a greater concourse of Englishmen', so that they 'might possess, as it were, Italy and England together'. Nonetheless, deprived of patronage for the first time in their lives, he and Marianne felt 'strange enough, seeking a home by ourselves in a foreign land'.

On the streets of Genoa the talk had been of 'nothing but money'; Hunt took it as a good omen that the first words he heard on the streets of Florence were 'fiori' and 'donne' – 'flowers' and 'women'. After spending their first night in a hotel, and delighting in the street musicians outside their window, he found rooms at first in the Via delle Belle Donne and then in a corner of the Piazza Santa Croce, beside the church where Michelangelo, Botticelli, Galileo and Machiavelli lie buried. Hunt's landlord was a Greek called Dionysus, who lived up to his name as 'a proper Bacchanalian, always drunk'. His mother, 'old and ugly', was called Bella.

It did not take long for the Hunts, in accordance with their 'rustic propensities', to leave the town for the countryside, and a village two miles outside Florence called Maiano, where Florence lay 'clear and cathedralled' beneath them. Here they took rooms in the Villa Morandi, where the daughters of the house recited poetry by day while by night the parents held alfresco musical soirées.

Fond, playful letters from Mary Shelley paint a vivid picture of the life in Albaro they had all left behind. 'You rose early, wrote, walked, dined, whistled, sang and punned most outrageously, the worst puns in the world . . .' She pictured Marianne, cradling her 'new darling' while urging her husband to lift his eyes to the beauty of the light in the hills. She imagined the children playing, and suggested an idyllic summer together in Susa, a 'divine spot' in which she proposed to stay some three months, inviting the Hunts to join her. 'There are no gentlemen's seats or palazzi, so we will take a cottage, which we will paint and refit, just as this country inn is in which I now write – clean and plain. We will have no servants, only we will give out all the needlework. Marianne shall make puddings and pies, to make up for the vegetables and meat which I shall boil and spoil.'

All their children would have domestic roles. 'Thorny shall sweep the rooms, Mary make the beds, Johnny clean the kettles and pans, and then we will pop him into one of the many streams hereabouts, and so clean him. Swinny being so quick shall be our Mercury, Percy our gardener, Sylvan and Percy Florence our weeders, and Vincent our plaything; and then to raise us above the vulgar, we will do all our work keeping time to Hunt's symphonies; we will perform our sweepings and dustings to the March in *Alceste*, we will prepare our meals to the tune of the *Laughing Trio*, and when we are tired we will lie on our turf sofas, while all our voices shall join in chorus to *Notte e giorno faticar*.'

But it was not to be. Italy was not living up to Hunt's romantic expectations. The idyllic country envisaged in a mind swirling with Italian poets had stubbornly failed to materialise. The landscape around Pisa had left 'a certain hard taste in the mouth'; its mountains were 'too bare, its outlines too sharp, its lanes too stony, its voices too loud, its long summer too dusty'. Above all, it was too hot. Coming almost to hate Italy, the land of his beloved poets, Hunt was 'ill, uncomfortable, in a perpetual fever', and sorely homesick for London – especially the cool, green, wooded expanses of Hampstead.

There were occasional consolations: 'You learn for the first time in this climate what colours really are . . . A red cap in Italy goes by you, not like a mere cap, much less any thing vulgar or butcher-like, but like what it is, an intense specimen of the colour of red. It is like a scarlet bud in the blue atmosphere.' The spirit of Boccaccio infused the mountain air of Maiano: 'I lived with the divine human being, with his friends of the Falcon and the Basil, and my own not unworthy melancholy.' But he walked the lanes and hills around Fiesole 'solitary' and 'sick at heart': 'In looking back to such periods of one's existence, one is surprised to find how much they surpass many seasons of mirth, as in some fine old painting.'

In this restless and disconsolate mood, Hunt published much less than usual during 1823. The *Examiner* had suspended publication at the end of 1822, after 779 issues over fifteen years, during which Hunt had made more than fourteen hundred editorial contributions. (Soon revived in modified form, the Hunt brothers' creation would eventually outlive them both, surviving until 1881.) Apart from occasional 'Indicator' essays in its new offshoot the *Literary Examiner*, and his work for the *Liberal*, Hunt's only published work that year was a pamphlet, his elaborate, ultimately ill-judged satire on Gifford, *Ultra-Crepidarius*.

Whereas all Gifford's assaults on Hunt had been published anonymously, this was far from the first time Hunt had replied to his long-standing nemesis under his own name. For all the work's neo-Juvenalian exuberance, its 'Cockney classicism', taking this elaborate sledgehammer to an elderly nut, not long for this world, could not but reinforce the impression – then as now – that 'Hunt is more fascinated by Gifford . . . than Gifford is by him.' The stream of gleeful squibs about shoes and cobblers commenced in the title – of humble Devon origins, Gifford began as an apprentice shoemaker – soon pall. Late in life, Hunt himself offered a semi-apology for the work by explaining to readers of his memoirs that 'in these kindlier days of criticism' they would have 'no conception [of the extent] to which personal hostility allowed itself to be transported in the periodicals of those times'.

Although first drafted five years earlier, *Ultra-Crepidarius* found its way into the *Literary Examiner* (which would last twenty-six issues before expiring within the year), as did Hunt's prophetic 'Sonnet to Percy Shelley':

> Hast though from earth, then, really passed away,
> And mingled with the shadowy mass of things
> Which were, but are not? Will thy harp's dear strings
> No more yield music to the rapid play
> Of thy swift thoughts, now thou art turned to clay?
> Hark! Is that rushing of thy spirit's wings
> When (like the skylark, who in mounting sings)
> Soaring through high imagination's way,
> Thou pour'dst forth thy melody upon the earth,
> Silent forever? Yes, wild ocean's wave
> Hath o'er thee rolled. But whilst within the grave
> Thou sleepst, let me in the love of thy pure worth
> One thing foretell, – that thy great fame shall be
> Progressive as Time's flood, eternal as the sea!

The more Hunt missed Shelley, the more he seems to have reheated his profound affection for his sister-in-law Bessy, whom he had not now seen for nearly three years. This was the year that Elizabeth Kent published her *magnum opus*, *Flora Domestica*, which owed much to Hunt and those of his friends she had met, not least Keats and Shelley – whom she remembered 'returning home with his hat wreathed with briony or wild convolvulus; his hand filled with bunches of wild-flowers plucked from the hedges as he passed, and his eyes, indeed every feature, beaming with the benevolence of his heart'. For this and her subsequent *Sylvan Sketches*, published two years later, Hunt supplied his sister-in-law with a wealth of poetic quotations and classical allusions, sharing her delight in flowers despite the fact (which we know from his son Thornton, not from Hunt himself) that he had no sense of smell. 'Unable to perceive the smell of flowers,' Thornton tells us, Hunt 'habitually strove to imagine it.'

Was it more than a mutual love of flowers which united Hunt and his wife's sister? His letters to Bessy at this time are so desperate as to suggest a greater closeness between brother-in-law and sister-in-law than would at the time (or indeed at any time) have been thought appropriate. Just as he did with the details of many financial loans to his father, Thornton Hunt deleted in purple ink all suggestive exchanges between his father and Bessy when editing Hunt's correspondence for posthumous publication. But they survive in the original documents, many of them now in the Carl H. Pforzheimer Collection in the New York Public Library.

Even before Shelley's death Hunt had been making such mysterious remarks to Bessy as 'I have not forgotten Monday night,' adding: 'Here is an eyelash for you, fastened by a piece of wafer.' Already he hoped for his sister-in-law's arrival in Italy. While sharing Mary Shelley's house he had confided to Bessy how 'painful' daily life was made by her 'extreme and apparently unmitigated bad temper'. Now, in his grief and loneliness, with a sick, tetchy Marianne beginning to drink more than she should, Hunt's longings for Bessy become acute.

At first he tries to keep his feelings under control: 'The longer I am in Italy, the more reason I see to expect you soon; and depend upon it. I shall lose no time in hastening your arrival.' By November 1822 he was wishing he could 'send you as many actual kind looks and caresses in return for your kindest letter as I wish heartily to give you'. That autumn he advanced from 'Our love of flowers is one of our pleasantest links' to

'Take a pat, madam, on the shoulders, and this kiss' and '20 kisses for you . . . [I] never had greater affection for you since I knew you.'

By May 1823, after Mary Shelley's departure, Hunt is telling Bessy how he wishes he could 'touch up my portrait for you, and animate it into a second self, warm and moving. Give it a kiss on the lips for me, and imagine I return it.' After reproving himself – 'I must not talk thus' – he is soon wondering 'Why cannot I run underground and issue forth in the shape of a little plant for you?' That March, from Florence, he is to be found rhapsodising: 'I think the trees and flowers now belong to you and me, par excellence, for we have said more about them than any persons living and the world seriously ought to be very grateful to us . . .' before again losing his self-control: 'I give you the tenderest of embraces in the most beautiful of spots.' The following winter, in a postscript also deleted by Thornton, Hunt implants a kiss on the notepaper, with: 'Here is a kiss, as long as I can make it. Does it do you good or harm? Tell me truly.'

There is more, much more, in this vein, often echoing the conspiratorial note in that last postscript. Did Bessy feel guilty about reciprocating the affections of her sister's husband? Her replies do not survive. And there is no other evidence that Hunt, as had been noised abroad during the 'Cockney School' furore, was emulating his fellow freethinkers by himself indulging in the incestuous relations he had celebrated in his *The Story of Rimini*. Bessy had always had eyes for him, from the moment he had walked into the Kents' house in Marylebone and fallen for her sister. She had shared many hours alone with him in his prison cell, during the absences enforced on Marianne by their children's ailments. Bessy had continued to live with the Hunts until ugly rumour had forced her out. Were she and her brother-in-law guilty of anything more than epistolary passion? The only contemporary to address the notion was Haydon, who knew Hunt well enough to adjudge him 'abandoned in principles without ever having the courage to be so in body'.

In his heart Hunt must have known that propriety would prevent his beloved 'Bebs' joining them in Italy – quite apart from the ailing Marianne's threat that her sister would be faced with more than her share of needlework. For now, she would remain beyond his unhappy reach.

Bessy Kent was in fact one of the first friends on whom Mary Shelley called upon reaching England again, and each joined others such as Lamb and the Novellos in sending Hunt a torrent of news-laden letters from London, which only added to his growing homesickness. Lamb had taken a house in Islington; that 'saturated blackguard' Theodore Hook had moved to Hunt's very own Vale of Health; at the Hunter home in Marylebone, 'Your piping Faun and kneeling Venus are on the piano; but from a feeling of delicacy they are turned with their backs to the company.' Mary had taken tea with the Hunters and Bessy; Cowden Clarke had dined with the Lambs; and Lamb was praising Hunt's contributions to an anthology edited by Hazlitt, *Select British Poets, or New Elegant Extracts*. It also contained Byron, Scott, Crabbe and Montgomery, but Hunt's work – culled from *Rimini, Foliage* and *Amyntas* – had pleased Clarke most. When he asked Mary Shelley whether people made puns in Italy, she replied: 'Yes, now Hunt is there.'

That October Lamb was extolling Hunt (amid some gentle criticism of *Rimini*) in an open letter to Robert Southey published in the *London Magazine*. Lamb was not going to let Southey get away with cheap gibes about Hunt's religious views: 'Accident introduced me to the acquaintance of Mr L.H. – and the experience of his many friendly qualities confirmed a friendship between us.' Lamb deplored the 'calumnies which have been spread abroad respecting this gentleman', whom he knew from years of acquaintance to be 'in his domestic relations as correct as any man'. Hunt was not merely 'a man of taste, and a poet'; he was 'better than so . . . one of the most cordial-minded men I ever knew, and matchless as a fireside companion . . .

'I have a letter from Italy, received but the other day, into which L.H. has put as much heart, and as many friendly yearnings after old associates, and native country, as I think paper can well hold . . .'

Mary Novello sent Hunt a boisterous account of a birthday party held in his honour that October, with Mary Shelley and Jane Williams, Clarke, Robertson, the Novellos and others: 'We had bay in honour of our poet, laurustinus, Cuba japonica, &c . . . Your name ran through the room like a charm, and your spirit seemed to animate them all. As though they could not better manifest their devotion, an universal spirit of enjoyment broke loose; puns – good and bad – badinage, raillery, compliments; but, above all, music was triumphant': Mozart, Haydn, Handel, Beethoven 'until nearly midnight'. Hunt's friends celebrated him in his absence, toasting him in a dozen bottles of (British) champagne. 'Many tears were shed by friendly eyes' as 'your health was drunk *con amore*; and by this time, being pretty well elated with so many excitements, they sang around the table *Beviamo, How Sweet is the Pleasure* and many other musical merriments; in short, they were in "excellent fooling", and declared unanimously that such an evening had never been spent before . . .'

Hearing all this, which naturally made him feel all the more marooned in Italy, Hunt had the consolation of visits from Fanny Burney's niece, who brought news of the Lambs; and Charles Armitage Brown, friend of Keats and commentator on Shakespeare's sonnets, who briefly took lodgings in a convent near Maiano – 'We discoursed of love and wine in the apartments of the Lady Abbess' – before moving into Florence. While visiting Brown there, Hunt also enjoyed the company of the English artist Seymour Kirkup and the poet Walter Savage Landor, 'to whose genius I had made the *amende honorable* the year before'. Now he paid Landor the high compliment of a Huntian nickname, 'Wat Sylvan', and found him 'like a stormy mountain pine, that should produce lilies. After indulging the partialities of his friendships and enmities, and trampling on kings and ministers, he shall cool himself, like a Spartan worshipping a moonbeam, in the patient meekness of Lady Jane Grey.'

Landor, for his part, became fond enough of Hunt to give him some poems for the resuscitated *Examiner*, and write him a verse about the lock of Lucrezia Borgia's hair in his collection, stolen by Byron from an Italian museum:

> Borgia, thou once wert almost too august,
> And high for adoration – now thou'rt dust!
> All that remains of thee these plaits infold –
> Calm hair meand'ring with pellucid gold!

Hunt laid it beside the lock of Napoleon's hair – pride of place went to Keats's and Shelley's – which already lay on his desk, amid the chaos of books, paintings, flowers and ornamental vases. For all such inspir-

iting company, however, and such a re-creation of his Hampstead parlour, Hunt sorely missed his London coterie. 'Tell me when are you
coming?' he wrote to Bessy and the Novellos. '*When*, WHEN, WHEN
do you come?' But the Novellos were as married to London as to each
other, not to mention the circle of metropolitan friends so sorely
missed by Hunt.

Idly, dogged by continued illness, a frustrated and increasingly
depressed Hunt beguiled the time by embarking upon 'the lightest
and easiest translation I could think of', Francesco Redi's *Baccho in
Toscana* (*Bacchus in Tuscany*). For the *Examiner* he showed signs of his
homesickness with the series of essays about London published under
the title *The Wishing Cap*, later developed into his collection *The Town*,
full of fond, vivid memories of the streets of London. 'I used to feel as
if I actually pitched my soul there, and that spiritual eyes might have
seen it shot over from Tuscany into York Street, like a rocket.'

Plans to make extra money compiling an edition of the English journals for expatriates – there were some two hundred British families
resident in Florence at the time – foundered on the objections of the
Italian censors, who wanted no politics or religion 'creeping in'. But it
was also at Maiano, in 1823, that Hunt climaxed a period of religious
reflection with a monograph entitled 'Christianism, or Belief and
Unbelief Reconciled', as yet for private circulation only. While insisting on some sort of afterlife, in which 'we shall all yet be comfortable
and together' (as he wrote to Bessy, enclosing her copy), the pamphlet
reflects Hunt's rejection of any systematic religion for 'a sense of the
wonders and beauties of the sacred creation', in which he did believe.
If all religions were in need of 'formulas' to be of use to congregations
or individuals, Christianity was 'defective in those particulars, chiefly
of meditations, and putting its conclusions into no practical shape – in
other words, into ritual', argued the high-church preacher's son.
Although, as yet, he had come up with no practical alternative, Hunt
would in later life expand the work into a quasi-religious manual.

So ill did he feel at the time that he thought he might be dying: 'I
wrote it because I was in a state of health which I thought might terminate fatally, and I was anxious before I died to do what good I
could . . .' News of an actual death now arrived in metaphorical,
almost psychic form, if the spiritualist Mary Howitt is to be believed

(and Edmund Blunden, for one, is 'not prepared to deny . . . that good woman'). In the spring of 1824 Hunt and some expatriate companions including the sculptor Richard Westmacott were taking the evening air when a large black butterfly 'of remarkable beauty' fluttered around them, eventually settling nearby 'for an unusual length of time'. They watched it with awe, to the point where Hunt began musing upon the 'Psyche of the Greeks'. The date was 19 April 1824 — the day of Byron's death in Greece.

When the news reached him Hunt took it as some kind of omen. He must try to let the beauty of his surroundings help him surmount his own seemingly permanent difficulties. For all his physical and spiritual ailments, Hunt had formed a deep bond with Florence, in which he saw 'nothing . . . but cheerfulness and elegance': 'I loved the name; I loved the fine arts and the old palaces; I loved the memories of Pulci and Lorenzo de Medici, the latter of whom I could never consider in any light than that of a high-minded patron of genius, himself a poet; I loved the good-natured, intelligent inhabitants, who saw fair play between industry and amusement; nay, I loved the Government itself, however afraid it was of English periodicals; for at that time it was good-natured also, and could "live and let live", after a certain quiet fashion, in that beautiful by-corner of Europe, where there were no longer any wars, nor any great regard for the parties that had lately waged them, illegitimate or legitimate . . .'

His only disappointment was the Medici Venus: 'How shall I venture to express what I felt? how own the disappointment? . . . When I saw the face, all the charms of the body vanished . . . It is the face of a foolish young woman, who thinks highly of herself, and is prepared to be sarcastic on all her acquaintance.'

Otherwise lost amid his raptures in the Uffizi, Hunt was brought back to earth with a bump by financial news from his brother John. With Leigh making only occasional contributions, while John held the fort back in London, their publishing house was not in good shape. Nor, for the first time in their long and eventful partnership, were relations between them. Leigh thought he owed John some £800; now he learnt, to the dismay of both, that the figure had risen to £1790 19s 10d.

In a letter containing a breakdown of this sum, John reported that 'the *Liberal* volumes may or may not be turned to some account. The *Literary Examiner* does not at present quite pay its way, though it rises gradually . . . The *Examiner* after nearly a year (owing to the change of price) yielding absolutely nothing, is now getting up again, and producing profits; and, under all the circumstances of the last two years – as well as the present state of the paper and your entire secession from it – I should like to hear your opinion as to the extent of the claim on your part.'

Mary Shelley had evidently been telling John that Leigh still expected to rely on the *Examiner* for regular income, perhaps forgetting that he had agreed to withdraw as its proprietor after John's last incarceration. So the ownership of the paper was at best ambiguous. With Leigh of late writing so much less than usual, John's good nature was stretched to its extreme when he was asked by his brother to forward more funds: 'You will perceive from the accounts that you have drawn a considerable sum for your own use in Italy – that is, considering the source from which it comes, and the value of money in Italy, which is, I find, *at least double* what it is in England . . .'

While suggesting various money-spinning projects to Leigh – an edition of Chaucer, perhaps (as suggested by Hazlitt), or a 'philosophical poem' called 'Jesus' (along the lines of Pope's *Messiah*) – John proposed bringing in an independent arbitrator to settle their financial differences. He, for his part, would contentedly respect the ruling of Novello or Bryan Procter, or both. Leigh opted for Novello, who reported in December that John was willing to pay his brother an annuity of £100 a year from the *Examiner* 'in consideration of your former exertions in raising the reputation of the paper', plus separate payments for any contributions. Novello had suggested a system of bonuses for Leigh if the paper's circulation rose above certain levels – to which John had readily agreed. Clearly, John was having an unhappy time trying to make his brother see financial sense. According to Novello, 'your brother . . . manifested the most unequivocal disposition to conciliate matters and to meet all your wishes if possible'.

John had leant over backwards to be generous. But still Leigh procrastinated – more out of desperation than any less seemly motive. He was ill again, and writing little; no doubt this accounts for Mary

Shelley's mounting desperation as she waited in vain for the 'notice' he had promised for her husband's 'Posthumous Poems'. This glaring omission on Hunt's part – there is no need to spell out how sorely he would wish to have been the prime introducer of his best friend's works – is a sorry measure of how low his spirits had sunk. Having had to give up on him, and write an introduction herself, Mary was generous to point out the conspicuousness of Leigh Hunt's absence from the volume, which she hoped would be remedied in future editions.

'Constant anxiety in a foreign land for the very subsistence of my family' was not, by Hunt's own account, conducive to work; before long, indeed, it was 'not to be borne any longer'. The review Hunt finally wrote of Shelley's 'Posthumous Poems' never in fact appeared in his lifetime; scheduled for publication in an 1825 issue of the *Westminster Review*, it was eventually rejected after a complex episode revolving around the antagonism of Thomas Love Peacock.

In a spirit less generous than it should have been, given that he had little choice, Hunt 'provisionally' accepted John's annuity and a fee of two guineas over the next two years for each in the series of essays known as the 'Wishing-Cap Papers'. There were sorry disputes between the Hunt brothers on the irregularity of their appearance in the paper, due as much to Leigh's unwonted inconsistency as to John's equally uncharacteristic 'press of temporary matter'. Hunt believed that he 'never wrote better prose in my life', without admitting that its production grew increasingly spasmodic. By mid-1824 John was writing that, 'solitary as my nature is, I have been obliged to admit a widower and his three children to board and lodge in my house'.

Just a few days later, after noting that Byron's remains had arrived back in England and were to be buried in Poet's Corner in Westminster Abbey, John is reporting the final settlement of the lawsuit against him as publisher of *The Vision of Judgment*: a fine of £100 and sureties totalling £2000. 'Of course the death of Lord B. is a heavy blow to me, as I had only just begun to obtain some advantage from the connection . . .'

Relations between the brothers continued to deteriorate, for all John's efforts on the distant Leigh's behalf. Mary Shelley, despite her own disappointment, had 'put your *Bacchus in Tuscany* into the hands of a printer' and now begged Hunt for an introduction to Shelley's collected prose. John pressed her case, tartly pointing out that the volume was 'shortly to go to the press', while firmly instructing him to cease drawing bills on 'us'. John urged Leigh to accept an offer from the magazine and book publisher Henry Colburn of £150 a year for verse and prose contributions to his *New Monthly*, while continuing to contribute a 'Wishing-Cap Paper' a fortnight to the *Examiner*. Their merchant friend Charles Brown, reported John, had urged him to 'cancel' all Leigh's debts to him, still exceeding £2000; but John candidly said he 'could say nothing about it till the arrangement between us is completed'.

Brown had been studying the Hunt accounts, which he felt moved to describe as 'the most perplexing papers ever laid before me'. To John's surprise, Brown took Leigh's part in the dispute over the technicalities between the roles of editor, proprietor and publisher. Brown told John that he had acted 'wrongly, in my opinion . . . in having assisted his brother when his income was more than sufficient' and that such assistance had 'fostered his imprudence'. Brown was 'aware how bitter a thing it is to hear that our best actions have been real injuries'; nevertheless, it would have been better 'had [Leigh] endured an ounce of suffering at first than thus be crushed with a ton at last'.

Hazlitt and Kirkup assented in this view, despite a paper produced by John offering 'Proofs that L.H. has forfeited (not *given away*) his proprietorship'. Typical of the happy chaos of Leigh Hunt's life is the fact that, amid this maelstrom, John should choose this moment to publish Leigh's *Bacchus in Tuscany*, only to find himself its dedicatee, in terms arriving from Italy apparently oblivious of all that was raging between them: 'May it give you a hundredth part of the elevation which you have often caused to the heart of your affectionate brother, Leigh Hunt.'

In February 1825 Hazlitt fetched up in Florence, and Hunt rushed to greet him. Together they excoriated Gifford, and those of Byron's friends who had persuaded him to kill off the *Liberal*, but Hazlitt found it hard to raise Hunt's spirits; he was 'dull as a hen under a penthouse on a rainy day'. The author of *Rimini* declined Hazlitt's suggestion of a visit to Rimini, or indeed to Venice. 'Moulting', as Hazlitt put it, Hunt preferred to remain in his hill-top fastness, where Marianne was still coughing up blood – and where Hazlitt came visiting with his new bride, Isabella Bridgwater, who recorded her husband's amusement when confronted with some mild criticism of him published by Hunt in one of his many literary guises. 'God, sir, there's a good deal of truth in it!' he exclaimed, good-natured through all. (This may well have been Hunt's article in the first issue entitled 'My Books', in which he accuses Hazlitt of failing to return books he has borrowed: 'W.H., I believe, has no books except mine.')

Since their intense partnership on the *Examiner* and subsequent books and periodicals, dating back to the days of Hunt's imprisonment, Hunt and Hazlitt had enjoyed a relationship as combative as admiring. Six months before leaving England, Hunt had felt obliged to take Hazlitt to task in print for an assault on his beloved Shelley. A thinly veiled satire on himself and his foppish ways, as in Hazlitt's essay 'People with One Idea', Hunt could shrug off, for all the hurtful identity of himself with Hazlitt's musings that 'There are persons who . . . though not dull and monotonous . . . are vivacious mannerists in their conversation, and excessive egotists. Though they run over a thousand subjects in mere gaiety of heart, their delight still flows from one idea, namely themselves . . .' That he let pass. But a wholesale assault on Shelley's reputation, after the publication of his *Prometheus Unbound*, could not be allowed to go unanswered.

A stern letter of 20 April 1821 earned a prompt, conciliatory response freighted with strategic flattery: 'My dear Hunt, I have no quarrel with you. You are one of those people that I like, do what they will: there are others that I do not like, do what they may. I have always spoken well of you to friend & foe, viz. I have said you were one of the pleasantest & cleverest people I know . . . As to Shelley, I do not hold myself responsible to him.' Hazlitt's postscript – 'I want to know why everybody has such a dislike to me' – earned an equally swift, even longer response, distilled in Hunt's opening: 'I have always said, to my own mind and to those few to whom I am in the habit of speaking such things, that Hazlitt might play me more tricks than any man; and I conceive you have played me some . . . The tears came into this coxcomb's eyes when he read the passage in your letter where you speak of not having a soul to stand by you.' Largely avoiding the substantive issues between them, beyond quibbling over the *Examiner*'s coverage of

Hazlitt's lectures on the English poets, they remained an unlikely mutual support team. Of the loner Hazlitt and the gregarious Hunt, Hunt emerges better from the exchanges, restating his loyalty and passionate liberalism to the point of making Hazlitt appear tetchy and self-pitying.

There had been further spats, usually over Hunt's pointedly impartial reviews of Hazlitt's lectures and writings, before Hazlitt became distracted by marital dramas and exhaustion brought on by his love of rackets. But they had since collaborated memorably, even at a distance, on the *Liberal*, with Hazlitt publicly rushing to Hunt's aid when Byron withdrew his support.

Now, for all the volatility of their long, complex relationship, Hunt and Hazlitt clearly enjoyed each other's company in Italy. It was in the wake of this visit – and perhaps with consciously punning references to Hunt's 'vinous' mind and the 'intoxication' it could ferment in company – that the teetotal Hazlitt wrote a portrait of him, in *The Spirit of the Age*, as vivid (and candid) as any we have:

> He improves upon acquaintance. The author translates admirably into the man. Indeed the very faults of his style are virtues in the individual. His natural gaiety and sprightliness of manner, his high animal spirits, and the *vinous* quality of his mind, produce an immediate fascination and intoxication in those who come in contact with him, and carry off in society whatever in his writings may to some seem flat and impertinent. From great sanguineness of temper, from great quickness and unsuspecting simplicity, he runs on to the public as he does at his own fireside, and talks about himself, forgetting that he is not always among friends. His look, his tone are required to point many things that he says: his frank, cordial manner reconciles you instantly to a little over-bearing, over-weening self-complacency. 'To be admired, he needs but to be seen': but perhaps he ought to be seen to be fully appreciated.

After Hazlitt's departure, bereft of friends and funds, and desperately homesick, Hunt found life in Italy intolerable. 'The dinner of the family is one dish of the cheapest kind,' reported Charles Armitage Brown. 'They sit over a shivering fire during the bitter cold of an

Italian winter.' Hunt was desperate to escape. But there was no sign, however hard he worked, of accumulating enough money to finance a return to England.

By now Hunt was returning to something approaching his usual prolix standards, with a 'Wishing-Cap' a fortnight for the *Examiner*, and 'The Family Journal' under the pen-name of Harry Honeycomb for Colburn's *New Monthly Magazine*. 'Vellutti to his Revilers', a defence of an operatic castrato then taking a critical mauling, was his last substantial poem to be published in the *Examiner*, 'Caractacus' among his finest for the *New Monthly*. To his brother he meanwhile sent the manuscript of his religious meditations; it was not in his power, replied John, to offer any advance for them. 'If you please, I will print and publish them at my own risk, and share with you whatever profit may arise,' he wrote, adding (perhaps somewhat patronisingly): 'There is a novelty in them which may strike.'

For once it was not John, but Henry Colburn, who was to prove Hunt's saviour. A publishing advance of £200, in the form of a virtual mortgage on future literary productions, gave him the means to escape his grim Italian exile and return to the England he so sorely missed. 'I shall set him down as the most *engaging* of publishers,' Hunt was enthusing of Colburn in June 1825. 'What I mean to do for him is infinite . . .'

But there was a stern price to pay. Colburn wanted a life of Byron – a critical, gossipy one, to counter all the idolatry filling the bookshops since his premature death. Hunt was too anxious to head home to England to consider the cost. 'Mud – mud is our object,' he wrote back, little anticipating the double meaning the word was soon to carry. On his last day in Italy, at last in 'jovial' spirits, he 'cracked a bottle in high style' with a stranger in Florence: 'He ran against me with a flask of wine in his hand, and divided it gloriously between us. My white waistcoat was drenched into rose colour.' It was impossible to be angry with a face so good-humoured; they parted 'on the most flourishing terms'. That evening Kirkup and Brown came up to Maiano to say their farewells.

At six the next morning, 10 September 1825, Hunt took his leave of Maiano 'with a dry eye', piling his family aboard the *vettura* which would take them all the way to Calais. For a progress of thirty to forty miles a day in this horse-drawn carriage, its box converted into a canopied chaise, with a hearty breakfast and dinner provided on the road, and five beds at night for a party of ten (counted as six 'because of the children'), Hunt paid eighty-two guineas for the entire trip. Four rest days, wherever and for as long as the passengers saw fit, were also built into the price. 'Our bargain', even to Hunt's spendthrift thinking, was 'a good one', not least because he saw in his 'rogue' of a *vetturino*, Gigi, a promising resemblance to Lamb, whose countenance, 'a little jovialized', he 'engrafted upon an active little body and sturdy pair of legs, walking about in jackboots as if they were pumps'.

As the vines and olive trees gradually disappeared along the road from Florence to Bologna, Hunt was able to admit that he found it a relief. Soon he was pleased to behold 'proper swelling Apennines, valley and mountain, with fine sloping meadows of green, interspersed with wood'. Past Reggio, birthplace of Ariosto, to the Po – and the Alps, on first sight 'classical, and Italian, and northern', making Hunt feel 'we were taking a giant step nearer home'. In Turin he beheld 'the finest dancer I have ever seen', in Susa brooded upon that 'nobody' Augustus, before finally reaching 'a sight worth living for': the passage through the Alps, filled with admiring memories of '*Napoleone di felice memoria*': 'You look up towards airy galleries and down upon villages that appear like toys, and feel somewhat disappointed at rolling over it all so easily.'

And so into France, through 'glorious' Savoy – a 'wonderful inter-mixture of savage precipices and pastoral meads' – to Chambéry, where he could not resist visiting Rousseau's house, through Lyons and Auxerre to Paris. Just past Lyons, in a quintessentially Huntian episode, they encountered an equestrian statue of Louis XIV coming the other way, en route to 'overawe' that city; looking as it did, under its wrapping, like 'some mysterious heap', Hunt fancied that 'Don Quixote would have attacked it, and not been thought mad'.

Mont Blanc looked like a 'turret in the sky, amber coloured, golden, belonging to the wall of some ethereal world'. During two days in Paris Hunt could think of little but the Revolution and Molière. Relishing the city's profusion of bookstalls, he also visited the site of the guillotine, reflecting that those who had died there, both innocent and guilty, were 'all victims of a reaction against tyranny, such as will never let tyranny be what it was, unless a convulsion of nature should swallow up knowledge, and make the world begin over again. These are the thoughts that enable us to bear such sights, and that serve to secure what we hope for.'

It was 'a blessed moment' when Hunt led his family ashore back in England on 14 October, after the best part of four years away, and a journey during whose final leg the steamboat had 'energetically trembled' beneath them, 'as if its burning body partook of the fervour of our desire'. After a long, eventful and largely wretched exile, Hunt was back in his beloved London. 'May we never be without our old fields again in this world, or the old "familiar faces" in this world or the next.'

10

'A poetical Tinkerdom'

1825–34

Before leaving Italy, Hunt had received a letter from Mary Novello warning him 'against expecting London on your return to be what it was'. He came back to find that the city had indeed been transformed by the new industrial age. Amid his beloved 'bosky bourns' were 'clouds of dust' arising from macadamised roads and 'endless projections' so that 'everything is to be improved, but no time for enjoying those improvements'. This was the backdrop against which Hunt, sole survivor of the heady literary moment of Shelley, Keats and Byron, would write his way on into the Victorian era, looking increasingly 'at odds with the thrusting commercial and imperial spirit of the times'.

After lodging at first in Hadlow Street, Bloomsbury, where the Novellos had found him temporary accommodation, Hunt was drawn ineluctably back to the northern fringes of London, this time to the semi-rural village of Highgate. Here he took a brief break from his usual frantic workload – the only one in his life, as it transpired, so exultant was he to be home – and seized the chance to re-establish his literary salon. Soon, to fill the gaping holes left by Keats and Shelley, such steadfast friends as Hazlitt and Cowden Clarke would be supplemented by new ones such as Carlyle and Macaulay, as well as longer-standing acquaintances from the old days in Sydenham twenty years earlier, not least Thomas Hill of the *Monthly Mirror*.

It is from Tommy Hill that we have one of the most potent of all Leigh
Hunt anecdotes, concerning the day that his publishers, Smith, Elder
and Co., gave Hunt a cheque for £100. 'He didn't know what to do with
it, and did not understand "presenting" it at a bank, so they cashed it for
him and gave him bank-notes, which he put in an envelope. On reaching home he threw it on the table and his wife later flung it into the fire.'
Hunt told his publishers about the incident, and they took him to the
Bank of England; on the way he 'purchased a little statue of Psyche
which he nursed on his arm. In the course of the Bank interview he
walked up to one of the officials and said: "And this is the Bank of
England. And do you sit here all day and never see the green woods and
the trees and the flowers and the charming country? Are you contented
with such a life?" And all the time he nursed his little Psyche.'

Hunt's innocence with money would eventually return to haunt
him, in ways beyond the merely fiscal. 'He had no grasp of things
material,' by the account of his son Thornton, 'but exaggerating his
own defects, he so hesitated at any arithmetical effort that he could
scarcely count.' Was it really exaggeration? There are several witnesses
to the story that Hunt, while trying to make 3s 6d out of some half-
crowns and shillings, protested that he was unable to find the odd
sixpence. Hence, as Thornton adds, 'the stewardship [of his household]
was all performed by others'.

Before reaching a terrible climax, the coming three decades would
increasingly see Hunt's literary character and reputation all but identified with his attitude to money, which remained an urgent problem
when Julia Trelawny Leigh Hunt was born in 1826, within a year of her
parents' return to England. Their eighth child, and second daughter,
Julia was born in the same year as the premature death of their son
Swinburne, aged only eleven. Two years later, perhaps to replace him,
the grieving Marianne gave birth to their ninth child, another daughter,
whom they called Jacintha. 'It was on a May morning,' wrote Hunt of
Jacintha's birth in their cottage atop Highgate Hill, 'in a cottage flowering with greengage in the time of hyacinth and new hopes, when the
hand that wrote this took the hand that had nine times lain thin and delicate on the bed of a mother's endurance; and he kissed it, like a
bride's.' Both the Hunts were devoted parents – Marianne was to have
yet one more child, a daughter named Arabella, who would die in

infancy – but Leigh seems to have been especially fond of Jacintha, 'born, so to speak, under a bed of hyacinths'.

Despite continuing money worries – 'the necessity to borrow shillings to get a dinner or tea with, constant dunnings at the door, withholdings of the family linen by the washerwoman, the sight of my children in rags' – these were some of Hunt's happiest months since the seemingly long-lost days of Hampstead, Keats and Shelley – less, in truth, than a decade earlier. 'Pleasant were the walks and talks taken arm-in-arm with such a host and entertainer as Leigh Hunt,' recalled Cowden Clarke's wife, Mary. 'He also shone brilliantly in his after-breakfast pacings up and down his room. Clad in the flowered wrapping-gown he was so fond of wearing when at home, he would continue the lively subject broached during breakfast, or launch forth into some fresh one, gladly prolonging that bright and pleasant morning hour . . .'

Highgate also gave him Coleridge as a neighbour: 'fat . . . and lament[ing], in very delightful verses, that he was getting infirm'. One day Hunt heard the great man, 'under the Grove at Highgate, repeat one of his melodious lamentations, as he walked up and down, his voice undulating in a stream of music, and his regrets of youth sparkling with visions ever young'. On first visiting Coleridge's room, which 'looked upon a delicious prospect of wood and meadow, with coloured gardens under the window, like an embroidery to the mantle', Hunt saw him as an abbot-like figure; when they talked poetry he deemed Coleridge 'as great a high priest as Spenser' of 'the Muse's mysteries'. With a 'triumphant' eloquence Coleridge asked Hunt 'what chastity itself were worth, if it were a casket, not to keep love in, but hate, and strife, and worldliness?' On the same occasion, Coleridge 'built up a metaphor out of a flower, in a style surpassing the famous passage in Milton; deducing it from its root in religious mystery, and carrying it up into the bright, consummate flower, "the bridal chamber of reproductiveness"'. Forlornly, Hunt looked back to the day he had somehow contrived to be in the wrong room at Byron's home in Piccadilly as Coleridge recited his *Kubla Khan*; Byron emerged 'highly struck with his poem, and saying how wonderfully he talked. This was the impression of everybody who heard him.' After an unproductive final decade Coleridge was to die here in Highgate in July 1834.

Hunt, too, had been uncharacteristically unproductive of late. But soon, having published nothing at all in 1826–7, for all his obligations to Colburn, he was finally back at work. For long enough he had placated his publisher and creditor by bringing him the work of others, such as the momentous memoirs of Michael Kelly, the Irish tenor who had known Mozart and befriended the young Hunt more than twenty years earlier. But the projects Hunt had in mind, though close to his literary heart, were not those agreed with Colburn while still in Italy.

'At the time of which I am speaking,' continues Mary Cowden Clarke, 'Leigh Hunt was full of some translations he was making from Clément Marot and other of the French epigrammatists; and as he walked to and fro he would fashion a line or two, and hit off some felicitous turn of phrase, between whiles whistling with a melodious soft little birdy tone in a mode peculiar to himself of drawing the breath inwardly instead of sending it forth outwardly through his lips . . . He was also cogitating the material for a book which he purposed naming "Fabulous Zoology"; and while this idea was in the ascendant his talk would be rife of dragons, griffins, hippogriffs, minotaurs, basilisks . . .' He also began work on a historical novel about a nobleman in the time of Charles II.

It was at this time that Hazlitt's encomium to Hunt in *The Spirit of the Age* was published. Beyond the warm, if qualified, personal praise already quoted, there were some professional compliments especially welcome from so esteemed a colleague, now also a neighbour in Highgate: 'He is the only poet or literary man we ever knew who puts us in mind of Sir John Killigrew or Carew; or who united rare intellectual acquirements with outward grace and natural gentility. Mr Hunt ought to have been a gentleman born, and to have patronized men of letters. He might then have played, and sung, and laughed, and talked his life away; have written mainly prose, elegant verse; and his "Story of Rimini" would have been praised by Mr Blackwood. As it is, there is no man now living who at the same time writes verse and prose so well, with the exception of Mr Southey (an exception, we fear, that will be little palatable to either of these gentlemen).' Hunt had never thought much of Southey; and the feeling was distinctly mutual.

So Hazlitt and Hunt were colleagues again, along with Lamb, thanks to one of the long-standing Sydenham friends reintroduced into Hunt's

Highgate circle: Thomas Campbell, editor of the *New Monthly Magazine*, who now boasted with some justice that he had the 'three best essayists in England' among his contributors. Another habitué, Bryan Walker Procter (Barry Cornwall), enjoyed the lively interaction of this eminent triumvirate: 'Each of them understood the others, and placed just value on their objections when any difference of opinion (not infrequent) arose between them.'

One of the many old companions who rejoiced in Hunt's return, Procter was soon revelling with him in affectionate anecdotes about mutual friends: 'Have you seen the caricature of Charles Lamb? I went into the shop of a printseller (whom I know) and remonstrated with him on the heinousness of selling such a libel – but he attempted to justify himself by saying that it was not intended as a piece of scandal or libel – that it was done by an acquaintance of C.L. who did not *intend* to libel him – and finally that he had sold all the copies he had of this eminent critic and essayist!'

Blackwood's was, of course, equally glad to see Hunt back, so as to pepper him with more savage fusillades about his 'Cockney' poetry and 'heretical' beliefs. But there were signs that, even in his early forties, the only surviving Romantic was already turning into something of a national treasure. He was now celebrated enough to invite imitation and gentle, affectionate parody, plus dedications – such as that of the anonymous *Day in Stowe Gardens* (which Lamb described as 'a day ill-bestowed'). He was still seen as the peer of Keats and Shelley – and not only in Bessy Kent's *Sylvan Sketches*, a companion volume to her *Flora Domestica*, in which naturalists and poets alike assemble to admire trees; Hunt was of their company, along with his late, much lamented friends. 'The familiar love between British botany and verse at that period would occupy inquiry agreeably for many a winter's evening,' suggests Blunden, 'and it is singular to see how widely the words and names of the Romantic poets travelled by the indirect means of works like *Sylvan Sketches*.'

The only cloud over Hunt's life at this time was an estrangement from his brother John, whose door was one of the few in London firmly closed to him, and who avoided even the slightest chance of any meeting. Beyond the dispute over ownership of the *Examiner*, and the huge, unsettled debts arising therefrom, we have no documentation as to the precise cause of John's grave disenchantment – unusual in so good-natured a man and fraternal a brother. Most likely, it still rankled that the arbitration in the *Examiner* dispute had gone against him, seemingly in defiance of the facts of the case, involving him in a modest public humiliation while writing off his not so modest subsidies to his brother.

For Leigh this breach was more than privately upsetting; it was publicly uncomfortable, for John was still a popular and respected figure in literary circles – 'a man of greater probity I never knew,' testified Cyrus Redding of the *New Monthly* – with powers of patronage beyond Leigh's mere imprimatur. And there was no way that their differences could be kept private; John's refusal of any invitation to any function where Leigh might be present was the talk of the town. So the younger brother had to go to reluctant public lengths to explain away the elder's conduct towards him, reminding all enquirers that, in the matter of the *Examiner*, impartial investigators had found in his favour. That it should come to this with these brothers who once shared noble imprisonment for their beliefs: this sorry episode would have bruised Hunt's gentle soul.

As did Hazlitt's assault on Shelley in 1826 – swiftly compensated for, from Hunt's point of view, by a touching reminder of his dead friend's affection in the shape of a letter from Mary Shelley announcing that she intended to honour her husband's unwritten pledge to bequeath Hunt £2000. 'I shall be bound to pay you by the laws of honour instead of a legal obligation,' Mary wrote. 'I have as yet made no will but if in the meantime I should chance to die, this paper may serve as a legal document to prove that I give and bequeath to you, dear Leigh Hunt, the sum of two thousand pounds sterling. But I hope we both shall live – I to accomplish our Shelley's intentions, you to honour me so far as to permit me to be the executor.' Touching as her sentiments were, Mary's undertaking was dependent on the supposedly imminent death of her baronet father-in-law – who in fact survived another eighteen years, rendering Mary's charming notion of £2000 no more than that.

Just, of course, Hunt's luck. Already, in the *New Monthly*, he had shared wistfully with the world another of Shelley's promises that now had no chance of being fulfilled. Of Penshurst Place in Kent, the castellated residence of the descendants of Shelley's kinsman Sir Philip

Sidney, which had been bequeathed to him by its then incumbent, Hunt wrote: 'That house was to have become the property of a beloved friend, now no more. He promised me a turret of it, which was to be called by my name; "and here," said he, "if there is such a thing as heaven upon earth, will you and I realize it." We were to have had books infinite, horses, a boat. The manor-house supplied us with excellent neighbours. "If I happen," said my friend, "to die in the midst of our enjoyments, I will stay and live with you still in spirit, for a diviner corner than this I cannot imagine." Alas! he died before he entered into possession, and I am not rich enough to inherit it for him. But if I am rich in any thing, it is in memory and affection.'

Imagining that he now lived nearby, Hunt continued: 'I sit looking at it, as I used to do at Claude's picture of the Enchanted Castle; and fancy my departed friend still living with me according to his promise. He will not do so the less, because my enjoyments are disappointed. I delight to sit here on warm sunny days, and build all sorts of imaginations. I fancy my friend with me. Sometimes we live in the castles of Ariosto; sometimes in the East amidst enchanted gardens; sometimes with Theocritus in Sicily, with Plato in Greece. We often visit Lemnos, to comfort Philoctetes . . .'

The Shelley money, in whatever form, might (as so often) have saved Hunt from himself, for now was the time that the publisher Colburn reminded him of the contract which had financed his return from Italy. His writing career mortgaged to the hilt to Colburn, Hunt had no option but to come up with something along the lines promised: a couple of volumes on Italy and an anthology of his own writings, including some sort of personal memoir about Keats, Shelley and above all Byron. Recognising that there was no way even Hunt could deliver on all this, their original agreement, now some two years old, Colburn negotiated a compromise: a large volume of autobiography with an especial emphasis on Byron, whose name alone was still turning books into gold mines.

Hunt set about his task with an energy feverish even by his usual standards. 'Frustration must be retrospective,' as Blunden notes. 'There is no greater source of prolix phraseology than a bitter confidence that one has been wronged.' Soon the *New Monthly* and others in Colburn's stable of magazines began to *bouleverse* the London literary

scene with the first wholesale assaults on Byron to have appeared since
his death in Greece four years earlier, in 1824. Outraged that Byron
had been sanctified in death, extolled as the European poet of his age,
hailed as an exemplary nobleman and Christian, his vices and misde-
meanours whitewashed – and all at the expense of his beloved Shelley –
Hunt set to with a will. Still estranged from his brother, and now from
his mother-in-law (who was engaged in a long-running dispute with
Bessy), he felt he had nothing to lose. What would soon become a
book, a much-reviled book, began as a series of articles for Colburn's
journals with an uncomfortably personal edge to their revelations
about the noble poet.

'Lord B. had a particular way of marking the pages that pleased
him,' observed one such, referring to the occasion Byron had borrowed Hunt's copy of Cotton's *Montaigne*. 'He usually made a double
dog's-ear, of a very tight and, as it were, irritable description; folding
the corner twice, and drawing his nail with a sort of violence over it,
as if to hinder "the dog"'s escape from him. I will begin the extract with
one that he has marked with a *triple* dog's-ear. The reader will observe
in it a very obvious application to himself. I must premise that these
dog's-ears are the only marks: so that the reader must notice for himself such passages as he thinks the noble poet may have had more
particularly in view. There is another dog's-ear two pages further
on . . .' The passage then quoted is an analysis of literary egotism.

Huntians may find this mordantly witty, but Byron partisans will
now – as then – write it off, with some justice, as the petty indiscretion
of a slighted man out for vengeance. As Hunt recycled these articles
among other previously published material, anecdotes and reminiscences into a hastily cobbled-together potboiler, Haydon was among
the first to express scandalised indignation. 'Have you read Leigh
Hunt's last hit on Byron in *Campbell's Magazine*? If not, read it without
further fatal procrastination. "The noble lord," says Leigh Hunt "com-
plains in *Don Juan* that he could never make a lady tell her age! But,"
says the amiable and chivalrous Leigh, "*we* have been more fortunate
with our informants than the noble lord." Oh! Heavens! *His* fair informants! Who be they? Mrs Gliddon, the tobacconist's wife, or the lady of
"Hampstead ponds", who, in trying to be pathetic, and hoping she
might *not* be drowned, threw herself off a wooden footpath into a

Hampstead puddle where it was six inches deep . . . Poor Leigh! Why does he write such twaddle? He is now writing his life, which will be a monkish mixture of petticoat twaddling and Grandison cant.'

Hunt had not seen Haydon since his return from Italy. But Haydon had been seeing Hazlitt, who arrived back in England just two days later (minus, according to form, his latest wife). The temperamental painter's worst suspicions about Hunt had been confirmed by Hazlitt's light-hearted account of Hunt's Italian sulks; Haydon it was who passed on Hazlitt's testimony that Hunt could not be budged from his Tuscan mountain top, had failed even to visit the Louvre as he returned home via Paris. Even before Hunt's Byron book, an embittered Haydon had confided to his diary: 'Sorry I am to write so much of a man in whose acquaintance I can no longer feel any pride. He ruined Keats; he has injured me; he perverted Byron. Poor Shelley was drowned in going back from visiting him. Like Scylla, where he comes grass never grows; and when he treads on what is growing, it withers, as if the cloven hoof of hell had poisoned it . . . I can never think of Leigh Hunt again without sorrow.'

But Hunt had worse enemies than Haydon lying in wait. As Colburn began excited pre-promotion of his forthcoming volume, Thomas Moore, self-appointed keeper of the Byron flame, pre-empted it in *The Times* with a bitterly sarcastic verse fable entitled 'The Living Dog and the Dead Lion'. Hunt replied with one entitled 'The False Lion and the Real Puppy'.

'It is for slaves to lie, and freemen to speak truth,' read a defiant quotation from Montaigne on the title page of Leigh Hunt's *Lord Byron and Some of his Contemporaries, with Reflections of the Author's Life and of his Visit to Italy*, published by Henry Colburn of New Burlington Street, London, in January 1828. On the facing page sat a plumpish Byron in profile, a sneer on his lips, a jaunty cap on his head and a riding crop nonchalantly tossed over his shoulder – a silhouette cut by Marianne, and reckoned by impartial observers to be an excellent likeness, a welcome antidote to the succession of fawning portraits which had so swiftly romanticised the Byron cult.

The tone for the book was set in its overly apologetic preface, in which Hunt wriggles with discomfort even as he begins to sink his teeth into his subject. What began life as a memoir, he explains, has turned into the collected lives of several poets with special reference to one, leaving the material in less than satisfactory shape. 'Time . . . as well as place, is violated,' he confesses, making no effort to shirk the blame, but confessing to 'bad habits of business and the sorriest arithmetic' – an all but open acknowledgement that money was a more pressing motive than any literary imperatives. By focusing on the one poet, Byron, he had added to the 'attractions of the title-page' while giving the book an 'altogether different look' from that he had first contemplated. 'My publisher thought it best,' he shrugs, continuing in overly confessional mode: 'Such is my dislike of these personal histories that, had I been rich enough, my first impulse on finishing the work would have been to put it in the fire.'

This ambivalence about his own work came down to 'a conflict of principles'. On the one hand, Hunt's version of events should 'put an end to a great deal of false biography'; on the other, 'it has long ceased to be within my notions of what is necessary for society to give an unpleasant account of any man'. But to write truly of the Noble Poet 'involved of necessity a painful retrospect'. 'Humanize as I may, and as I trust I do', in renewing his intercourse with Byron, even in his imagination, Hunt had 'involuntarily felt a re-access of the spleen and indignation which I experienced, as a man who thought himself illtreated. With this, to a certain extent, the account is coloured, though never with a shadow of untruth.'

Truth, truth was to blame. 'O Truth! what scrapes of portraiture have you not got me into!' laments Hunt after page upon page parading examples of Byron's self-love, self-pity, vanity and above all his professional and pecuniary meanness to fellow poets, schoolfellows, mistresses, the Greeks and indeed the author himself. The agonies caused Hunt by the writing of such charges remain all too visible, to the point where he protests too much; he would not say anything about Byron's meanness, 'nor about twenty other matters, but that they hang together more or less, and are connected with the truth of a portrait which it has become necessary to me to paint. It is fortunate that there are some which I can omit.'

It is hard to conceive what Hunt could have left out, given what he includes. 'His failure in the House of Lords is well known'; 'His

Lordship was one of a management that governed Drury-lane Theatre [who] made a sad business of their direction'; he was one of those 'who only seek personal importance in their generosity'; one whose superstition was 'petty and old-womanish'; one whose 'love of noto-riety was superior even to his love of money'; one who was 'far the pleasantest when he had got wine in his head'. Byron 'did not care for the truth'; he felt 'jealous of the smallest accomplishments' and 'impa-tient of any despotism not his own'; Christian 'he certainly was not', nor indeed as 'brave' as he had been portrayed: 'I doubt greatly whether he was a man of courage . . . I suspect, that personal anxiety, coming upon a constitution unwisely treated, had no small hand in has-tening his death in Greece.' As for the received wisdom that Byron was an 'apostle of liberty', he would have been 'a very unwilling apostle, had he known he was also to be a martyr'.

Even the poet's nose, 'though handsome in itself, had the appearance when you saw it closely in front, of being grafted on the face, rather than growing properly out of it'. Did Byron have no redeeming fea-tures? He rode well, was a strong swimmer and did not fear big dogs. But his 'predominant' characteristic was 'an indulgence of his self-will and self-love united, denying himself no pleasure that could add to the intensity of his consciousness, and the means of his being powerful and effective, with a particular satisfaction in contributing as little as possible to the same end in others'. Hunt permitted himself to surmise that the noble Lord had never enjoyed the good fortune of 'knowing what real love is' – a cardinal sin, of course, in a Romantic poet – while sinking as low as to quip that he enabled his 'adoring' female admirers 'to discover that a great man may be a very small one'.

The first third of Hunt's nine-hundred-page book was dedicated to his assault upon Byron, the rest comprising his own memoirs in the shape of 'detached', gentler portraits of others, from Coleridge, Lamb and the brothers James and Horace Smith to Keats and Shelley. Here again Hunt runs the danger of doing himself a disservice. Of Shelley he writes in the same wide-eyed superlatives – 'He was like a spirit that had darted out of its orb, and found itself in another planet' – as he had just bemoaned in hagiographers of Byron. And his portrait of Keats contains inaccuracies based on hearsay, from 'the poor boy who mirac-ulously makes good' to 'the over-sensitive soul martyred by a harsh world', which have coloured all subsequent biography; to this day, in the words of one disgruntled Keatsian, these 'myths' and 'fables' are 'embedded into a body of Keats legend which is . . . very difficult to shift'.

For all Hunt's professed misgivings, the book was an instant success, reprinting within the year and enjoying rapid translation into French. While Hunt was reviled on all sides, for ingratitude towards a man who had offered him substantial patronage, his bestseller was as avidly (if guiltily) read as are all such indiscreet memoirs of the famous. Hunt was reversing the trend of Byron idolatry, involving wholesale suspension of critical faculties, which had begun in his lifetime and grown beyond all proportion since his death. In truth, this was a timely corrective to Byron studies, as sales of the book demonstrated, but the plain fact remains that Hunt was the wrong man to make it; known to have accepted Byron's hospitality and substantial financial support, he could not but appear an ungrateful wretch, out to settle petty scores. The book made Colburn a fortune; while paying off Hunt's debt to his publisher, however, it did his reputation grave damage.

Given what we know of Hunt's strained relations with Byron in Italy, the truth seems to be that the 'wren' misjudged his posthumous assessment of the 'eagle' less out of malice than mere miscalculation. 'It is unlikely,' as Blunden puts it, 'that Hunt's rendering of their relations was seriously inexact. The narrative was garrulous, petty, perplexed, but Hunt was not a liar. In the tumult of his troubles, the feeling that Byron was the cause of most of them disordered his judgment, and deformed his style.' But it was not the 'substance of his statement' that could justly be condemned; there was a misperception at the time of the book's publication that Hunt, with his innocence of the *Examiner*'s financial plight, had broken some moral obligation to Byron – rather than the other way around, i.e. that Byron, with his high-handed treatment of Hunt, was guilty of 'commonplace calculation'. The 'noble imagination' was found 'wholly wanting'. But even this most sympathetic of Huntians concedes that 'this fact needed no such irritable compilation of minor casualties as Hunt produced for Colburn; a short and striking chronicle of the main promise, risk, undertaking and disappointment would have done good'.

Anecdotes would also have been perfectly acceptable – 'and Hunt had many to tell, some laughable, some pathetic' – had he not made them 'texts for rambling sermons, if indeed in his fevered tenacity he did not mismanage them altogether'. For instance, Byron had one day scolded Hunt's mischievous young son John: 'You must take care how you get notions in your head about Truth and Sincerity, for they will hinder your getting on in the world.' This 'artful and well-meant' remark was now being interpreted by Hunt as an attempt 'to corrupt a poor child'.

The tragic subtext of it all was that the friendship between Hunt and Byron was potentially one made in heaven. 'Hunt would have gloried in Byron, had not certain characteristics on both sides clashed, and obscured the view.' Hunt was by nature effusive, 'and probably that spoiled all'; he was a vociferous idealist, and Byron 'was not built that way'. Hunt had desperately hoped, at first tried, to see the best in Byron; but his characteristically virtuous, anticipatory smile 'made Byron, still a mischievous boy, play at showing off his worst'. As a result, Hunt was now reduced to writing sentences frankly unworthy of him, such as 'Lord Byron was always acting, even when he told the truth.'

A less charitable twentieth-century view is that of the Byron partisan Peter Quennell: 'Warped by the author's self-pity, and tinged with envy, the portrait would be more amusing and far more damaging if the prejudice that informs it were less solemnly self-centred, and more convincing if it included a greater degree of sympathy. But how should Hunt, impoverished, ailing, worried, feel sympathy for Lord Byron, rich, celebrated, care-free, pampered by his servants, adored by his mistress, spoiled, courted, admonished by his fashionable London friends?'

To another of Hunt's latter-day champions, J.E. Morpurgo, such verdicts are unjust but inevitable. Byron's biographers 'cannot hide his weakness and, in consequence, they are almost reasonable in their counter-blows against the hard-hitting author of Lord Byron and Some of His Contemporaries. They do not deny the power of Hunt, but instead, they fling around their twentieth-century shoulders the lordly cloak of their hero – they praise, they patronize and then they gibe; but only the gibes cling.'

* * *

This proved equally true at the time, as Hunt's world temporarily caved in. Typical of the outraged reviews were the gleeful sneers of Lockhart in the *Quarterly Review*, his long-standing case against Hunt finally proven; this was 'the miserable book of a miserable man: the little airy fopperies of its manner are like the fantastic trip and compulsive simpers of some poor worn-out wanton, struggling between famine and remorse, leering through her tears'. This 'unhappy', 'unfortunate' man had filled page after page, through a long quarto volume, with the meanest details of private gossip:

> dirty gabble about men's wives, and men's mistresses – and men's lackeys, and even the mistresses of the lackeys – and with anecdotes of the personal habits of an illustrious poet, such as could never have come to the knowledge of any man who was not treated by Lord Byron either as a friend or as a menial.
>
> It is really too bad that Lord Byron, in addition to the grave condemnation of men able to appreciate both his merits and his demerits, and well disposed to think more in sorrow than in anger of the worst errors that existed along with so much that was excellent and noble – it is by much too bad that this great man's glorious, though melancholy, memory –
>
> Must also bear the vile attacks
> Of ragged curs and vulgar hacks
>
> whom he fed; that his bones must be scraped up from their bed of repose to be at once grinned and howled over by creatures who, even in the least hyena-like of their moods, can touch nothing that mankind would wish to respect without polluting it.

Lockhart could only hope and trust that the public reception of this 'filthy gossip' would be 'such as to discourage any more of these assaults upon Lord Byron's memory'.

Even to some of Hunt's friends, it was an 'underbred' book, unworthy of the otherwise generous, gentle spirit they knew. Chief among his critics, of course, was his erstwhile friend Tom Moore, from whom he had drifted even further apart since the Italian episode. It was not just

that Moore had been privy to – indeed, as subsequently published letters showed, the prime recipient of – Byron's withering wisecracks
about Hunt and his family. Already, even before Hunt went to Italy,
long gone were the heady days when an admiring Moore had brought
an equally admiring Byron to visit Hunt in jail; during the intervening
years of his Hampstead friendship with Keats and Shelley, Hunt's relations with Moore had soured as the Irishman (and inferior poet) chose
to move in London social circles Hunt shunned. Chief among them was
the so-called 'Holland House' group, an alliance of Whigs under the
patronage of Henry Richard Vassall Fox, third Baron Holland, which
Hunt had declined to join for fear of compromising his independence
as a political journalist.

It was not that Hunt had anything against Lord Holland himself, a
nephew and disciple of Charles James Fox, a patron of Godwin and
political ally of Byron. Quite the reverse; in 1817 Holland's study of
the Spanish nobleman and poet Guillén de Castro had so excited him as
to keep him awake 'two hours . . . the other night, unable to cease
thinking of the filial gallantry of the Cid', as he wrote excitedly to
Holland at the time. (This was not just another bout of fawning politeness to an aristocrat; in his autobiography Hunt recalled 'about thirty
years ago, being sleepless one night with a fit of enthusiasm, in consequence of reading about the Spanish play of *The Cid*, in Lord Holland's
Life of Guillen de Castro'.)

'The name of Lord Holland has always presented to my mind that
mixture of the genial and intellectual, which renders respect affectionate,' Hunt ended his letter in March 1817 – and he meant it. He
never blamed Holland personally for the negative effect on his career
caused, as he believed, by his refusal to join the Holland House group.
Holland had 'courteously sent me his publications, and never ceased,
while he lived, to show me all the kindness in his power'. Hunt was
'far, therefore . . . from supposing that the silence of the Whig critics
respecting me was owing to any hostile influence which Lord Holland
would have condescended to exercise'. Because of his refusal to visit
Holland House, 'I dare say I was not thought of; or if I was, I was
regarded as a person who, in shunning Whig connections, and perhaps
in persisting to advocate a reform towards which they were cooling,
might be supposed indifferent to Whig advocacy.'

Hunt believed that Whig journals such as the *Edinburgh Review* might have noticed his books 'a little oftener' had he been a member of the Holland coterie. 'I am sure it would have done me a great deal of worldly good . . . and in itself no harm in these progressing days of criticism. But I said nothing on the subject, and may have been thought indifferent.'

In 1828, however, in the section of his *Byron* concerning Shelley, Hunt's mood led him into somewhat more ambiguous remarks, albeit veiled, on the Holland House group: 'The family connexions of Mr Shelley belonged to a small party in the House of Commons, itself belonging to another party. They were Whig aristocrats; a distinction that, within a late period, has been handsomely merged by some of the bearers of it into the splendour of a more prevailing universality.'

All this was symptomatic of a broader ideological split with Moore in the years before Hunt's departure for Italy. While Hunt had aligned himself with Shelley, Hazlitt and others in a broad manifesto of sweeping political, social and ideological reforms, Moore had become increasingly identified with less radical Whig magnates such as Holland and the Marquis of Lansdowne, who shared Hunt's views on parliamentary reform, Catholic emancipation and a handful of other basic political changes, but stopped short of more radical notions about society. Moore was not, in short, 'an ideological reformer'. In 1803, moreover, he had accepted a government position – a 'sinecure' of the very kind Hunt loathed and had vigorously attacked in the *Examiner*.

This was the background against which their relations deteriorated yet further in the build-up to the launch of the *Liberal* – when Moore had joined, both publicly and privately, in the chorus of those deploring the potentially 'dangerous' influence on Byron of Shelley and Hunt. After the journal's failure Hunt attacked Moore as the 'son of a grocer' in the preface to his assault on Gifford, *Ultra-Crepidarius*. Now, in his *Byron*, after recalling their earlier, more pleasant relations, Hunt accused Moore of sabotaging the *Liberal* by trying to persuade Byron that there was 'a "taint" in it'; Moore, sneered Hunt, had sacrificed his 'free sentiment on the fat altars of the aristocracy'.

All the more reason that the publication of Hunt's *Byron* galvanised Moore into bringing forward plans of his own to edit a collection of Byron's letters and journals. Murray, too, was irritated enough to agree to rush out *The Letters and Journals of Lord Byron: with Notices of His Life*, edited by Thomas Moore (with a fawning dedication to Sir Walter Scott), hastily published in two volumes in 1830 before the full seventeen-volume edition of 1832–3.

In his personal commentary on the Byron documents, Moore let Hunt have it with both barrels. More in anger than in sorrow – subtlety was not his forte – Moore recalled visiting Hunt in prison with Byron, on that occasion when he was irritated that Hunt permitted others, against Moore's express wishes, to be present. Among them was John Scott, proprietor of the *Champion*, who had subsequently published 'severe' attacks on Byron – but at least while he was still alive. 'It is painful to think,' wrote Moore, 'that among the persons then assembled round the poet, there should have been one so soon to step forth, the assailant of his living fame, while another, less manful, was to reserve the cool venom for his grave.'

Of that man, and the book in which he now thought it 'decent to revenge upon the dead the pain of those obligations he had, in his hour of need, accepted from the living', Moore declared himself 'luckily saved from the distaste of speaking at any length' by 'the utter and most deserved oblivion into which his volume has fallen'. Never, indeed, had 'the right feeling of the world upon such subjects been more creditably displayed than in the reception given universally to that ungenerous book'. Even those least disposed to think approvingly of Byron had 'shrunk back from such a corroboration of their own opinion as could be afforded by one who did not blush to derive his authority, as an accuser, from those facilities of observation which he had enjoyed by having been sheltered and fed under the very roof of the man whom he maligned'.

With respect to the 'hostile feelings' manifested by Hunt towards himself, the 'sole revenge' Moore proposed to take was to lay before his readers the passage in one of his letters which appeared to have provoked them. This, at least, could claim the merit of not being a covert attack; throughout all his letters remonstrating with Byron on the subject of his new literary allies, whether Shelley or Hunt, he had no reason to imagine – from 'long knowledge' of his friend – that Byron would 'instantly, and as a matter of course' share them with their victims. There followed the passage which Byron, as Moore assumed, had shown to Hunt (and to which one of his letters to Moore, dated 20 February 1821, specifically refers):

'I am most anxious to know that you mean to emerge out of the *Liberal*. It grieves me to urge anything so much against Hunt's interest; but I should not hesitate to use the same language to himself, were I near him. I would, if I were you, serve him in every possible way but this – I would give him (if he would accept of it) the profits of the same works, published separately – but I would not mix myself up in this way with others. I would not become a partner in this sort of miscellaneous "pot au feu", where the bad flavour of one ingredient is sure to taint all the rest. I would be, if I were you, alone, single-handed, and, as such, invincible.'

So that was where Hunt had got hold of the word 'taint'. While on the subject of Hunt, Moore now proposed to avail himself of the opportunity to introduce extracts from a letter 'addressed to a friend of that gentleman by Lord B., in consequence of an appeal made to the feelings of the latter on the score of his professed "friendship" for Mr Hunt'. Even Moore conceded that its contents were 'startling, and must be taken with more than the usual allowance, not only for the particular mood of temper or spirits in which the letter was written, but for the influence also of such slight casual piques and resentments as might have been, just then, in their darkening transit through his mind – indisposing him, for the moment, to those among his friends whom, in a sunnier mood, he would have proclaimed as his most chosen and dearest'.

There followed a passage from a letter from Byron to an unnamed Mrs —— on a date unspecified by Moore (but presumably in March 1823):

I presume that you, at least, know enough of me to be sure that I could have no intention to insult Hunt's poverty. On the contrary, I honour him for it; for I know what it is, having been as much embarrassed as ever he was, without perceiving aught in it to diminish an honourable man's self-respect. If you mean to say that, had he been a wealthy man, I would have joined in this journal, I answer in the negative . . . I engaged in the journal from goodwill towards him, added to respect for his character, literary and personal; and no less

for his political courage, as well as regret for his present circumstances: I did this in the hope that he might, with the same aid from
literary friends of literary contributions (which is requisite for all
journals of a mixed nature), render him independent.

I have always treated him, in our personal intercourse, with such
scrupulous delicacy, that I have forborne intruding advice which I
thought might be disagreeable, lest he should impute it to what is
called taking advantage of a man's situation . . .

As to friendship, it is a propensity in which my genius is very limited. I do not know the male human being, except Lord Clare, the
friend of my infancy, for whom I feel anything that deserves the
name. All my others are men-of-the-world friendships. I did not
even feel it for Shelley, however much I admired and esteemed him;
so that you see not even vanity could bribe me into it, for, of all
men, Shelley thought highest of my talents – and, perhaps, of my
disposition.

I will do my duty by my intimates, upon the principle of doing as
you would be done by. I have done so, I trust, in most instances. I
may be pleased with their conversation – rejoice in their success – be
glad to do them service, or to receive their counsel and assistance in
return. But as for friends and friendship, I have (as I already said)
named the only remaining male for whom I feel anything of the
kind, excepting perhaps Thomas Moore. I have had, and may have
still, a thousand friends, as they are called, in life, who are like
one's partners in the waltz of this world – not much remembered
when the ball is over, though very pleasant for the time. Habit,
business, and companionship in pleasure or in pain, are links of a
similar kind, and the same faith in politics is another.

Moore's relish in his revisionism was not sated yet. In a footnote to
another letter from Byron he now chose to make public – that from
Venice on 1 June 1818, calling Hunt 'a good man' but a 'martyr', a
'charlatan', a 'coxcomb' and 'a very vulgar person' whose poetry
amounted to 'a trash of vulgar phrases tortured into compound barbarisms' – Moore ingenuously declared that he had originally planned
to omit 'the whole of this caustic, and perhaps over-severe character of
Mr Hunt', but had been persuaded otherwise by 'the tone of that

gentleman's book having, as far as himself is concerned, released me from all those scruples which prompted the suppression'. He had therefore considered himself 'at liberty to restore the passage'. So angry was he, indeed, that in the throes of embarrassing Hunt further by publishing Shelley's begging letter to Byron on Hunt's behalf – 'I am so much annoyed by this subject that I hardly know what to write' – he managed to date it 15 February 1823, eight months after Shelley died.

Basking in the reflected glory of his friendship with Byron, Moore regarded himself as the keeper of His Lordship's flame; he of all men, and indeed poets, was always going to defend Byron's honour – by whatever means seemed necessary. At the time he also appeared to have right on his side. But posterity has gradually swung Hunt's way. If Hunt's strictures about Byron were out of character, written before he had allowed time for his Italian miseries to subside, his portrait of the noble poet turns out largely to have stood the test of time. 'The records and opinions of others who knew Byron in Italy . . . have confirmed the chief burden of Hunt's portrayal,' writes one twentieth-century Romantic scholar. At the time the formidable society hostess Lady Blessington was one of the few eyewitnesses with the courage to back Hunt, even adding some 'psychologically subtle' observations of her own which were 'quite as damaging' as his. According to Crabb Robinson, not always Hunt's closest ally, Her Ladyship 'went so far as to say that she thinks Leigh Hunt gave in the main a fair account of Lord Byron'.

More characteristic of Hunt was his contribution at the end of 1828 to a Christmas anthology entitled *Keepsake*, edited by Harrison Ainsworth. To a relieved Blunden this is *le vrai* Hunt. 'Perhaps I err,' he confesses, 'perhaps without the surge and speed of common demands he could not have achieved the tenderness, the fullness of these carecharming dreams' – as he goes on to quote what this, his greatest twentieth-century champion, considers Hunt's style as 'it should have been, could life have let him write when and how he desired': 'Sometimes music poured in, as from a hundred fountains; and sometimes a goddess called. Not a leaf then stirred; but the silence trembled. I heard Venus speak; which was as if there should never be sorrow more.'

And perhaps Blunden's sensibility, for all its First World War battering, was closer to Hunt's florid sentimentality than the less indulgent tastes of subsequent generations. His own dismay with Hunt's *Byron* was relieved by its more generous sections on other poets – 'his unlucky quarto was redeemed by the beautiful utterances on Shelley, Keats, Coleridge and Lamb' – and one virtue of Hunt's assault was that it drew attention away from Byron towards other second-generation Romantics to the point where the works of Shelley and Keats were first bracketed with those of Coleridge in a volume published by Galignani the following year.

Whatever the rights and wrongs of Hunt's evisceration of Byron's personality, there is no doubt that, having earlier been one of the first to praise his work, he was ahead of his time – as he always had been, since their first emergence in his life – as a connoisseur of the genius of Shelley and Keats. Already, in his Italian sonnet, he had predicted Shelley's immortality; as for Keats, it would take a century and more to acknowledge the truth of Hunt's 1828 prophecy that he would find a lasting place in English poetry, let alone 'be known hereafter in English literature, emphatically, as the *young* poet'.

The months following publication of *Lord Byron and Some of His Contemporaries* saw Hunt feverishly defending himself against a host of accusations in long, draining articles for the *Examiner* and the *Morning Chronicle*, while contributing more relaxed essays to a short-lived but significant weekly under his editorship called the *Companion*. Here he also published a delightful poem, 'The Royal Line', guying the monarchy via the mnemonics of school history lessons. But Colburn wisely talked him out of including his further thoughts on Byron in the second edition of the book, along with a candid 'attempt to estimate my own character', on the self-evident grounds that it would do 'more harm than good'.

Not published until thirty-four years after Hunt's death, in the *Athenæum*, and then in a turn-of-the-century study by R. Brimley Johnson, Hunt's assessments of himself would really better have lain unpublished for ever. 'I am at once the sickliest and most sanguine of my race, the liveliest and most thoughtful, the most social and the most solitary, the most indolent and the most laborious,' he opines. 'I am not naturally a teller of truth . . . In a family of men remarkable for their bravery, I am a timid person.'

Denied the gratification of offering such ammunition to his enemies, a far from timid Hunt instead went on the offensive in his preface
to the second edition, branding his *Blackwood's* hecklers 'unprincipled
cowards' and dismissing his *Quarterly* critic (Gifford) with a haughty 'I
am noticing this born slave more than I intended,' while writing off
Moore as a 'turn-spit'. That said, he gave ground by conceding that his
'spleen' perhaps made him 'undervalue' Byron's 'genius' – before
handing himself on a platter to one future literary opponent, then still
a teenage schoolboy, by owning somewhat archly that: 'The commonest rules of arithmetic were omitted in my education.'

He said much the same to Francis Jeffrey, former editor of the
Edinburgh Review and now Lord Advocate of Scotland, in a long letter
soliciting work. 'My education was in one respect remarkable, nay singular, perhaps unlike that of one man in educated millions; & that is, that
by a very singular chance I received instruction in everything except the
commonest grounds of arithmetic. I taught myself addition, long after
everybody knows it; but to this day I cannot do a multiplication sum, nor
any other.' Pleading his case at great autobiographical length, avowing that
he became 'an author by choice, a politician by accident', Hunt went on:
'Money, for a long while, I literally never thought of, either to get or to
keep'; now, finding himself £800 in debt, he poured his heart out in
confessional detail to a Scottish grandee whom he had no reason to suppose sympathetic beyond a kind word or two about him from a mutual
friend. Telling Jeffrey more than he could possibly want to know about his
eight surviving offspring, Hunt even confessed that he had so many children only because of a prediction that his wife would die when she ceased
bearing children. There is, throughout, a note of real desperation:

> Mental labour, as to the degree of it which I undergo, is only trying
> to me because it is accompanied by bad health & unceasing anxiety.
> I have to run a race with daily wants, burthened with a large family,
> whose education I am forced to suspend, & not sure that I shall
> have bread for them any week to come. I mean, that if I break down
> from illness, and as I sometimes do, I have no receipts to look to
> (except what a slow & small subscription is now producing); & then
> debts, however small, accumulate; & these are added to the bur-
> thens with which I begin again; and thus for years past, I have been

making my new Pilgrim's Progress, running my race, falling & running again, with an addition to my load each time, & only saved from
destruction by the love of those whom I carry, and an invincible
delight which I take in the beauties of the creation round me. I love
& admire that creation, & think the very best of this world & its
capabilities, and am heartily willing, & accustomed, to attribute my
mischances to my own want of thought in the first instance, and to
evil in nothing. All I wish is, that after great suffering and patient
effort, I should be put in a way, if possible, of securing myself work,
without the drawbacks that tend to deprive me of the fruits of it.

There is no record of any answer. Hunt was so hard up at this time
that he was obliged to give houseroom to a bailiff. The family, Marianne
wrote pseudonymously to Brougham, was enduring 'great privation:
indeed, he has not means to provide for the *coming week. Such is the
fact* . . . a friend called some days ago, & found him writing hand wrapt
up in blankets, not allowing himself a fire, meat is an article seldom
seen on the table'. Hunt was 'the same as ever', Mary Shelley told
Trelawny, 'a person whom all most love & regret'.

The death of his old enemy George IV in 1830, swiftly followed by
the second French Revolution, moved Hunt to a burst of political
zeal – 'What hope in it! What an anticipation of centuries!' – and
level-headed pessimism about the future of the monarchy: 'We hold it
to be the inevitable course of things that the example of the Anglo-
Americans will go round the globe, and that men will govern
themselves.' Otherwise, with significant exceptions such as Ireland
and political reform, poverty would see him increasingly embracing the
'cheerful sentimentalism' in his nature, and his writing, at the expense
of his former political animus. He could not now risk libel costs, let
alone imprisonment, so instead he risked his health with constant out-
pourings reflecting 'the sunny side of everything'.

Since the Byron book, he had worked as hard as ever, launching new
journals such as the (weekly) *Companion* (which lasted from 9 January
to 23 July 1828), the (weekly) *Chat of the Week* (5 June to 28 August
1830) and the (daily) *Tatler* (4 September 1830 to 13 February 1832).
He also contributed more 'Wishing Cap' papers to *Tait's Edinburgh
Magazine* and miscellaneous articles to the *True Sun*. In the fourteenth

edition of the *Tatler* he mourned the death of Hazlitt, with whom he had shared so long and fruitful a dialogue. 'I did it all myself, except when too ill,' he recalled of his work on the *Tatler* at this desperate time, 'and illness seldom hindered me either from supplying the review of a book, going every night to the play, or writing the notice of the play the same night at the printing-office. The consequence was that the work, slight as it looked, nearly killed me.' Illness and exhaustion had also seen him 'obliged for some time to be carried every morning to the *True Sun* offices in a hackney-coach'.

Twice he had moved to cheaper lodgings, from Cromwell Lane, Old Brompton to 18 Elm Tree Road, St John's Wood, and thence back to York Buildings, Marylebone, where he had lived in 1818. But still he could not win the eternal battle to house and feed his family. Only in such dire straits could Hunt have written so demeaning a letter – and started selling his beloved books, including even his trusty *Parnaso Italiano*, a collection of the Italian poets running to fifty-two volumes. 'This book aided Spenser himself in filling my English walks with visions of gods and nymphs, of enchantments and magicians,' he said forlornly. 'The reader might be surprised to know to what a literal extent such was the case.' The pain of giving it up was 'like that of a violinist parting with his instrument'.

Hunt's older sons were now leaving their teens, yet still not financially independent of their long-suffering parents. In 1831, when their eldest child, Thornton, turned twenty-one, Mary Shelley sighed that 'Leigh Hunt's sons, now young men, do not contribute a penny towards their own support.' Thornton himself had taken art lessons, thinking to become a painter, but soon found himself feeling sick at the smell of paint. He was still chiefly occupied anyway as secretary to his father – as he would remain for another five years, until he followed him into journalism after marrying and making Hunt a grandfather.

In 1834 Thornton wed Katharine (Kate) Gliddon, whose brother John would later marry the Hunts' eldest daughter, Mary (the child delivered by Hunt himself in the Surrey jail). Even after his marriage Thornton continued to live at home with his parents, enforcing another move to a larger house in the 'unfashionable, rustic' district of Chelsea, 4 [now 22] Upper Cheyne Row. After the birth of his first child Thornton took gainful employment on the staff of the *Constitutional*, then edited by his father's friend Laman Blanchard. Not until 1838, when he was a twenty-eight-year-old father of two, did Thornton finally leave home – and then only because his work took him north to Stockport, as editor of the *North Cheshire Reformer*. 'My hand-in-hand companion has at length quitted me for the first time in his life,' sighed his father. 'You may judge how I feel; but it is for the best.'

In 1840 Thornton returned to London to join the staff of the *Spectator*; fifteen years later, to his father's personal pride, he would become editor of the *Daily Telegraph*. Back in the 1830s, however, Thornton seems to have inherited Hunt's sickly timidity rather than his professional prowess. In 1833, when he was twenty-two, Hunt sent him to visit friends in Scotland. He got as far as Edinburgh before turning back, pleading illness, nervous fatigue and homesickness.

Thornton's intended destination was Dumfries, and Craigenputtock, home of his father's new friends Thomas and Jane Carlyle. In February of the previous year Carlyle had invited Hunt to tea. Eighteen thirty-two was already an *annus mirabilis* for Hunt, with its combination of the Reform Bill, first publication by Edward Moxon of his collected *Poetical Works* and the appearance of his only work of prose fiction, *Sir Ralph Esher*, which survived mixed reviews to go through three editions in four years. Hunt had in fact finished his 'sort of literary historical essay – a species of unconcealed forgery, after the manner of a more critical and cultivated Pepys' all of two years earlier, but Colburn had withheld it in the wake of the Byron furore; even now he insisted on publishing it anonymously.

Hunt's introduction to his 1832 *Poetical Works*, much admired to this day, constituted his poetical credo: 'The first quality of a poet is imagination, or that faculty by which the subtlest idea is given us of the nature or condition of any one thing, by illustration from another, or by the inclusion of remote affinities.' The volume was supported by a subscription which garnered some illustrious names: Coleridge and Wordsworth, Godwin and Southey, Isaac D'Israeli and Francis Jeffrey, the Lords Holland, Dover and Mulgrave. Perhaps, as in his teens, all this unwonted success briefly went to his head. In the wake of the Reform Bill and these rare literary triumphs, 'Leigh Hunt's self-importance' seemed 'ludicrous' to Brougham's secretary, Sir Denis Le

Marchant, at a party at Bulwer-Lytton's. Hunt apparently spoke of the 'persecution' he had suffered and 'observed that it had great results', crowing, 'Yes, we worked this revolution . . .'

It took the previous generation – like Brougham himself – to know that, more than most, Hunt really had suffered in the vanguard of reform. In time (all of five years later), no less a figure than John Stuart Mill would apologise to him in writing that he and others had missed the chance to put on record 'my sense of your great merits as a political journalist, & of what you have done & suffered in the cause'.

If, at the time, Hunt made a meal of his long-awaited moment of triumph, Carlyle was just the man to bring him back down to earth. This welcome new arrival in Hunt's social life, still somewhat dislocated by the response to his assault on Byron, was the courteous Scotsman's response to a letter from Hunt – though one of many, from admirers including Macaulay, Macvey Napier and Mill – in praise of his article in the *Edinburgh Review* entitled 'Characteristics', still arguing the case for political reform. After this, their first meeting, Carlyle noted in his journal that he found Hunt 'a pleasant, innocent, ingenious man, filled with Epicurean philosophy', but 'likeable for all that'.

Hunt's charm must have come as a surprise; a decade earlier Carlyle had written sourly to his future wife that 'Leigh Hunt writes "wishing caps" for the *Examiner*, and lives on the lightest of diets at Pisa.' Five years on, in a letter to his brother, he noted the 'continued abuse' Hunt was enduring for his 'Byron' book.

Carlyle was thirty-six, Hunt now forty-seven. The dour Calvinist and his formidable wife Jane, both strict Scottish Presbyterians, made unlikely new friends for the vaguely 'deist' Hunt, who had sent a copy of his own 'Christianism' with his letter to 'the writer of the article in the *Edinburgh Review*'. Hunt, for instance, still followed Shelley in advocating 'open' marriages, even if he did not himself practise what he preached; Carlyle, nonetheless, took an immediate liking to this 'most interesting, pitiable, loveable man'. Besides, he had met Hunt's old foe Lockhart the previous year, over a London dinner table filled with the exiled Scottish literary mafia, about whom he fumed in his journal: 'Literary *men*! They are not worthy to be the valets of such.'

On first meeting him, Hunt noted that 'the finest eyes, in every sense of the word, which I have ever seen in a man's head' – and he had

'seen many fine ones', not least Wordsworth's – 'are those of Thomas
Carlyle'. Carlyle, for his part, seemed to take to the entire Hunt
brood. Even of young Thornton he observed: 'There looks through
him that fair openness of soul which, besides its intrinsic price and
pricelessness, I have found a sweet presage of other gifts.' Hence the
invitation to Craigenputtock, whither the Carlyles had already planned
to retreat from London in the spring of 1832, just after this first meeting with Hunt. But the two writers stayed in touch by letter, their
topics ranging from Diderot and Goethe, Schiller and Shelley to the
French Revolution and the sanctity of marriage. In mid-1833 Hunt
would seem to be pushing his luck when he writes to the doctrinaire
Carlyle of marriage as 'an experiment which I should hardly think can
be said to have succeeded in the world, even in this chaste & hypocrit-
ical & Mamma-sacrificing country of England', where 'a sixth part of
the poor female sex' (i.e. prostitutes) were sacrificed 'for the conven-
ience of prudential young gentlemen & the preservation of chastity in
the five remaining classes of shrews & scolds, & women good & bad, &
wives happy, unhappy, & crimcon-ical'. But still Carlyle indulged this
libertine. 'We make an exception of him,' he wrote to his brother
Jack, 'tho' nowise of the doctrine as held by him.'

When Carlyle returned to London two years later, in 1834, it was
with Hunt that he went house-hunting in Chelsea. On hearing that he
planned to move back south, Hunt had written recommending Chelsea,
where he himself now lived in 'a delightful house, big enough for ten children . . . all wainscoted &c for 30 guineas'. Hunt was asked to 'fish'
Chelsea for a similar one for the Carlyles. In vain did the frugal Carlyle
himself search Bayswater and Kensington before setting out to explore
Chelsea with Hunt. En route he took tea *chez* Hunt, leaving a vivid
description of their 'indescribable, dreamlike household':

'The Frau Hunt lay drowsing on cushions "sick, sick" with a thousand
temporary ailments, the young imps all agog to see me jumped hither
and thither, one strange goblin-looking-fellow about sixteen, ran min-
istering about with tea-kettles for us: it was all a mingled lazaretto and
tinkers' camp, yet with a certain joy and nobleness at the heart of it;
faintly resembling some of the maddest scenes in *Wilhelm Meister*
[Goethe's novel, which Carlyle had translated in 1824], only
madder . . .' As the Hunt children gave him tea, and 'would fain have

given me the Husband's shoes', Carlyle concluded they were treating him 'à la Shelley', for 'I was to be the new Shelley.'

He soon 'got out' with Hunt, Carlyle told his wife, 'in wide quest of houses. Chelsea lies low close by the side of the river; has an ancient, here and there dilapidated look; the houses apparently a tenth cheaper; some market articles, especially coals said likewise to be cheaper. I liked it little; and, to say truth, cared not to be so near the poetic Tinkerdom.'

Nonetheless, after further consultations with Jane ('Let Hunt say what he will'), Carlyle soon settled for a house round the corner at 5 Cheyne Row, then available for £35 a year. The following May, after another visit to the Hunt ménage at Upper Cheyne Row, he found that little had changed: 'Hunt's household in Cheyne Row, Chelsea. Nondescript! Unutterable! Mrs Hunt asleep on cushions; four or five beautiful, strange, gipsy-looking children running about in undress, whom the lady ordered to get us tea. The eldest boy, Percy – a sallow, black-haired youth of sixteen, with a kind of dark cotton nightgown on, went whirling about like a familiar, providing everything . . .'

But Carlyle was not going to let his neighbour's domestic style – 'hugger-mugger, unthrift, and sordid collapse, once for all' – get in the way of a stimulating friendship. Within days of their arrival Hunt was continually sending round notes; most evenings he would come round in person 'before bedtime, and give us an hour of the prettiest melodious discourse'. Two weeks later: 'Hunt is always ready to go and walk with me, or sit and talk with me to all lengths if I want him. He comes in once a week (when invited, for he is very modest), takes a cup of tea, and sits discoursing in his brisk, fanciful way till supper time, and then cheerfully eats a cup of porridge (to sugar only), which he praises to the skies, and vows he will make his supper of at home.' Closer acquaintance had Carlyle deeming Hunt 'a man of thoroughly London make, such as you would not find elsewhere, and I think about the *best* possible to be made of his sort: an airy, crotchety, most copious clever talker, with an honest undercurrent of reason too, but unfortunately not the deepest, not the most practical – or rather it is the most unpractical ever man dealt in. His hair is grizzled, eyes black-hazel, complexion of the clearest dusky brown; a thin glimmer of a smile plays over a face of cast-iron gravity. He never laughs – can only titter, which I think indicates his worst deficiency . . .'

Soon Hunt was round at the Carlyles' 'almost nightly', at least three or four times a week. He turned up 'always neatly dressed, was thoroughly courteous, friendly of spirit and talked – like a singing bird. Good insight, plenty of a kind of humour, too; I remember little warbles in the turns of his fine voice which were full of fun and charm. We gave him Scotch porridge to supper ("nothing in nature so interesting and delightful"); *she* played him Scotch tunes, a man he to understand and feel them well.' His talk was 'often enough (perhaps at first oftenest) Literary-Biographical, Autobiographical, wandering into Criticism, Reform of Society, Progress, etc etc – on which latter points he gradually found me very shocking I believe – so fatal to his rose-coloured visions on the subject. An innocent-hearted, but misguided, in fact rather foolish, *un*practical and often much-suffering man.'

Alongside the qualified affection in which he held Hunt, Carlyle retained a rather grim fascination with the style in which he chose to live. To Hunt himself, his Chelsea house had a 'sense of quiet and repose', not least in the small upstairs room which he cordoned off as 'a sanctum, into which no perturbation was to enter, except to calm itself with religious and cheerful thoughts (a room thus appropriated in a house appears to me an excellent thing)'. Carlyle saw it through different eyes:

His house excels all you have ever read of – a poetical *Tinkerdom*, without parallel even in literature. In his family room, where are a sickly large wife and a whole school of well-conditioned wild children, you will find half a dozen rickety old chairs gathered from half a dozen different hucksters, and all seeming engaged, and just pausing, in a violent hornpipe. On these and around them and over the dusty table and ragged carpet lie all kinds of litter – books, paper, egg-shells, scissors, and last night when I was there, the torn half of a quartern-loaf.

His own room above stairs, into which I alone strive to enter, he keeps cleaner. It has only two chairs, a bookcase and a writing-table; yet the noble Hunt receives you in his Tinkerdom in the spirit of a king, apologizes for nothing, places you in the best seat, takes a window-sill himself if there is no other, and there folding closer his loose-flowing 'muslin cloud' of a printed night-gown, in which he always writes, commences the liveliest dialogue on philosophy and the prospects of man (who is to be beyond measure 'happy' yet); which again he will courteously terminate the moment you are bound to go.

He added that Hunt was 'to be used kindly but with discretion'.

Carlyle considered it 'rather a comfort' to have such 'honest, friendly people' as neighbours – 'at least an honest, friendly man of that sort'. As if strangely fascinated, he further described Hunt at this time as a 'chivalrous' figure: 'Dark complexion (a trace of the African, I believe), copious clean strong black hair, beautifully-shaped head, fine beaming serious hazel eyes; *seriousness* and intellect the main expression of his face (to our surprise at first).' Hunt would 'lean on his elbow against the mantelpiece (fine clean, elastic figure too, he had five feet ten or more), and look round him nearly in silence, before taking leave for the night: "as if I were a *Lar*," said he once, "or permanent Household God here!" (such his polite Ariel-like way)'. On another occasion, 'rising from his *Lar* attitude', Hunt took his leave – 'voice very fine, as if in sport of parody, yet with something of very sad perceptible' – with 'While I to sulphurous and penal fire', leaving Mrs Carlyle 'almost in tears' at the thought of the home life to which Hunt must return.

Himself a volatile, temperamental man, Carlyle would occasionally lose patience with Hunt's eccentricities, which saw them estranged for a while that summer. 'His theory of life and mine have already declared themselves to be from top to bottom at variance, which shocks him considerably; to me his talk is occasionally pleasant, is always clear and lively, but all too *foisonless*, baseless, and shallow. He has a theory that the world is, or should be, a gingerbread Lubberland, where evil (that is, pain) shall never come: a theory in very considerable favour here, which to me is pleasant as streams of unambrosial dishwater, a thing I simply shut up my mouth against, as the shortest way.'

In time Carlyle would reach a 'settled tolerance' of Hunt's sunny utopianism, a philosophy very different from his own. In the interim he occasionally lost patience with him, confiding harsher judgements to his journal: 'Hunt is limited, even bigoted, and seeing that I utterly dissent from him, fears that I despise him; a kindly clever man, fantastic, brilliant, shallow, of one topic, loquacious, unproductive.'

Carlyle's wife was simultaneously losing patience with Hunt's. In a letter that autumn to her mother-in-law, Margaret, complaining at the want of Scottish thrift in English housewives, Jane Carlyle reported that she had told Mrs Hunt one day that she had been very busy painting. 'What?' asked Marianne, 'is it a portrait?' Oh no, replied Jane Carlyle, 'something of more importance: a large wardrobe'. Marianne responded that she could never imagine herself undertaking that kind of work: 'How could I have patience for such things?'

'And so,' continued her irritated neighbour, 'having no patience for them herself, what is the result? She is every other day reduced to borrow[ing] my tumblers, my teacups, even – a cupful of porridge, a few spoonfuls of tea are begged of me, because "Missus has got company and happens to be out of the article" – in plain unadorned English, because "Missus is the most wretched of managers and is often at the point of having not copper in her purse."'

Like Haydon's nearly twenty years before, Jane Carlyle's patience with Marianne's 'borrowing' was swiftly wearing thin. Two months later she is telling her mother-in-law: 'Mrs Hunt I shall soon be quite terminated with, I foresee. She torments my life out with borrowing. She actually borrowed the brass fender the other day and I had difficulty in getting it out of her hands – irons, glasses, tea-cups, silver spoons are in constant requisition – and when one sends for them, the whole number can never be found.' Some of Mrs Carlyle's remarks suggest that Marianne had also taken to the bottle by now; that this may have been the case for some years, as yet unknown to her husband, is suggested by an 1828 letter from Mary Shelley referring to Marianne's 'consolation'.

'Acid-tongued' Jane Carlyle could be equally scornful about Marianne's husband, now her own husband's close friend. The following year, while Carlyle was away on an extended trip to Scotland, his wife paused for light relief in an otherwise testy letter by telling him anecdotes about the 'devilish' and 'drunkish' Marianne Hunt at a tea party given by her friend Susan Hunter. But her real venom was reserved for Leigh Hunt, who himself had behaved little better. Ever flirtatious, Hunt

sang, talked like a pen-gun [a toy air-gun made from a quill] even to [Susan Hunter], who drank it all in like nectar, while my mother looked cross enough, and I had to listen to the whispered confidences of Mrs Hunt.

But for me, who was declared to be grown 'quite prim and elderly', I believe they would have communicated their mutual experiences in a retired window-seat till morning. 'God bless you, Miss [Hunter],' was repeated by Hunt three several times in tones of ever-increasing pathos and tenderness, as he handed her downstairs behind me. [Susan], for once in her life, seemed past speech. At the bottom of the stairs a demur took place. I saw nothing; but I heard, with my wonted glegness – what think you? – a couple of handsome smacks! and then an almost inaudibly soft, 'God bless you, Miss [Hunter]!' Now just remember what sort of looking woman is [Susan Hunter]; and figure their transaction! If he had kissed me it would have been intelligible, but Susan Hunter of all people!

Beyond her irritation at having had to listen to Marianne's 'whispered confidences', is there a note of jealousy in the righteous indignation of Jane Carlyle (known to her husband and close friends as 'Jenny')? Somehow it must have reached Hunt's ears, evidently causing him some amusement. Three years later he braved Jenny's Scottish wrath in a charming little verse conceit entitled 'Rondeau', first published in the *Monthly Chronicle* of November 1838, which has since joined 'Abou Ben Adhem' as one of Hunt's few poems to merit such descriptions as 'best-known', even 'best-loved', certainly 'most anthologised':

> Jenny kissed me when we met,
> Jumping from the chair she sat in;
> Time, you thief, who love to get
> Sweets into your list, put that in:
> Say I'm weary, say I'm sad,
> Say that health and wealth have missed me,
> Say I'm growing old, but add
> Jenny kissed me.

Whether or not Carlyle's crusty old wife actually had given Hunt a kiss, let alone leapt from her chair to do so, we will never know; no such unlikely moment is documented in any of the relevant parties' letters or journals. Carlyle himself testifies that Hunt was always 'chivalrous, polite, affectionate, respectful (especially to her)'. But Hunt could also be flirtatious; all his life, without having to make much effort, he was capable of bewitching women. We have Thornton Hunt's word for it that his father's 'animation, his striking appearance, his manly voice, its sweetness and flexibility, the exhaustless fancy to which it gave utterance, his almost breathlessly tender manner in saying tender things, his eyes deep, bright and genial, with a dash of cunning, his delicate yet emphatic homage' all combined to make him a 'dangerous' man among women.

But Hunt was also a bit of a prude. He would shrink back from such danger, 'the quickest to take alarm, confessing that "to err is human" as if he *had* erred in any but the most theoretical or imaginative sense'. At the slightest suggestion of impropriety he would 'give you a sermon on the sins of the fancy, hallowed by quotations from the Bible – of which he was as much a master as any clergyman – and illustrated by endless quotations from the poets, to prove the fearful peril of the first step; and *also* to prove that, though men, they were not bad men – that it is not for us to cast the first stone, and that, probably, if they had been different, their poetry would have suffered, to the grievous loss of the library and mankind . . .'

Despite all this, it is intriguing to note that in Hunt's original manuscript version of the poem, before publication, the kisser's name was originally 'Nelly'; and that perfect word 'weary' in its charming fifth line began life as 'jaundiced'.

In a subsequent meditation on the whole subject of *rondeaux* ('pray pronounce the word in good honest old French', he required, 'with the *eaux*, like the beating up of eggs for a pudding'), otherwise buried deep in an essay on Pope, Hunt claimed that his was the first to be written since the Augustan era. The form had fallen into desuetude 'owing to the lesser animal spirits prevailing in this country'; of several reasons why it was worth reviving, the fifth and most important was that 'love sometimes makes people imprudent'.

His own 'Rondeau', Hunt avowed, 'was written on a real occasion, and therefore may be presumed to have had the aforesaid impulse. We must add, lest our egotism should be thought still greater on the occasion than it is, that the lady was a great lover of books and impulsive writers: and that it was our sincerity as one of them which obtained for us the delightful compliment from a young enthusiast to an old one.'

'A sort of literary Robin Hood'

1834–40

'We have a kindness for Mr Leigh Hunt,' wrote Thomas Macaulay in the *Edinburgh Review* of January 1841. 'We form our judgment of him only from events of universal notoriety, from his own works, and from the works of other writers, who have generally abused him in the most rancorous manner. But, unless we are greatly mistaken, he is a very clever, a very honest, and a very good-natured man. We can clearly discern, together with many merits, many faults both in his writings and his conduct. But we really think that there is hardly a man living whose merits have been so grudgingly allowed, and whose faults have been so cruelly expiated.'

This most elegant and fair-minded of tributes ushered in a decade which would gradually treat the ageing Hunt more kindly, seeing his fortunes rise to the point of his becoming a grand old man of letters with a state pension, a candidate for the poet laureateship on the deaths of Southey and Wordsworth. In the meantime the 1830s remained an incessant struggle to stay financially afloat – though continuing propitiously enough, for now, with some unexpected public compliments to mark his fiftieth birthday (and the launch of his latest magazine) in the autumn of 1834.

'Fortune has not smiled upon him,' sympathised *Fraser's Magazine* while according Hunt a niche in its hallowed 'Gallery of Literary

Characters' and the accolade of an engraving by the cartoonist of the moment, Daniel Maclise. 'The party to which he formerly attached himself is in power, but all his old labours in the libel line on their behalf are forgotten. Those who abused the Prince Regent with far greater virulence than Hunt ever did are high in office, and glorying in their elevation. They have of course left him to struggle as they can. We hope that his struggling is successful – we understand, indeed, that his *Journal* has, as it deserves to have, a prosperous sale. It is as refreshing as his former productions, and of a pleasanter spirit. He has been an excessively ill-used man in many respects, and by none more than by Lord Byron, and those who panegyrise his lordship.'

This welcome reassessment was echoed by similar sentiments in, of all places, *Blackwood's*. Under the penname 'Christopher North', John Wilson decided that Hunt's fiftieth birthday was the right moment to make amends for his part in Lockhart's fusillades of twenty and more years earlier:

Shepherd: Leigh Hunt loved Shelley.
North: And Shelley truly loved Leigh Hunt. Their friendship was honourable to both, for it was as disinterested as sincere; and I hope Gurney will let a certain person in the City understand that I treat his offer of a review of Mr Hunt's *London Journal* with disdain. If he has anything to say against us or against that gentleman, either conjunctly or severally, let him out with it in some other channel, and I promise him a touch and a taste of the crutch. He talks to me of Maga's desertion of principle; but if he were a Christian – nay, a man – his heart and head too would tell him that the Animosities are mortal, but the Humanities live for ever – and that Leigh Hunt has more talent in his little finger than the pulling prig, who has taken upon himself to lecture Christopher North in a scrawl teeming with forgotten falsehoods. Mr Hunt's *London Journal*, my dear James, is not only beyond all comparison, but out of all sight, the most entertaining and instructive of all the cheap periodicals; and when laid, as it duly is once a week, on my breakfast-table, it lies there – but is not permitted to lie long – like a spot of sunshine dazzling the snow.

The first edition of *Leigh Hunt's London Journal* was published on 2

April 1834. The magazine's masthead proclaimed it strictly non-controversial, aspiring only 'to assist the enquiring, animate the struggling, and sympathize with all'. Full folio size, costing three-halfpence and printed by his friend Charles Reynell, Hunt's umpteenth attempt to make money from his journalism swam into the mainstream of 'popular literature' then being made popular by such publishers and editors as Charles Knight and (in Edinburgh) the Chambers brothers. He was given a poem by Carlyle, and several from Landor, whose 'Ode to a Friend' was addressed directly to the journal's eponymous editor:

> And live, too, thou for happier days
> Whom Dryden's force and Spenser's fays
> Have heart and soul possessed:
> Growl in grim London, he who will;
> Revisit thou Maiano's hill,
> And swell with pride his sunburnt breast.
> Old Redi in his easy chair,
> With varied chant awaits thee here,
> And here are voices in the grove,
> Aside my house, that makes me think
> Bacchus is coming down to drink
> To Ariadne's love.

But Hunt, as always, did most of the work himself, commissioning and editing the few contributions he did not write personally – most famously, in this instance, his commentary on Keats's poem 'The Eve of St Agnes', which he reprinted in full in the course of his own astute appraisal, still well ahead of its time in its appreciation of Keats's significance. As so often, however, his efforts were ultimately in vain; for all its high-quality content, the journal lasted barely a year before being obliged to merge at the end of May 1835 with Knight's *Printing Machine* – an unhappy marriage which ended in oblivion by the end of that same year.

The journal had given Hunt the chance for some legitimate boasting about his past talent-spotting successes – 'The Editor of this Journal believes he may say that, in the various periodicals which he has conducted, it has been his good fortune to introduce more talent and

genius to the public than any other' – while wryly conceding the lim-
itation of his own creative talents: 'It has ever been his boast that he has
been a sort of literary Robin Hood, and got companions to act under
him who have beaten him at his own weapons.'

The timing of this latest literary failure could not have been worse.
Long accustomed to financial hardship, the Hunt household now
entered sharp decline, in direct proportion to Marianne's swift descent
into alcoholism, which saw her behaving ever more erratically and
soliciting handouts from her husband's friends behind his back. In
1835, with the couple still in Upper Cheyne Row, the marriage was in
such bad shape that Marianne began keeping a defensive, self-pitying
diary: 'I commence this journal for three reasons: first, because it will
be to a certain extent a memorandum book in matters of business, and
secondly, because it is a great settler of disputes; and thirdly, because it
is a great help to the regulation of one's conduct and feeling and a check
upon bad passions etc.'

Years of stress, struggle and illness had finally taken their toll on the
Hunts' marriage. Always very different characters, who had found
some common way through so much adversity, Leigh and Marianne had
now become what, in their son Thornton's words, they had long been
without acknowledging it: strangers. 'The inevitable dictates of daily
life, it is true – instincts of affection, the call of hunger, the need for
clothing and lodging, the attractions of society – had a power over
both, but in the most remarkably opposite degrees and modes; the
same thing which to one was aliment and grave delight affording to the
other no more than "amusement"; and of course with thoughts and sensations so diverse, they were actuated by motives so different, that
lengthening years only made them, in the longer portion of their faithful and unsevered union, strangers.'

By that summer, while Hunt was on an extended visit to Wales with
a young new friend named Egerton Webbe (a musician and poet who
was to die tragically young), matters had evidently reached some sort
of impasse. As Hunt charmed a potential patron in Mrs Anna Maria
Dashwood, a wealthy admirer, his letters to family and friends arrived
with instructions that they should not be shown to Marianne. 'I am sent
to Coventry!' she complained to her diary. 'Sometimes I believe my
Henry believes me to be made of stone & that I have not the common

feelings and emotions of my sex – What can I do? I am up in the morning to have his breakfast by *seven*. I cook his dinner to have it as nearly as possible by 3 – I make his bread – I abstain from going to see my mother and my dear sister Nancy to please him. Oh Henry you may get a cleverer, you may get a handsomer wife, but you will never get one to *love* you dearer than your despised Marianne.'

Contemporary accounts suggest that Hunt, however irritated by his wife's behaviour, did not himself notice a decline in her health and household management all too evident to others. Even her drinking she managed to keep from him; or perhaps he turned a supposedly innocent blind eye. One visitor at this time spoke of Hunt's 'mismanaging, unthrifty wife, the most barefaced, persevering, pertinacious of mendicants. Whenever she made a good collection she was sure to be seen the next day, with her daughters and a son or two, driving about London in what the French call a *voiture de remise*, and what we used to designate a "glass coach".'

In her own son's description, Marianne Hunt was 'the reverse of handsome, and without accomplishments; but she had a pretty figure, beautiful black hair, which reached down to her knees, magnificent eyes, and a very unusual turn for plastic art. She was an active and a thrifty housewife, until the curious malady with which she was seized totally undermined her strength.' So what was this mystery ailment? Her discreet husband blamed 'a well-intended but ill-advised treatment of her constitution in girlhood' that had 'brought on a life-long spitting of blood, which was only lessened by the years of acute rheumatism, that in depriving her of all power of locomotion ultimately killed her'. If Marianne's condition was truly consumption, as this passage has led some to conjecture, it is indeed 'surprising that she should have survived to the age of sixty-nine'.

So what kept this unlikely couple together all those storm-tossed years? After the deaths of both parents, Thornton painted a very candid portrait of his mother:

Fate joined [Leigh Hunt] with one who shared his taste for plastic art, with a greater natural aptitude, but without culture or the power of acquiring it; with a child-like sense of verse, never matured; with an almost equally child-like sense of economy which the bookworm long believed to be nearly perfect. United by strong affection and love for their progeny, what had this couple in common? He was regarded as a stranger to real life, and he learned to be content with a total ignorance of the sphere comprising 'the butcher and the baker'; she could follow a little way into the domain of sculpture and painting, a still less way into the English library; but could not, even from his full conversation, which seldom drew from her any steadfast attention, form so much as a conjecture of the fields around Parnassus which were his pasture and habitual haunt.

Did Hunt need Marianne to share his love of poetry? One skill of hers in which he delighted was the early-nineteenth-century art of cutting profiles. Those still in existence include studies of Byron, Keats and Hunt himself, who proudly boasts that she 'surprised everybody with her ability in cutting profiles of her friends in paper, so true to the spirit as well as letter, as to make them laugh at the instantaneous recognition of the likeness'. The Scottish painter Sir David Wilkie, Haydon's friend, said 'he couldn't but wonder to think how *the hard scissors* could treat the lips in particular with so much expression'. When writing his memoirs, Haydon himself paid Marianne the compliment of asking her for a silhouette or 'pen sketch' of Byron. She was also a proficient sculptress, producing a bust of Shelley of which copies were made in 1830, at their request, for Carlyle and the rising young poet Robert Browning. Hunt used to say that the likeness was so strong as to 'startle' him from time to time.

It was around this time that Hunt's troubles with Marianne, which would never again quite ease, were compounded by even more wayward behaviour from their son John, who was embarked upon a downward spiral which would have impressed Hogarth. 'After breakfasting with a friend,' according to the engraver W.J. Linton, a family friend, John 'would borrow a book, and pledge it at the nearest pawnbroker's; he would try to borrow money in his father's name from his father's friends'; on one such occasion Hunt himself was in the house when John came calling, so he beat a hasty retreat. According to his brother Thornton, John 'used his father's means, and sometimes his father's name; and it is almost certain that this abuse was extended to cases which have never been traced. The consequences visited Leigh

Hunt, sometimes in money lost, sometimes in more painful forms.' If Hunt knew about this at all, let alone its full extent, he kept it firmly to himself. But John's behaviour at home grew so wild that his father was forced into one of the least characteristic acts of his life; in 1834 he excluded John from the household.

A bad year was crowned at its close by the death of Charles Lamb, Hunt's most steadfast friend and colleague since their schooldays at Christ's Hospital. '[Lamb] was only at his ease in the old arms of humanity,' wrote a forlorn Hunt in the first issue of his *London Journal* for 1835, 'and she loved and comforted him like one of her wisest, though weakest children'. Hunt's obituary of his friend ended with a vision of Death looking benevolently at Lamb and claiming his kind word, for 'now and then, as if he would cram into one moment the spleen of years, he would throw out a startling and morbid subject for reflection, perhaps in no better shape than a pun; for he was a great punster'.

For some mutual friends, notably Procter, this hastily written assessment did Lamb's memory scant service; Hunt was roundly told of universal dismay that he had treated their late friend so coldly. So, at an already difficult time, he found himself drawn into a public row he would much rather have avoided. 'What man,' he protested to Forster, 'has praised him more frequently and warmly than myself in his life-time?'

Hunt's mind was elsewhere. England was at peace, as it had been throughout the two decades since Waterloo; two more such would follow, as it transpired, before war in the Crimea. But it was a fragile peace; the English remained suspicious of the French and a new enemy was emerging in the shape of an increasingly belligerent Russia. In 1830–1 British public opinion had been outraged by the ferocity with which the Russians put down a Polish revolt, moving the *Edinburgh Review* to declare that 'two great antagonist principles now divide Europe – freedom and despotism'. Now, in the mid-1830s, the British Mediterranean Squadron was on stand-by to defend Constantinople in the event of a Russian attack.

Hunt made no mention of these matters in his *London Journal*, pre-ferring to maintain its tranquil atmosphere. 'There are green fields in the world, as well as fields of battle,' he wrote in the issue of 3 September 1834, recalling his days as more of a polemicist: 'It would not be difficult for us, old soldiers as we are, and accustomed to rougher labours in former times, to summon up a little of our old battle-grip . . . But *cui bono*? Where would be the good of it? . . . We are at peace with all.'

By 4 March 1835, however, he was apologising to his readers for the absence of his usual leading article because he had been hard at work on a new poem – one of the finest he would ever write. 'Captain Sword and Captain Pen' would not be appearing in his *London Journal*, wrote Hunt the following week, because 'the Editor is determined to keep [the magazine] sequestered and serene from all sound of trouble and controversy, however conscientiously executed.' Intended 'to show the horrors of war, the false ideas of power produced in the minds of its leaders, and, by inference, the unfitness of those leaders for the government of the world', the poem was published as a separate volume by Charles Knight, to be reprinted four years later and republished, with voluminous notes, in 1849; Hunt also included an extract in his 1844 *Poetical Works*, reprinting it in full in the 1857 and 1860 editions.

The composition of his great pacifist poem, in the tranquillity of his 'sanctum' atop Upper Cheyne Row, cost Hunt dear. 'I was several times forced to quit my task by accesses of wonder and horror so overwhelming as to make me burst out in perspiration . . . Men of action are too apt to think an author, and especially a poet, dares and undergoes nothing as he peacefully sits by the fireside "indulging his muse". But the muse is sometimes an awful divinity.'

Driven by an ideological passion unusual in Hunt's verse, 'Captain Sword and Captain Pen' vividly depicts the horrors of war, for all its surface glamour, while maintaining his passionate conviction that the day will inevitably be won by 'all that is noblest in the human spirit'. His own fortunes were again at a low ebb, with debtor's jail a very real prospect, and his health suffering accordingly; somehow this seems to have contributed to the white heat in which the poem was forged. He was also squabbling with his neighbour Carlyle, who described him at this time as 'the miserablest man I ever sat and talked with', who nevertheless 'talks forever about happiness'. This eternal paradox in Hunt – a belief in the ultimate victory of the good, amid so much evidence in his life to the contrary – may be what Carlyle called 'innocent-hearted', but in this poem it combines with his uncomplicated sense of man's duty to combat evil to produce one of the most compelling and effective of all his works.

Hunt was not worried about any immediate prospect of war so much as the return to political power of 'Military Toryism'. With the dismissal in November 1834 of the Whig government which had enacted the Reform Bill, he saw the new Tory Prime Minister, Peel, as the poodle of the party's grand old man, the Duke of Wellington, who did indeed act as caretaker leader while Peel hurried home from an Italian holiday. 'Notwithstanding his abilities', warned Hunt in his postscript to the poem, Peel would turn out to be 'nothing but a servant of the aristo-cracy, and (more or less openly) of a barrack-master . . . Do we want a soldier at the head of us when there is nobody abroad to fight with?'

The poem's title may have been suggested to Hunt by the 'Captain Swing' riots of 1830 (so called because so many agrarian protesters 'swung' from the gallows if not deported). But Captain Sword is clearly modelled on Wellington, whose conservatism Hunt deplored while admiring his personal courage and sincerity. Hence, for all the Captain's ugly belligerence in the poem, there 'hasteth a tear from his old grey eye' as he looks on the battlefield piles of the dead, just as Wellington had wept after Waterloo. As for Captain Pen: apart from Hunt himself – and he does recall his own parade-ground days in some early lines – one obvious inspiration is the poem's dedicatee, Henry, Lord Brougham, who had defended Hunt in his youthful libel trial and gone on to become Lord Chancellor in Grey's Reformist ministry. In 1828 Brougham had attacked Wellington in the Commons, soon after he had become Prime Minister, in terms which might well have pro-vided the wellspring for Hunt's poem:

These are not times when the soldier only is abroad. Somebody of more importance has risen, who has reduced the soldier to nothing, even if he were ten thousand times more potent than he is. In the nineteenth century, new power bears sway: the Schoolmaster is abroad. [Cries of *Hear! Hear!*]. I will trust more to him, armed with his primer, than to the soldier with his bayonet. [*Hear! Hear!*]

Hunt's dedication hailed Brougham as 'The Promoter of Education; The Expediter of Justice; the Liberator from Slavery; And (What is the Rarest Virtue in a Statesman) Always a Denouncer of War.' But he had another, even more personal inspiration: 'The author of the present poem believes that he owes the worst part of his constitution to the illness and anxiety caused to one of the best of mothers, by the American War.'

If his mother's memory always kept Hunt in close touch with his feminine side, it also bred in him a constant readiness – highly unusual for his time – to acknowledge the literary work of women. In his *Companion* essays of the late 1820s he had not shrunk from identifying the weaknesses of some female poets and artists; now, given the unprecedented strength of women writers on the literary scene, his next publication was a gentler, female version of *The Feast of the Poets*, entitled *Blue-Stocking Revels, or, The Feast of the Violets*. Those admitted to Phoebus' Hall of Fame this time around ranged from Elizabeth Barrett ('I took her at first for a sister of Tennyson') via many less remembered names (Felicia Hemans, Letitia Landon, Hannah More, Mary Robinson, Anna Seward, Charlotte Smith, Mary Tighe) to his own Marianne ('But, what pleased me hugely, he called to my wife, / And said, "You have done Shelley's mood to the life"'). Softening his criticisms of earlier years, Hunt reserves his highest praise for Lady Ann Barnard, Anne Finch (Countess of Winchelsea) and above all Anna Letitia Barbauld.

The poem was intended for the *New Monthly Magazine*, but in 1836 its editorial chair was taken over by Hunt's long-time foe Theodore Hook; so he withdrew it. *Leigh Hunt's London Journal* had closed, after ninety-one numbers, in December 1835. Now, as fate would have it, a consortium of owners of the *Monthly Repository*, a flagging journal for 'progressive' (and largely female) minds, made a gift of it to Hunt. With his printer friend Reynell, he decided to try to 'make something of it'; contributors under his editorship included Landor, Carlyle, Browning and its previous editor, Richard Hengist Horne, an adventurer and critic who swiftly became a close friend.

Landor canvassed on its behalf, as did the literary hostess Lady Blessington, and at first Hunt saw the circulation grow 'imperceptibly, almost like a flower'. But the magazine's long-standing association

with the Dissenters proved fatal; after less than a year under his stewardship the *Repository* became the latest in his long line of literary
casualties. Hunt had 'done no better', noted Horne with unbecoming
satisfaction, in shedding its sectarian stigma; within a year, however,
Horne had developed something approaching hero worship for Hunt,
survivor of a greater literary age, to whom he dedicated his play *The
Death of Marlowe* as one who had 'long assisted largely and most successfully to educate the hearts and heads of both old and young'.

Blue-Stocking Revels Hunt dedicated to 'A.M.D.' – Anna Maria
Dashwood, the Welsh admirer who had granted him an annuity of
£100; when, upon her remarriage, she asked to be released from the
commitment, Hunt brusquely removed the dedication from the
poem's 1844 reprint. By now he had another welcome source of
income, thanks to the decision of his thirty-four-year-old publisher and
friend Edward Moxon to abandon writing his own poetry and concentrate solely on publishing. Described by Hunt as 'a bookseller
among poets, and a poet among booksellers', Moxon swiftly built a
reputation as a publisher with excellent taste in poets; thanks to Hunt's
counsel, his list soon included Hunt himself, Shelley, Keats, Coleridge,
Lamb, Southey, Clare, Wordsworth, Tennyson and, later, Browning.
'Moxon has no connexion,' joked Hunt, 'but with the select of the
earth.'

Tennyson was just the latest in the long line of young poets Hunt
had encouraged at the outset of his career, having been sent his first
published works by his friend Arthur Hallam. 'A genuine young poet,
who will by and by be an eminent one,' Hunt had taken the time and
trouble to write to Tennyson's publisher, William Tait, amid his own
financial crisis of 1832; five years later he would be referring to
Tennyson as 'our best living poet, next to Wordsworth'. Now his
dealings with Moxon coincided with what he regarded as a renewed
lease on his own poetic life. In the wake of 'Captain Sword and
Captain Pen', Hunt returned to more familiar themes, both lyrical and
playful, with a sudden burst of verse for the *New Monthly*. 'The stream,
or brooklet of poetry that is in me (such as it is) appears to me to have
got a new & stronger run in my old age,' he wrote to his latest new
friend, the 'literary and legal lion' Thomas Noon Talfourd, in the
summer of 1836. 'By and by, I will muster up confidence enough to

shew you a sample of it.' Besides his 'Songs and Chorus of the Flowers'
he had written some sonnets on 'Fish', 'which surpassed to my own
feeling at the moments, & its truth, fluency & facility, all that I ever
wrote [of] verse before. I have got a notion that my true vein is lyrical, mixed up with Indicatorial, & that I shall do something in verse
yet . . .'

The sonnets to which he refers, collectively titled 'The Fish, the
Man and the Spirit', first appeared in the *New Monthly* of June 1836.
Eight years later he would confide to G.J. De Wilde, editor of the
Northampton Mercury, that these were among his 'favourite' works,
rating them even above his *Foliage*. They have since joined the ranks of
his most anthologised.

> You strange, astonished-looking, angle-faced,
> Dreary-mouthed, gaping wretches of the sea,
> Gulping salt-water everlastingly,
> Cold-blooded, though with red your blood be graced,
> And mute, though dwellers in the roaring waste;
> And you, all shapes beside, that fishy be, –
> Some round, some flat, some long, all devilry,
> Legless, unloving, infamously chaste: –
>
> O scaly, slippery, wet, swift, staring wights,
> What is't ye do? What life lead? eh, dull goggles?
> How do ye vary your vile days and nights?
> How pass your Sundays? Are ye still but joggles
> In ceaseless wash? Still nought but gapes, and bites,
> And drinks, and stares, diversified with boggles?

A FISH ANSWERS

> Amazing monster! that, for aught I know,
> With the first sight of thee didst make our race
> For ever stare! O flat and shocking face,
> Grimly divided from the breast below!
> Thou that on dry land horribly dost go
> With a split body and most ridiculous pace,

Prong after prong, disgracer of all grace,
Long-useless-finned, haired, upright, unwet, slow!

O breather of unbreathable, sword-sharp air,
How canst exist? How bear thyself, thou dry
And dreary sloth? What particle canst share
Of the only blessed life, the watery?
I sometimes see of ye an actual pair
Go by! linked fin by fin! most odiously.

THE FISH TURNS INTO A MAN AGAIN, AND THEN INTO A SPIRIT, AND AGAIN SPEAKS

Indulge thy smiling scorn, if smiling still,
O man! and loathe, but with a sort of love;
For difference must its use by difference prove,
And, in sweet clang, the spheres with music fill.
One of the spirits am I, that at his will
Live in whate'er has life – fish, eagle, dove –
No hate, no pride, beneath nought, nor above,
A visitor of the rounds of God's sweet skill.

Man's life is warm, glad, sad, 'twixt loves and graves,
Boundless in hope, honoured with pangs austere,
Heaven-gazing; and his angel-wings he craves: –
The fish is swift, small-needing, vague yet clear,
A cold, sweet, silver life, wrapped in round waves,
Quickened with touches of transporting fear.

This and the 'Songs and Chorus of the Flowers' always remained high on the list of his poems with which Hunt was most pleased. The following year, when compiling the *Book of Gems* with the publisher S.C. Hall, he confided that the second half of the 'Songs and Chorus', entitled the 'Chorus of the Flowers', was 'the best poem I ever wrote'. This anthology also gave Hunt another chance to speak up for Keats, whose reputation had yet to be made. 'His fame does not yet stand high enough,' agreed their mutual friend Charles Brown, now a teacher and magazine editor in Plymouth, in a letter offering Hunt unpublished poems were it not for an embargo imposed by Keats's brother George. If he could not publish hitherto unseen work, Hunt could at least take the chance to correct misapprehensions about Keats recently compounded by, among others, Coleridge, who had spoken of the poet's 'laxity' in his *Table-Talk*. 'He had any thing in his dress and general demeanour but that appearance of "laxity", which has been strangely attributed to him in a late publication,' wrote Hunt, also at pains to correct the pervasive view that Keats had been killed by his critics. 'In fact he had so much of the reverse, though in no unbecoming degree, that he might be supposed to maintain a certain jealous care of the appearance and bearing of a gentleman, in the consciousness of his genius, and perhaps not without some sense of his origin. His face was handsome and sensitive, with a look in the eyes at once earnest and tender; and his hair grew in delicate brown ringlets, of remarkable beauty . . .'

He also made the most of his personal knowledge in a companion volume on Shelley: 'Mr Shelley was tall, and slight of figure, with a singular union of general delicacy of organization and muscular strength. His hair was brown, prematurely touched with grey; his complexion fair and glowing; his eyes grey and extremely vivid; his face small and delicately featured, especially about the lower part; and he had an expression of countenance, when he was talking in his usual earnest fashion, which had been described elsewhere as giving you the idea of something "seraphical".'

Amid discussions of his dead friends' qualities as poets, Hunt used the *Book of Gems* to promote the qualities of new writers such as Tennyson, who had yet to win a wide following: 'He is of the school of Keats; much, however, as he reminds us of Keats, his genius is its own: he would have written poetry had his precursor written none; and he has, also, a vein of metaphysical subtlety in which the other did not indulge.'

Here, too, came the first appearance between hard covers of what was to become Hunt's most celebrated poem. First published in Hall's the *Amulet* in 1834, 'Abou Ben Adhem' contained the characteristically simple, innocent line that would become Hunt's own epitaph:

> Abou Ben Adhem (may his tribe increase!)
> Awoke one night from a deep dream of peace,

And saw, within the moonlight in his room,
Making it rich, and like a lily in bloom,
An angel writing in a book of gold: –
Exceeding peace had made Ben Adhem bold,
And to the presence in the room he said,
'What writest thou?' – The vision raised its head,
And with a look made all of sweet accord,
Answered, 'The names of those who love the Lord.'
'And is mine one?' said Abou. 'Nay, not so,'
Replied the angel. Abou spoke more low,
But cheerly still; and said, 'I pray thee then,
Write me as one that loves his fellow-men.'

The angel wrote, and vanished. The next night
It came again with a great wakening light,
And showed the names whom love of God had blessed,
And lo! Ben Adhem's name led all the rest.

Two years after the latest published collection of Hunt's *Poetical Works*, this stand-alone *pièce d'occasion* seems to have been inspired by a renewed burst of interest in all things oriental, especially Islamic myths and the 'sensual' delights of Arabia – partly inspired, in turn, by a letter from Calcutta informing him, to his evident delight, that his *Collected Poems* were 'subscribing well' in India. The poem's wide-eyed faith in a secular humanity could not be more characteristic.

Hunt's advance through his fifties to the status of literary institution increasingly saw him chosen as the dedicatee of works by admirers and friends, the latest example being Horne's *The Death of Marlowe*; in 1870, eleven years after Hunt's death, and thirty-two since its original publication in 1838, the play's fourth edition was still inscribed by Horne to Hunt's 'dear memory – deservedly dear to all who knew him, and to a world of others who know his books'. Horne developed something close to Huntolatry for 'one of the most amiable and widely-sympathizing men that ever lived', possessed of 'boundless charity', a 'religious passion in his soul' and a political and literary courage that Horne was uncomfortably aware he himself lacked.

As he visited the shambling, chaotic household so vividly described by Carlyle, with its paterfamilias toiling away in the midst of its squalid, child-infested chaos, Horne became a fertile source of the kind of anecdotes which uniquely seem to attach themselves to Hunt. On one occasion Horne found him 'in all seriousness entreating a poor man who perhaps could not find the price of a few flowers to take his wife home a handful of grass'. On another he 'heard him discourse while standing in front of a bed of winter cabbages covered with a sparkling hoar-frost, as though it were Nature's jewellery of emeralds and diamonds set in frosted silver'.

It was also Horne who found Hunt one cold winter day 'playing and warbling' at a grand piano he had dragged close to a roaring fire. 'But, Hunt, you'll ruin the piano!' exclaimed Horne. 'I know, I know,' came the reply, 'but it's delicious!' Horne claimed to have heard Hunt apologise to his wife and daughters for having spent eighteen pence at a second-hand bookstall, explaining how 'useful and valuable' the work would be to him – 'and this at a time when the improvidence of others had brought him into trouble'. With 'bad health, incipient old age, and thriftless imbecility all around him,' observed Carlyle at this time, 'Hunt has the sorriest outlook; yet keeps his heart up amazingly.'

After paying a visit to the Hunts' Chelsea home in 1837, the poet and painter William Bell Scott described his host as 'inseparable' from his upstairs eyrie with its 'venerable' piano and his beloved *Parnaso Italiano* (now repurchased). 'Mrs Hunt I never saw but once by chance on the staircase.' Primroses in a jar, a 'Petrarchan' inkstand . . . 'On the hob a small iron pot simmered, with a kind of bread pudding in it. A cup of tea was the only refreshment. Hunt did not gloss his poverty. He said he should like to spend a few shillings on old books – "but I can deny myself even that".'

But Hunt, as yet, was no recluse; his 'salon' years were far from over. In the late 1830s he found a new friend and admirer in Browning, who was drawn into a Hunt circle now centred around Horne and Talfourd but also including such other new literary talents as the novelists Charles Dickens, William Makepeace Thackeray and Edward Bulwer (later, as of 1843, Bulwer-Lytton, author of popular romances and editor of the *New Monthly*), the poets Walter Savage Landor and Richard Monckton Milnes (later Baron Houghton), the Irish painter

Daniel Maclise, the actor Charles Macready and the essayist and biographer John Forster.

Browning acknowledged that Hunt was the only poet before him to
attempt to convey the sound of music in poetry – with some success,
as the American poet and critic John Hollander concedes while lamenting the 'smarmy German manner' of Hunt's 'The Lover of Music to his
Pianoforte' (published in the *Athenæum* of 7 July 1832). But two blank-
verse exercises, 'A Thought on Music' (1815) and the recent 'Paganini'
(1834), earn Hollander's detailed approval, as they did Browning's.
This new visitor also liked Hunt for his 'child-like' nature and his collection of hair.

Like other visitors to Hunt's study, Browning had been given a
guided tour of the collection of locks of hair, begun by that kindly Dr
Batty forty years before with Milton. Batty 'had it from his father-in-
law, who had it from Hoole the translator, who had it from Johnson',
Hunt would tell his guests. 'The link of evidence is here lost; but
Johnson was famous for his veracity, and he would not have given it to
Hoole as Milton's hair, had he not believed it to be genuine . . . There
is no grey in the lock. It must have been cut when the poet was in the
vigour of life, before he wrote "Paradise Lost"; and we may indulge our
fancy by supposing it was cut off as a present to his wife. Love and locks
of hair, the most touching the most beautiful, and the most lasting of
keepsakes, naturally go together . . .'

Milton's lock, the pride of Hunt's collection, had earlier moved
him to one of his better sonnets:

> It lies before me there, and my own breath
> Stirs its thin outer threads, as though beside
> The living head I stood in honoured pride,
> Talking of lovely things that conquer death.
> Perhaps he pressed it once, or underneath
> Ran his fine fingers when he leant, blank-eyed,
> And saw in fancy Adam and his bride
> With their heaped locks, or his own Delphic wreath.
>
> There seems a love in hair, though it be dead.
> It is the gentlest, yet the strongest thread

Of our frail plant, – a blossom from the tree
Surviving the proud trunk; as if it said,
Patience and gentleness in power. In me
Behold affectionate eternity.

Alongside Milton's lay samples of Swift's and Johnson's hair (also from Dr Batty), Napoleon's and Lucrezia Borgia's (both from Byron). Over the years Hunt had added Keats and both Shelleys, Maria Edgeworth, Procter, Lamb, Hazlitt, Coleridge and Wordsworth. Soon he would solicit samples from both Brownings, Robert and Elizabeth Barrett. As they listened to the detailed provenance of each sample, Hunt's more eminent visitors must have looked at his scissors with apprehension.

After seeing less of Carlyle in the mid-1830s – the Scotsman thought Hunt had been put off by his 'Cameronian rigour' – Hunt renewed relations with his neighbour in 1838 by reviewing his ambitious series of lectures on the history of European literature in *The Examiner*. Walking across Battersea Bridge years later, after Hunt's death, Carlyle succumbed to an uncharacteristic bout of nostalgia when recalling his walks in the area with his neighbour. Hunt was 'sweet and dignified', he told his companion, his talk 'like the song of a nightingale'. Although 'delighted' with everything in the Carlyle household – his wife's playing of Scottish melodies, Scotch broth for supper – he found 'I was not a Shelley – had a foundation of Presbyterianism which was not agreeable to him. He met with much contradiction and ceased to come to walk with me.' Now, it seems, Hunt was trying to mend fences.

He had further reason to have distanced himself from the Carlyles, when mortified to discover that his son John had begged them for money after being barred from the family home. Although Carlyle had handled this delicate matter tactfully, Hunt now allowed no personal sentiment to cloud his judgement of the lectures, which continued into the following year, ranging from the Reformation to the French Revolution.

At times Hunt seemed to damn with faint praise. 'There is frequently a noble homeliness, a passionate simplicity and familiarity of speech in the language of Mr Carlyle, which gives startling effect to his sincerity,' he wrote. 'The effects of hearty convictions like these, uttered in such simple, truthful words, and with the flavour of a Scottish accent (as if some Puritan had come to life again, liberalized by German philosophy and his own intense reflections and experience), can be duly appreciated only by those who see it. Every manly face among the audience seems to knit its lips, out of a severity of sympathy, whether it would or no; and all the pretty church-and-state bonnets seem to trill through all their ribbons.'

But Hunt did not shrink from open dissent from some of Carlyle's conclusions, as when he pronounced a victory in battle to be a 'judgement of God' and, in his third lecture (on Cromwell and Puritanism), 'hampered himself with denouncing falsehood in Charles I, and allowing it in his successful adversary – Cromwell'.

Carlyle's most recent biographer, Rosemary Ashton, commends this as 'an early recognition of Carlyle's propensity, which increased with the years, to argue for the rightness of might'. But Carlyle himself was irritated by what he considered Hunt's nitpicking, and put it down to pure jealousy. Hunt's remarks, he observed in his journal, were 'no longer *friendly*, not so in spirit, tho' still in letter, a shade of spleen in it . . . He finds me grown to be *something* now.' When Hunt took him to task for praising Roman thrift in his third lecture, Carlyle drily observed: 'His whole way of life is at death-variance with mine. He expresses himself afflicted with my eulogy of *thrift*, and two days ago he had, *multa gemens* [groaning mightily], to borrow two sovereigns of me!'

The story of the sovereigns was to become legendary, to the point where one wonders if an irritated Carlyle might have been embroidering the truth. It comes down to posterity via Augustus Hare, a notoriously gossipy writer (mostly of travel books) whose memoirs cite the evidence of a Scottish poet and critic named James Hannay. 'Mr Hannay knew Carlyle very well, and often went to see him, but in his poorer days . . .' (By now Carlyle had become relatively prosperous; his lectures alone, for instance, had earned him £260.) 'One day when Mr Hannay went to the house, he saw two gold sovereigns lying exposed in a little case on the chimney-piece. He asked Carlyle what they were for. Carlyle looked – for him – embarrassed, but gave no definite answer. "Well, now, my dear fellow," said Mr Hannay, "neither you nor I are in a position to play ducks and drakes with sovereigns;

what *are* these for?" "Well," said Carlyle, "the fact is, Leigh Hunt likes better to find them there than that I should give them to him.'"

Perhaps it was Hare, rather than Carlyle himself, who had reason to tinker with retrospective truths. Elsewhere Hannay himself testifies that Hunt 'outlived his early faults. He developed successfully all the nobler parts of his nature . . . Leigh Hunt, then, was no parasite.' He goes on to note that 'our own' Carlyle was among the men of letters who 'stuck by him . . . for a considerable time, among the red-brick terraces and quiet trees of Chelsea'. And he writes sympathetically of the 'several sly stabs' Hunt suffered at the hands of the *Athenæum*. 'Having lived down so much, he also lived down those things.' Of Hunt's attitude to money, Hare also quotes an unknown 'Mr Bourton' as saying: '[Hunt] is the only person, I believe, who, if he saw something yellow in the distance, and was told it was a buttercup, would be disappointed if he found it was only a guinea.'

In December 1837, with his usual generosity, Hunt brought his new literary protégé Horne round to Cheyne Walk to meet the Carlyles. Another guest on that occasion was Harriet Martineau, the formidable authoress and economist, who noted the contrast between her host's 'rugged genius' and Hunt's 'homely manliness'. Thereafter Hunt's visits again became less regular. Carlyle thought Hunt had been 'repelled' – if 'more in sorrow than in anger' – by his rigorous 'Cameronian' rejection of his ideology; he remembered Hunt calling his views 'Scotch, Presbyterian, who knows what'; even in his wife's 'brilliancy and faculty', which Hunt had been quick to recognise, 'none better', there had been 'something of positive, of practically steadfast, which scared him off'. In his journal for 15 May 1838, Carlyle wrote that 'happily', these days, 'I have next to nothing to do with Hunt.'

Yet in early March 1839 Hunt is reported as a late arrival at a Carlyle dinner party in Cheyne Walk for a visiting mutual friend, the Scottish publisher John Hunter. '[Hunt] joined us about nine o'clock and gave a livelier and happier tone to the conversation,' noted Hunter, reporting that the topics of conversation ranged from the Scottish Kirk, Wordsworth, Petrarch, Burns, Knox and Hume, the Church of England, Dante, heaven and hell to the macabre mummification of Jeremy Bentham's corpse.

According to Hunter, Carlyle and Hunt were 'determined disputants';

both, that night, 'were in great force, and came out in their full strength'. They formed 'decided contrasts to each other in almost every respect'; the occasional 'collisions' between them 'drew out the salient points and characteristic powers of each in the most striking manner possible . . .' Hunt was 'all light and air, glancing gracefully over all topics, and casting the hues of his own temperament on every subject that arose'. He told a story, for instance, about Lamb, to whom someone had been talking about eternal punishments 'and the like'; Lamb rounded on him with, 'No, that won't do for me. I can't give up my hell.'

When Carlyle, in chauvinist as much as Calvinist mode, argued Burns's merits over Wordsworth's before dismissing Petrarch's 'weak, washy twaddle about another man's wife', Hunt countered: 'Well, that's very good. Carlyle knocks down all our idols with two or three sweeps of his arm, and having so far cleared his way to us, he winds up by knocking down ourselves; and when we cry out against his rough work, he begins to talk of – politeness!' There were peals of laughter, in which Carlyle joined, confessing: 'I believe, after all, you are quite right . . . I honour and love you for the lesson you have taught me.' To which compliment Hunt responded in kind: 'There is Carlyle all over. That's what makes us all love him. His darkest speculations always come out to the light by reason of the human heart which he carries along with him. He will at last end in glory and gladness.'

So Hunt and Carlyle were friends again; they could disagree happily on all sorts of topics. One such difference arose in early 1840 after the trial of John Frost and others, sentenced to death for their role in attempting to free a Chartist prisoner from Monmouth jail. When Hunt's friend Linton, who had engraved many a drawing for his books, came calling on both with a petition against the death sentence, Carlyle refused to sign, saying: 'No! Force must be met by force; who took the sword must expect to perish by the sword' (or, according to Linton, 'words to that effect'). Linton then went to Hunt, who signed immediately. But to Linton, as he walked away, there was 'something in the manner of Carlyle's refusal' – a 'deep-heartedness' – which touched him more than Hunt's 'prompt acquiescence'.

Though no more Carlyle's neighbour, Hunt was soon a regular visitor again at Cheyne Row, talking incessantly ('melodious as a bird on a bough'), relishing his free porridge and listening 'with real feeling' to his hosts' Scottish tunes. Soon after, according to Horne, they were all part of a group walking home together one starry night, when Hunt began waxing eloquent about the 'sweet influences of which the heavens were telling, of the music of the spheres, and destined Shelleian transcendencies of consciousness'; when he finally paused, Carlyle interposed: 'Man, it's a sad sight.' For once lost for words, Hunt 'sat down on a stone step'. Also from Horne comes the touching tale of Lady Airlie, who had known Hunt in her childhood; once, talking to her in his garden, he had asked what she thought heaven would be like. Whatever the child replied, Hunt said: 'I'll tell you what I think it will be like: I think it will be like a most beautiful arbour all hung with creepers and flowers, and that one will be able to sit in it all day, and read a most interesting novel.'

For all his permanent money worries, Hunt was back on top form in his mid-fifties, writing as prolifically and fearlessly as ever, surrounded by stimulating (and largely adoring) friends, and finally back on terms with his brother John, who had retired to the West Country. There was even a brief (but vain) glimmer of hope that his son John, who was now married, might make something of his life. Hunt's lawyer brother Stephen was by now dead; his other brother, Robert, once the art critic of the *Examiner*, whose only claim to fame was a scornful review of William Blake, had grown old and solitary, with a dozen years left before dying in the Charterhouse, where Hunt's petition to the Queen had earned him a place.

In 1840 Hunt's health and financial problems forced yet another move upon him: from Chelsea to 5 Edwardes Square, Kensington, where his daughter, Mary Florimel, had just moved into number 45 with her husband John Gliddon, soon joined by Thornton and his wife Kate (née Gliddon). Four years earlier Thornton and Kate had given Hunt his first grandchild, Margaret, followed two years later by Walter; only then, in 1838, had they finally found a home of their own.

Within a year Thornton and his family had moved down the road to Church Lane (now Kensington Church Street); another three years, and he and Kate would join forces with Mary and John to share a household in Bayswater. Here, as of 1844, they embarked on their experiment in 'Phalanstery', or communal living, which would end in scandal when Thornton's friend G. H. (George) Lewes eloped with the novelist George Eliot. Much though he may have approved, Hunt himself had never practised the morality he preached, and wasn't going to start now. For once, the Hunt patriarch stayed put, moving from 5 to 32 Edwardes Square within a year, but then remaining there for the next decade – the longest he would ever live at one address.

Named in honour of William Edwardes, first Baron Kensington, Edwardes Square was built at the beginning of the nineteenth century to designs in the French style by the architect Louis Changeur, for the purpose of housing French officers after Napoleon had conquered England. A plaque in its lively pub, the Scarsdale, recalls to this day Hunt's description of the square as 'a French Arcadia' in a series of articles about Kensington for Dickens's magazine *Household Words*. 'It would never,' he mused, 'have occurred to an English mind to design it.'

It was during the Edwardes Square years that the Irish poet William Allingham, a member of Rossetti's Pre-Raphaelite circle, spoke of Hunt as looking 'wonderfully different in the street from in the house. There, a spare old man in a frock coat and black stock, with weak eyes and rather careworn look; here, a young man (though of sixty), with luxuriant if grey locks, open shirt collar and flowing dressing-gown, bright face, and the easiest way of talking in the world.' Bumping into Hunt in Piccadilly one day, Allingham found himself thinking, 'If I ever have any doubts about him, they vanish at one glance from his eye.'

Forty years younger than Hunt, and grateful for his introductions to 'several of the great men of the time' (not least Carlyle, Dickens, Browning and Thackeray), Allingham is one of several young admirers to have left a vivid account of his first meeting with Hunt in Edwardes Square. 'I was shown into the study, and had some minutes to look round the book-cases, busts, old framed engravings, and to glance at some of the books on the table, diligently marked and noted in the well-known neatest of hand-writings. Outside the window climbed a hop on its trellis. The door opened and in came the Genius Loci, a tall-ish young old man, in dark dressing-gown and wide turned-down collar, his copious iron-grey hair falling almost to his shoulders. The friendly brown eyes, simple yet fine-toned voice, easy hand-pressure, gave me greeting as to one already known to him.'

They talked at first of reason and instinct. 'He maintained (for argument's sake, I thought) that beasts may be equal or superior to men. He has a light earnestness of manner, and toleration for almost every possible different view from his own.' Of free will Hunt said, 'I would much rather be without it. I should like to feel myself taken care of in the arms of beneficent power.' The subject turned to the Italian violin virtuoso Niccolò Paganini, then visiting London, whom Hunt declared 'incomparable . . . When he came forward and struck the first chord, my neighbour in the opera pit (an Italian) exclaimed in a low voice, "O Dio!" Violin, or better violino, is the name for his instrument. Common English players *fiddle*, it is a good word for their playing.' Similar distinctions could be made about the stage. 'Macready is not a genius, he is our best actor now because there is no other. He keeps a fine house, but is not in what I call the best society.'

The following week Allingham visited Hunt again. His host was tired, but asked him to stay, evidently in late-night, discursive mode. 'I hate Dante: in reading him I first found that a great poet can be an unamiable man.' Wordsworth, too, was 'personally very disagreeable'. He had been asked to meet Hans Christian Andersen, then in London. 'Can't understand why people want to see *me* – I am used to myself. O yes, I like to see some men of letters. Dislike mountains, can't bear height, my legs shudder at the thought of it. London is the best place for you; why don't you try and live in it? Walk back . . .'

Another young visitor at this time was the aspirant writer Coventry Patmore, who leaves a remarkably similar account – with a pleasant twist at the end. 'I was informed that the poet was at home, and asked to sit down until he came to see me. This he did after I had waited in the little parlour at least two hours, when the door was opened and a most picturesque gentleman, with hair flowing nearly or quite to his shoulders, a beautiful velvet coat and a Vandyck collar of lace about a foot deep, appeared, rubbing his hands and smiling ethereally, and saying, without a word of preface or notice of my having waited so long, "This is a beautiful world, Mr Patmore!"'

Patmore was so struck by this remark that it 'eclipsed my memory of what occurred during the remainder of my visit'. Told this story by the

Victorian critic and biographer Sir Edmund Gosse, who received it in a letter from Patmore, Max Beerbohm is said to have remarked: 'There was nothing wrong with the words themselves; they were exactly, exquisitely the right words; but they should have been said sooner.'

But Hunt's 'beautiful world' hid shadows of which he himself was unaware in the shape of ever more shameless borrowing by Marianne. As if his own financial incompetence were not enough, his wife's increasingly erratic behaviour was stretching the patience of some of his closest friends. Horne was one of several, including Dickens, who raised and administered a fund for Hunt known as the 'Private List'. Younger writers' admiration in acknowledging a distinguished literary career was mingled with some embarrassment about so senior a member of the profession they sought to enhance leading so publicly down-at-heel a life. In attempting to help out Hunt, however, they had reckoned without his indigent, irresponsible wife. A letter dated 6 June 1840 shows Horne's frustration at Marianne's profligate, if not downright dishonest ways:

My dear Mrs Hunt,
. . . I am still in debt £10 to Mr Kirkman for the old 'Private List' account, Mr Blanchard not having yet paid me, – and of course I cannot ask one who has been so kind and true in his feelings to you all. He is himself in great difficulties just now. I received a letter from a subscriber to the 'Private List' *some weeks ago* who asked if it was true that you had received nothing from the 'Private List' fund for these *last eight months*? As you received the weekly payments up to the week when Mr Hunt's play came out, this report is rather vexatious. Can you at all conceive who could have set it afloat? . . .
R. H. Horne

As the Lity. Fund gave £50 last year, it would be of no use to apply again so soon – indeed, it would be injurious, as they would perhaps make troublesome inquiries, with regard to the Queen's donation &c. In short, as I said, the affair is altogether most confusing.

Another trustee of the private list was Talfourd, who found himself 'obliged to return many, and more abrupt refusals to Mrs Hunt'.

The play mentioned in Horne's letter was *A Legend of Florence*, which earned Hunt a surprise success at Covent Garden in 1840 – gratifying with rare ease his long-standing wish to succeed with a verse drama. Hunt had written plays before, without managing to find a management willing to stage them; this time he experimented by trying out his work-in-progress on his friends before submitting it to a theatre. During the play's gestation Hunt performed histrionic readings for various groups of indulgent friends; one such, at Carlyle's house, where guests included the literary historian George Craik, was described by John Hunter of Craigcrook: 'Carlyle, Craik and I arose; on which Hunt said, "I am satisfied with my verdict, and care not what any person may say of my play. I know it has life in it, since it has touched all of you." Carlyle spoke earnestly and candidly of it; told him it was a piece of right good stuff, solid and real, with a pulse of life and play of passion in every scene and line, and capitally dramatized.' When they ventured one lone objection – 'that we all thought the conclusion might be better brought out in *action*, so as to have more of dramatic interest than it has at present, by a long, but most admirable and indeed Shakespearean speech from a Cardinal giving judgement as to the divorce' – Hunt 'at once acquiesced, and said he would endeavour to alter it agreeably to our suggestions'.

Hunt's drama criticism (and supposedly private conversations) had already made him an enemy in the actor Macready – of whose mere 'merits' he had spoken and written, as opposed to Kean's 'genius'. Hunt, the younger Macready had complained to his diary, 'seemed to hold my destinies in his grasp'. Now it was one of Macready's rivals, the Irish actor Sheridan Knowles, who helped Hunt out by commissioning a reading to which he could invite Dickens, Procter and other influential friends. The result was a formal reading for the management of Covent Garden, where it was 'received with acclamation'. The face of Ellen Tree, whom Hunt longed to see as the heroine, was 'bathed in tears' as he read. Another of those present, the house dramaturge J.R. Planché, was impressed by Hunt's impassioned performance but concerned about his stagecraft: 'Hunt had the wildest ideas of dramatic effect, and calculated in the most Utopian spirit upon the intelligence of the British public. As I often told him, if he read his scenes himself, the magic of his voice, the marvellous intonation and variety of expression in his delivery would probably enchain and enchant a general audience as it did us; but the hope of being so interpreted was not to be entertained for a moment.'

However mixed Hunt's feelings about Dante, his torrid melo-drama – made all the more so by the 'solemn and affecting strains' of music he commissioned from Novello and Webbe – clearly owed him a considerable debt. Agolanti is obsessively jealous of his wife Ginevra, who is loved by Antonio Rondinelli. Moved by her misery at her husband's remonstrations, Rondinelli tries to mediate; amid the ensuing argument Ginevra is reported dead. The night after her funeral she knocks at her husband's window; believing her to be a ghost, he closes the shutters. So she takes herself off to Rondinelli, announcing that she was 'buried, but not dead'; when Agolanti hears the news and comes to demand her return, he winds up dead and she in a nunnery.

So impressed was the poet Sir John Hanmer by Hunt's versification and stagecraft that he wrote to the publisher Moxon: 'If Bulwer[-Lytton] sets up for *the* dramatist of this day, he must hide his diminished head . . . I am inclined to think that, among the many semi-Elizabethan attempts of Victorian dramatic poets, *A Legend of Florence* is eminent for emotion, movement and unpretentious dignity of style.' The owners of Covent Garden, Mr and Mrs Charles Matthews, evidently agreed; they paid Hunt an advance of £100, requested an option on his next play and scheduled *A Legend of Florence* for the 1840 season. Then they threw him on the mercy of their formidable manager for that season, Madame Vestris (an actress and producer born Lucia Elizabetta Bartolozzi), who promptly came up with all sorts of unwelcome suggestions. 'Now, Hunt,' she ventured, 'if you will change the movement and close of the last act, it will be far more popular and profitable.' Madame Vestris wanted a happy ending, with Agolanti's wife restored to him. If he would just make this minor amendment, she insisted, 'your play will run for a hundred nights'. Hunt refused to change a word. 'Impossible!' he railed, 'I can't give him back Ginevra.' And he was tri-umphantly proved right.

On 1 November 1839, after 'sitting silent for an hour', Wordsworth suddenly told the visiting Horne: 'I wish I could be in London in January.' When Horne asked why, the great man replied: 'To make my hands burn in welcoming Leigh Hunt's play.' Hunt's latest literary

excursion was winning back old acquaintanceships, even ending petty
feuds. Out walking that winter he met Haydon, whom he had not
seen for many years. Haydon found Hunt looking 'hearty, grey and a
veteran'. Said Hunt: 'Haydon, when I see you hosts of household
remembrances crowd my fancy.' Replied Haydon: 'Hunt, I am going to
write my life, and I'll do *you* justice. You would have been burnt at the
stake for a principle, and would have feared to put your foot in the
mud.'

'Affected', Hunt asked if Haydon would come to see his play. 'I'll
applaud you to the skies,' his old sparring partner replied. 'Bring
your wife,' said Hunt, 'I'll put your names down.' And Haydon was
indeed among those at Covent Garden on the first night, 7 February
1840, to see Ellen Tree triumph as Ginevra and lead a standing ovation for the author at the curtain call. He looked 'grey, sturdy, worn
and timid' to Haydon, whose turn it now was to be 'much
affected . . . Think of poor Hunt being ruined for telling mankind
what George IV was ashamed they should know, but was not
ashamed to do before his Maker, provided it was unknown to his
people.'

'Do tell me how you felt when you heard your name ringing
through the walls of the great theatre,' Laman Blanchard asked Hunt.
'Are you aware that when you came on, you stood on your head instead
of your heels? . . . Did you feel at all like a man who stands silent
upon a peak in Darien?' According to Thornton's friend Lewes, 'It was
really an exciting scene, that first night! So many of us were intensely
anxious for the success of the poet; so many were delighted to see the
poetical drama once more triumphing.' But, he added, 'the tears and
the plaudits of that night, genuine though they were, had something
feverish and exaggerated in them'. Another first-nighter, Linton,
thought Hunt's play 'too refined and purely beautiful for general appreciation'. Hunt's luck was anyway running true to form. With a long
run apparently in prospect for the play, the previous commitments of
the leading lady forced its closure after only two weeks. Undeterred,
Hunt determined to write more plays.

'The author of one successful piece,' as he put it, 'is easily persuaded to write another.' But Lewes was to be proved right; lightning
failed to strike twice. Emboldened to write several more verse dramas,

Hunt could not get them staged. 'The success sufficed to inspire Leigh Hunt with the hope that he had at last found his real vocation, and a profitable mine,' recalled Lewes. 'For some years he devoted himself to the composition of plays, and had to endure the tortures of an unacted dramatist, for not one of these plays could he get produced.' Instead a disappointed Hunt had to fall back on editing the plays of others. Old rivalries from the Regency era were forgotten with a preface, albeit lukewarm, to the comedies of Sheridan (Hunt was 'conscious of a want of enthusiasm for [his] genius'), followed by an edition of Wycherley, Congreve, Vanbrugh and Farquhar for Moxon's 'Dramatic Library' series.

The publishers chose to dedicate the volume to Thomas Moore, to coincide with the publication of his Collected Poems; when Moore did not shrink from including his verses attacking Hunt over his Byron biography, Hunt was as surprised as he was hurt. He had supposed their differences to have been buried since 1832, when Moore had subscribed for five copies of his *Poetical Works* after tactfully asking Mary Shelley whether Hunt would mind. Hunt, in turn, had included a compliment to the 'wit and festivity' of Moore's poetry in the preface to that volume; and when one of Moore's colonial staff had absconded, leaving him with a £6000 debt, Hunt had offered to start a subscription by selling his piano.

So now, one last time, he felt moved to respond:

I confess I should almost as soon have expected their republication in your collected works (a packet for posterity) as I should have thought of repeating the letters from the *Tatler* in the selection of [my] papers recently published under the title of the *Seer* . . . If, indeed, any imaginary circumstance should have induced you to misconstrue these evidences of goodwill, all I can say is that I have never written a syllable, during these late years, with the intention of wounding you, and that I never utter a syllable in private at variance with what I write. How could I renew hostilities after consenting (permit me to use that word on the present occasion) to receive a favour from you – the subscription to my *Poems*? And allow me to ask, how could you, after I had received the favour, suffer the attack on me to be reprinted . . .

Moore evidently regretted including the poems; in June 1841 he wrote to Hunt begging him finally to forget their quarrel over Byron. At much the same time unwelcome memories of the past also resurfaced in the shape of the pseudonymous Christopher North, John Wilson, co-author of some of the 1818 *Blackwood's* attacks; it took much of Hunt's energy, now in ever shorter supply, to talk Horne out of an ironic dedication of his play *Gregory VII* to 'North' (who had savaged his book *The Exposition of the False Medium*) for fear of reopening old wounds.

Despite the all too brief success of *A Legend of Florence*, Hunt was especially tickled by the fact that the Queen herself had come to see it more than once. On her second visit, he noted, 'when the lovely organ strain composed by my friend Vincent Novello began to double the tears of the audience, a fair hand was observed to come from behind the royal curtain and press the congenial arm next to it, as if in recognition'.

Victoria had been on the throne since June 1837, when she had succeeded her uncle, William IV, at the age of eighteen. In the autumn of 1840, on the birth of her first child, some verses by Hunt in the *Morning Chronicle* greeted the arrival of the Princess Royal:

> Welcome, bud beside the rose,
> On whose stem our safety grows;
> Welcome, little Saxon Guelph;
> Welcome for thine own small self
> Welcome for thy father, mother,
> Proud the one and safe the other;
> Welcome to three kingdoms; nay,
> Such is thy potential day,
> Welcome little mighty birth,
> To our human star the earth . . .

And so on in such vein for another seventy dispiriting lines. The Poet Laureate, Southey, being too ill to perform his duties, Hunt appeared to be appointing himself as stand-in. 'Glanced over the paper and seen some verses, which I did not read, from the republican Leigh Hunt to the Queen on her infant!' snorted Macready in his diary. So Hunt's youthful assault on the Prince of Wales had not been forgotten; thirty years on, this ardent royalist was still being mistaken for a republican.

Two years later, undeterred, Hunt followed this dreadful doggerel for the infant princess with 'Three Visions on the Birth and Christening of the Prince of Wales', also published in the *Morning Chronicle*. An equally feeble paean soon greeted the Queen's birthday and the birth of Princess Alice. Cynics like Macready, who saw Hunt's dire ditties as a blatant job application, for once had a point.

1 2

'A track of radiance'

1841–52

'I heard the other day, from one of poor Southey's nephews, that he cannot live many weeks,' wrote Macaulay to Hunt in March 1841. 'I really do not see why you might not succeed him. The title of Poet Laureate is indeed ridiculous. But the salary ought to be left for the benefit of some man of letters. Should the present government be in office when a vacancy takes place, I really think that the matter might be managed.'

Writing from his desk at the War Office, Macaulay was actually in a position to 'manage' that sort of thing. The prospect went to Hunt's head. Following his sycophantic verse greetings to the infant Prince of Wales, he dedicated his 1842 poem 'The Palfrey' (a 'love story of old times') to the Queen herself, in a remarkably embarrassing 'Envoy':

> To HER, who loves all peaceful glory,
> Therefore laurelled song and story;
> Who, as blooming maiden should,
> Married blest, with young and good . . .

Hunt even felt moved to confess, *en passant*, that he had not sought the monarch's permission for the dedication:

> And yet how to beg it for one flower
> Cast in the path of Sovereign Power?

But it was not to be. This time around, when Southey died, the job went to seventy-year-old William Wordsworth. Fifty-six-year-old Hunt could have no objection to that; but it might not be too long, he no doubt reflected, before the poet laureateship would again be vacant.

Back in 1813, Hunt's younger self had railed in the *Examiner* against the poets Southey and Wordsworth accepting office under government 'of such a nature as absolutely ties up their independence' – Southey the poet laureateship, Wordsworth a position in the Stamp Office (as Distributor of Stamps for Westmorland and part of Cumberland). Now the one had succeeded the other in an office Hunt himself openly coveted, somewhat humiliating himself in the process. This curious whim of his was clearly a yearning for some sort of establishment recognition, after a lifetime as a maverick-of-all-trades drowning in debt.

All he could do to assuage his disappointment, while continuing to live in hope, was continue to pour out a wide range of verse of his own and astute appraisals of the work of others. But still these and his other endeavours did not make enough money to keep Hunt and his brood afloat. 'It is easy to say to a man – Write such and such a thing, and it is sure to sell. Watch the public's taste, and act accordingly. Care not for original composition; for inventions or theories of your own; for aesthetics, which the many will be slow to apprehend. Stick to the works of others. Write only in magazines and reviews. Or if you must write things of your own, compile. Tell anecdotes. Reproduce memoirs and topographies. Repeat, in as many words of your own as you can, other men's criticisms. Do anything but write to the few, and you may get rich.'

These were lessons Hunt refused to learn. 'A man can only do as he can, or as others will let him.' If the last two decades of Hunt's life were to see him as fertile and prolific as ever, the quality of his work showed no decline. Quite the reverse; in the recent words of one connoisseur, 'The period between 1844 and 1859 is in no way a denouement but in fact one of the most important and productive of his long and varied career.'

In 1844 Hunt's sixtieth birthday was marked by another edition of his *Poetical Works*, of which Moxon printed all of two thousand copies. Despite yet another revision of the lengthy *Rimini*, and additions to his 1836 piece 'Our Cottage', it was a pocket-sized volume, of 'companionable' proportions, but Hunt was still not sure that he had been selective enough. 'Should you ever meet with it,' he told William Allingham, 'I hope you will tear it to pieces . . . I always long to make my editions just half or a fourth part of what they are, to give myself a better chance of life. I should like to be a thin, very thin little book, which people would carry in their pockets, like Gray and Collins. The most flattering of my dreams is, that by and by perhaps somebody may pare me down to this.'

A city clerk and 'dabbler' in literature named Thomas Powell had recently lent Hunt £40, accepting as security a prose manuscript entitled *True Poetry*. Powell, Hunt joked, had often wondered whether it was worth £40. But George M. Smith Jr. of Smith, Elder and Co. now repaid Powell his £40, and Hunt £60 more, to publish an extended version of the essay under the title 'An Answer to the Question: "What is Poetry?"', by way of an introduction to an anthology entitled *Imagination and Fancy*. The objects of the volume, whose introductory essay has since become a classic, were threefold: 'to present the public with some of the finest passages in English poetry, marked and commented; to furnish such an account, in an essay, of the nature and requirements of poetry as may enable readers in general to give an answer on those points to themselves and others; and to show, throughout the greater part of the volume, what sort of poetry is to be considered as poetry of the most poetical kind . . . in its element, like an essence distilled.' Regarded as his finest work of theoretical criticism, Hunt's essay 'What is Poetry?' has now come to overshadow his intriguing selection of poets, which included Spenser, Marlowe, Shakespeare, Jonson, Beaumont and Fletcher, Middleton, Dekker, Webster, Milton, Coleridge, Shelley and Keats – but omitted Byron. 'It will,' remarked Elizabeth Barrett Browning, 'be a companion to me for the rest of my life.'

Published in 1844, reprinted in 1846 and frequently thereafter, the anthology's success moved Hunt to plan more such collections, taking as his themes 'Action and Passion', 'Contemplation', 'Wit and Humour' and 'Song'. But ill-health again put paid to his hopes. *Wit and Humour* proved the only subsequent volume in the series to make it as far as publication; its scope was billed as ranging from 'Chaucer to Byron', but Byron, again, was mentioned only in the Introduction, not quoted in the anthology itself.

Aware that Hunt still laboured under heavy debts, for all his industry, Mary Shelley now wrote to him of her hopes of honouring her husband's promise of an annuity; the present baronet, Sir Timothy, was finally sinking: 'Ere long there will be a change.' The £2000 originally promised by Shelley would no longer be possible; but Mary proposed that after Sir Timothy's death she would give directions to her banker to honour Hunt's cheques for £30 a quarter; this would be secured not only to Hunt, but also to Marianne, should she survive him. Percy Shelley, her son and heir, had read her letter and approved the grant. 'I know your *real* delicacy about money matters, and that you will at once be ready to enter into my views; and feel assured that if any present debt should press, if we have any command of money, we will take care to free you from it.' This time around, having lingered such an inconveniently long time, Sir Timothy did indeed pass on, and Hunt finally had his £120 a year.

All this time Forster and others had been trying to negotiate Hunt a state pension (then not uncommon for writers and other creative artists). But if Hunt felt sorry for himself, which he rarely did, the newspapers for June 1846 brought news that others were faring far worse; misquoting *King Lear* – 'Stretch me no longer on this rough world' – Haydon had shot himself. 'I have just read of poor Haydon!' Hunt wrote to Forster. 'How dreadful! how *astonishing*! for he is one of the last men of whom I should have expected such a thing. I looked upon him as one who turned disappointment itself to a kind of self-glory – but see how we may be mistaken. Poor fellow! but then, poor *family*! That is the worst.'

Hunt's own fortunes, by contrast, seemed at last to be on the rise. Horne's *A New Spirit of the Age*, an update of Hazlitt almost twenty years later, mentioned him in the same breath as Wordsworth. 'In religious feeling, [Hunt] has been misrepresented. It is certain that no man was ever more capable of the spirit of reverence; for God gifted him with a loving genius – with a genius to love and bless. He looks full tenderly into the face of every man, and woman, and child, and living creature; and the beautiful exterior world, even when it is in angry mood, he smoothes down softly, as in recognition of its sentiency, with a gentle caressing of the fancy – Chaucer's irrepressible "Ah, benedicite" falling for ever from his lips.'

Appreciative as he was, Hunt must have been chagrined to be acknowledged less for his own work than the inspiration he had offered others. 'He is an original writer,' opined Horne, 'his individuality extending into mannerism . . . When he says new things, he puts them strikingly; when he says old things, he puts them newly – and no intellectual and good-tempered reader will complain of this freshness, on account of a certain "knack at trifling" in which he sometimes chooses to indulge.' If there is a somewhat patronising note in all this, Horne rather lazily concludes his tribute by quoting himself (without attribution) from the dedication of his *The Death of Marlowe*: 'You have long assisted, largely and most successfully, to educate the hearts and heads of both old and young; and the extent of the service is scarcely perceptible, because the free and familiar spirit in which it has been rendered gives it the semblance of an involuntary emanation. The spontaneous diffusion of intelligence and good feeling is not calculated, however, to force its attention upon general perception, etc.' Because Hunt had no 'system', and no 'sustained gravity of countenance', Horne went on, 'the fineness of his intellect and the great value of his unprofessor-like teaching' had been 'extremely underrated'. Significantly, and fruitfully, he also reiterated 'this disgrace to the age – which shall be as distinctly stated as such a disgrace deserves – that while the public generally takes it for granted that Mr Leigh Hunt is on the Pension List, he most certainly is *not*, and never has been!'

Horne's tribute was soon followed by a charming compliment from the Scottish poet and critic George Gilfillan, in his own assessment of his contemporaries' place in literary history: 'Hunt, we need say, is *the* Companion. Most easy, and talkative, and good-humoured of companions, thou hast to us beguiled not a few hours while reading, and not a few while at present writing of thee. Our glad hours owe thee much, for thou hast gladdened them still more.

Our sad hours owe thee more, for thou hast soothed and brightened them at times.'

Amid these welcome rewards for his labours, Hunt now had to endure the bitter-sweet mixture of pride and sorrow which can befall all but the most fortunate parents; in 1846, soon after he had written a preface for a novel by Thornton, *The Foster-Brother*, his prodigal son John died at the age of thirty-two, leaving an impover-ished widow and several small children. 'He had been in low water for some time,' reports Blunden, who was privy to a letter from John to his mother, apparently dating from 1843, 'bitterly blaming her for instilling the worst opinions of him into the mind of Leigh Hunt' and for refusing him help. 'Does he know that I write for *Cleave's Gazette* at one shilling per column? *No*. But he *is* told I write petitioning letters – and therefore thinks I won't work . . . I am dreadfully ill. I see only something worse at hand than this starv-ing . . .' Thornton, who assisted John's destitute family until they emigrated to Australia, wrote of his brother that 'from the very earliest to the very latest, he never lost a sense of deference and affection for Leigh Hunt'.

Thornton himself was now more prosperous (if no more careful with his money) than his father. 'The beatitude,' Hunt had written after the Shelley bequest, 'of actually paying as I go, and incurring no more bills!' As usual, he proved far too optimistic; within a year he was applying to the new baronet, Sir Percy, for leave to draw a year's advance on the annuity; it would seem to be no coincidence that his latest book, *Stories from the Italian Poets*, was dedicated that same year to Sir Percy Shelley Bt., by 'your Father's Friend'.

With Marianne's domestic mismanagement growing worse, and her secret borrowings from his friends blackening Hunt's name behind his back, institutional help was finally at hand. On 22 June 1847 Hunt received a very welcome letter from Downing Street:

Sir, I have much pleasure in informing you that the Queen has been pleased to direct that, in consideration of your distinguished liter-ary talents, a pension of Two Hundred Pounds yearly should be settled upon you from the funds of the Civil List. Allow me to add, that the severe treatment you formerly received, in times of unjust

persecution of liberal writers, enhances the satisfaction with which
I make this announcement.

Lord John Russell, PM.

'I feel,' said Hunt, 'as if history itself were deigning to speak to me
as a friend.'

History was not his only friend. Hunt's state pension – 'a most
welcome and gratefully acknowledged compensation', to Thornton,
'of time and money torn from him in early years' – was the result of
more than a decade of lobbying by a legion of admirers and acquaintances, dating back to an application on his behalf from the
well-connected diplomat, linguist and writer Sir John Bowring in
1836 – and beyond.

Had Haydon, himself no stranger to debt and its consequences,
put in a good word for his friend while painting Melbourne's portrait
in 1832? It seems unlikely, though his sitter had asked about Hazlitt,
Hunt, Keats and Shelley, and 'seemed much amused at my anecdotes'. Six years later Forster, Horne and Talfourd, while promoting
that 'Private List' of annual subscribers to a Hunt fund, also
approached Lord Melbourne about his case for a pension. But
Melbourne, as Macaulay indiscreetly wrote to Hunt in March 1841,
was 'not so much of a Maecenas as might be expected from his
understanding, his numerous accomplishments and his kind nature.
To get anything from him, for a man of letters, is almost as difficult
as to get a Dukedom.'

In his next letter, holding out hope of the laureateship, Macaulay
went so far as to enclose some cash. 'I am sorry and ashamed for my
country that a man of so much merit should have endured so much distress,' he told Hunt, inviting him to call on him in Whitehall. 'I am far
from rich, but can at present spare without inconvenience the sum
which I enclose.' Hunt's 'distress and gratitude', Macaulay told a colleague three days later, were 'really heart-breaking'. By August he was
sadly telling Hunt: 'I'm afraid I have no good news for you.' He had
urged Melbourne 'as strongly as I could' at the last Cabinet meeting,
but the Prime Minister was 'beset' by requests with 'scarcely anything
left to give'.

Lord and Lady Holland now lent their names to the cause, soon followed by Forster. Even the frugal Carlyle had drawn up 'Memoranda concerning Mr Leigh Hunt', whose sixth clause argued that 'such a man is rare in a nation, and of high value there; not to be *procured* for a whole nation's revenue, or recovered when taken from us, and some £200 a year is the price which this one, whom we now have, is valued at'. With such a sum he would be 'lifted above his perplexities, perhaps saved from nameless wretchedness'. Carlyle could think of no other way £200 could 'abolish as much suffering, create as much benefit to one man, and through him to many and all'. So why had public recognition taken so long? Hunt had simply lived too long, according to the literary historian J.E. Morpurgo. 'Hunt had outlived his generation, and in living too long, had lost the attention and the respect of his accidental contemporaries and slipped the plaudits of posterity.'

But even a state pension was not going to stop Hunt working. Horne had him collaborating with Wordsworth, Landor and others on a new 'translation' of Chaucer, for which Hunt 'modernised' *The Squire's Tale* and *The Friar's Tale*. In his introduction Horne ascribed the 'great advances in versification' to Coleridge, Shelley, Hunt and Tennyson. Despite irritating disputes with Horne over fidelity to the original, Hunt's contribution proved the most admired. One review described Hunt as 'the most constant and enthusiastic lover of Chaucer in the nineteenth century'. When an ugly moment from the past seemed to resurface with Henry Chorley's sneer in the *Athenæum* that Chaucer had been 'brought down to Cockney comprehension', Hunt was specifically exempted. It was Horne's version which did Chaucer a 'stumbling, tampering' disservice while Hunt's were more faithful, with 'an easy, colloquial air'.

Eighteen forty-seven proved an especially prolific year, with publication of a collection of Hunt's critical essays under the title *Men, Women and Books*, a series of essays for the *Atlas* entitled 'Streets of London' (posthumously published in 1861 as *A Saunter Through the West End*) and a further collection of essays about poetry billed as *A Jar of Honey from Mount Hybla*. Walking down Piccadilly one day, Hunt spotted a blue jar in the window of Fortnum and Mason labelled 'Sicilian Honey'. 'You may imagine what a world of southern beauty & luxury two such words would suggest to a spectator of any fancy,' he enthused

to Harrison Ainsworth, in whose eponymous magazine he would publish the subsequent 'offerings' from his fantastical jar before they were
collected in book form. Dedicated to his old friend and perennial
champion Horace Smith, *A Jar of Honey* was chosen by Smith and Elder
as their 'Christmas book', sent to favoured clients and authors. One of
the recipients of this collection of 'essays on pastoral poetry and
kindred pleasures', in an edition with a decorated binding, showing 'a
blue jar wreathed with green tendrils against a honey-yellow background, all framed by ivy', was the Smith and Elder author Charlotte
Brontë.

In a covering letter written on Christmas Day 1847, with which she
returned the corrected proofs of the preface to the second edition of
Jane Eyre, Brontë wrote: 'Permit me to thank you for your present
which reached me yesterday. I was not prepared for anything so truly
tasteful, and when I had opened the parcel, removed the various
envelopes, and at last got a glimpse of the chastely attractive binding,
I was most agreeably surprised. What is better; on examination, I find
the contents fully answer to the expectation excited by the charming
exterior; the *Honey* is quite as choice as the *Jar* is elegant. The illustra-
tions too are very beautiful – some of them peculiarly so. I trust the
Public will shew itself grateful for the pains you have taken to provide
a book so appropriate to the season!'

Eighteen forty-eight saw publication in two volumes of *The Town*,
also from Smith and Elder, subtitled 'Its Memorable Characters and
Events: St Paul's to St James's', of which Charlotte Brontë wrote: 'I
took up Leigh Hunt's book 'The Town' with an impression that it
would be interesting only to Londoners, and I was surprised, ere I
had read many pages, to find myself enchained by his pleasant,
graceful, easy style, varied knowledge, just views and kindly spirit.'
She found 'something peculiarly anti-melancholic in Hunt's writings – and yet they are never boisterous – they resemble sunshine –
being at once bright and tranquil'. Another contemporary declared
that Hunt 'had illuminated the fog and smoke of London with a
halo of glory, and peopled the streets and buildings with the life of
past generations'.

That autumn, while working on a play entitled *The Secret Marriage*
(commissioned by Sadler's Wells, but never staged), Hunt was visited

by Ralph Waldo Emerson, the first of several eminent Americans who
would come to pay their respects in his later years. 'Hunt charmed
him,' reports Emerson's host, Alexander Ireland, editor of the
Manchester Examiner and Times (and father of the composer John
Ireland). 'His courteous and winning manner was on this occasion
tempered by a certain delicate reverence, indicating how deeply he felt
the honour of being thus sought out by his distinguished visitor.'
Emerson later opined that De Quincey and Hunt had the finest manners of any literary men he ever met.

As eminent contemporaries came calling, still Hunt's guidance and
blessing was sought by aspirant writers – and never denied. One such
request now arrived from twenty-year-old Dante Gabriel Rossetti,
enclosing a sheaf of poems with a plea for advice and assistance. As
always, Hunt responded as helpfully as he could: 'I guess indeed that
you are altogether not so musical as pictorial.' He discerned 'an
unquestionable poet' in Rossetti, 'thoughtful, imaginative, and with
rare powers of expression. I hailed you such at once, without any mis-
giving.' But he also warned: 'Poetry . . . is not a thing for man to live
upon while he is in the flesh, however immortal it may render him in
the spirit.'

Now in his mid-sixties, Hunt was reaching the age when things
new-born all too often coincide with those dying. The autumn of
1848, specifically 7 September, brought news of the demise of his
doughty brother John, with whom he had been through so much.
'There was one man, and one man only, towards whom Hazlitt
seemed to cherish a feeling of unmingled personal affection and
regard,' wrote P.G. Patmore, an early contributor to the *Examiner*.
Added Horace Smith: 'Calm, firm, upright, he reminded you of
Horace's "justum et tenacem propositi virum", though perhaps his
character might have found a better prototype in the republican than
the imperial days of Rome.' The *Examiner*'s obituary of its founder was
written by Albany Fonblanque.

His devotion to truth and justice had no bounds; there was no peril,
no suffering, that he was not ready to encounter for either. With resolution and fortitude not to be surpassed, he was one of the gentlest
and kindest of beings. His own sufferings were the only sufferings to

which he could be indifferent . . . We never heard him repine; seldom, on the other hand, had he occasion to rejoice, and never for long. He took whatever befell him calmly, as his portion, and with a manly yet sweet resignation . . . Unconscious prejudice might enter into his views occasionally: but they were honest, according to his lights; and in the days of martyrdom a martyr he would cheerfully have been for what he deemed the truth. John Hunt never put forth a claim of any kind on the world. He had fought the battle in the front ranks when the battle was the hottest: but he passed into retirement in the very hour of victory as if he had done nothing, and deserved nothing of the triumphant cause . . .

Six months later there was happier domestic news, with the marriage in 1849 of the Hunts' twenty-one-year-old daughter Jacintha to twenty-six-year-old Charles Smith Cheltnam, a pupil of that family friend W.J. Linton, the wood-engraver. Cheltnam soon gave up engraving for writing, eventually becoming manager of the *Morning Chronicle* when his brother-in-law Thornton Hunt was its editor.

In the absence of more vivid descriptions from Carlyle, no longer a neighbour of the Hunts, Edmund Blunden has painted a fanciful picture of the Hunt household in Kensington at this time:

Hunt, with his 'singing robes' about him, is striding up and down his study, dictating to his helper Vincent, who looks haggard, and coughs now and then. But Vincent will not be excused duty. 'Let's go on.' Or else, Leigh Hunt is having his supper, and recommending it to his visitor – dried fruit, bread, and water; or three boiled eggs. Perhaps some of his children have come in. The pure-hearted Vincent is almost certainly there, talking to his sister Julia, the girl with the sparkling black eyes and a fine soprano. Henry, when he sings, has a fine tenor . . . There is also Jacintha. Captain Thomas of the Bengal Lancers thinks of writing a poem on her; but Leigh Hunt observes 'Jacintha is herself a verse.' Captain Thomas punningly hopes not . . .

We do not expect to see Thornton. He is a busy man, both at the newspaper offices and at his large house on Sunday nights – bread and cheese and beer for revolutionary refugees, emancipated novelists, clergymen with Socialist views, painters. We do not see Mrs Hunt; it is hinted that she dislikes any exertion, and she remains in her room. You never know, however, what celebrity may walk in. Procter, Mr and Mrs Browning, Allingham, Lewes – it is an unusual parlour in this as in other respects . . .

A less whimsical, more informed vignette of Hunt at this time comes from his 'busy' son Thornton, beginning with the memorable line: 'He saw everything through books, or he saw it dimly.' Thornton's father

failed in practical life, because he was not guided in it by literature. He could only apprehend so much of it as he found in the cyclopae-dia. On the other hand, he could render all that literature could give. His memory was marvellous; and to try him in history, biog-raphy, bibliography or topography, was to draw forth an oral 'article' on the topic in question.

Ask him where was the Ouse, and he would tell you of all the rivers so called; what were the books on a given subject, and you had the list; 'Who was Colonel O'Kelly?' and you had a sketch of the colonel, of the horse 'Eclipse', of Epsom, and of horse-racing in general, as distinguished from the racing of the ancients or the modern riderless races of Italy – where, as in Florence, may still be seen a specimen of the biga sweeping round the meta *'fervidis evitata rotis'*.

Hunt's conversation was 'an exhaustless *Curiosities of Literature*. The delighted visitor *read* his host – but it was from a talking book, with cordial voice naturally pitched to every change of subject, animated gesture, sparkling eyes, and overflowing sympathy.' In society Hunt was 'ever the perfect gentleman, not in the fashion, but always the scholar and the noble-minded man. But his diffidence was disguised, rather than removed, by his desire to agree with those around him, and to fall in with the humour of the hour. He was better known to his reader, either in his books, or, best of all, in his home, where familiarity tested his unfailing courtesy, daily intercourse brought forth the persevering goodness of his heart and conscience, and poverty did but fetch out the thorough-going generosity that not only "*would* share" but did share the last crust.'

At sixty-five Hunt was continuing to pour out the collections which had helped turn round his fortunes since their low point in the mid-1830s, when he had first gathered some previously published essays between hard covers in *The Indicator and the Companion* (1834). This proved successful enough to be followed by such collections as *The Seer* (1840, mostly from *Leigh Hunt's London Journal*); *Essays by Leigh Hunt: The Indicator, The Seer* (1841), *Men, Women, and Books* and *A Jar of Honey from Mount Hybla* (both 1847) and *The Town* (1848). Now, in 1849, came *A Book for a Corner*, subtitled 'Selections in Prose and Verse from Authors the Best Suited to That Mode of Enjoyment, with Comments on Each and a General Introduction', and *Readings for Railways*, or 'Anecdotes and Other Short Stories, Reflections, Maxims, Characteristics, Passages of Wit, Humour and Poetry, etc., Together with Points of Information on Matters of General Interest collected in the course of the Author's own reading'. He was meanwhile contributing poems to *Ainsworth's Magazine* and the *New Monthly*. But above all, in the autumn of 1849, he was at work on his memoirs.

Published in three volumes in 1850, the *Autobiography* of Leigh Hunt is generally adjudged his best book, though he was highly reluctant to accept Smith and Elder's commission. Shamelessly recycling much of his 1828 account of Byron and other contemporaries, Hunt more or less admitted in the preface that he had done it only for the money: 'The work . . . was commenced under circumstances which committed me to its execution, and would have been abandoned at almost every step, had those circumstances allowed.' Much of it proved 'painful' to write. But, in one twentieth-century judgement, 'the dignity and poetry of the autobiographer transform the pain into the reader's easy and beautiful travel'.

And the exercise at last gave Hunt the chance finally to make his peace with such erstwhile *bêtes noires* as the late King George IV, his attack upon whom (as Prince Regent) had made his name. 'Neither have I any quarrel, at this distance in time, with the Prince Regent; for though his frivolity, his tergiversation, and his treatment of his wife, will not allow me to respect his memory, I am bound to pardon it as I do my own faults, in consideration of the circumstances which mould the character of every human being. Could I meet him in some odd corner of the Elysian fields, where charity had room for both of us, I should first apologize to him for having been the instrument in the hand of events for attacking a fellow creature, and then expect to hear him avow as hearty a regret for having injured myself, and unjustly treated his wife.'

Having long since made his peace with Tom Moore, now sunk into senile dementia, Hunt also sought some settlement with the shade of Byron: 'I wrote nothing that I did not feel to be true, or think so. But I can say . . . that I was then a young man, and that I am now advanced in years. I can say that I was agitated by grief and anger, and that I am now free from anger. I can say that I was far more alive to other people's defects than to my own, and that I am now sufficiently sensible of my own to show to others the charity which I need myself. I can say, moreover, that apart from a little allowance for provocation, I do not think it right to exhibit what is amiss, or may be thought amiss, in the character of a fellow-creature, out of any feelings but unmistakable sorrow, or the wish to lessen evils which society itself may have caused . . . I am sorry I ever wrote a syllable respecting Lord Byron which might have been spared.' Gifford alone was refused Hunt's farewell pardon, as 'the only man I ever attacked, respecting whom I have felt no regret'.

Among those to whom he sent copies were the Carlyles, from whom he had become somewhat estranged since his move from Chelsea to Kensington. Praised in the book for his 'honesty and eloquence' while rebuked for his 'habit of denouncing', Carlyle wrote a fulsome letter of thanks, describing Hunt's volume as 'by far the best book of the autobiographic kind' in English. This emboldened Hunt to invite himself to visit them in Cheyne Row to 'take my good old North-British supper with you'. He duly went on 25 June and had a plate of porridge.

'I have just finished your *Autobiography*, which has been most pleasantly occupying all my leisure these three days; and you must permit me to write you a word upon it, out of the fullness of my heart, while the impulse is still fresh to thank you,' Carlyle had written to Hunt the previous week. 'I call this an excellently good Book, by far the best of the autobiographic kind I remember to have read in the English Language; and indeed, except it be Boswell's of Johnson, I do not know where we have such a picture drawn of a human life as in these three volumes. A pious, ingenious, altogether *human* and worthy book, imaging, with graceful honesty and free felicity, many interesting objects and persons on your life-path – and imaging throughout, what is best of all, a gifted, gentle, patient and valiant human soul, as it buffets its way thro' the billows of the time, and will not drown, tho' often in danger; *cannot* be drowned, but conquers, and leaves a track of radiance behind it . . .'

This elegant and generous image, Carlyle assured Hunt, 'comes out more clearly to me than in any other of your books; and that, I can venture to assure you, is the best of all results to realize in a book or written record'. Hunt's memoirs had been 'like an exercise of *devotion*' to Carlyle: 'I have not assisted at any sermon, liturgy or litany, this long while, that has had so *religious* an effect on me. Thanks in the name of all men. And believe along with me that this book will be welcome to other generations as well as to ours. And long may you live to write more books for us; and may the evening sun be softer on you (and on me) than the noon sometimes was!'

Carlyle was not alone in his high estimation of Hunt's memoirs. Charles Kent, editor of *The Times* for twenty-five years, considered the book had a 'right to be placed upon the same shelf with Lockhart's Scott, and even with Boswell's Johnson'. Said the Duke of Devonshire: 'I do not like to have received so much pleasure and amusement from the perusal of a book, as your *Autobiography* has given me, without making my acknowledgements to you. And though you tell in it, it was a task unwillingly performed, the success of its execution calls for the sincere congratulations of your friends . . .' In the back of his presentation copy, after the closing pages summing up the author's simple, unselfish, ever optimistic philosophy of life, Hunt's friend and admirer R.H. Horne wrote: 'And if you, brave and tender-hearted Leigh Hunt, had never written anything but the concluding pages of this book, you would nevertheless deserve to rank among the greatest benefactors of mankind.'

As always with Hunt, however, something had to go wrong. Amid lavish praise on all sides, he had inevitably upset some of his readers, even friends and acquaintances. Forster was put out by his 'insufficient' mention, as was the playwright Douglas Jerrold, who threatened to throw away all the books by Hunt in his library. There were others who saw the book, not without reason, simply as a job application for the poet laureateship.

In April 1850, just as the *Autobiography* was emerging, Wordsworth died at the age of eighty. Hunt's disappointment ten years earlier lingered in the minds of some of his admirers. One was herself now a candidate, Elizabeth Barrett Browning, who preferred Hunt for the post ('if one discounted his lack of delicacy and good taste'), on the grounds that he was 'a great and good man who had been long neglected by the world'. To her friend Mary Russell Mitford she wrote: 'I think he has been wronged by many, & that even you, your own just truthful & appreciating self, do not choose soft words enough to suit his case.' Citing a disagreement over Hunt's *Rimini*, Mrs Browning rejected the notion that the poem had an 'immoral' tendency. 'Indeed my belief is exactly the reverse. The final impression of that poem, most beautiful surely as a poem, appears to me morally unexceptionable. The "poetical justice" is worked out too from the *sin itself*, – & not from a cause independent of it, after the fashion of those pseudo-moralists who place the serpent's sting anywhere but in the serpent. We are made to feel & see that apart from the discovery, apart from the husband's vengeance on the lover, both sinners are miserable & one must die. *She* was dying, without the blow – The sin involved the death-agony! – Who can read these things tearless, & without a deep enforced sense of "the sinfulness of sin"?'

As he published an 'Ode to the Sun', a meditation on 'Death' and his vivid Gothic ballad 'Wallace and Fawdon' in the *New Monthly*, Hunt's old foes at the *Athenæum* predictably launched a vigorous campaign against the laureateship as a 'meaningless, offensive, intellectually servile appointment' that no self-respecting poet should consider. The only remedy was the abolition of the title. Failing that, the main thing was that it should not go to Leigh Hunt, who already enjoyed a state pension. 'Mr Hunt should not have a double benefice.'

Eventually Hunt himself went public on the matter – given his 'particular reasons for wishing to give his opinion on the subject' – with the view that 'if the office is in future really to be bestowed on the highest degree of poetical merit, and on that only, then Mr Alfred Tennyson is entitled to it above any other man in the kingdom; since of all living poets he is the most gifted with the sovereign and poetical faculty, Imagination'.

In the 1850 version of Hunt's autobiography (omitted in its 1860 reissue), half the final chapter finds Hunt explaining at some length why he feels no claim to the laureateship 'as has been thought by many'. In the process he reprints his patriotic effusions of the previous decade and insists that he is a 'royalist of the right English sort'. When Tennyson was indeed named Poet Laureate that November, Thackeray wrote to William Allingham, whom he had met through Hunt: 'I hope dear old Leigh Hunt won't take the loss of the laurels to heart after bidding for them so naively as he did in those pleasant memoirs.'

After the publication of *In Memoriam*, his monumental elegy for his friend Arthur Hallam, Tennyson's standing was at its highest. Twenty-five years Hunt's junior, he effectively ended whatever hopes Hunt had of landing a comfortable sinecure to which he would have been well suited. There is nothing to suggest that Hunt was especially downcast to miss out again, or indeed that he resented Tennyson's appointment; quite the reverse, as he had done much to promote a younger poet he genuinely admired.

If it was establishment recognition for his life's work that Hunt was craving by none too subtly campaigning for the post in such demeaning style, there is no doubt that his hopes were effectively rendered null and void by his youthful offences against royalty, of which his memoirs had recently informed those too young to remember them. As another door was closed against him, he still had other battles left to fight.

Throughout 1850, his sixty-sixth year, Hunt increasingly felt 'ratherish unwell'. In July 1851, after ten years in Edwardes Square, he moved his family the short distance across Kensington to Phillimore Terrace (now Allen Street), off Kensington High Road (now Street). As the new decade began, Hunt became 'more and more sedentary'. Illness even prevented him, much to his disappointment, visiting the Great Exhibition of 1851. Such occasional outings as he did make at this time were all chronicled for Dickens's magazine *Household Words*, and eventually published in book form as *The Old Court Suburb* (1855), full of such charming fancies as: 'When we quit Piccadilly for Hyde Park Corner, we always fancy that the air, somehow, feels not only fresher but *whiter*.'

He also recounted meeting a woman who, on meeting Coleridge walking through Edwardes Square, had been honoured with a kiss. Of the French architect who had built the square, Hunt imagined him musing: 'Here shall be cheap lodging and *fête champêtre* combined; here, economy indoors, and Watteau without; promenades; *la belle passion*; perusal of newspapers on benches; an ordinary at the Holland Arms – a French Arcadia, in short, or a little Palais Royal, in an English suburb.'

But Hunt's Arcadia was clouded by his youngest son Vincent's serious illness. For more than a decade, since Thornton's departure, he had relied on this 'willing and sweet-tempered young man' for companionship and assistance with his work. Like his aunt Bessy, Vincent wrote about flowers; he had published some sonnets in the *Athenæum*; he played the piano, like his father, with more 'rapture' than skill. One evening Vincent wrote a touching sonnet about his father snoozing over his book:

> The firelight flickers on the wall of books,
> While my dear father slumbers in its shade,
> And leaning as he sits, his head he's laid
> 'Gainst his beloved Spenser; and he looks
> As though his mind through those delicious nooks
> Of Fairy-land with perfect Una stray'd, –
> List'ning to all the lovely things she said
> In a voice far sweeter than Spenserian brooks.
> Alas! that that so loved fine face should be
> Scor'd by life's sufferings more than by its years,
> So that in calmest sleep it is not free
> From sorrow-marks that dim mine eyes with tears:
> And yet (thank God!) that patient kind face wears
> A youthful vigour still, divine to see.

Vincent's illness stemmed from a ride on an omnibus in the winter rain; his reward for giving his seat to a washerwoman and riding on the top deck, open to the elements, was tuberculosis. Throughout the summer of 1851 his life was in danger; but that autumn he rallied, and his father took him to the healthier air of Ewell, in Surrey, for the three months before Christmas. They returned to Kensington with high hopes, only to find them dashed by the family doctors, George Bird and Southwood Smith. Vincent 'faded with the leaves', and died early the following year, not yet thirty. Wrote Hunt: 'It was a colder break of dawn than usual, but equally beautiful, as if, in both respects, it came to take him away, when my son died. His last words were poetry itself. A glass of water had been given to him at his request; and on feeling the refreshment of it, he said "I drink the morning."'

Hunt's friend Francis H. Grundy, their host in Ewell, considered Vincent 'the best of all Leigh Hunt's children'. Whether or not he was Hunt's 'favourite' child, as has been suggested, there is no doubt that Vincent's death affected Hunt deeply. 'For nearly two years I saw him fading before my eyes; and a like time elapsed before he ceased to be the chief preoccupation of my thoughts.' Henceforth Hunt became more reserved and reflective, more spiritually inclined than ever. He started keeping private notebooks filled with 'lamentations and hopes and apprehensions of the immortals in the universe'.

As Vincent lay dying, Hunt had managed to produce yet another collection, *Table-Talk* ('to which are added Imaginary Conversations of Pope and Swift') and launch one last periodical, *Leigh Hunt's Journal*, a 'Miscellany for the Cultivation of the Memorable, the Progressive, and the Beautiful'. It lasted from 7 December 1850 to 29 March 1851 before closing the long list of his publishing casualties. As Morpurgo charmingly puts it of Hunt's many forays into the publication of periodicals, he was 'always too brilliantly discursive and too violently partisan to receive the mediocre applause of a successful circulation'.

The project had been the idea of a young man from Manchester known as 'Turpentine' Smith; having made a fortune in cotton, he had written a life of Mirabeau and come to London with literary aspirations. Smith had attempted to edit his own journal, *Social Aspects*, before seeking out Hunt with what was left of his capital. Hunt solicited contributions from Landor, Allingham, Carlyle and Tennyson;

all but the last complied. But Smith felt that Hunt was paying his contributors too much; after only four months he decamped back to Manchester, where he found therapy by publishing a series of stinging attacks on Leigh and Marianne Hunt before giving up literature and returning to his more lucrative calling.

Amid a year of political turmoil which saw the resignation of Palmerston, the defeat of Lord John Russell and the advent of a new Tory government under Lord Derby, with Disraeli as Chancellor, Hunt and his circle appear to have been more exercised about the politics of the recently founded London Library. Hunt had congratulated the Library's founding fathers in his preface to *Stories from the Italian Poets*, published five years after its foundation in 1841; now he was able to order books to be sent to his home, rather than consulting them in the British Museum, which was 'highly desirable' for literati, like himself, prone to illness or constraints of time and distance. So he lent his support to a campaign led by Carlyle, one of the Library's founding fathers, to prevent the Italian-born James Lacaita, a protégé of Gladstone, being appointed its new librarian; his efforts met with success on 12 June 1852, when Lacaita (whom Carlyle dubbed 'the Signor of merit') was defeated by William Bodham Donne.

Thanks to the industry of the American scholar David H. Stam, formerly director of the Syracuse University Libraries and the Research Libraries of the New York Public Library, we have a fascinatingly detailed picture of Hunt's use of the London Library during the 1840s, when he was often ill at home while remaining remarkably prolific. A self-styled 'glutton for books', Hunt borrowed no fewer than 238 volumes from the London Library in the period from December 1844 to June 1846, many connected with his work on *Stories from the Italian Poets*.

While finding 'neither a treasure-trove of rich annotation, nor a smoking gun of library abuse', Stam discovered interesting examples of 'Leontine graffiti' in at least twenty-five of the books Hunt borrowed. 'Untrue', for example, in the margin of Henri Beyle's (Stendahl's) *Life of Haydn . . . followed by the Life of Mozart* (1817), as regards the argument that 'composers have advantages over other artists because their productions are finished as soon as imagined'. In Richard Brathwait's

bilingual edition of *Barnabee's Journal* (1818), adjacent to a passage on
'doleful teares', Hunt had written: 'Yet you continue them, reinvent
them 20 years after? This cannot have been Barnabie.' On page 16 of
Moses Samuels's *Memoirs of Moses Mendelssohn, the Jewish Philosopher*
(1827), he drew a vertical line beside the following passage, under-
scoring its last two words: 'There was not a branch of mathematics to
which Mendelssohn did not now apply himself; his knowledge of alge-
bra, fluxions, and judician astronomy is said to have been
considerable . . . we mention his peculiar skill in *mercantile accounts*'
(Hunt's emphasis).

Stam, who regards Hunt as 'a guileless innocent, an often naïve
optimist throughout many travails, and an astute critic of various
aspects of nineteenth-century English life', is touched by his response
to a philosopher's skill with accounts; a career librarian himself, he par-
dons Hunt's 'innocuous' marginalia as 'a few minor indiscretions, of
which any of us might be guilty'.

Now sixty-two, Hunt had become an elder statesman of English
letters – unchanged in his outlook on life, but a very different figure
from the fiery days of his radical youth. His few surviving friends from
the first two decades of the century, early champions of the liberal
reforms which had now largely come to pass, were as elderly and
demure as Hunt had himself become, while never quite losing the mischievous twinkle in those observant brown eyes. To the up-and-coming
young writers of the mid-century Hunt was something of an icon, the
only remaining link with the glory days of Shelley, Keats and Byron, the
recipient of many humble petitions for advice and assistance, which was
always freely on offer.

Tennyson and Rossetti, for instance, were but two of the then rising,
now established writers who owed Hunt as much as, in their day, did
Keats and Shelley, not to mention Wordsworth. 'Wherever one looks
in the nineteenth-century literary scene in England,' in the words of
one contemporary scholar, 'Leigh Hunt's influence is apparent.'

It was because of his literary standing that Hunt was one of those
approached in mid-1852 by the bookseller John Chapman, publisher of
'free-thinking' books, and new owner of the *Westminster Review*, to lend
his name to a campaign Chapman was mounting against the Booksellers
Association, the price-fixing cartel then preventing small publishers

from offering discounts of more than 10 per cent on the published price of books.

At a protest meeting organised at Chapman's bookshop in the Strand on 4 May, a letter of support from Hunt was read out amid others from Carlisle, Gladstone, Mill and Cobden. In the chair was Charles Dickens, still only in his mid-thirties but already one of the most successful writers of the day. Dickens was yet another of the literary men with good reason to be grateful for Hunt's support and friendship as he started out on his career. But he was to repay Hunt's generosity in wholly unexpected and undeserved terms.

13

'A perfect child'

1852–3

Fifteen years earlier, in December 1837, Dickens had asked his close friend and eventual biographer John Forster to 'tell Leigh Hunt when you have an opportunity how much he has affected me, and how deeply I thank him for what he has done – you cannot say it too strongly'.

Hunt had written some 'delicately chosen words' about the inscription Dickens composed for the grave of his wife's sister, Mary Hogarth, whose recent death at the age of seventeen had affected him deeply. Hunt's 'beautiful passage', wrote Dickens, 'has given me the only feeling akin to pleasure – sorrowful pleasure it is – that I have yet had, connected with the loss of my dear young friend and companion for whom my love and attachment will never diminish'.

We can but wonder why Dickens – so devoted to his late sister-in-law as to express a wish to be buried with her – chose to ask a mutual friend to convey his thanks to Hunt rather than taking the trouble to do so himself. But his letter serves as some indication of the regard in which the rising twenty-five-year-old novelist held the fifty-three-year-old man of letters. Hunt was in turn beguiled by the precocious author of the previous year's *Pickwick Papers* – despite the intriguing fact that he himself had been high on the publisher Chapman and Hall's original list of potential authors to embellish the 'Nimrod Club' drawings of the cartoonist Robert Seymour. 'What a face is his to meet in a drawing-room!' Hunt wrote of Dickens to Forster, after he had introduced them earlier that year. 'It has the life and soul in it of fifty human beings.'

This was generous of Hunt, to whom Dickens owed more than either cared to admit. More than one critic has suggested that the influence of Hunt's fluent style as a prolific essayist can be divined in the *Sketches by Boz* which first brought the young Dickens to the attention of its publishers, Chapman and Hall, in the mid-1830s. In 1833–4, several years before Forster introduced them, Hunt was a regular contributor (under the name of 'The Townsman') to the *True Sun*, the radical journal on which Dickens first worked as a general reporter; a copy of *The Town*, the book in which Hunt collected these and later articles expressing his 'Townosophy', was listed as being in Dickens's library at the time of his death. The novelist Harrison Ainsworth once wrote to Hunt: 'I firmly believe that you paved the way to Dickens' great popularity. He has derived some of his best notions from you, and is, so to speak, reaping your harvest.' Later Edmund Blunden would go so far as to invite his readers to 'compare Hunt's writings on Christmas with those of Dickens'.

In 1836, before Boz's true identity was generally known, the editor of the *Court Journal*, Laman Blanchard, told a friend of Dickens – 'as a mighty secret' – that Boz was in fact his own friend Leigh Hunt. 'Knowing fellow, is he not?' Dickens commented sourly. Nonetheless, Dickens's diary and his correspondence with Hunt attest that, once Forster had brought them together, a lively and affectionate relationship developed between the young novelist and his ageing colleague. They met regularly, often over 'intemperate' dinners; they sent each other copies of their books as they appeared; and Dickens was clearly anxious for the approval of the 'old stager', as he rather boldly called Hunt.

'You are an old stager in works, but a young one in faith – faith in all beautiful and excellent things,' Dickens wrote to Hunt in July 1838, seeking his approval of *Oliver Twist* and *Nicholas Nickleby*. 'If you can only find it in that green heart of yours to tell me one of these days that you have met, in wading through the accompanying trifles, with anything that felt like a vibration of the old chord you have touched so often and sounded so well, you will confer on [me] the truest gratification.'

At this early stage of his relations with Hunt, Dickens was wide-eyed enough to want to follow where Keats, Shelley and Byron had once trod. Here was a fellow poet, if a lesser one, who had enjoyed intimate friendships with all three icons of the second generation of the Romantic movement, all of whom had died while Dickens was barely in his teens. Hunt's early years were by now the stuff of legend. And this was the man now publicly greeting him and his own work in such terms as: 'If ever a man of genius appeared whose lot would seem an enviable one, it is that of Mr Dickens; for he has been acknowledged as such at once, is young, popular, prosperous, *and doing good*. Of what other writers in the annals of literature could this be said?' Privately, meanwhile, Hunt wrote to Dickens: 'Your books – How much I wish I could say all I think & feel about them! . . . I admire you for your wit & humour, & love you as a humanist.'

So 1839 saw Dickens, who had by then known him three years, happily subscribing five guineas to the fund organised by a committee of Hunt's literary friends and admirers with the 'excellent object' of ensuring him an income of £3 a week. So close were they becoming that Dickens celebrated his twenty-seventh birthday that same year with 'only my own folks, Leigh Hunt, Ainsworth and Forster'. A month later, on 30 March, Macready reports Hunt as one of the guests of honour, along with Thackeray and Landseer, at a Shakespeare Club dinner chaired by Dickens.

The following year Dickens is sending Hunt a 'crowd' of thanks, 'treading on each others' heels and tripping one another up most pleasantly', for copies of his poems 'The Walk' and 'The Dinner', in such playful detail as to confirm that they had by now enjoyed many a walk and dinner together. Two months later he is to be found recommending Hunt's son Thornton to the committee of the Western Literary Institution as its librarian, for reasons beyond the 'great esteem and regard' in which he held his father. The postscript in the covering letter with the copy he sent Hunt suggests they had enjoyed a 'merry meeting' only the previous evening: 'I fancied there was the slightest possible peculiarity in your speech last night – just an elaborate show of distinctness – a remarkably correct delivery – an exquisite appreciation of the beauty of the language, with the faintest smack of wine running through it. This was mere fancy, I suppose?'

In January 1841, as Dickens struggled to finish *The Old Curiosity Shop*, there is a note of mutual affection in his remark to Forster that he was in 'what Leigh Hunt would call a kind of impossible state' while trying to come up with 'what on earth Master Humphrey can think of through four mortal pages'. In April of the following year he is citing Hunt's name and keeping him informed of progress in his copyright battle with American publishers during his first tour of the United States (chronicled in his *American Notes*). That July, back in London, he is complaining that Hunt has not sent him his play *A Legend of Florence* or his latest poetical work, *The Palfrey*, while admitting that he has obtained copies of both – and would like Hunt to sign them for him 'when that leg of mutton does come off (Good God, how long it has been unamputated!)'.

Other such ebullient letters precede what appears, in light of subsequent events, to have been a rather more significant one that December, in which Dickens writes to Hunt: 'I have received your letter – and received it with some pain. In heaven's name, don't imagine there is any man alive from whom you could possibly, if you knew his heart, accept a favour with less reason for feeling it a burden or a cause of uneasiness, than your faithful friend, C.D.'

Hunt's original letter to Dickens was no doubt destroyed in the novelist's notorious bonfire of his correspondence in 1860; but it is all too clear that he was thanking him for a loan – if 'a small one', according to the Oxford editors of Dickens's correspondence, since it was 'not shown in [Dickens's] accounts'.

Whatever his self-confessed failings with money, Hunt had always been scrupulous about repaying such loans, large or small, however long it might take him. As since the days of Shelley, a gift was one thing, accepted with thanks, but a loan quite another. A year later, in January 1844, Hunt was advanced the substantial sum of £200 by an aristocratic admirer, the Duke of Devonshire, for a period of two years. On the very last day of the due period, 12 January 1846, the Duke was astonished to receive the sum due, in full, whereupon he promptly went round to Hunt's house to return it to 'poor, noble, honourable' Hunt as a gift, remarking that he was 'himself Hunt's debtor' and that 'never before had borrowed money come back' to him. Similarly, in his journal for 15 July 1850, Macaulay notes with some irritation that 'Leigh

Hunt called – Talked all sorts of mawkish nonsense and paid me the £50 which he borrowed three years ago on solemn promise to pay in three months.' At least Hunt *had* repaid the debt, however belatedly, as John Hunter and others could testify from this rare moment of financial stability.

Beyond his father's permanent poverty, and his own early memories of debtor's jail, Hunt's attitude to matters material was shaped as far back as his schooldays – when, on an impulse, he once gave away a book he had borrowed from another boy. 'I made a present of it,' recalled Hunt (in a passage from his autobiography which he deleted from the second edition, perhaps because of its uneasy pre-echo of subsequent events). 'The wish to give was irresistible, and I gave.' When the book's rightful owner publicly accused him of theft, Hunt was 'ashamed; very sorry; very full of remorse'. But the offended party overplayed his hand, making too much of the matter with noisily scornful complaints to the point where the sympathy of Hunt's schoolfellows swung his way; suddenly other boys were siding with the self-confessed 'offender', restoring Hunt's self-respect and giving him a sense that perhaps he had, after all, been in the right. 'I left the school-room that morning with a particular air of self-resumption, putting on my gloves at the door, & cherishing a book under my arm, as if nothing had happened.'

With hindsight Hunt could see that this had proved 'an ill & dangerous process', leaving him with a sense that little or no reciprocal obligation need flow from the generosity of others. With Shelley, for instance, he shared just such a view: that Shelley had intermittent access to far greater means, and would share them with Hunt whenever he was able, without expecting any pecuniary return. If Hunt set no great store by money, it has been argued, it is because he was more used to receiving than giving it. Yet it is not just in Shelley's case that such financial generosity was amply repaid in kind, to the point where helping out his friend Hunt gave Shelley especial satisfaction. Many others, from Keats to numerous lesser writers, had reason to be grateful to Hunt. 'No man,' as Blunden puts it, 'was more generous in act so far as he had the means of serving another man. Shelley and Keats made his home theirs when they wished, and Haydon acknowledged the assistance that both John and Leigh Hunt gave him . . .'

R.H. Horne spoke of the 'minute critical labour' that Hunt was happy to lavish on manuscripts or proofs submitted for his appraisal. He has also explained – in a wholly indulgent tone of voice, for all Hunt's improvidence – how Hunt did not feel 'grateful' in the common sense of the word. 'He was incapable of feeling that he had himself conferred obligation, and he thought that at any rate the spirits of finer tone whom he met also avoided that idea. It was delightful to do well, and that virtue was its own reward.' Horne further maintains that 'Hunt, having received a benefit, was apt to be irritated when the doer asked for a service in return.'

On the rare occasions he had any money, moreover, Hunt would readily share it with others in distress. Haydon's journal is full of grateful entries: 'A friend came forward only to the extent of his power'; 'the Hunts nobly assisted me at cost of great personal deprivation'; 'Many friends forbore to press [payment of debts], the Hunts the foremost'; 'Helped as I was by John and Leigh Hunt, to the best of their limited means . . .'

Back in 1823, when his friend Byron was treating Hunt in such cavalier fashion in the wake of Shelley's death, Trelawny offered to lend Hunt money. 'No,' Hunt replied, 'I *will* take the money when I feel it in justice due to me, and I will *not* take it from a generous man who has already but too little to spare. You will therefore not think of sending it from Leghorn [Livorno], as it will only put me to the trouble of sending it you back again in Greece.'

Twenty years later, in 1843, a comedy of manners saw Hunt repay a loan from Macaulay, only for Macaulay to send back his cheque, which Hunt duly returned, Macaulay sent back again and Hunt returned again. Four years later the editor of the *Northampton Mercury*, G.J. de Wilde, noticed a certain 'weariness' in Hunt's journalism; on hearing that the doyen of his profession was ill and impoverished, de Wilde proposed the setting up of a fund on Hunt's behalf, and sent him a cheque for £5 to launch it. 'You must not think ill of me for returning the five-pound note,' Hunt wrote to his would-be benefactor. 'Should occasion render its re-appearance advisable, I promise you I will let you know; and I esteem and regard you so much, that were you a man of princely fortune I would not hesitate to accept a hundred times as much from you; but poets and humanists like my friends de Wilde and

[J.W.] Dalby . . . must have thousands of things to do with the fruits of their industry, which, short of the most loving necessity, must not be interfered with; and therefore you must be content with resuming the money, and leaving the obligation on my heart. *That* it shall never part with.'

Two years later in 1846, when the Shelley family had finally settled on Hunt his annual allowance of £120 – not the £2000 prescribed in the poet's will more than twenty years earlier, but it helped – Dickens had been among the first to congratulate him: 'No-one who knows and cherishes you can be better pleased . . . than I am.' In his autobiography Hunt paid due thanks by hailing the new baronet Sir Percy, Shelley's son by Mary, as 'worthy' of all the 'lustre' of his descent by virtue of 'his own intelligent and liberal nature'.

In July of that year, six months after his attempt to repay the Duke of Devonshire, Hunt also repaid Dickens's smaller loan of four years before. 'I was not glad to receive your letter,' came Dickens's acknowledgement. 'It affected me at first, with a sensation of pain that you should have so carefully remembered what I had so utterly forgotten.' But Hunt's financial problems persisted. And now his son John, also an indigent writer, had appalled Dickens's sense of propriety by himself applying for funds to such worthies as the Duke of Devonshire.

'One of the most persistent begging-letter writers in London', as John was described in the Casebook of the Literary Fund, Hunt's impoverished son was in the habit of using his father's name in such applications. Not until John's death had Hunt finally discovered this. When Dickens heard of it, he sympathised. 'I don't know what I should have done,' he told Forster, 'if I had been poor Hunt.'

When 1846–7 again saw Hunt losing the constant struggle to house and feed his large family, Dickens came to his rescue. In his dual roles as colleague and friend, Forster was more aware than most of Hunt's plight. An affectionate admirer of Hunt as 'the first distinguished man of letters I ever knew', who 'confirmed me in adopting literature as a profession', it was Forster who persuaded Dickens to come to Hunt's aid by organising and himself acting in four benefit performances 'to honour all the good work [Hunt] has done' – two of Ben Jonson's *Every Man in His Humour* in Manchester and Liverpool, and two of Shakespeare's *The Merry Wives of Windsor* in London, at Covent Garden.

While working in Broadstairs on *Dombey and Son*, Dickens put considerable time and energy into personally rounding up a pro-am cast of talented professionals and stage-struck writers – not least himself as Ben Jonson's Captain Bobadill – while drafting and distributing circulars and broadsheets advertising the forthcoming performances in honour of 'one of the most genial and graceful writers in the language; who has ever laboured for the welfare and improvement of mankind; who, in poetry, and in prose, has charmed and improved hundreds of thousands of readers . . .' He continues in this vein for some time, before ending: 'Mr Leigh Hunt, grown grey in such service, is in unprosperous worldly circumstances, and in bad health. He needs respite from labour, and relief from anxiety.' Seat prices ranged from two shillings to five guineas.

Hunt's claims 'upon his country', the advertisement continued, had 'long been under the consideration of the country's government during so many years that it becomes necessary, pending any permanent provision . . . to afford his well-wishers some opportunity of recognizing those claims for themselves'. As fate would have it, this was the very month that Lord John Russell's government chose, with Dickens's eager preparations well under way, to announce that Hunt had been awarded a state pension of £200 a year for life. The wind somewhat taken from his sails, Dickens was forced to readjust; he cancelled the London performances of *The Merry Wives*, but persisted with the plans to take the Jonson to the north-west, partly because it was too late to back out, partly because he knew Hunt needed more than the government's £200 to get himself back on his feet.

'For the private information of the committee,' Dickens wrote to the wealthy merchant heading his Liverpool fund-raising team, 'Mr Hunt's circumstances are really in that condition that he cannot enjoy the gift he has received, without such assistance as you can help us to give him. But not wishing – for reasons that will be sufficiently plain to you – to put this consideration prominently forward, we would rather make our effort in his behalf one, as it were, of congratulation.' Before long Dickens further announced that it had been decided to share the proceeds of the benefit performances between Hunt and another needy writer, John Poole.

Asked his opinion of Dickens at this time – by Allingham, the Irish poet, during his visit in June 1847 – Hunt replied: 'A pleasant fellow, very busy now.' The following month, just before Dickens and friends headed north for the theatricals, he and Hunt were among a group who dined in Putney Heath *chez* Douglas Jerrold. Forster had brought the actor Macready, who still did not care for Hunt. That evening, according to his diary, Macready found Hunt *'particularly disagreeable*. Disputative and tedious – affecting great benevolence and arguing most malevolently. He is a good-tempered coxcomb – but coxcomb heart and soul – not meaning any harm to any, but a coxcomb.' Two years earlier, after dinner at Forster's, Macready had echoed Byron again: 'Hunt is a *bore*.'

There is no suggestion, as yet, that Dickens shared Macready's irritation with Hunt. Quite the opposite. With other friends and admirers of Hunt in the cast – Forster (as Kitely), Jerrold, Lewes, Cruikshank and Leech, the Jonson was duly performed in Liverpool on 26 July, and Manchester two days later, preceded by a prologue written by Talfourd and declaimed by Lytton:

> The base may mock, the household asp may sting,
> The bard, like Lear, is 'every inch a king.'
> Want but anoints his head with holier balms –
> He claims your tribute, not implores your alms!
> Mild amidst foes, amidst a prison free,
> He comes – our grey-hair'd bard of *Rimini*!
> Comes with the pomp of memories in his train,
> Pathos and wit, sweet pleasure and sweet pain!

Hunt was duly sensible of the honour done him by the generosity of such eminent friends, and equally grateful for the proceeds of £250 – which were, he later wrote, 'of great use to me'. Their generosity continued into the autumn; on 15 September there was a benefit dinner in Hunt's honour at the Museum Club, which required him to make a rare public speech; it took the shape of literary reminiscences which, by one account, 'made a profound impression on his audience'. Hunt's health was proposed that night by Jerrold (who had yet to be offended by his 'insufficient' mention in Hunt's *Autobiography*): 'Even in his hottest warfare his natural sense of beauty and gentleness is so great that, like

David of old, he arms his sling with the shining pebbles of the brook, and never pelts even his fiercest enemy with mud.' Said Hunt in reply: 'If my friend Jerrold has the sting of the bee, he also has his honey.'

So Hunt's latest circle of friends had good reason to suppose his problems at last solved. Before the year was out, however, Hunt was appealing to those same friends for a further £500. This time Dickens was not sympathetic. To one pained enquirer he replied:

> I cannot, of course, speak decisively as to the feeling that may exist among Hunt's literary friends in reference to his new application [but] my impression is that it will be extremely difficult, if not absolutely impossible, to call forth any general answer among them to the present appeal.
>
> My own conviction of the hopelessness of the five hundred pounds required doing any real service to anyone on earth, even if the sum were raised tomorrow, is so strong that I do not feel justified in drawing on any literary man who can ill afford the money, by putting down my own name for £5. Nor could I do anything in such a case, but bring up the rear of the subscription if it approached the desired amount – and then in spite of my persuasion – my certainty – that it is an absurdity, and that, for any good it will do Hunt, it might as well be left alone . . .
>
> I was one of some five or six who, not quite a year ago, when we were about to act those plays in the country, did, again and again, ask Hunt what money would set him clear of the world. Advancing on what we could get out of him, considerably, we put that sum at £250. Those £250 were got, and paid to him. We went into debt £50 to make up the money. For that sum we are responsible, and it is not paid yet, out of our acting proceeds.

When, that November, Hunt appealed directly to Dickens for another benefit, his reply was understandably direct: 'I grieve to say that such a performance is impracticable. Firstly, because if I played at all, to get money, I am bound and pledged to play for another purpose. Secondly, because such a proceeding would not be well judged in reference to yourself, and would not – I believe most confidently – succeed.'

The letter was written on mourning paper. At the top, apparently as an afterthought, Dickens scribbled and framed in a square: 'If I could think of the kindest word in the language, I'd put it here, to begin with.'

All too soon, however, he was writing many more words which could not have been less kind.

For the next four years relations between the two writers appear to have proceeded much as normal, with Dickens quoting Hunt affectionately in his correspondence, inviting him to rehearsals of his amateur theatricals at the home of that same Duke of Devonshire, and giving him work by publishing his poems and essays in his new magazine, *Household Words*, whose launch in 1850 was marked by one of Hunt's genial *pièces d'occasion*:

> As when a friend (himself in music's list)
> Stands by some rare, full-handed organist,
> And glorying as he sees the master roll
> The surging sweets through all their depths of soul,
> Cannot, encouraged by his smile, forbear
> With his own hand to join them then and there;
> And so, if little, yet add something more
> To the sound's volume and the golden roar;
> So I, dear friend, Charles Dickens, though thy hand
> Needs but itself, to charm from land to land,
> Make bold to join in summoning men's ears
> To this thy new-found music of our spheres,
> In hopes that by thy Household Words and thee
> The world may haste to days of harmony.

But when another impoverished writer, James Devlin, applied to Dickens for financial help – apparently at the suggestion of his friend Hunt – Dickens's patience appeared to snap. He curtly declined, wondering aloud: 'Am I a beast whom begging letters have made out of a beautiful prince?' His next novel was to offer an unequivocal answer.

In March 1852, when *Bleak House* began to appear in twenty monthly instalments, Dickens had just turned forty. Already he had progressed

Lifelong friends: Charles Lamb
(above) and William Hazlitt.

Previous page: Hunt drawn by
J. Hayter.

The painter Benjamin
Haydon (top) and musician
Vincent Novello.

Marianne Hunt and the silhouettes she made of her husband (top right),
Byron (bottom left) and Keats.

Victorian friends: Thomas
Carlyle (top left) and the
Brownings, Robert and
Elizabeth Barrett.

Tennyson (top) and
Charles Dickens, who
based Harold Skimpole
in *Bleak House* on Hunt.

'Coavinses' (*Bleak House*): Dickens told 'Phiz' to make Skimpole short and fat in contrast to Hunt, who was tall and thin.

JAMES HENRY
LEIGH HUNT,
BORN OCT? 19. 1784,
DIED AUGUST 28. 1859.

"WRITE ME AS ONE
THAT LOVES HIS FELLOW MEN."

Leigh Hunt aged sixty-six, and his tombstone in Kensal Green cemetery
(before the bust was stolen by vandals).

from *Boz* and *Pickwick* via *Oliver Twist*, *Nicholas Nickleby* and *The Old Curiosity Shop* to *Barnaby Rudge*, *A Christmas Carol*, *Dombey and Son* and *David Copperfield*. Dickens was by now rich and world-famous; Hunt was a respected, even loved, if sick and increasingly reclusive man of letters approaching seventy – working as hard as ever but still in debt.

As the first instalment of *Bleak House* appeared, Hunt's son Vincent lay dying – with the result, as Hunt himself later testified, that this was the first of Dickens's books he did not read as it was appearing. The second episode, published in April, introduced a character named Harold Skimpole, who is characterised by John Jarndyce as 'a child . . . I don't mean literally a child, not a child in years – he is at least as old as I am – but in simplicity, and freshness, and enthusiasm, and a fine guileless inaptitude for all worldly affairs, he is a perfect child.'

Skimpole, continued Jarndyce, was also 'a musical man . . . a man of attainments, and of captivating manners, he has been unfortunate in his affairs, and unfortunate in his pursuits, and unfortunate in his family'. His 'dozen' or so children seemed to have 'tumbled up somehow or other' – 'but he don't care – he's a child'.

Had Dickens been reading Byron's letters? 'In the affairs of the world he himself is a child,' Byron had written to Murray from Genoa on 9 October 1822, in the wake of Shelley's death. The letter had first been published in 1834, eighteen years before Dickens began writing *Bleak House*, in Moore's *Letters and Journals of Lord Byron*. Esther Summerson's narrative also portrays Skimpole as 'child-like'. He was: 'a little bright creature with a rather large head; but a delicate face, and a sweet voice, and there was a perfect charm in him. All he said was so free from effort and spontaneous, and was said with such a captivating gaiety, that it was fascinating to hear him talk . . . There was an easy negligence in his manner, and even in his dress . . . which I could not separate from the idea of a romantic youth who had undergone some unique process of depreciation.'

By his own contented admission, Harold Skimpole was 'a mere child in the world', who confesses (in the third person) to two of its 'oldest infirmities . . . One was, that he had no idea of time; the other, that he had no idea of money. In consequence of which he never kept an appointment, never could transact any business, and never knew the value of anything!'

The very first time the reader meets Skimpole, evidently a regular freeloader at Bleak House, he is within no time cadging money from the novel's young innocents – Esther, Ada Clare and Richard Carstone – to avoid arrest for debt. As they happily hand over their collective life-savings, Skimpole prattles on as if he were doing them a favour rather than the other way round: 'I envy you your power of doing what you do. It is what I should revel in, myself. I don't feel any vulgar gratitude to you. I almost feel as if you ought to be grateful to me for giving you the opportunity of enjoying the luxury of generosity. I know you like it. For anything I can tell, I may have come into the world expressly for the purpose of increasing your stock of happiness. I may have been born to be a benefactor to you, by sometimes giving you an opportunity of assisting me with my little perplexities. Why should I regret my incapacity for details and worldly affairs, when it leads to such pleasant consequences? I don't.'

Skimpole's subsequent soliloquy on 'the overweening assumptions' of bees – a *tour de force* in which he 'had no objection to honey . . . but he didn't see at all why the busy bee should be proposed as a model to him; he supposed the bee liked to make honey or he wouldn't do it' – seemed like a painfully obvious reference to the title of Hunt's recently published work, *A Jar of Honey from Mount Hybla*.

A few nights after Esther has met Skimpole, she is called upstairs to find a bailiff arresting him for debt. Like Hunt, Dickens would have known such a dreadful summons from his own childhood; but he would also have known that this was a not uncommon occurrence in the adult Hunt's household. 'Last Friday I was sitting down to dinner, having just finished a most agitated morning, when I was called away by a man who brought an execution into my house for forty shillings,' he had recently complained. 'It is under circumstances like these that I always write.'

For two mutual friends privy to Dickens's manuscript before publication, Forster and Bryan Waller Procter, the character of Skimpole was so clearly based on Hunt that they felt obliged to intervene. The likeness was 'too like' for Forster, whose unexpected objections put Dickens on the defensive. As Forster wrote much later, 'Hunt's philosophy of money obligations, always, though loudly, half jocosely proclaimed, and his ostentatious wilfulness in the humouring of that or any other theme on which he cared for the time to expatiate, had so often seemed to Dickens to be whimsical and attractive that . . . this of Hunt occurred to him . . . and he yielded to the temptation of too often making the character speak like his old friend.'

Dickens relented to some extent, 'toning down' a few passages and changing Skimpole's first name from Leonard to Harold (or, in effect, from Leigh to Hunt). By some accounts the character's original name had been even more thinly disguised as Leonard Horner. Although the surname Horner appears nowhere in the text, the forename Leonard survived throughout one instalment; Dickens had altered it in the proofs of Chapter Six, but in Chapter 31 (No. X, published on 1 December) absent-mindedly reverted to 'Leonard' in several places, having overlooked the change at proof. Skimpole's first name was finally changed throughout to Harold only in the errata to the first edition published in bound book form.

On the eve of the serial, in early March 1852, Dickens reported to Forster that 'Browne has done Skimpole, and helped to make him singularly unlike the great original.' This was Hablot K. Browne, alias the cartoonist 'Phiz', whose second plate (entitled 'Coavinses') made Skimpole a short, tubby, round-faced figure where Hunt was tall and slender. 'Look it over,' Dickens continued to Forster, 'and say what occurs to you . . .'

A week later, on 17 March 1852, Dickens again wrote to Forster, apparently after further disagreement. 'You will see from the enclosed, that Procter is much of my mind. I will nevertheless go through the character again in the course of the afternoon, and soften down words here and there.' But Procter made further protests to Dickens later that same day, which led Dickens to tell Forster next morning: 'I have again gone over every part of it very carefully, and I think I have made it much less like . . . I have no right to give Hunt pain, and I am so bent upon not doing it that I wish you would look at the proof once more, and indicate any particular place in which you feel it particularly like. Whereupon I will alter that place.'

Two years later, when the identification of Skimpole with Hunt became all too public, and Hunt privately declared himself 'pained and perplexed', Dickens would apologise in his own pained terms: 'Separate in your own mind what you see of yourself from what other people tell you that they see. As it has given you so much pain, I take it at its worst, and say I am deeply sorry, and that I feel I did wrong in doing it. I should otherwise have taken it at its best, and ridden off upon what I strongly feel to be the truth, that there is nothing in it that should have given you pain.' The character of Skimpole, Dickens seeks to reassure his old friend, 'is not you, for there are traits in it common to fifty thousand people besides' – and, he continues, in somewhat giveaway vein, 'I did not fancy you would ever recognise it.'

Between publication and that weaselly letter, on 21 September 1853, Dickens had inadvertently betrayed himself to posterity in another, rather more gleeful letter to his close friend Mrs Richard Watson, the dedicatee (with her late husband) of *David Copperfield*.

In 'confidential reply to your enquiry', Dickens boasts: 'Skimpole. I must not forget Skimpole – of whom I will now begin to speak as if I had only read him, and had not written him. I suppose he is the most exact portrait that ever was painted in words! I have very seldom, if ever, done such a thing. But the likeness is astonishing. I don't think he could possibly be more like himself. It is so awfully true that I make a bargain with myself never to do so, any more. There is not an atom of exaggeration or suppression. It is an absolute reproduction of a real man. Of course I have been careful to keep the outward figure away from the fact; but in all else it is the Life itself.'

Throughout 1853, as *Bleak House* continued to appear in monthly instalments, relations between Dickens and Hunt appear to have proceeded much as normal, with Hunt writing for Dickens's *Household Words* the series of articles on Kensington later collected as *The Old Court Suburb*. Among Hunt's other writings at the time were two historical poems, 'Kilspindie' and 'The Trumpets of Doolkarnein', which Dickens was pleased to publish.

The 'airy' and 'whimsical' character of Harold Skimpole, meanwhile, grew steadily darker. In episode XIV, which appeared that April, Esther's narrative takes the reader into Skimpole's home, whose 'state of dilapidation' lent it a distinct resemblance to 4 Upper Cheyne Row, as so vividly described by Hunt's neighbour Carlyle some twenty years earlier. With its 'sickly large wife . . . asleep on cushions', 'strange, gipsy-looking children running about in undress' and host in 'his loose-flowing muslin-cloud of a printed night-gown', Hunt's home was 'a poetical Tinkerdom, without parallel even in literature' – until Dickens took up the challenge. Had Carlyle been talking to Dickens about Hunt? The Scottish sage had presciently written of Hunt to his brother Jack: 'I never in my whole life met with a more innocent child-like man: transparent, many-glancing, really beautiful, were this Lubberland or Elysium, and not Earth or England. His family also are innocent, tho' wholly foolish and do-nothings.'

In *Bleak House*, after the door has been answered by a 'slatternly' maid, Skimpole is found in his cosy inner sanctum – much like Hunt's celebrated 'salon', where Dickens had been a frequent visitor – behaving like the foppish aesthete Hunt could often himself seem. Reclining on a sofa in his dressing gown at midday, drinking some 'fragrant' coffee from an old china cup, Skimpole is contemplating some wallflowers while consuming a hearty breakfast of beef and mutton.

Hunt could be accused of numerous shortcomings, but never of idleness and rarely of excess. As for self-indulgence, we have his son Thornton's explanation of any wrong impressions:

> He inculcated the study of minor pleasures with so much industry that his writings have caused him to be taken for a minor voluptuary. His special apparatus for the luxury consisted in some old cloak to put about his shoulders when cold – which he allowed to slip off while reading or writing; in a fire – 'to toast his feet' – which he let out many times in the day, with as many apologies to the servant for the trouble; and in a bill of fare, which he preposterously restricted for a fancied delicacy of stomach, and a fancied poison in everything agreeable, and which he could scarcely taste for a natural dullness of palate . . .
>
> The Epicurean in theory was something like a Stoic in practice; he would break off an 'article' on the pleasures of feasting to ease his hunger, literally, with a supper of bread; turning round to enjoy by proxy, on report, the daintier food which he had provided for others.

As this touching filial piety testifies, Hunt had all his life cherished and toiled to support those numerous children who had, in Dickens's

hurtful phrase, somehow 'tumbled up'. Skimpole now seeks to introduce some of them to his visitors. His sons, according to a brutal aside,
had 'run away' – as, Dickens would know, had poor dead John Hunt –
'but here were his daughters Arethusa, Laura and Kitty'. In his original manuscript Dickens gave Laura and Kitty the names Juliet and
Susannah, but changed them – no doubt at Forster's and Procter's
insistence – because of their all too clear resemblance to the names of
Hunt's own daughters Julia and Jacintha.

But there is no mistaking Mrs Skimpole, who now puts in her only,
brief appearance. She 'had once been a beauty, but was now a delicate
high-nosed invalid suffering under a complication of disorders'. This
might as well have been a portrait from life of Marianne, Hunt's invalid
wife of nearly half a century, who was to die within four years. As his
work progressed Dickens had all but given up bothering to try to disguise Skimpole's 'great original'. He was even privy to a dark secret
still unknown to Hunt himself, that his wife had taken to borrowing
money behind his back; from the corner in which Mrs Skimpole lurks,
the visitors 'could not help hearing the chink of money'.

That July, in a letter to W.H. Wills, his sub-editor and general fac-
totum on *Household Words*, Dickens spluttered: 'Look at the enclosed
from Hunt! I declare I don't know what to say, and have not answered
it! Can you devise any means of getting out of the matter privately and
confidentially?'

Again Hunt's original letter does not survive, but it is not difficult to
guess what had so irritated Dickens. Hunt had 'probably' asked him,
surmise the editors of his letters, 'to commit himself to publication of
his whole series of seven articles on Kensington . . . and to pay him in
advance'. Can it entirely be coincidence that the very next episode of
Bleak House to appear, on which Dickens would have been working at
the time, sees Skimpole degenerate into an arrant villain? He it is who
betrays little Jo to Inspector Bucket, in return for a financial 'consideration', leading eventually to Jo's demise – a poignant one even by
Dickens's schmaltzy standards. And he it is, again for backhanders, who
draws poor, deluded Richard Carstone deeper and deeper into the
interminable Chancery case of Jarndyce v Jarndyce – to the point
where this, too, proves fatal.

That August, as Skimpole's betrayal of Jo was appearing in print,

Dickens was to be found complaining to Wills that Hunt's latest sub-
mission to *Household Words*, another Kensington essay entitled 'Gore
House', was 'very poor. Page 591, first column. Stop at the Graces,
and delete the rest of that paragraph. It is Skimpole, you know — the
whole passage. I couldn't write it more like him.'

When 'Gore House' was republished in book form in *The Old Court
Suburb*, two years later, Hunt naturally restored the excised passage,
giving us the rare treat of seeing what Dickens had found so Skimpole-
ish: 'All good things, as well as all bad things, hold together; truth,
strength, right, perceptions in art; falsehood, weakness, bad taste.
Truth, in any one respect, is good for truth in other respects . . .'

Not Hunt at his best, granted, if entirely characteristic of his
dreamier modes. Two days later Dickens is instructing Wills to 'hold
over' Hunt's latest Kensington piece, 'certainly for a number. O
Heaven, Hunt's not lounging' – a caustic reference to his earlier article 'Lounging through Kensington' – but 'being in earnest'.

At the time, Dickens would have been putting the finishing touches
to the final double instalment of *Bleak House*, which appeared that
September. In our last, posthumous glimpse of Skimpole, who has
died 'heavily' in debt to John Jarndyce, he is revealed to have
denounced his great benefactor, the genial character at the heart of the
novel, as 'the Incarnation of Selfishness'.

Esther discovers the remark in Skimpole's diary, which had been
published, 'and which showed him to have been the victim of a combination on the part of mankind against an amiable child'. Hunt's own
autobiography had been published just three years earlier, twenty-two
years after the biography of Byron so widely perceived as an act of
ingratitude to a man from whom he had received financial support and
hospitality. In that autobiography, ironically enough, Hunt mentions
that a 'distinguished economist' had recently chosen to refer to him as
the 'spoiled child of the public' – 'a title', he smiled innocently, 'I
should be proud to possess'.

Five years later, revising his autobiography in the penultimate year of
his life, Hunt still seems to have felt sufficiently hurt by the Skimpole
episode to address it for posterity.

At the time of the publication of *Bleak House*, he writes, he had finally managed to free himself of all financial obligations for the first time in his adult life, and had returned to his social round. 'I was sincerely congratulating myself on this new and unlooked for condition, and on the prospect which it opened to me of reappearing among my friends, and obtaining all the additional comfort and diversion of my thoughts, which town and their society would afford me, when I received a blow that threw me back on my tendency to be haunted by a painful idea, and that was of a nature which I had never dreamed of having to bear.'

An 'acquaintance' had drawn his attention to 'an alleged attack on me by a friend in one of his novels, but [I] had treated it as a thing impossible, and laughed at it. I had not only never said anything [to] this friend, myself, having ever held friendship to be a thing sacred from evil-speaking: I had spoken, and written, nothing but good and kind of him publicly or in private, contributing what I could to his stock of glory and honour, and this too of late years, out of gratitude for his own kindness, as well as admiration of his genius.'

Hunt goes on to acknowledge the unnamed author as having had 'the main hand' in the benefit performances which enabled him to clear his debts. 'I had therefore reckoned myself in as sure possession of his regard, as he was owner of mine; and the report of his attack on me seemed the most ridiculous thing conceivable . . . I could on no account believe him capable of attacking me at all, much less on the score that he was charged with.'

There might the matter have rested, Hunt continues, with him disbelieving (and thus ignoring) an unworthy slur on both his friend and himself, had not the matter been raised in a 'malicious' way in an American newspaper, and thus found its way across the Atlantic into a Scottish paper – though not yet, to his relief, into the London press.

By his own account Hunt had still not read the book when 'a young stranger' one day introduced himself and repeated the rumour, now the talk of the town, that he was the original of Skimpole – adding that a mutual friend, of whom Hunt thought 'highly', believed it to be 'well-founded'. The character in question, however, was not meant 'to apply to me in the darker parts, but only in the lighter'.

So Leigh Hunt finally read *Bleak House* and met Harold Skimpole. 'I began to consider,' he recalled, 'in what possible way I could have offended the friend who thus unaccountably assailed me. My conduct towards himself, as I have shown, was spotless. At least I had thought so. In what respect could I have been mistaken? I had never supposed him petulant, suspicious, apt to take offence, or given to any other weakness not common to a genius like his. What was it? He could not be jealous of any little attention shewn me in great quarters, for he possessed heaps of it. Envy was out of the question from a man prosperous like himself towards one in a state of adversity. I was old and he young; sick, and he healthy; in sorrow, and he happy. What could it be?'

Hunt's own immediate suspicion was that he had failed – for entirely Skimpole-ish reasons, vagueness and want of money – to join the Guild of Literature and Art, a society recently founded by Dickens and Bulwer-Lytton with a view not merely to helping writers in distress, but to raising the lowly status of writers in polite society. It would seem no coincidence that Dickens chose to dedicate *Bleak House* to his 'friends and companions in the Guild of Literature and Art' – which Hunt had not only failed to join, but was signally letting down with his Skimpole-ish begging letters and down-at-heel lifestyle. Perhaps Hunt, he reflected, had asked Dickens for one too many loan, when the Guild had been formed to aid writers without the good fortune of a state pension.

Otherwise baffled, Hunt was for a while reduced to fretting that Dickens had heard that he did not have too high an opinion of his acting skills. Others suggested that Dickens had been as hurt as Forster and Jerrold (who went so far as to write a letter of complaint to the *Athenæum*) that Hunt had barely mentioned them in his autobiography – omissions he later corrected.

Whatever had so irritated Dickens, the obvious explanation (as Forster concluded) was that the novelist simply got carried away with the excitement of his own depictive powers. There were no protests, for instance, that the character of Lawrence Boythorn was so clearly based on the personal traits of Walter Savage Landor. But Boythorn was a harmless enough bit-player in the drama, whereas Skimpole was assigned, in Forster's own words, 'a part in the plot which no fascinating foibles could redeem from contempt'. Dickens's closest friend thus charged him with 'want of consideration' for another mutual friend, even of doing him 'radical wrong', but insisted that his intention was 'not at first, or at any time, an unkind one. He erred from thoughtlessness only.'

If so, it is worth recording on Hunt's behalf that none of his own meditations and protestations about the matter was ever published – or, therefore, used publicly to bring Dickens to account – in his lifetime. Even after his death, when Thornton edited his autobiography for publication – as he also did two volumes of his father's letters, which involved him in some dealings with Dickens – that passage did not appear. It exists only in manuscript form, in Hunt's own hand, in the British Museum.

That Hunt only once took the matter up with Dickens face to face we know from Wilkie Collins, who wrote in the margin of his edition of Forster's biography: 'At Dickens's own house, when Leigh Hunt was one of his guests at dinner . . . Hunt directly charged Dickens with taking the character of Harold Skimpole from the character of Leigh Hunt, and protested strongly.' Collins was not himself present, he adds, 'but Dickens told me what happened'.

On 8 November 1854 Dickens received a letter from an ailing Hunt, evidently dictated to Marianne, inviting him to call at his modest rented house in Hammersmith, west London, 'to have a little conversation with you quite by ourselves'. What he had in mind, he continued, was 'business of no ordinary kind, and such as when you have heard it out, I think you wd be sorry to have missed hearing'.

Hunt would have been aware that Dickens was a regular visitor to Hammersmith, where a home for the rehabilitation of prostitutes, founded at Shepherd's Bush by Angela Burdett-Coutts, was one of the prime causes to attract his philanthropic interest. 'No, I won't come and take tea with you,' Dickens nonetheless replied a week later, launching into another jaunty metaphor about legs of mutton finally being amputated, and insisting that Hunt come to him instead, along with Forster, on an imminent date to be mutually agreed. 'I will place a little pill-box on wheels, which staggers about town with Mrs Dickens, at your disposal, to bring you here as snugly as it can, and take you home again.' As well as adding a third party, to defuse a potentially embarrassing conversation à deux, this blithe reversal of Hunt's invitation takes no account of the elder man's poor health, and his inevitable reluctance to travel on a cold winter evening.

Twelve days later Dickens apologises to Wills for having to postpone their usual lunch meeting at *Household Words* 'as I have no less a person than Leigh Hunt (!) asking me to give him something soft to eat tomorrow'. (Hunt had by now lost most of his teeth, and could eat only 'soft' food). In Forster's presence, Dickens seized the opportunity to insist to Hunt, once and for all, that 'there are many remembrances of [you] in little traits of manner and expression in that character, and especially in all the pleasantest parts of it, but that is all'.

Dickens thereafter began to avoid Hunt. Weeks would go by with continual postponements of promised meetings and meals, while overly jolly letters, all avoiding the dread subject, continued occasionally to arrive. In January 1855 he is to be found telling Hunt about an imminent visit to Paris, promising on his return 'to shake your hand speedily'. But there follows only silence until May, when Dickens thanks Hunt for sending him a copy of his latest volume, *Stories in Verse*: 'I have been so constantly engaged and occupied since I came home from Paris, that I have never (as you know) got to your teapot, though I have often (as you don't know) paved the road to Hammersmith with good intentions.'

By the end of June 1855 Dickens finally promises to call on Hunt in Hammersmith for an hour the following Monday evening (which then gets postponed to Tuesday) – 'but I hope you will not now think it necessary to renew that painful subject with me. There is nothing to remove from my mind – I hope, nothing to remove from yours.' He reminds Hunt that he has just given his *Stories in Verse* a 'highly favourable' review in the *Examiner*. 'In that better and unmistakable association with you, let all end.' There is evidence that Hunt proposed to ask Dickens for a public apology – or at least a public denial – before he died. Unsurprisingly, he does not seem to have succeeded.

The following week Hunt told their mutual friend Charles Ollier of 'some delightful hours' spent with Dickens, to whom he has inscribed his latest book, *The Religion of the Heart*: 'To C.D., from his obliged and affectionate friend.' Writing to thank him, Dickens enthused: 'I don't know when I have talked so much at a sitting, as with you on Tuesday night. Either there is some remarkable chirruping quality in your tea – or in you – for I seem to have been transformed into a sort of cricket.'

There is no record of any further meetings or indeed dealings between them for the next three years, until the summer of 1858, when Dickens wrote to thank Hunt for a note of sympathy following the announcement of his separation from his wife. 'Your letter has moved me very much . . . It is worth suffering something, to be so remembered.'

There was to be but one more exchange, on 23 June 1859 – two months, as it transpired, before Hunt's death – and it did indeed concern Harold Skimpole, with whom Hunt had again been identified in a London newspaper. Knowing he was on his deathbed, Hunt was evidently asking Dickens one last time either to rewrite the text, or to disclaim the identity with him in a new preface. Dickens, predictably enough, declined: 'Believe me, I have not forgotten that matter; nor will I forget it. To alter the book itself, or to make any reference in the preface of the book itself, would be to revive a forgotten absurdity, and to establish the very association that is to be denied or discarded.

'In the matter of the smitten cheek, I hold you to be thoroughly right in principle. But be sure that you do not give importance to what is worthless and insignificant, or drag any obscure person or thing into your own light. That is always the risk when a man of your mark honours Grub Street with a look.'

These were the last words to pass between Dickens and Hunt. 'I little thought I should never see his bright face again,' Dickens wrote to Thornton immediately after his father's death. 'I hope I shall never forget, or be undeserving of, his gentle and affectionate consideration.'

Posterity has had mixed views on this last sentiment, as indeed did Dickens's contemporaries. Obituaries of Hunt inevitably mentioned the Skimpole connection, and Dickens found himself denounced on all sides for his 'heartless calumny'. He dismissed the attacks as 'contemptible trash', telling Forster: 'What I told Hunt, and what I promised Hunt, when you were by, to tell anybody, I will not reserve, qualify, or in any way with-hold. I am quite sure Thornton Hunt will be manful and open with me, and he may rely on my being so with him.'

Distressed by the references to Skimpole in Hunt's obituaries, such old friends of his father's as Dalby urged upon Thornton the 'necessity of something being done'. When Hunt had 'so feelingly complained of "the great blow" which came so unexpectedly and so staggeringly upon him, ought not Mr Dickens to have told the world that it was never aimed? To me his silence then and now appears unaccountable, unexplainable, inexcusable – and see what rascally inferences are drawn from it.'

The pressure on Dickens grew to the point where, by the end of the year, four months after Hunt's death, he did finally feel compelled to make one definitive public statement on the matter, in the shape of a warm review in his own magazine *All the Year Round* of Thornton Hunt's posthumous edition of his father's autobiography. As 'one who knew Leigh Hunt well', Dickens saw it as 'an act of plain, clear duty' to testify that 'his life was of the most amiable and domestic kind, that his wants were few, that his way of life was frugal, that he was a man of small expenses, no ostentations, a diligent labourer, and a secluded man of letters'. He went on to recall Hunt's 'wrong and sufferings in the days of the Regency' and 'the national disgrace of his imprisonment', before proceeding to the main burden of his article – not so much an obituary as (in his own title) 'A Remonstrance'.

The rumours that Leigh Hunt was the original of Harold Skimpole, as first reported in the American press soon after the publication of *Bleak House*, were 'more surprisingly destitute of all foundation in truth than the wildest delusions of the wildest lunatics'. For that reason, while Hunt was alive Dickens had 'let the thing go by'. But since Hunt's death the charge had been revived in England. The plain fact, insisted Dickens, was that 'exactly those graces and charms of manner' recalled in the loving passages he quoted from Thornton's memoir of his father 'were remembered by the author of the work of fiction in question, when he drew the character in question'.

'Above all other things,' continued Dickens, speaking of himself in the third person,

> that sort of gay and ostentatious wilfulness in the humouring of a subject, which had many a time delighted him, and impressed him as being unspeakably whimsical and attractive, was the airy quality he wanted for the man he invented . . . Partly for this reason, and partly (he has since often grieved to think) for the pleasure it afforded him to find that delightful manner reproducing itself under

his hand, he yielded to the temptation of too often making the character speak like his old friend.

He no more thought, God forgive him!, that the admired original would ever be charged with the imaginary vices of the fictitious creature, than he has himself ever thought of charging the blood of Desdemona and Othello on the Academy model who sat for Iago's leg in the picture. Even as to the mere occasional manner, he meant to be so cautious and conscientious, that he privately referred the proof sheets of the first number of that book to two intimate literary friends of Leigh Hunt (both still living), and altered the whole of that part of the text on their discovering too strong a resemblance to his way.

Dickens's protestations of innocence have not, on the whole, convinced posterity any more than they did his contemporaries. 'An odd declaration by Dickens,' wrote Macaulay in his diary, 'that he did not mean Leigh Hunt by Harold Skimpole. Yet he owns that he took the light externals of the character from Hunt, and surely it is by those light externals that the bulk of mankind will always recognize character.' To Horne, the caricature was accurate only 'in a very limited degree; and all the rest, comprising all the most important things – utterly false'.

To one of Dickens's first biographers, A.W. Ward (1882), the novelist's own explanation 'only helps to prove the rashness of the offence. While intending the portrait to keep its own secret from the general public, Dickens at the same time must have wished to gratify a few keen-sighted friends . . . A wound was needlessly inflicted, if not upon Leigh Hunt himself, at least upon all who cherished his friendship or good name.' Skimpole, in short, was 'a mistake' which constituted 'an unfortunate incident in Dickens's literary life'.

In his own life of Dickens (1872–4), Forster essentially dodged the issue. He knew too much. He might as well have been writing of himself as of his friend when he conceded that 'nothing remained to Dickens but what amounted to friendly evasion of the points at issue'.

'The simple and final reply,' wrote Algernon Charles Swinburne in the *Quarterly Review* of July 1902, 'should have been that indolence was the essential quality of the character and philosophy of Skimpole, and that Leigh Hunt was one of the hardest and steadiest workers on record, throughout a long and chequered life, at the toilsome trade of letters; and therefore to represent him as a heartless and shameless idler would have been as rational an enterprise, as lifelike a design after the life, as it would be to represent Shelley as a gluttonous, canting hypocrite or Byron as a loyal and unselfish friend.'

To the *Westminster Gazette*, in reply to Dickens's 'Remonstrance', Swinburne wrote later that month: 'I wish I could think that I had always been wrong in thinking or feeling that Dickens' rejoinder to the charge of libel on the character of Leigh Hunt was singularly incomplete, ineffective and awkward. I am old enough to remember its appearance, and the fact that I never met anybody at the time who did not think it more and worse than adequate as an apology. "God forgive him," by all means; but mere men, I fancy, will as a rule agree with me that the due reply should have been the shorter and more straightforward one, which would at once have indicated and established the outrageous absurdity of the libellous imputation.'

To the literary historian Sir Arthur Quiller-Couch, in 1927, 'Nothing, least of all its verisimilitude, can excuse the outrage perpetrated upon Hunt in the mask of Skimpole . . . Hunt, who (with all his faults) never lacked generosity, had been among the first to hail and help Dickens, was (as often happens) the last to recognize himself for the intended victim . . . [But] the wound went deep.' Dickens's apology 'could not . . . amount to more than kindly evasiveness. He was guilty and he knew it. Hunt had been wounded in the house of his friend.'

Stephen Leacock is careless enough to write of 'Horace' Skimpole when excusing Dickens in his 1936 study: 'The name of Leigh Hunt has drifted so far back into obscurity that the controversy loses its interest.' Dickens, Leacock concludes, 'probably' meant Skimpole to be 'a charming and loveable character, which he certainly is not. Dickens failed in his aim.' G.K. Chesterton lazily hid behind the word 'alleged', as in 'the character whose alleged likeness to Leigh Hunt has laid Dickens open to so much disapproval'. By 1949 Hesketh Pearson could concede that the portrait was both malicious and intentional, but defended it on the intriguing grounds that 'bad taste is one of the diagnostics of genius'.

Of recent Dickens biographers, only Fred Kaplan tackles the issue with any rigour, arguing that Dickens is venting his spleen on Hunt – for 'tactlessly' returning to friends for financial help after being granted a state pension – by making Skimpole 'the irresponsible artist whose sponging self-indulgence is immoral'. But Skimpole's 'hypocrisy, immorality and oily rhetoric', Kaplan concedes, 'were Dickens' invention, not Hunt's characteristics'. Dickens was 'slow in making redress' and 'resentful in being called to account'.

It seems surprising that none of Dickens's other recent biographers, from Edgar Johnson to Peter Ackroyd, treats the Skimpole episode in much detail, or cares to portray Hunt as much more than a pesky irritant who may or may not have been the original of one of their man's most vivid creations. Or perhaps it is not. As long afterwards as 1932 a newspaper article on Hunt's home in Hammersmith was headlined 'Harold Skimpole's house', perhaps sustaining the thesis of the novelist Martin Amis in his memoir *Experience*: 'Of course, only a semiliterate would say that Harold Skimpole is Leigh Hunt . . . of course, even the most precisely recreated character is nonetheless recreated, transfigured; of course, autobiographical fiction is still fiction – an autonomous construct.'

As Dickens would himself argue in that disingenuous letter of apology to Hunt, two years after the event: 'Everyone in writing must speak from points of his experience, and so I of mine with you; but when I have felt it was going too close I stopped myself, and the most blotted parts of my MS are those in which I have been striving hard to make the impression I was writing from, unlike you . . . Under similar disguises my own father and mother are in my books, and you might as well see your likeness in Micawber.'

This is the only other recorded example of Dickens conceding that he based any of his fictional characters on real people from his own experience. Yet in the December 1840 instalment of *David Copperfield*, the 'personal deformities' of Miss Mowcher were recognised as her own by Mrs Jane Seymour Hill, a diminutive London manicurist and chiropodist. Mrs Hill threatened to sue Dickens for 'great mental torture and agony' unless he agreed to make specific alterations to the character. Three months later, in the eleventh instalment, Miss Mowcher suddenly became the heroic figure responsible for the arrest of Littimer, and is permitted a moral homily on stature: 'Try not to associate bodily defects with mental, my friend, except for a solid reason.'

Leigh Hunt, alias Harold Skimpole, was granted no such reprieve.

14

'One that loves his fellow-men'

1853–9

It was in the spring of 1853, as he approached seventy, that Hunt had moved two miles west to Hammersmith, to what proved the last of the twenty or more London addresses of his adult lifetime – a modest cottage at 7 Cornwall Road (now 16 Rowan Road, on the west flank of St Paul's Girls' School). 'Reckoning that his family had somewhat diminished in numbers, my father removed to a smaller house,' testified Thornton, in a kindly euphemism for the truth that Vincent's death had robbed Phillimore Terrace of its sometime charms. Daily life there had simply become too painful. Hunt worked out his grief in verse:

> Waking at morn, with the accustomed sigh
> For what no morn could ever bring me more,
> And again sighing, while collecting strength
> To meet the pangs that waited me; like one
> Whose sleep the rack hath watched: I tried to feel
> How good for me had been strange griefs of old,
> That for long days, months, years, inured my wits
> To bear the dreadful burden of one thought.
> One thought with woeful need turned many ways,
> Which, shunned at first, and scaring me, as wounds
> Thrusting in wound, became, oh! almost clasped

> And blest, as saviours from the one dire pang
> That mocked the will to move it.

Unsurprisingly, domestic economics were another reason for the move from Kensington to a significantly less expensive home. The researches of Molly Tatchell, tireless archivist of Hunt's few years in Hammersmith, reveal that the rateable value of the Cornwall Road house in 1853 was £17, compared with £42 for that in Phillimore Terrace; so, as she concludes, 'there must have been a corresponding saving in rent'.

Now it was not so much Hunt as his increasingly wayward wife who was accumulating bills and debts. So it was prudent of him to put some distance between Marianne and the Kensington tradesmen whose patience had long since worn thin, not to mention the friends from whom she had recently been begging loans – usually, as we know from a shocked Macaulay, among others, without her husband's knowledge.

For some years now Marianne's mental and physical condition had been deteriorating to an alarming degree; two years before, in 1851, the family doctor had adjudged her 'an intemperate woman and sodden from drink'. In a letter to Hunt's grandson forty years after Hunt's death, Dr George Bird (who had taken over as the family doctor after the retirement of Southwood Smith) pointed to Marianne as the main source of the misrepresentations of Hunt's character still flowing from the Skimpole caricature. 'In my opinion, she was mendacious, self-indulgent and incapable of controlling her household.' How much her husband knew of her drink problem he could not say. One day Hunt had asked the doctor: 'Isn't a bottle of brandy a day, which I hear you have ordered my wife, too much?' In fact, reported Dr Bird, he had ordered complete abstention from 'spirituous' drinks.

On another occasion, as he walked into his wife's room Hunt kicked over a bottle of foaming beer, partly hidden under the bed. 'It's milk, my dear,' said Marianne – and, according to the doctor, Hunt 'accepted the explanation, with what reservations of his own I cannot tell'. Hunt's lifelong loyalty to Marianne survived this most supreme of tests. Horne, more candidly, said that he had never heard Hunt say one word in anger about Marianne, or indeed any of their children, no matter how provoked he may have been. Even in his autobiography, which he was revising when she was at her most difficult, Hunt remained unswervingly loyal to his increasingly troublesome wife – who, 'for many years', by Horne's account, 'had been no companion and no help to her husband'.

In the Kensington years, according to Linton, this 'stout, genial, motherly woman, of whom no-one could have supposed that in her young days she had been consumptive', had pealed walnuts for her husband while listening to the 'pleasant, wise talk' of this 'most delightful of old men'. That endearing picture seems to have faded by the time the Hunts moved to Hammersmith. Now bedridden, Marianne had become 'a grievous trial to her husband, himself old and ailing'. She may, in Hunt's view, have deserved his indulgence for surviving 'the worst storms of our adversity', but she was now little more than a worrisome burden. One of the few Hammersmith visitors to catch a glimpse of her testifies that she had 'become so stout, and disliked any exertion'.

Hunt developed an obsessive fear that Marianne would set the house on fire; each night he searched the place for unsafe lamps and candles. This 'morbid dread', revealed Thornton, meant that for many years Hunt 'never went to bed without visiting the whole house to see that the lights were out; and he has told me that he never left home to return at night without a dread lest he should see the house in flames. This fiend of fear which dogged his steps was connected with other domestic anxieties . . .'

'Alas,' Hunt wrote to John Hunter in 1855, reluctantly unable to accept an invitation to stay, 'to be in Craigcrook I must have a wife healthy and unrheumatised, to be able to take care of herself in case of alarms, and fires, and other domesticities; and as this cannot be, neither can I be where otherwise I would.' The following year: 'Mrs Hunt [is] so helpless in limbs, I have never been able to be comfortable away from her at night-time. I become haunted with fears of fires etc.' To Ollier: 'I have been in the midst of many anxieties and calls upon me . . . Mrs Hunt is going on or rather, sitting still, well – wonderfully well, indeed, as she always is, "considering"; and indeed, after a little while, when not "considering" . . .'

Few visitors to the Hunts' Hammersmith home now caught so much as a glimpse of Marianne. The parlour her husband had characteristically made cosy was a room that 'her rheumatism has never allowed her to behold', he wrote to the American artist and author William Wetmore Story, 'since the day when we first came to this house'. Rheumatism, indeed. Hunt was hiding behind the instructions of the retired doctor, Southwood Smith, that his wife 'should guard the hands, arms, chest and indeed every part of the body from contact with cold air. She should therefore never sit up in bed without having on a sleeved jacket except when properly covered with the bed-clothes.' For he was also hiding Marianne's true condition – chronic alcoholism – from the world, perhaps from himself.

Against this dark backdrop there were other reasons for Hunt to choose Hammersmith, beyond its supposedly healthy climate and its proud radical traditions (later to be upheld, beyond Hunt's death, by William Morris at nearby Kelmscott House). In Hunt's outspoken youth the locals had been vociferous supporters of the Prince Regent's estranged wife, the wayward Queen Caroline, who had spent her declining years at Brandenburgh House near Hammersmith Bridge. Hunt recalled that, as a schoolboy contemplating a dip in the Thames with some chums, he had received a 'stern lecture' there from no less than the Margravine of Anspach (Lady Craven), Caroline's companion.

In the 1840s there was a Chartist branch in Hammersmith, whose record of support for the Reform Bill and repeal of the Corn Laws would have appealed to Hunt. But the most obvious, more personal motive was that his daughter Jacintha now lived there, with her husband Charles Smith Cheltnam; only the previous year they had moved the short distance from Stamford Brook to Cornwall Road. Now her father moved in a few doors away with her ailing mother and spinster sister Julia. According to Francis H. Grundy, Julia Hunt at thirty was 'fascinating and wayward'. A lively spirit with a fine soprano voice, she would corral her brother Henry into dressing as opera singers and performing in the street, to the point where they were occasionally recognised and invited into neighbouring homes; until his recent death she had also been 'dragging her sick brother Vincent off to parties when he should have been in bed'.

Small and graceful, with dark but sparkling eyes, Julia was 'one of the most dangerous coquettes of her day'. Soon other members of the family would arrive in the same modest terrace. This branch of the

Hunt family would remain there long after its patriarch's demise; his granddaughter, Marian Spencer Leigh Hunt, was buried in Hammersmith cemetery in 1927.

As for the area's supposedly healthy air: about this Hunt was decidedly mistaken. He was not alone in believing Hammersmith, along with Kensington, Chelsea and Knightsbridge, to be districts almost as salubrious as Hampstead — as evidenced by the number of summer houses kept in these outlying districts by the aristocracy and the wealthy. In *The Old Court Suburb*, compiled after he had moved there, Hunt quoted a poem by a Dr Samuel Garth, commending the health-giving properties of the Kensington gravel pits; it was believed that 'the emanations from carts bearing the newly-turned gravel to London were peculiarly beneficial'.

He would have done better to read the report of the Sanitary Commissioners for 1849, which spoke of 'an open ditch' on the western side of Brook Green, 'wide, stagnant and with a large accumulation of foul deposit, receiving the drainage of most of the houses in its vicinity . . .' This was the year of a cholera epidemic in London, with three hundred deaths a day recorded in September. A drainage plan was not implemented until 1855, two years after Hunt had moved in. 'The air can scarcely have been salubrious,' as Tatchell puts it, 'but the Victorian nose was no doubt accustomed to noxious smells . . . As far as can be ascertained, Leigh Hunt had no complaints to make on this score.'

In 1853, in the wake of the Skimpole episode, Hunt could be forgiven for looking 'a little bowed, a little disheartened', as Blunden pictures him in Hammersmith. But he had his books, as always, around him in his new home; and he had a few propitious prospects to cheer him. The Queen had commanded his play, *A Legend of Florence*, to be performed at Windsor (though there was no invitation, it seems, for the playwright himself); and Forster had offered to underwrite publication of his life's thoughts on matters religious under the title *The Religion of the Heart*, a much-expanded version of his privately published pamphlet 'Christianism', written in his Italian exile in 1823.

At that time, in his 'Grace before Meat', Lamb had made an oblique reference to Hunt's quasi-religious musings. 'I own that I am disposed to say grace upon twenty other occasions in the course of the day besides my dinner . . . commending my new scheme for extension to a niche in the grand, philosophical, poetical and perchance in part heretical liturgy, now compiling by my friend Homo Humanus, for the use of a certain smug congregation of Utopian Rabelaisian Christians, no matter where assembled.'

Thirty years on, it again seems to have been Vincent's death – if not intimations of Marianne's and his own mortality – which set Hunt to musing again upon the afterlife, in a spiritual (as opposed to dogmatically Christian) version of which he believed. While not repudiating his lifelong, Shelley-induced unorthodoxy in matters religious, Hunt had always believed in a 'spirit-world' where he would be reunited with his loved ones after death. Even so, he took some persuading to put his name to the book, apparently fearing that it might 'mar' its influence by 'causing it to be considered as one of an author's numerous productions, not worse perhaps than the rest, but no better'. He thought of it less as a book, in fact, than a 'little heaven down below'.

To combat charges of blasphemy, or merely of being irreligious, Hunt goes to some pains in the preface to explain that 'the object of this book is to supply the wants of one class of religious persons, and not to give more offence than can be helped to others . . . The point for reflection is whether the matter is in earnest and is needed; whether the book finds its response in the heart; whether readers felt it to be good for them, good for their families, for parents who would cease to fear questions respecting God and eternity; for heart that would fain see the final separation of religion from repulsiveness; for understanding, during an age of transition, perplexed between the two extremes of faiths which despise reason, and a reason exasperated or mechanicalized into no faith at all.'

A 'natural piety, no less than cheerfulness', had always pervaded his own writings. 'The cheerfulness indeed was a part of the piety, flowing from the same tendency to love and admire.' His personal aspiration was 'not that all should think alike in particulars, but that all should feel alike in essentials, and that there should be no belief or practice irreconcilable with the heart'. The heart, to Hunt, was 'intimately associated with happiness, cheerful thinking and piety'. With this in mind he asked the printer, John Chapman, to emboss a heart on the cover of the book, encircled with a wreath of mingled thorns and flowers (to represent, respectively, the pains and pleasures of duty). He also asked for the cover to be dark crimson or purple, to look as much as possible like a prayer book without being black.

Although reviewed by the *Athenæum* 'like an old lady removing a dead rat with a pair of tongs', Hunt's theistic manual was pious enough; it began with a creed, continued with some forms of daily and weekly service and concluded with a series of short homilies which he billed as 'exercises of the heart in its duties and aspirations'. The red meat follows with a paean to Confucius amid a selection of 'The Only Final Scriptures', followed by Hunt's personal selection of religious texts, counting Jesus as an 'Oriental fabulist' among a varied list including Confucius again, Socrates, Epictetus, Marcus Aurelius, St Francis de Sales, Bishop Whichcote, Shaftesbury, Emerson and Carlyle. Poets also figure as sages, ranging from Wordsworth and Coleridge to Keats, Shelley and Tennyson, and not excluding the author himself: 'Nor shall a false modesty hinder us from saying that passages for discourse might be found in the *Indicator* and the *Seer*.'

By way of conclusion, in a poetic form of prose, Hunt thinks aloud about the afterlife :

What is it we shall first look at? which way turn? what life lead, and how long? and after that life whither go, ever hand in hand, to another? on what electrical wings? from what planet to planet and sun to sun, each sun being a heaven (for does not the sun look like a heaven, with all that beauty and goodness?) and then, when we seem to have got to our final heaven, or to one in which we can feel but one mightiest desire to go further, whither shall we find ourselves once more, and once for all, travelling? whither still going? where arriving? what unspeakable vision at last circuiting, closer and closer; yearning towards it more and more; drawn irresistibly towards it, but with perfect love and transport, and no fear, and all still together; – towards what? – towards WHOM?

While he was writing this, news arrived of the death of his old friend Talfourd, from whom he had latterly been estranged. Thanks to his lifelong rapport with younger men, Hunt was not exactly without friends; but now it seemed as if the mainstays of his life were being removed one by one. It was more than thirty years since the deaths of Keats and Shelley, fifteen since he had mourned the loss of Hazlitt and Lamb in an 1840 essay: 'Ah, dear Hazlitt and Lamb, old tea-drinking friends and teachers! Must he that writes this learn no more from you, in voice, as well as from mute books? Is it true, as sometimes he can hardly think it is, that neither of you is again coming down the street to his door, nor he to yours?' However well meant, and gratefully received, a respectful visit from Hazlitt's grandson, William Carew Hazlitt, was simply another reminder that there were friends who could never be replaced. It was all the more gratifying to hear from Glasgow that a City Hall audience of 3500 'glistened with interest and enthusiasm' at a service using Hunt's home-made prayers from his *The Religion of the Heart*.

Such were the mysteries exercising Hunt as the grand (if rather shabby) old man of English letters received a respectful stream of visitors – notably the American novelist Nathaniel Hawthorne, then US consul in Liverpool. Hawthorne, who came to pay his respects in 1855, professed himself shocked to find this august literary giant occupying 'a very plain and shabby little house' in a terrace with 'no prospect but that of an ugly village street, and certainly nothing to gratify his craving for a tasteful environment, inside or out'. The door was answered by a 'slatternly' maidservant – that Dickensian word again – to reveal Hunt, 'a beautiful and venerable old man, buttoned to the chin in a black dress-coat, tall and slender, with a countenance quietly alive all over, and the gentlest and most naturally courteous manner'.

Hunt ushered Hawthorne and his companions – 'a lady and a young girl', whom neither identifies – into 'a little study, or parlour, or both – a very forlorn room, with poor paper-hangings and carpet, few books, no pictures that I remember, and an awful lack of upholstery'. He mentioned these 'external blemishes' and this 'nudity of adornment' only because 'Leigh Hunt was born with such a faculty for enjoying all beautiful things that it seemed as if Fortune did him as much wrong in not supplying them, as in withholding a sufficiency of vital breath from ordinary men.'

This passage surprises, as all other accounts of the Hammersmith home have Hunt surrounded, as always, by 'mountains' of books, pictures, busts and other ornate decorative objects. Perhaps Hawthorne called on a bad day. But his visit was worth it for his most touching description of Hunt two years before his death: 'I have said that he was a beautiful old man. In truth, I never saw a finer countenance, either as to the mould of the features or the expression, nor any that showed the play of expression so perfectly without the slightest theatrical emphasis. It was like a child's face in this respect . . .' (Had the author of *The Scarlet Letter* been reading *Bleak House*?)

'At my first glimpse of him, I discerned that he was old, his long hair being white and his wrinkles many . . . But when he began to speak, and as he grew more earnest in conversation, I ceased to be sensible of his age; sometimes, indeed, its dusky shadow darkened through the gleam which his sprightly thoughts diffused about his face, but then another flash of youth came out of his eyes and made an illumination again. I never witnessed such a wonderfully illusive transformation, before or since.'

Leigh Hunt, Hawthorne continued, 'loved dearly to be praised'. By which he meant only that Hunt 'desired sympathy as a flower seeks sunshine', and 'perhaps profited by it as much in the richer depths of colouring that it imparted to his ideas'. When praised to his face, not least by Hawthorne's female companions ('the fit ministers at such a shrine'), Hunt's face 'shone, and he manifested great delight, with a perfect and yet delicate frankness, for which I loved him . . . He smiled, making himself and the poor little parlour about him beautiful thereby.

'It is usually the hardest thing in the world to praise a man to his face; but Leigh Hunt received the incense with such gracious satisfaction (feeling it to be sympathy, not vulgar praise), that the only difficulty was to keep the enthusiasm of the moment within the limit of permanent opinion.' A storm had been brewing as they talked; suddenly 'the rain poured and the lightning flashed, and the thunder broke; but I hope, and have great pleasure in believing, that it was a sunny hour for Leigh Hunt'.

To an English visitor, Robert Bell, who now sought his help with an edition of the English poets, Hunt had 'gone to live a long way off, near Hammersmith Broadway'. His health 'rarely permitted him to come to town', so Bell contentedly went to see him – usually at 8 p.m., 'which was his hour for a friendly compromise between tea and supper, or, rather, a union of both, "the cup that cheers but not inebriates" being always accompanied by some light and delicate fare, such as lamb cutlet and salad'. Sighed Hunt, himself, an ailing old man with a bedridden wife: 'I am always to be found alone, and visitors do me good.'

All his life Hunt had enjoyed visits from Americans, with whom his parental roots lent him a special kinship. George Ticknor, the Boston publisher, had come calling as early as 1819, the lawyer and writer Benjamin B. Thatcher in 1838. After visiting Hunt in Chelsea in 1839, Charles Sumner, later US Senator for Massachusetts, reported him 'truly brilliant in conversation', adding: 'He lives more simply, I think, than any person I have visited in England; but he possesses a palace of a mind.'

Recently the New England poet and critic James Russell Lowell had spent an 'entertaining' hour talking with Hunt of poets and poetry. A correspondence with the Boston editor S. Adams Lee had resulted in the gift of a lock of George Washington's hair — which Hunt rewarded, to Lee's astonished delight, with a fragment of Keats's handwritten manuscript of *Hyperion*.

Now came another American publisher, James T. Fields (later editor of the *Atlantic Monthly* and co-founder with Ticknor and others of the American publishing house Houghton Mifflin.) Fields shared Hawthorne's dismay at the cottage but conceded that the view appealed to his author, as if his imagination were still performing the same quantum leaps as during his youthful imprisonment: 'When he looked out of his dingy old windows on the four bleak elms in front of his dwelling, he saw, or thought he saw, a vast forest, and he could hear in the note of one poor sparrow even, the silvery voice of a hundred nightingales.'

In one of a spate of letters to Ollier, written in the small front parlour which had become his study, Hunt himself gives his imagination such free rein. 'By a curious effect of the evening sunshine my little homely black mantelpiece, not an inelegant structure, you know, in itself, is turned, while I write, into a solemnly glorious presentment of black and gold . . . How rich are such eyes as yours and mine, how rich and how fortunate, that can see visitations so splendid in matters of such nine-and-twopence!'

Wednesday was 'Ollier day', when Hunt looked forward to the visits of his oldest surviving friend. But the 'rainy and un-omnibused roads' of winter all too often meant Ollier could not make the journey. When they could not meet, the two exchanged playful letters, predominantly about their respective states of health. 'I have just got a "railway wrapper",' writes Hunt in November 1853, 'which has brought greater comfort to my knees than anything I have had yet. It is the *Knee*-plus-ultra.'

Hunt's diet at this time seems to have been frugal, probably as much for health as economic reasons. One visitor reported that 'a cup of tea was my only entertainment, brought on a tray, and that rarely; his own food seems to be a panade – some sort of bread stuff, like Beranger's simple diet, which he used to simmer in a small iron pot on the hob'. Another visitor has left a rather different account of Hunt's 'odd' eating habits: 'He would "take a fancy", and indulge freely night after night in a thoroughly indigestible supper of anything which accident or circumstance might have suggested, from corned beef to Welsh rarebit or Scotch porridge . . . Then, after a week or so of indulgence, he would have brought on a fit of indigestion, upon which he would abuse the innocent, if indigestible cause of his illness "up hill and down dale".' Hunt was also described as 'eating and praising 3 eggs boiled hard with bread and butter . . . next time Welsh rarebit with mustard etc. . . . his longest love – dried fruit, bread, water – his Italian memory'.

Ever the eccentric in medical matters, seventy-year-old Hunt now decided to grow a beard – not for aesthetic reasons, nor even to spare himself the trouble of shaving, but because he had read in a newspaper that beards had a beneficial effect on coughs, colds and chest complaints: 'Physicians proclaim it to be a natural respirator . . . Railway conductors, I understand, are fast adopting the beard.' Soon Ollier grew one, too, and decided he looked 'thrice his age'.

In early-Victorian England, beards had yet to come into fashion, let alone become a commonplace – as they would do after 1856, with the return of unshaven troops from the Crimean War. But Carlyle, too, followed Hunt's example, causing great controversy among his family and friends. '[Hunt] complained that there were two drawbacks,' a good-humoured Carlyle wrote to his friend Lord Ashburton (who had also joined what they called 'the beard-movement'). 'First, the little boys laughed at him; second, the beard abolished an uncommonly sweet smile he was understood to have. That latter evil will not apply to me . . .' This would be the last conversation between Hunt and

Carlyle; his visits had become 'almost pathetic' to both Carlyles, leaving the 'Jenny' whose kiss he had immortalised in tears as he took his leave – 'kind and pitying', in her husband's words, 'to the now weak and time-worn old man'.

Hunt's beard was pure white. Thackeray's daughter, Lady Ritchie, described him at this time as 'romantic' and 'foreign-looking', with 'a cloak flung over one shoulder'. The would-be man of letters Frederick Locker-Lampson, who visited Hunt in the last year of his life, found him 'tall, dark, grizzled, bright-eyed and rather fantastically dressed in a sacerdotal-looking garment'.

Hunt received Locker-Lampson, an amateur poet come to 'inflict' his verses on the great man, 'with cordiality, tinged with ceremony'. He describes the elderly Hunt as 'not wholly in the busy world, not quite beyond it' and as 'proud of his old age, speaking with a smile of his *soixante et mille ans*'. Giving the impression of being 'rich in the milk of amiability and optimism', Hunt reportedly acknowledged the amateur verses with 'gusto' and criticised them with 'tenderness'.

Soon it was less poetry than the weather which came to dominate Hunt's social life. 'Well, winter is now gone, surely, and the very word *spring* is good (though we must not cease to guard against colds),' he wrote to Ollier in early 1855. Health, which meant survival, was becoming a major issue for both of them. 'And we two are vital men, and must look forward to *June*, JUNE JUNE. You note the crescendo of that vociferation.'

Hunt's voluminous correspondence with Ollier that winter also reveals that he contemplated leaving Hammersmith and returning to Kensington; but nothing came of the idea, as Wednesday was still 'Ollier day' in Hammersmith two years later, in 1857, and indeed in 1858, when June – 'including certain powers of cross-country cabs' – was still the month to which both frail old men were looking forward.

By now their sons were working together on the *Leader*, the paper edited by Thornton, who had given Edmund Ollier a job. 'Good news, that,' Hunt enthused to Ollier père. 'Sons of you and me ought to go together, ought they not? Aye, and grandsons and great-grandsons, in *saecula saeculorum*.'

For all his growing infirmity, Hunt's bibliography shows him as prolific as ever in 1855, which saw publication of *The Old Court Suburb* (a

collection of his prose writings about London), *Stories in Verse* (a col-
lection of his narrative poetry, dedicated in florid style to the Duke of
Devonshire) and a bowdlerised edition of the works of *Beaumont and
Fletcher* (dedicated to Procter).

As noted during the post-Skimpole controversy, Dickens arranged
for *Stories in Verse* to enjoy a favourable review in his *Household Words*,
written by Henry Morley under the headline 'By Rail to Parnassus'.
Imagining a conversation in a railway carriage, in which the reader
tells a fellow passenger of 'a book of stories, all of them good ones,
written in such verse as may be read by rich and poor with almost equal
pleasure', Morley speaks for Dickens's guilty conscience in a passage
about the book's author – 'a pure-hearted man, beloved of poets in his
youth and in his prime, now worthy to be loved of all mankind'.

The metaphor developed in the ensuing passage takes the art of
non-apology to bizarre extremes. 'Of him,' continues the traveller,
'there are fewer to speak ill than even of Robin Hood, when not a soul
in Locksley town would speak him an ill-word; the friars raged; but no
man's tongue nor even feature stirred; except among a very few, who
dined in the abbey halls; and then with a sigh bold Robin knew his true
friends from his false.' There follows an aside from the reader: 'I had
been thinking about Leigh Hunt to myself, and went on reading to
myself of those unfaithful comrades, Roger the monk, and Midge, on
whom Robin had never turned his face but tenderly; with one or two,
they say, besides – Lord! that in this life's dream men should abandon
one true thing, that would abide with them.'

Amid proxy trash of this order, Dickens's dogged hypocrisy continued with more refusals to visit Hunt in his 'Lilliputian bit of a
house' in Hammersmith, or discuss the Skimpole matter further.
What would he have made of an episode at this time not revealed until
several years later, after Hunt's death, by his fellow novelist Elizabeth
Gaskell? In the summer of 1856 William Wetmore Story, a mutual
friend of Hunt and Gaskell, was commissioned by a grateful Adams
Lee to spend $500 on 'something of value' and 'ask [Leigh Hunt's]
acceptance of it'. Hunt's reply to Story's letter conveying the offer,
according to Gaskell, 'declined receiving the money in *any* shape –
statue, cash, books – in the firmest & most graceful manner'. The circumstances in which he had once been 'glad & thankful' to receive

such offerings from friends had recently been 'cruelly misunderstood & misrepresented'. He now felt it 'due to himself to reject material kindness, while he was fully alive as ever to the nobleness of heart which offered it'.

To the stream of pilgrims to his 'far-flung' cottage, Leigh Hunt was no Harold Skimpole. He was 'an old man with snowy hair, but his eyes were still brilliant, and the fascinating grace of his manner was unimpaired. He was naturally rather tall and of a slender figure, but incessant daily toil at the desk caused him to stoop somewhat . . .

'He was then living in a small house . . . which presented few external attractions either to a worldly or aesthetic observer, but Leigh Hunt was there like a prince in hiding. The same treasures were round him, too, which lighted Keats's fire of song. The Greek casts, Sappho's meek head, Great Alfred too . . . In themselves they were but a few casts, a few engravings, a few sketches in colour, a number of well-worn books, with windows full of flowers and no heavy draperies to keep away heaven's light. The fresh white muslin curtains swayed in the summer breeze as Leigh Hunt talked . . .'

The Bostonian Mrs James T. Fields, the 'beautiful and accomplished' young Annie Fields, also professed herself thrilled to have been admitted to 'the interior that had inspired Keats', mistaking Hunt's modest Hammersmith parlour for that of his Hampstead home some forty years earlier. Hunt spoke of Keats and Shelley, she wrote, 'as if they had just closed the door by which we entered'. More elegantly, she described Hunt as wearing 'the dignity and sweetness of a man not only independent of worldly ambitions, but of one dependent upon unworldly satisfactions . . . Although our visit to Leigh Hunt was within a few months of his death, the native elasticity of his mind and the living grace of his manner were undimmed.'

Her publisher husband meanwhile made their visit worthwhile by suggesting an anthology of Hunt's prose and verse, which he proceeded to busy himself editing throughout 1856. Apart from some 'new papers of Londiniana', this was otherwise a less productive year than usual. Looking back over his earlier work, without undue self-indulgence, Hunt now saw *The Story of Rimini* as 'conventional, not rich and aromatic, and tending to prose'. He declared himself 'not unwilling to be judged' by such poems as 'Abou Ben Adhem' and some of his other smaller pieces. 'In truth,' in the verdict of the sympathetic Blunden, Hunt had in later life become 'a poet not remarkably strong and glowing, but clear, various and following his own course'.

In December 1856 both Hunts were unwell, 'she with a cough as well as rheumatism, and I with a cough and bronchorroea'. A steady decline in Hunt's own health, these days more genuine than imaginary, was probably accelerated by the rapidly worsening condition of Marianne.

Even the ministrations of Hunt's devoted friend Southwood Smith, whom he immortalised in a sonnet –

> Ages will honour, in their hearts enshrined,
> Thee, Southwood Smith, physician of mankind . . .

– could not now prolong her increasingly wretched life. After almost forty-eight years of marriage to Leigh Hunt, Marianne died on 26 January 1857, in her seventieth year. She was buried with their son Vincent in Kensal Green cemetery.

Built in the 1830s on the model of Paris's Père-Lachaise cemetery, and made fashionable by the choice of George III's sixth son, Prince Augustus Frederick, Duke of Sussex, to be buried there, soon to be followed by his sister, Princess Sophia, this was the final resting-place Hunt had now chosen for himself.

'My wife,' wrote her ever-devoted widower, 'was a woman of great generosity, of great freedom from every kind of jealousy, great superiority to illusions from the ordinary shows of prosperity. In all the hazards to which I put our little means in the pursuit of what I thought it my duty to do in furtherance of social advancements, and all the injury which really resulted to them, she never uttered a word of objection.' Marianne, he pretended, unable to resist a sentimental trip down memory lane, had been 'as uncomplaining during the worst storms of our adversity as she was during those at sea in our Italian voyage'.

Only after her death did Hunt begin to realise that Marianne had been borrowing money in his name, without his knowledge. An appalled exchange of letters with Procter, for example, revealed that there had been 'three or four sums sent to poor Mrs Hunt, amounting altogether to £140', followed by 'a trifle or two – I do not know what – something – almost nothing'. Like many of Hunt's friends, poor Procter was tongue-tied with mortification on his behalf. 'The last time I had any communication, I grieve to say that I got angry and wrote angrily to her – Forgive me – I did not know then – as I know now – what a host of faults I myself had – what a host of faults everybody has – and what *trouble* – but I will say nothing, lest I should say something to give you pain, and God knows that is not my intention.'

Liberated, in truth, by Marianne's death, Hunt again contemplated moving back into London proper from Hammersmith, where he felt so cut off from literary and social life. According to Thornton, he liked the idea of returning to the area of New Road (now Marylebone Road), where he had lived so many years earlier; Thornton's son Walter testifies that his grandfather asked him to inspect a house in St John's Wood. Either way, Hunt was evidently in nostalgic mood about an earlier, happier time in his life. Wanting 'a tree and a bit of a garden', he even wondered aloud about moving in with Thornton and his family, to share the domestic expenses. As it turned out, unsurprisingly, the cheapest option was to stay where he was, soon to be joined by other children and grandchildren.

Hunt's eternal financial difficulties were now somewhat relieved by the unexpected arrival of £50 from the Queen's private purse. Forty more was all he received for a successful West End production of his play *Lover's Amazements*. Although it was well received at the Lyceum Theatre in January 1858, involving the author in another gratifying curtain-call ovation, the producer, Charles Dillon, somehow contrived to go bankrupt, forcing the closure of both play and theatre.

Just, as ever, Hunt's luck. As was the fate of a collection of sonnets he had spent two years gathering and editing, with another elegant and perceptive introduction, to a commission from Adams Lee. Soon after receiving Hunt's parcel in Boston in 1857, Lee was hospitalised for dementia. He later said he had entrusted a return parcel to Hunt to a friend travelling to Europe, but had been swindled; both courier and parcel had disappeared. Whether or not we choose to believe this, Lee somehow managed to relocate the parcel by 1867, eight years after Hunt's death, when he published it as *The Book of the Sonnet*, crediting himself as Hunt's co-editor.

Now, in his semi-invalid state, Hunt took the chance to reread favourite books yet again while keeping up with the publications of the day. His copy of Chaucer bears an inscription dated 1 September 1857: 'Finished my third regular reading of this great poet and good-hearted man, whom I admire more than ever.' On 23 January 1858, in Spenser's *Faerie Queene*, he wrote : 'Finished with greater reluctance, far greater – for the more I read Spenser, the more I see in him – and get out of him, as out of an ever growing, and superabounding forest of orchards – my third regular reading of the divine poem – wondering after all that it is only the third, for I read him always . . . What a consolation has my perpetual wandering in his enchanted ground been to me! I seem to possess it like a property, to which I wish to shut myself away (as much as it is possible for me to do so) from care and sorrow. Here, if anywhere, I have attained the end of the "wings of the dove", and "been at rest".'

After signing this, he added as if for posterity: 'No disparagement the above effusion to those whom I love and have loved, and without whose companionship my being can never be but wanting, here or hereafter. But love itself is often full of anxiety (what so full?) and the remote enchantment must be flown to, to tranquillize perseverance . . . Same day and moment. *Absentes lugens, omnia est post mortem sperans.*'

In the margins of his copy of Hazlitt's *Political Essays, with Sketches of Public Characters* (1819), Hunt relives his differences with Byron and his alliance with Shelley: 'It is a pity Mr Hazlitt could not leave his greater brother-reformer alone!' In his copy of Shakespeare he specifies his own examples of the Bard's 'mirror, as it were, held up to nature': 'In three instances during my life have I known what it is to undergo the anguish of an impatience with the ordinations of Providence – a feeling, the absurdity of which was speedily subjected to the consideration that Providence itself gave me the very humanities which resented its apparent cruelty. One only of the occasions was a real one. It was when I stood on the sea-coast of Lerici, during the search for the body of my drowned friend. The two others were the catastrophe (the sepulchre-scene) of *Romeo and Juliet*, and the scene in *Lear* when he comes in with the body of his daughter.'

Holding Hunt's well-worn copy of Pope's letters, some sixty years after his death, Blunden felt a palpable sense of the 'almost tranced' state which overcame Hunt with a favourite book in his hand. 'The world became a duodecimo, and he had no bad dreams in it, or very few, at such times. He is unbodied, except for the hand that holds the pen, and in the fullest significance enters into the spirit of the intellectual universe. His private marks and monologues in the margin prove his happiness.'

Reading was one consolation of an increasingly reclusive life, about which Hunt was wryly self-conscious, as in a letter of December 1857 thanking Procter's daughter Adelaide, herself a poet, for visiting Cornwall Road with friends bearing the touching gift of an illuminated copy of his best-known poem, 'Abou Ben Adhem'. With a promise to hang it up in his study, Hunt's thank-you letter had him wondering 'what the young ladies thought of the strange, battered-looking old cosmopolite who came staring again into the world out of his hermitage'.

The penultimate year of Hunt's life was marred by a 'wild' biography of Shelley by Hogg, his old sparring partner, whom he was now moved to take on again by an indignant letter from Shelley's son, Sir Percy, wishing to dissociate himself from the book – not least its dedication to him. Sir Percy wrote to inform Hunt of 'the history of it, because without some explanation you may consider me and my wife (whose names figure in the dedication) responsible for the bad taste and contemptuous tone of scurrility with which the book is filled – to say nothing of the reckless publication of letters, which ought to have been considered confidential'. This proved the first of a stream of letters enlisting Hunt's help in 'saving Shelley's beloved memory from such handling as Hogg'.

In a long, angry reply to Sir Percy, Hunt denounced the 'enormities and vagaries' of Hogg's book as the work of a madman. Of sundry inaccuracies, even imputations as to Shelley's honesty, he declared: 'During the whole time that I knew your father, I never knew him violate the truth in the slightest degree, either in letter or in spirit. My faith in his veracity was so great that a single shadow of incompatibility with it in a letter respecting myself, which was republished the other day by one of his premature biographers (to say nothing of other reasons), instantly renewed my opinion of its being a forgery . . .

'This foolish book of an imbecile pretender, whose misdirected absurdities have made me in my own old age speak of a fellow-creature in a manner to which I thought I had bidden a long adieu, and for whom those three poor human words, *old age* and *imbecile*, may after all furnish an excuse, which I have not sufficiently borne in mind . . .'

Hunt's letter proved 'very acceptable' to the Shelley family, who accepted his advice not to pursue Hogg with a public protest. Instead the family would publish a 'little volume', in which Hunt's letter might be inappropriate; but Sir Percy urged him to publish it – 'as a sort of notion of Hogg's *Life*' – in a magazine or journal. Around this time, by bizarre coincidence, Hunt's heady memories of Shelley were further stirred by a letter from a postal clerk informing him of the discovery of a 'remarkable' letter from Shelley to Mary, written forty-two years earlier but only now, in some 'unaccountable' manner, 'reposted, and returned to the office as "unknown at this address"'. It proved to be the letter of 16 December 1816 in which Shelley paid tribute to Hunt's kindness and hospitality during the trauma of Harriet Westbrook's death: 'Leigh Hunt has been with me all day, and his delicate and tender attentions to me, his kind speeches of you, have sustained me . . .'

A few months later, in April 1859, Hunt was duly gratified by a letter from an American cousin, a Mrs Swift, inviting him to visit the United States, where his reputation was steadily growing as Lee, Fields and others continued to publish more of his work. 'My object in writing now is to persuade you to visit America. A cordial welcome would await you wherever you might go. The name and fame of Leigh Hunt is known and appreciated by every reading American. It is the land of your forefathers – your dear mother's natal home. What shall I write more to induce you to come?' He knew, she continued, what a 'golden harvest' Thackeray had gathered there by his American lectures. 'Think if you were to come to us.' Hunt's health would not, of course, permit him to contemplate the journey. The American ambassador to London had recently told him that his name was 'a household word, from one end of the United States to the other'; but, unlike such contemporaries as Thackeray and Dickens, Hunt would never visit the land of his fathers.

Still, marooned in remote Hammersmith, he wrote on tirelessly, now in the *Spectator* (usually under the heading of 'The Occasional').

Here, on 26 March, appeared the last of his published poems, 'To Poerio and his Fellow-Patriots', a final assault on princely autocracy. Here also appeared his farewell tribute to Ollier – Hunt's friend of fifty years, who died in June 1859 – and two further papers on Shelley, embellishing his tirades against Hogg with the judgement that he was 'no more entitled to write about Shelley than Caliban to follow Ariel's flights of fancy'.

His lifelong stream of letters continued with messages of support to Mazzini in Italy and the heirs of Daniel O'Connell in Ireland, amid affectionate musings to family and friends. But his main energies in these last few months of his life were devoted to an article he would never see in print: a reply, posthumously published in *Fraser's Magazine* that December, to an assault on the 'wantonness, voluptuousness and debauchery' of Keats and other Romantic poets by Cardinal (Nicholas) Wiseman, first Catholic Archbishop of Westminster, who had collected a series of sermons, lectures and addresses during a tour of Ireland the previous summer into a hefty, outspoken book.

In 'English Poetry versus Cardinal Wiseman', Hunt wrote for the last time of an age now long gone:

I knew Keats himself as well as his poetry; knew him both in his weakness and his strength; know how far removed both of them were from want of impressibility by his fellow-creatures; know in particular how he felt for those connected with him by ties of natural affection, and with what 'glow' and 'emotion' [the Cardinal's words] he has written of the best moral principles, public and private.

My own feelings I shall endeavour to content with observing that a robust, prosperous and satisfied elderly gentleman might have spared, if he could not pity or do justice to the inspired and impassioned youth whose death was embittered by the agonies of a love which he was never to enjoy, and the like of which, in reverence to the maiden sincerity of the Catholic priesthood, his Eminence is to be supposed never to have felt – certainly never gave way to.

It seems supremely appropriate that Hunt's farewell to literary arms was a final tribute to his beloved Shelley in the *Spectator*: 'Great men of advanced and unworldly natures need the growth of time to do them justice equal to their greatness.'

As he wrote these, his last public words, in the summer of 1859, Hunt had high hopes of an invitation to visit Shelley's heirs at their country seat, Boscombe, that August. Since Marianne's death, loneliness had been a recurring theme of his letters to friends from Hammersmith. By Thornton's account, his father had all but given up going out. 'He sat surrounded by his books, and while he paced the room, while he conversed or meditated, or allowed his eyes to wander upon objects within the house or without it, the contents of those familiar volumes were present to his mind as if the pages had stood open before him.'

But he made the most of his tiny garden: 'There is a trellis on two sides of [the lawn],' he wrote to Hunter in Craigcrook, 'to hide outhouses and neighbours' paling, so that it makes a sort of garden box, *in* a garden box, and I sit out of doors in it on sunny west-wind days, and pretend to have an arbour, grass-plots and all, and to be remote, and horticultural, and impossible.'

And still he entertained, with his daughter Jacintha playing hostess, however imperfectly. Since Marianne's death, the impecunious Cheltnams had moved into 7 Cornwall Road, with their seven-year-old daughter Marian and three-year-old son Thornton. 'Good children, and a great relief to my weariness,' Hunt wrote of them to a friend. 'The older one grows, the fonder one grows of children. They help us to take an interest in little things and pleasant words.'

By June 1859 his son Henry Sylvan, now forty, had also moved into the terrace; he had married Rosalind Williams, daughter of Edward, the mutual friend who had drowned with Shelley. They brought six more grandchildren into Hunt's daily life, as well as further mixed memories of his salad days; besides being the son-in-law of Shelley's friend Williams, he was the stepson-in-law of Hogg, author of the recent memoir which had so outraged Sir Percy.

Early in 1859 Locker-Lampson describes tea *chez* Hunt being 'presided over by a nimble-fingered little nymph of a daughter in a stuff frock imperfectly hooked and eyed. She had not even the coquetry to pin her collar straight!' He could 'still hear' Hunt's 'Jacintha, give Mr Locker another cup of tea', delivered in a 'suave, almost stately manner, and in silvery tones . . .'

Lugubrious enough to rival Hunt at his worst, Lampson had observed that 'the surroundings of your specially interesting people are commonplace. Their intimates are nearly always dull fellows.' Now, while repeating this, he was anxious to make it clear that 'I am not in any way reflecting on the little Jacintha, who, if she had condescended, might have proved a very agreeable companion.' She was 'not exactly pretty, but, as the gallant Frenchman said of somebody else, "she had a particularly sweet expression in some of her eyes." Her tea was excellent!'

By the summer of 1859 the rapid decline in Hunt's health was evident to Hawthorne during a dinner in his honour at the home of Procter, who had first introduced them. Hawthorne was shocked by the sight of Hunt, able to stand only by leaning on a fellow guest's arm. He looked 'sadly broken down by infirmities'. The American's last recollection of the 'beautiful old man' had him 'arm in arm with, nay, if I mistake not, partly embraced and supported by, another beloved and honoured poet'.

That was Procter. But the American publisher Fields, also present with his wife, noted that Hunt's 'mercurial qualities' were 'even then perceptible in his manner'. It was a 'goodly companie' long to be remembered. Hunt and Procter were 'in a mood for gossip over the ruddy port'. As they talked in low tones, Fields saw the two old poets 'take hands more than once at the mention of a dead and beloved name'. It was a sight, he later told Hawthorne, 'I shall not soon forget'.

This was to prove Hunt's last evening out. By August 1859 his health had deteriorated to the point where his old friend Charles Reynell, his printer and benefactor for half a century, insisted that he abandon Hammersmith for his own home across the Thames in Putney, where the air was more salubrious. As a young man, before his marriage, Hunt had lived for some months in the Pimlico home of Reynell's parents, teaching the boy by way of rent; they had since become kinsmen when Hunt's brother John and Reynell's brother Carew had married sisters. Carew's daughter Catherine had subsequently married Hazlitt's son William Jr. Now some long-running wheel had turned full circle. Here at Woodlands Farm Hunt had spent the previous summer, with

Jacintha and her children, recuperating from his eternal chest trouble. Here again, perhaps, he could now regain what he seemed to be losing as he approached his seventy-fifth birthday: the will to live. Only recently, on losing the last of his teeth, he had smiled that he 'exulted' in this 'advance towards immortality'.

Hunt's last evening at his Hammersmith home, on 9 August, was shared by the poet and journalist Charles Kent, a friend of both his and Dickens's, whose account suggests that the fond old man was moved by premonitions of what was soon to come.

Kent had recently published a poem addressed to Hunt in *Bentley's Miscellany*:

> Hail! Grey beard stripling – young through seventy years,
> Lord of our laughter, master of our tears;
> One of those 'old familiar faces' all
> With pleasure from the radiant past recall . . .

This had precipitated an invitation from Hunt to visit him in 'the not very attractive suburbanity of Hammersmith'. Kent arrived to find his host 'seated in his easy-chair in his accustomed corner musing sadly in solitude'.

Between nostalgia and anticipation, Hunt ate a nectarine as he spoke of past and future – of his imprisonment, in light-hearted vein, and of his anticipated reunion with his loved ones. 'Leigh Hunt, though now nearly five years beyond the allotted age of man, still evidenced the same insatiable appetite as of yore for all the sugar-plums of life, "lumps of flowers", and snatches of melody . . .'

It was raining, 'with a subdued monotone in the sound that harmonized only too well with the evident sadness in the old poet's imagination'. As darkness fell outside, a barrel-organ down the street started playing – 'of all mal-à-propos airs in the world' – 'Home, Sweet Home'.

Hunt gathered together a bundle of books, as his own version of 'a bit of a home', and later that evening waved his daughters and grandchildren goodbye as his carriage departed for Putney. 'Like an old soldier upon his last march,' to the watching Kent, 'he had wrapped his cloak about him and gone forth, with his heart-strings torn and bleeding.'

Along with his bundle of books he took the proofs of the revised edition of his autobiography, with which he was still tinkering. From Putney he wrote his last letters, notably one to Lady Shelley, promising to send the two 'little articles I have written in the *Spectator*, on occasion of the notice of the *Memorials* in that paper'. Recognising that he would never be able to take up her invitation to Boscombe, Lady Shelley was gracious enough to pay him a visit in Putney; his letter of thanks, dated 24 August, apologised for still having failed to send her the promised papers, while gratefully remembering 'your bright countenance, smiling through its tears'.

Written in bed, 'with great internal pain' but the doctor telling him 'all will go well', this was the last letter Leigh Hunt would pen. 'The approach of my night-time,' he had recently written, 'is even yet adorned with a break in the clouds, and a parting smile of the sunset.'

In Thornton's words, 'The sense of beauty and gentleness, of moral beauty and faithful gentleness, grew upon him as the clear evening closed in.' In Putney, amid a spate of farewell letters, Hunt continued to work on his revised autobiography and the new edition of his poems then in prospect. 'Although his bodily powers had been giving way, his most conspicuous qualities, his memory for books, and his affection remained; and when his hair was white, when he had grown slender, when the very proportion of his height had visibly lessened, his step was still ready, and his dark eyes brightened at every happy expression, and at every thought of kindness.'

Other letters that month thanked some for their kindnesses, gave others his last blessings. 'We have real open fields to look upon,' he rejoiced, 'with trees, cattle etc.' Among his last letters was one to Jacintha, gamely expressing the hope of accepting the Shelleys' invitation to visit Boscombe 'before long'.

But Hunt knew his health was failing him for the last time. Soon he became 'mildly uneasy' at a shortage of breath, but was consoled by music 'from the next room'. While another son played for him, Thornton patiently answered his 'minute, eager and searching questions' about the condition of liberalism in Italy. Hunt all but achieved his wish, expressed nearly sixty years earlier, to die with his nose buried in a book: 'I may chance, some quiet day, to lay my over-beating temples on a book, and so have the death I most envy.' His last words were hopes for Italy's 'enlargement', his last breath 'uttering inquiries and messages of affection'. At the end Hunt believed that the spirits of his 'beloved dead' were in the room with him – anticipating, in the closing words of the autobiography he had only recently revised, the day when we may 'all meet in one of Plato's vast cycles of re-existence, experiencing the sum total of all that we have ever experienced and enjoyed before'.

'So gentle was the final approach,' witnessed Thornton, 'that he scarcely recognized it till the very last, and then it came without terrors.'

Death seems to have come as a kindness, perhaps a mercy, to a man who had maintained such a relish for life for so many long years through such mixed fortunes. Hunt's death, as Thornton put it soon afterwards, was 'simply exhaustion: he broke off his work to lie down and repose'. Thornton's note of the date is touchingly brief, and to the point: 'Sunday 28 August, 1859. Work unfinished.'

EPILOGUE

The world grows empty; fadingly and fast
The dear ones and the great ones of my life
Melt forth, and leave me but the shadows rife
Of those who blissful made my peopled past;
Shadows that in their numerousness cast
A sense of desolation sharp as knife
Upon the soul, perplexing it with strife
Against the vacancy, the void, the vast
Unfruitful desert which the earth becomes
To one who loses thus the cherished friends
Of youth. The loss of each beloved sends
An aching consciousness of want that dumbs
The voice to silence, – akin to the dead blank
All things became, when down the sad heart sank.

Cowden Clarke's sonnet 'On Hearing of Leigh Hunt's Death' was not the only one written as the word spread. 'I heard,' began another, 'and sudden clouds came o'er the day . . .' Henceforth, for the many friends he left behind, Hunt would live on via his own words about the authors he had loved: 'What a treasure is the possession of a friend's mind, when he is no more.'

Clarke and a handful of others were joined by younger admirers and the remaining relics of an older generation, Trelawny and Severn among them, at the funeral at Kensal Green, where he was buried with Marianne and Vincent. This was his 'beloved and flowery cemetery', to which he had often looked as his 'final bed-chamber, I trust, in this world' during 'solitary walks, with eyes at once most melancholy, yet consoled'.

That his last years in Hammersmith had been to some extent a 'posthumous life', as Keats had called his own final weeks in Rome, was confirmed by his obituary in the local paper, the *West London Observer*, which expressed mild surprise that this eminent local resident had still been alive. 'Some people will be surprised to hear not only that Leigh Hunt is dead, but that he only died on Sunday last. He had scarcely exceeded the age allotted to man, and yet to almost all but an inner circle of friends he was one of a generation long since passed away. Hazlitt, Lamb, Shelley, Byron – these are the names with which the name of Leigh Hunt will ever be associated.' At least there was no mention of Skimpole.

Hunt's assets were valued at less than £250. Unsurprisingly, he had neglected to make a will. To raise money for his children, especially his unmarried daughter Julia, Forster undertook to sell the celebrated collection of locks of hair. Hunt's beloved library, amounting to some two thousand volumes, was dispersed with almost indecent haste when Thornton, who had caught his father's habit of impecunity, sold the bulk of it to the American publisher Fields. Among the treasures which vanished across the Atlantic, where they lie scattered to this day, were signed copies of Coleridge, Shelley and Keats, all with Hunt's marginal annotations, Hunt's treasured editions of Chaucer, Shakespeare and Milton, and Shelley's copy of Diogenes Laertius' *Lives of the Greek Philosophers*.

Editor of the *Daily Telegraph* since 1855, Thornton became his father's ex-officio literary executor, preparing a volume of his collected poetry, finishing his revision of the autobiography and embarking on an edition of his letters. The revised *Autobiography* was the first to be published, in 1860, within a year of Hunt's death. Reading the proofs, Forster was moved to a pained protest that he himself still did not rate a mention: 'His silence, when a word would have been so grateful, is strange and unlike him.' Ever tactful, Thornton undertook to make good the omission in his introduction, a promise he fulfilled with as much delicacy as he handled all other aspects of his father's quirky legacy.

'Poor poet!' warbled Locker-Lampson. 'I like to think of thee as I saw thee on those two or three occasions, and not engulfed in draggle-tailed impecunity.' Already, as so often with such recollections, an unforgiving revisionism was setting in: 'People said that he would have been a happier man if he had not introduced disturbing forces into his lyrical life. We know that a poet filled the vestibule of his Gehenna with squalling children; and a prose philosopher says, "Avant de se marier il faut avoir au moins disséqué une femme"; that he had an incapacity for dealing with the ordinary affairs of existence, such as arithmetic and matrimony; but that he had a beautiful reliance on providence – which word, in this connection, I venture to spell with a little "p".'

One of the most eloquent of all posthumous tributes to Hunt is another essay by his eldest son, under the title 'A Man of Letters of the Last Generation', written for the first issue of the *Cornhill Magazine* in January 1860, at Thackeray's invitation:

Leigh Hunt belonged essentially to the earlier portion of the nine-teenth century; but . . . living among the old poets, and labouring to draw forth the spirit which the first half has breathed into the latter half of the century, he may be said to have been one of those true servitors of the library who unite all ages with the one we live in. The representative man of a school gone by, in his history we read the introduction to our own . . .

Leigh Hunt, although he dwelled and passed his days in the library, was no 'bookworm', divorced from human existence, its natural instincts and affections. On the contrary, he carried into his study a large heart and a strong pulse; to him the books spoke in the voices of his fellow-men, audible from the earliest ages, and he loved to be followed into his retreat by friends from the outer world . . . He brought to his labours great powers, often left latent, and used only in their superficial action; a defective perception of the tangible part of the subject; an imagination active, but overrat-ing its own share in the business; an impulsive will, checked by an over-scrupulous, over-conscientious habit of 'refining'; a nice taste, and an overwhelming sympathy with every form and aspect of human enjoyment, suffering or aspiration . . .

Elsewhere Thornton wrote of his father: 'The leading ideas of his mind were, first, earnest duty to his country at any cost to himself; next, the sacrifice of any ordinary consideration to personal affection and friendship; and lastly, the cultivation of "the ideal", especially as it is developed in imaginative literature.'

Thornton's next task was seeing through the latest edition of the *Poetical Works,* as gathered by Hunt himself before his death. The inscription 'Now Finally Collected' on the title page drew a protest from John Hunter, who bemoaned the absence of such poems as 'Talari Innamorati', 'Abraham and the Fire-Worshipper', 'The Fancy Concert' and others – rightly so, in Blunden's view: 'Those are poems of a decisive character, and such as cannot be imitated, however they may be surpassed in force of genius; for the spiritual and mental combination in them was peculiar to the author.' The issue was not satisfactorily resolved for another sixty years, until publication of the long definitive Oxford edition of Hunt's *Poetical Works* edited in 1923 by H.S. Milford.

Hunt's voluminous *Correspondence*, again edited by Thornton, was published in two volumes by Smith and Elder in 1862. A planned third volume never materialised. Given the chaos in which he was obliged to work – his father's papers were scarcely in apple-pie order – and the eccentric way in which he chose to arrange the book, grouping the letters by recipients and subject matter rather than chronology, with his own commentary to convert it into a quasi-biography, the result is far from satisfactory. Conspicuous by their absence, if for reasons beyond Thornton's control, are Hunt's letters to Keats and Byron, to his brother John, and many to Lamb, Hazlitt, Carlyle and Dickens.

Inheriting his father's penchant for haste at the expense of quality, Thornton also managed to upset many of the correspondents from whom he solicited contributions. Dickens, who had only recently thrown much of his correspondence on to that bonfire, wrote grudgingly that he had 'no sufficiently strong objection to the publication of the letter whereof you sent me a copy, since you desire to use it. I had many letters from your late father by me, but they were all destroyed a year or so ago in a general sacrifice of letters that I resolved to make.'

Browning, who had promised Thornton a letter from his father when 'locked up in Florence', was outraged to read another to Hunt from himself and his late wife, Elizabeth Barrett, published without his permission, and 'full of intimate talk about our child's illness, and other things which gave me real pain to read – the whole improved by such a series of blunders in the copying of my letter (being unused to my handwriting, I suppose, that the result is unintelligible beyond even *my* unintelligibility. He confesses it probably needs correction!). Think of doing this without one word of enquiry as to whether I would allow such a liberty – which means, taking care not to receive the inevitable refusal . . . It is as if some clownish person had thrown open the door of a bathing-machine in which I was undressing.'

Like father, again, like son. But Thornton was scrupulous about protecting his father's reputation. Forster supported him in editing out many potentially compromising passages in Hunt's letters to Bessy – who died not long after, in March 1861, having failed to fulfil her apparent literary promise. Since 1848, when she approached her in-laws in 'a state of distress', she had been taken in and cared for by her nephew Thornton. As for Thornton himself: he outlived his father by just thirteen years, dying on 25 June 1873 at the age of only sixty-two, after devoting the rest of his life to his father's memory and the service of the *Daily Telegraph* while failing to write ambitious books about 'the Progress of Society' and the Irish poet and journalist William Maginn (1793–1842).

That is the sum, at least, of Thornton's professional life. He was not a handsome man – 'monkey-face' was the verdict of his father's engraver friend Linton, who nevertheless seems guilty of understatement when adding that, 'in spite of his physiognomy', he had a 'way with women'. For literary history better remembers Thornton Hunt – married since 1834 to Katharine Gliddon, by whom he had nine children – as the lover of George Lewes's wife Agnes, by whom he had four more. Agnes Lewes already had four children by her husband, who was in turn the long-standing lover of Mary Ann Evans, better known as the novelist George Eliot. In a remarkable three-month period in 1851–2 Agnes Lewes and Kate Hunt gave birth to Thornton's offspring only three months apart; each also bore him another, a son and a daughter respectively, in 1853.

Friends since the 1840s, Thornton and Lewes had together founded the *Leader* as a platform for their progressive beliefs – among which was the view that marriage was 'a remnant of barbarism' and that 'wives, like worldly goods, were to be shared among friends'. While Thornton somehow managed to keep his marriage intact while doting on Agnes, Lewes abandoned her for Eliot, with whom he fled to Germany in 1854. Agnes's children by her husband were adopted by her father, who sent them to school in Switzerland, where Eliot grew deeply attached to them, coming to regard them as her own children.

Lewes, for his part, remained very close to Agnes (whom he called 'Rose', because of her unusually 'bright' complexion), visiting her in England regularly and treating her children by Thornton generously. With Thornton himself, however, Lewes's relations finally soured, not least because of his hereditary ineptitude with money. 'Have been agitated and distressed lately by finding Agnes £150 in debt, mainly owing to T[hornton]'s defalcations,' Lewes confided to his diary. There ensued an angry correspondence, during which Lewes refused to withdraw 'offensive expressions' to the point where Thornton challenged him to a duel. 'There is something ludicrous in the extravagance of this,' observed Lewes. 'A challenge from him to me, and on such grounds!'

Thornton's father made no recorded comment on all this, throughout his voluminous writings, whether private or public, much though it must have enlivened the last decade of his domestic life. Perhaps it was sheer exhaustion which saw Thornton Hunt so prematurely interred with his parents in Kensal Green in 1873, his funeral attended mostly by *Telegraph* journalists. Agnes outlived him by all of twenty-eight years; after Lewes's death in 1878, George Eliot undertook to support Agnes and her children financially, adopting Charles Lewes, Agnes's eldest son by her husband, as her heir.

Amid it all, Thornton proved a vigilant keeper of his father's flame, and one of his most eloquent obituarists, as in this unpublished homily:

> He was, in every sense of the words, a gentleman and a scholar.
> Cadet of a family broken by more than one revolution, he inherited

nothing more than the ambition to be a student and a patriot, but his uncompromising love of truth led him to be a questioner of dogma, even on his own side in politics and religion; while his indolence and still more his *indoles* – which we imperfectly call taste, genius or natural bent – led him to the lighter 'humanities'. A devoted idealist, he actually lived in the world of poetry, painting and music; coming into the real world only to play his part, confessedly with very elementary knowledge, in the stern unprofitable business of constitutional politics; and mingling in the business of common life only to treat his affairs on bookish principles and to invest his personal friends with ideal attributes; the tangible results of his conscientious endeavours being party persecution, imprisonment, embarrassment and disappointment. He seldom viewed anything as it really was, but as it looked under the atmosphere of poetry . . .

To Forster, there was never a man of 'so sunny a nature' as Hunt, 'who could draw so much pleasure from common things, or to whom books were a world so real, so exhaustless, so delightful. I was only seventeen when I derived from him the tastes which have been the solace of all subsequent years, and well remember the last time I saw him at Hammersmith, not long before his death, when, with his delicate, worn, but keenly intellectual face, his large, luminous eyes, his thick shock of wiry grey hair, and a little cape of faded black silk over his shoulders, he looked like an old French abbé. He was buoyant and pleasant as ever . . .'

Thornton's sometime colleague Edmund Ollier, son of Charles, wrote of Hunt senior that the 'qualities which make a man of genius what he is, are never to be met with again in precisely the same combination . . . Leigh Hunt has never had justice done him for the excellent sense and sanity of his mind.' In an introduction to a posthumous collection of Hunt's essays, the son of his lifelong friend and publisher left a judicious appraisal of the one literary skill at which, perhaps, Hunt excelled:

Now gay, now humorous, now witty, now reflective, now analytical, and inevitably literary, his essays pass through many lights and shades of feeling, and are at home in all. Addison had not half as much variety, and his views of life and nature had nothing like the subtlety and depth of Hunt's. Lamb had a richer humour, and a more singular personality, a more tragic intensity of pathos; but his range was less – his sympathies were not so catholic. Leigh Hunt's criticism may never have reached the majestic and sonorous heights of Hazlitt's masterpieces; it had less of eloquence and force; but it was more reliable, and more even.

Its quality was exquisitely refined and delicate – the result of a natural sensibility, educated and trained by long and careful study; but it is a mistake to suppose that its only characteristic was sympathy. No doubt, sympathy was a chief element; but not more so than judgment . . . Where Coleridge would rave, and Hazlitt be paradoxical, and Lamb grow hysterical with emotion, or beautifully quaint with fantastic eccentricities, Hunt seemed always to preserve the balance of his faculties. With great powers of admiration, a strong sense of enjoyment, and an ardent disposition, he nevertheless appeared to know the exact line beyond which literary worship passes into superstition.

Visited by Allingham in 1868, Carlyle reminisced about Hunt as 'a fine kind of man'. He had read the *Examiner* in Scotland 'with much interest' long before meeting him. 'Some used to talk of him as a frivolous fellow, but when I saw him I found he had a face as serious as death.' Five years later, on hearing of Thornton's death, Carlyle told Allingham that Leigh Hunt had once suggested to him 'what a fine thing it would be if a subscription could be made to abolish Hell'. Carlyle replied that it would be a 'decidedly bad investment' – which had 'grieved Hunt considerably'. As long after as 1888, Allingham was still talking about Hunt with the likes of Tennyson, then in his eightieth year. The Poet Laureate recalled a discussion with Hunt of the question 'How can a book corrupt?' Hunt had suggested that a boy, 'found out in vice', might ask: 'Why did you put such books into my hands?' Were these books necessary for the learning of Latin? Replied Tennyson, rather limply: 'There might be purified editions.'

To his friend Horne, Hunt was 'likely to be honoured with more love from posterity than he ever received from, or can hope to receive from, his contemporary public'. How wrong he was. Apart from Milford's

edition of his poems in 1923, Hunt's sole champion in the first half of
the twentieth century, apart from the French graduate student Louis
Landré, was his fellow Bluecoat, Edmund Blunden – but a doughty
defender he proved. To Blunden, Hunt's most conspicuous quality was

> his idealizing faculty, applied alike to social and intellectual situa-
> tions. From it he derived intense pleasure, and to it he might have
> learned to attribute much misery. He decorated his prison and
> forgot the painter's bill and the long strain of catching up again. He
> chose friends and intimates under the impression that they embod-
> ied a special capacity or virtue, which in fact was not their
> distinction or direction. He satirized those whom he judged to be
> asking for such treatment, because in his library there was an abun-
> dance of eighteenth-century satire, and it was amusing and brilliant;
> then he found that there are no unbreakable restrictions in warfare.
> He talked of himself and his own with his pen, spontaneously as a
> singing-bird hails a bright day, and was amazed, though never last-
> ingly instructed, to be ridiculed and struck at by those who had
> reasons to silence him, either as unnecessary or as monotonous.

There was one particular anecdote Hunt enjoyed telling against
himself. In a shop of plaster casts he had picked up the model of a hand,
beautifully turned, though he thought it 'somewhat too plump and
well-fed'. The fingers, however, were 'delicately tapered; the outline
flowing and graceful. I fancied it to have belonged to some jovial
beauty, a little too fat and festive, but laughing withal, and as full of
good nature.' He was told it was the hand of Madame Brinvilliers, a
notorious poisoner.

Something of this picture was simulated, to Blunden, 'when circumstance seemed to stretch a graceful and welcoming hand towards
him. The hand was perilous. It changed, and became deadly. In spite of
all his disasters, Hunt never really grew old. He was sure of the millennium, when every invitation, every conversation would lead only to
newer beatitudes and mutual illuminings. No new occasion dismayed
him because he had so often found himself in deep waters; no hatred of
life curved his lip, as he reached precarious safety and began his
progress once more.'

Among Hunt's few other twentieth-century champions, the name of the historian J.E. Morpurgo, then director-general of the National Book League, stands out for republishing an edition of his long out-of-print *Autobiography* in 1949. No single period of English literature, argued Morpurgo, is as full of luminaries as the first fifty years of the nineteenth century. This, perhaps, was Hunt's misfortune. 'Had there been no Elia, Leigh Hunt might have won the affection of a century for his personal essays. Had there been no Hazlitt, he might have figured as the critic of his day; as an editor he showed immaculate taste and immense strength . . . Hunt lived a Romantic, hopeful and graceful, dreaming always of possibilities that were unattainable.' The tragedy of his failure to reach the heights that had been forecast for him passed him by, for he believed that he had achieved his ambitions: 'To promote the happiness of his kind, to minister to the more educated appreciation of order and beauty, to open more widely the door of the library, and more widely the window of the library looking out upon nature . . .'

The mid-twentieth century also saw less gentle verdicts. In 1940, to Peter Quennell, biographer of Byron and Shelley, there were 'many admirable qualities' buried deep in Hunt's nature – 'but, wherever they grew upwards and outwards into his public life, they were apt to fritter themselves away in gush and artifice. Thus, for social purposes, his real devotion to a host of friends was transmuted into sentimentalism and vapid coterie-talk, while his knowledge and intense love of art and literature tailed off in the attitudinizing of a suburban *petit maître* . . . Under Hunt's touch, fancy was whimsy, and beauty prettiness . . . While Hunt chirped or carolled among his busts and vases, wreathed verses in true-love knots or gaily hummed the *motifs* of an Italian opera, there were often tradesmen at the door and always growing children to stamp or scream in the immediate background.'

By the 1970s Hunt had become a figure 'both famous and infamous in his own age, but often ignored or forgotten in ours', in the words of a short study by Professor James R. Thompson of Ohio University. It had proved Hunt's fate to live on in accounts of other writers' lives – 'in the odd corners of literary histories and of greater men's biographies', his name kept alive only by 'his extensive involvement with many writers of three vigorous literary generations.' Because of his close association with the celebrated writers of his day, Hunt lived continually in someone else's shadow. He was 'a child of the sunlit side of Romanticism; and, though he lived to see the darkness grow and the apocalypse denied, his simple humanism remained unshaken'.

Another late-twentieth-century hagiographer, Ann Blainey, felt moved to call Hunt 'the last survivor of a race of giants'. In a 1994 revaluation of Hunt's poetry, designed in part to show how 'grossly underrated the poems have been, and how fine they really are', the South African academic Rodney Stenning Edgecombe concluded that 'the multiplicity of [Hunt's] talents enabled him to tackle every literary enterprise known to humankind and reach a level of proficiency in all of them'; if literary history had denied Hunt 'due process', he had 'suffered as a result of his own generosity and self-effacement'. In 1998 the American scholar Jeffrey Cox concluded that 'in the love and camaraderie of the Hunt circle, in the solidarity of the Cockney School, [its members] found the faith to believe – in the face of oppression, imprisonment, death – that men and women might together still imagine and thus make a world of perpetual reform'.

In the last decade of the twentieth century Hunt found another significant new champion in Duncan Wu, whose eleven-hundred-page *Romanticism: An Anthology* republishes some of his best writing, and describes him as 'one of the most energetic and adventurous editors and publishers of the age, and the author of some enduringly entertaining poems and essays'. It's that word 'entertaining' which is so telling; even those who recognise how important was Hunt's contribution to other writers cannot quite bring themselves to use the same adjective of his own work. At the turn of the twenty-first century Nicholas Roe allowed himself no such cavil: 'Wherever one looks in the nineteenth-century literary scene, Leigh Hunt's influence is apparent.' Roe went on to echo Virginia Woolf by suggesting that Hunt's influence survived into the twentieth century, with such poets as John Betjeman and Philip Larkin adopting 'the domestic, suburban milieu and language of his poems'.

The editors of the six-volume *Selected Writings of Leigh Hunt* of 2003 are but the latest in a new and swelling wave of academics to come to the rescue of Hunt the 'editor, reviewer, critic, poet, satirist, cicerone, aesthete, essayist, radical, and much else'. Hunt's reputation, they maintain, was as cruelly and permanently damaged by the *Blackwood's*

attacks and the Skimpole caricature as by subsequent critical compar-
isons that 'insistently consign him to the second tier'. Hunt, they insist,
is 'a far more important and compelling figure than such assessments
allow, a remarkably multifarious voice of passion and insight that for
over half a century condemned corruption and inequality, and championed art, freedom, conviviality and tolerance'.

The name of Leigh Hunt may now be for ever 'written' in marble 'as
one that loves his fellow-men'; but he should also be remembered, for
all his very human flaws, as one equally loved by his fellow-men. If he
was not the greatest poet of his age, however game the attempts of academic revisionists, his was the innate generosity and sunny disposition
which brought together several of the most significant groups in the
history of English cultural life, owing their existence and cohesion to
his energy, intellect and charm. If Hunt's name is now overshadowed in
the literary pantheon by those of his greater contemporaries, it is
partly because he spread himself too thin, produced too much, moved
between too many different genres. But there can be no doubting (*pace*
Dickens) his strength of character, his importance in encouraging
better poets than himself to their best work, the high standing of his
reputation and influence for most of his life, and the almost universal
affection in which he was held by a remarkable range of eminent contemporaries.

It seems sadly Huntian that not until nearly a decade after his death
did it occur to anyone – S.C. Hall, as it happens, the editor of the *Book
of Gems* – to raise any kind of monument on Hunt's tombstone. A committee was formed, and a public subscription launched, with support
from such names as Dickens and Browning, Carlyle and Procter,
Cowden Clarke and Sir Percy Shelley, Forster and Tennyson. The
Kensal Green monument to Leigh Hunt, complete with the Durham
bust which has since gone missing, was unveiled on 19 October 1869,
ten years after his death, by the statesman Lord Houghton, alias the
poet Richard Monckton Milnes, friend and first biographer of Keats.

'You will live to write my epitaph,' Hunt had told his young friend
Allingham, the budding Irish poet with whom he had talked of Dante
and Wordsworth, Gray and Collins, Paganini and Hans Christian
Andersen. Now, in the *Athenæum*, Allingham duly obliged:

Our dear Leigh Hunt, whose earth lies here in earth,
Thyself, we trust, enjoying peace and mirth;
If thou from Heav'n behold, by leave Divine,
This tombstone (England's honour more than thine),
What wouldst thou we had carved thereon to praise
The Patriot's honest voice, the Poet's lays,
The subtle Critic, Essayist refined,
In all, brave, sympathetic, pungent, kind?
These words, methinks, Leigh Hunt, from thine own pen:
'Write me as one that loves his fellow-men.'
That *loves*, we say, not *loved*; a man like thee
Is proof enough of immortality.

CHRONOLOGY AND PUBLICATIONS

enlarged with a Preface and Additional Notes. By the editor of the 'Examiner' (London: John Hunt).

3 July: marries Marianne Kent; living at Gowland Cottage, Beckenham, Kent.

Father, Isaac Hunt, dies.

1810   A Reformist's Reply to the 'Edinburgh Review'.

10 September: Thornton Hunt born.

1811   The Reflector, a Collection of Essays on Miscellaneous Subjects of Literature and Politics; originally published as the commencement of a Quarterly Magazine, and written by the editor of 'The Examiner', with the assistance of various other hands (ed.), 4 issues, 2 vols. The Examiner prosecuted for libel over article on military flogging and acquitted. The Story of Rimini begun. First edition of The Feast of the Poets published in the Reflector. Moves from Beckenham to 37 Portland Street, Marylebone. Meets Shelley. The Prince of Wales becomes Prince Regent.

1812   22 March: 'The Prince on St Patrick's Day' published in the Examiner. 8 December: trial for libel.

John Hunt born. Moves from Portland Street to Hampstead.

The Prince of Wales v. the Examiner: A Full Report of the Trial of John and Leigh Hunt (London: John Hunt). Report on the Attorney-General's Information.

1813   3 February: imprisoned for two years in Surrey jail, Horsemonger Lane, Southwark. Writes Seven Sonnets to Hampstead in prison (1813–14). Birth of Mary Florimel Hunt.

1814   The Feast of the Poets, with Notes, and Other Pieces in Verse (London: James Cawthorn; New York: Van Winkle & Wiley; enlarged edition, London: Gale & Fenner, 1815). Writes The Descent of Liberty in prison while continuing to edit the Examiner. Mary Hunt born in the prison.

1815   3 February: leaves the Surrey jail.

Lives at 4 Maida Vale until October, then moves to Hampstead. Meets Wordsworth. The Descent of Liberty, a Mask (London: Gale, Curtis & Fenner; Philadelphia: Harrison Hall, 1816). 'The Round Table' series, co-written with Hazlitt, begins appearing in the Examiner.

1816   Living at Vale of Health, Hampstead. Meets Keats, re-meets Shelley. Poetical epistles to Byron, Field, Hazlitt and Moore in the Examiner. Prints sonnets by Keats in the Examiner. The Story of Rimini: A Poem (London: Printed by T. Davison for J. Murray;

Edinburgh: W. Blackwood; Dublin: Cummings; Boston: Wells & Lilly; Philadelphia: M. Carey). 'Young Poets' article in the *Examiner*. Birth of Swinburne Percy Hunt.

1817   April: Hampstead. July: 13 Lisson Grove North, Paddington.
The Round Table: a Collection of Essays on Literature, Men, and Manners, ed. William Hazlitt and Leigh Hunt, 2 vols. (London: Longman, Hurst, Rees, Orme & Brown; Edinburgh: Constable). *Blackwood's Edinburgh Magazine* launches series of attacks on the 'Cockney School' of poets. Birth of Percy Bysshe Shelley Hunt.

1818   Moves from Lisson Grove North to 8 York Buildings, New Road, Marylebone. February: sonnet contest with Keats and Shelley.
Foliage; or, Poems Original and Translated (London: C. & J. Ollier; Philadelphia: Littell & H. and E. Earle). *The Literary Pocket Book* (ed.).

1819   The *Indicator* launched. *Hero and Leander, and Bacchus and Ariadne* (London: C. & J. Ollier). *The Poetical Works of Leigh Hunt*, 3 vols. (London: C. & J. Ollier). Tragedy *The Cid* rejected by Covent Garden and Drury Lane. Shelley dedicates *The Cenci* to Hunt. November: Henry Sylvan Hunt born.

1820   April–August: 13 Mortimer Terrace, Kentish Town.
The Indicator (ed.), 2 vols., 1820–1. *Amyntas*, a Tale of the Woods; from the Italian of Torquato Tasso (London: T. & J. Allman). *The Literary Pocket Book* (1820) (ed.). Working on *Musical Evenings*, a miscellany of words and music.

1821   23 February: Keats dies.
Vale of Health. *The Months; Descriptive of the Successive Beauties of the Year* (London: C. & J. Ollier). *The Literary Pocket Book* (ed.). 'Sketches of Living Poets': four articles in the *Examiner*. Ceases connection with the *Indicator*. Portrait by Haydon.
November: departs for Italy; December: forced back to Ramsgate. John Hunt jailed again.

1822   Plymouth (–May). June: Genoa. July–September: Pisa. October–November: Albaro. November–December: Genoa. July: Shelley dies. September: first issue of the *Liberal*.

1823   February–August: Genoa and Albaro. September–December: Florence. Vincent Leigh Hunt born in Albaro. The *Liberal*, *Verse and Prose, from the South* (ed.), 2 vols. July–December: contributes to the *Literary Examiner, consisting of the 'Indicator', a Review of Books, and Miscellaneous Pieces in Verse and Prose*. *Ultra-Crepidarius: A Satire on William Gifford* (London: John Hunt).

1824   January–October: Florence and Maiano.

Visited by Hazlitt.

April: Death of Byron.

Engaged by Colburn to write for the *New Monthly Magazine*.
Hazlitt's *Select British Poets* (fifteen poems by Hunt).

1825   January–September: Florence. October: Paris. December:
London: 30 Hadlow Street, Bloomsbury.

Dispute with John Hunt over proprietorship of the *Examiner*. *The
Wishing-Cap*: a series of papers in the *Examiner* (28 March 1824–16
October 1825). *Bacchus in Tuscany, a Dithryambic Poem, from the
Italian of Francesco Redi, with Notes, original and select* (London:
J. Hunt). The *Family Journal*: a series of papers in the *New Monthly
Magazine*, under the signature of 'Harry Honeycomb'.

1826   July: moves from Hadlow Street to Highgate.

Birth of Julia Trelawny Hunt.

1827   September: death of Swinburne Hunt.

1828   9 January–23 July: ed. the *Companion*. *Lord Byron and Some of His
Contemporaries; with Recollections of the Author's Life, and of his Visit to
Italy* (London: Colburn; Philadelphia: Carey, Lea & Carey).

Birth of Jacintha Hunt.

1829   August–September: Woodcote Green, Epsom (home of friend
Charles Knight). Cromwell Lane, Old Brompton.

Birth of Arabella Hunt (d. 1830).

1830   5 June–28 August: *Chat of the Week* (weekly) (ed.), 4 September
–13 February 1832): the *Tatler, A Daily Journal of Literature and the
Stage, Veritas et Varietas*.

Death of Hazlitt.

1831   June: moves from Cromwell Lane to 18 Elm Tree Road, St John's
Wood. Horne and Talfourd administer a private fund on Hunt's
behalf; Macaulay (June) and Wordsworth (December) write to
promote an edition of Hunt's poems to be sold by subscription.

1832   5 York Buildings, New Road, Marylebone. William IV grants Hunt
£200 from Royal Bounty. Meets Carlyle (20 February), who intro-
duces him to Browning (November). Ceases connection with the
Tatler. Pamphlet *'Christianism'; or, Belief and Unbelief Reconciled;
being Exercises and Meditations* (London: Bradbury; revised and
enlarged as *The Religion of the Heart: a Manual of Faith and Duty*,
1853). *Sir Ralph Esher: or Memoirs of a Gentleman of the Court of
Charles II, including those of his Friend, Sir Philip Horne*, 3 vols.
(London: Colburn & Bentley; 2nd edition, 1836; 3rd edition

1850). *The Poetical Works of Leigh Hunt* (London: Moxon). Preface to Shelley's *The Mask of Anarchy* (London: Moxon).

1833   4 (now 22) Upper Cheyne Row, Chelsea (–summer 1840). January–September: contributes new series of the 'Wishing Cap Papers' to *Tait's Edinburgh Magazine*, 'Men and Books' to *New Monthly Magazine* and articles to the daily *True Sun* (16 August–26 December).

1834   2 April (–26 December 1835) *Leigh Hunt's London Journal, To assist the Inquiring, Animate the Struggling and Sympathise with All* (ed.), 2 vols. *The Indicator and the Companion: A Miscellany for the Fields and for the Fireside*, 2 vols. (London: Colburn; republished as *The Indicator: A Miscellany for the Fields and for the Fireside*, vol. 1, New York: Wiley & Putnam, 1845). June: Etching of Hunt by Daniel Maclise (*Fraser's Magazine*).

Carlyle becomes Hunt's neighbour in Chelsea.

1835   Summer: visits Wales. *Captain Sword and Captain Pen: A Poem, With some Remarks on War and Military Statesmen* (London: Knight). 6 June: first issue of *Leigh Hunt's London Journal and the Printing Machine*. Articles and Poems in the *New Monthly Magazine* (1835–6)

1836   Poems for the *New Monthly Magazine*. Contributions to the *True Sun*. Meets Dickens. Death of Godwin.

1837   July: Succeeds R. Horne as editor of the *Monthly Repository* (–March 1838). First version of *The Blue-Stocking Revels* published. Unfinished oil portrait by Samuel Lawrence.

1838   March (–June 1841): Articles in the *Monthly Chronicle, a National Journal of Politics, Literature, Science and Art*, including (October–January 1839) 'Notes to a Lover of Books'. April: the *Monthly Repository* ceases publication. November: poem 'Jenny kissed me' published in the *Monthly Chronicle*. 'Abou Ben Adhem' and notices of Keats and Shelley in S.C. Hall's *Book of Gems*.

1839   January–March: Writing for the *Musical World*. June: several of Hunt's tales reprinted in 'Romanticist and Novelist's Library'. Second edition of *Captain Sword and Captain Pen*.

1840   Moves from Chelsea to 5 Edwardes Square, Kensington. 7 February: *A Legend of Florence, A Play in Five Acts*, performed at Covent Garden; published by Moxon. *The Dramatic Works of Wycherley, Congreve, Vanbrugh, and Farquhar* (ed.) (London: Moxon). *The Dramatic Works of Richard Brinsley Sheridan* (ed.) (London: Moxon). *The Seer; or, Common-places Refreshed*, 2 vols. (London: Moxon; Boston: Roberts, 1864). 28

May and 5 November: congratulatory poems to Queen Victoria published in the *Morning Chronicle*.

1841   Moves from 5 to 32 Edwardes Square. *Essays by Leigh Hunt: The Indicator, The Seer* (London: Moxon). *The Seer*, vol. 2. Third edition of *The Round Table*.

1842   8 February: *Three Visions on the Birth and Christening of the Prince of Wales* published in the *Morning Chronicle*.

The Palfrey: A Love Story of Old Times (London: How & Parsons). W. Bell Scott etching *L.H. with G.H. Lewes, Vincent Hunt and W.B.S.*

1843   *One Hundred Romances of Real Life; comprising Remarkable Historical and Domestic Facts, illustrative of Human Nature* (ed.) (London: Whittaker).

1844   January–December: 'A Jar of Honey from Mount Hybla' in *Ainsworth's Magazine*. *Imagination and Fancy: or, Selections from the English Poets, illustrative of those First Requisites of their Art; with Markings of the Best Passages, Critical Notices of the Writers, and an Essay in Answer to the Question 'What is Poetry?'* (ed.) (London: Smith, Elder; New York: Wiley & Putnam, 1845). *The Poetical Works of Leigh Hunt, containing many Pieces now first collected* (London: Moxon; reprinted, 1846). *The Story of Rimini and Other Poems* published in USA (Boston: Ticknor). Receives annuity of £120 from Shelley family.

1845   Second edition of *Imagination and Fancy*. 'Lazy Corner; or Bed versus Business. A Poem from the Italian of Bernie', in the *New Monthly Magazine* (vol. 75, p. 143). Contributes preface to Thornton Hunt's novel *The Foster Brother*.

1846   *Stories from the Italian Poets: With Lives of the Writers*, 2 vols. (London: Chapman & Hall; New York: Wiley & Putnam). *Wit and Humour, Selected from the English Poets with an Illustrative Essay, and Critical Comments* (ed.) (London: Smith, Elder; New York: Wiley & Putnam, 1847). Contributes 'Table-Talk' weekly to the *Atlas* (ed. Thornton Hunt). Plans *A Book for a Chimney Corner*. Death of son John Hunt.

1847   *Men, Women, and Books: A Selection of Sketches, Essays and Critical Memoirs, from his uncollected Prose Writings*, 2 vols. (London: Smith, Elder; New York: Harper). *A Jar of Honey from Mount Hybla* (London: Smith, Elder). 'Streets of London' in the *Atlas* (posthumously published in 1861 in *A Saunter Through the West End*). 22 June: receives Civil List annual pension of £200. 26 and 28 July: benefit performances of *Every Man in his Humour* organized (and performed) by Dickens, Forster and others.

Queen Victoria awards £200 from the Royal Bounty. 15 September: congratulatory dinner for Hunt at the Museum Club, London. Forster becomes editor of the *Examiner*.

1848   *The Town: Its Memorable Characters and Events: St Paul's to St James's*, 2 vols. (London: Smith, Elder). November: working on play *The Secret Marriage* for Sadler's Wells (never produced).

1849   *A Book for a Corner, or Selections in Prose and Verse from Authors the Best Suited to That Mode of Enjoyment, with Comments on Each and a General Introduction*, 2 vols. (ed.) (London: Chapman & Hall; reprinted 1851 and 1858, 1 vol.; New York: Putnam, 1852). *Readings for Railways; or, Anecdotes and Other Short Stories, Reflections, Maxims, Characteristics, Passages of Wit, Humour and Poetry, etc., Together with Points of Information on Matters of General Interest. Collected in the course of his own Reading*. (London: Gilpin). Poems in *Ainsworth's Magazine* and the *New Monthly Magazine*. Working on *Autobiography*. Death of Mary Florimel Hunt.

1850   *The Autobiography of Leigh Hunt, with Reminiscences of Friends and Contemporaries*, 3 vols. (London: Smith, Elder; New York: Harper; revised edition, 1 vol, London: Smith, Elder, 1860). Contributes to the *New Monthly Magazine* and *Household Words* (ed. Dickens). January–July: Ainsworth reserves front page of the *New Monthly Magazine* for poems by Hunt. Portraits by W.F. Williams and G.F. Ford. 2nd edition of *Sir Ralph Esher*. Play *A Legend of Florence* revived at Sadler's Wells. Revising 'Christianism'. 7 December (–29 March 1851): *Leigh Hunt's Journal; A Miscellany for the Cultivation of the Memorable, the Progressive, and the Beautiful*. Thornton Hunt and G.H. Lewes found the *Leader*.

1851   January–March: play *Lover's Amazements*. 29 March: *Leigh Hunt's Journal* closed. July: moves from Edwardes Square to 2 Phillimore Terrace, Kensington. September–December: at Ewell, Surrey, for health of son Vincent. *Table-Talk, to which are added Imaginary Conversations of Pope and Swift* (London: Smith, Elder; New York: Appleton, 1879). *Essays and Miscellanies* (London: Smith, Elder).

1852   Moves from Kensington to 7 Cornwall Road (now 16 Rowan Road), Hammersmith. Death of Vincent Leigh Hunt. *Imagination and Fancy* republished. 4 and 18 September: poems in *Household Words* (ed. Dickens). March: Dickens's *Bleak House* begins to appear in twenty monthly instalments, with portrait of Hunt as Harold Skimpole.

1853   *The Religion of the Heart. A Manual of Faith and Duty* (revision of
        Christianism, 1824, 1832) (London: Chapman; New York: J. J.
        Reed, 1857). *Readings for Railways*, second series. August (–
        February 1854): papers on Kensington in *Household Words*. August:
        working on a play. *Bleak House* published in book form.

1854   Papers in the *Musical Times*. US publication of *The Works of Leigh
        Hunt*, 4 vols. (Philadelphia: Hazard).

1855   *Stories in Verse; Now First Collected* (London and New York:
        Routledge). *The Old Court Suburb; or, Memorials of Kensington, Regal,
        Critical, and Anecdotal*, 2 vols. (London: Hurst & Blackett;
        enlarged edition, 1855). *Beaumont and Fletcher, or The Finest Scenes,
        Lyrics, and Other Beauties of Those Two Poets, now first selected from the
        whole of their works, to the exclusion of whatever is morally objectionable;
        with Opinions of Distinguished Critics, Notes, Explanatory and
        Otherwise, and a General Introduction* (ed.) (London: Bohn).
        Revising *Autobiography*. Grant of £200 from the Royal Bounty.
        Visited by Nathaniel Hawthorne.

1856   Collecting poems and prose for US edition.

1857   26 January: Marianne Hunt dies.
        *The Poetical Works of Leigh Hunt: Now First Entirely Collected, Revised by
        Himself*, ed. S. Adams Lee, 4 vols. prose, 2 vols. verse; Boston:
        Ticknor & Fields). Working on essay on sonnets (posthumously
        published in *The Book of the Sonnet*, 1867).

1858   20 January: play *Lover's Amazements* produced at Lyceum Theatre.
        February, May: imitations of Chaucer and Shakespeare in *Fraser's
        Magazine*. March: working on 'West End' (posthumously published
        in 1861 in *A Saunter Through the West End*). September: at
        Woodlands Farm, Putney.

1859   15 January–20 August: 'The Occasional', a series of papers in the
        Spectator. 5 June: death of Charles Ollier.
        28 August: Hunt dies at 41 High Street, Putney, home of Charles
        Reynell. Buried at Kensal Green cemetery.

        Posthumous publications

1859   'English Poetry versus Cardinal Wiseman', *Fraser's Magazine*,
        December.

1860   *The Poetical Works of Leigh Hunt, Now Finally Collected, Revised by
        Himself, and edited by his Son, Thornton Hunt* (London and New
        York: Routledge, Warne & Routledge).
        The Autobiography of Leigh Hunt: a New Edition, Revised by the Author;

         with further Revision and an Introduction by his Eldest Son.

1861   *A Saunter Through the West End.* Papers originally published in the 'Atlas' newspaper, in 1847 (London: Hurst & Blackett).

1862   *The Correspondence of Leigh Hunt. Edited by his Eldest Son, Thornton Hunt,* 2 vols. (London: Smith, Elder).

1867   *The Book of the Sonnet,* 2 vols., ed. Leigh Hunt and S. Adams Lee, 2 vols. (London: S. Low, Son & Marston; Boston: Roberts).

1870   *A Day by the Fire; and Other Papers Hitherto Uncollected,* ed. Joseph Edward Babson (London: Sampson Low, Son & Marston; Boston: Roberts).

1870–2   *The Works of Leigh Hunt,* 7 vols. (London: Smith, Elder, 1870–2).

1873–4   *The Wishing-Cap Papers,* ed. Edward Babson (Boston: Lee & Shepard; London: Sampson Low, Marston, Low & Searle, 1874).

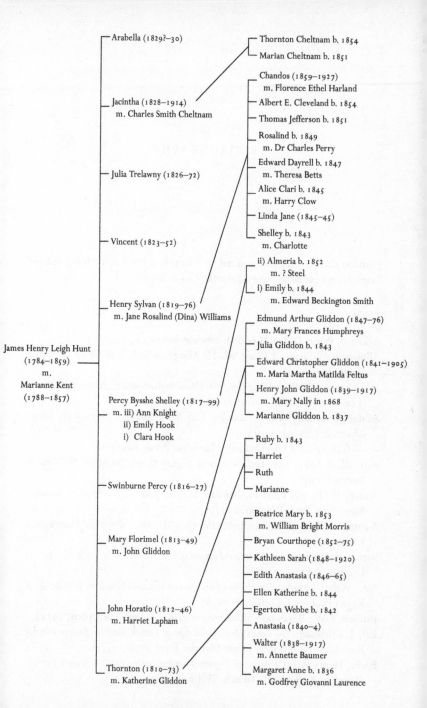

James Henry Leigh Hunt
(1784–1859)
m.
Marianne Kent
(1788–1857)

Arabella (1829?–30)

Jacintha (1828–1914)
m. Charles Smith Cheltnam
- Thornton Cheltnam b. 1854
- Marian Cheltnam b. 1851

Julia Trelawny (1826–72)
- Chandos (1859–1927)
  m. Florence Ethel Harland
- Albert E. Cleveland b. 1854
- Thomas Jefferson b. 1851
- Rosalind b. 1849
  m. Dr Charles Perry
- Edward Dayrell b. 1847
  m. Theresa Betts
- Alice Clari b. 1845
  m. Harry Clow
- Linda Jane (1845–45)
- Shelley b. 1843
  m. Charlotte

Vincent (1823–52)

Henry Sylvan (1819–76)
m. Jane Rosalind (Dina) Williams
- ii) Almeria b. 1852
  m. ? Steel
- i) Emily b. 1844
  m. Edward Beckington Smith

Percy Bysshe Shelley (1817–99)
m. iii) Ann Knight
    ii) Emily Hook
    i) Clara Hook
- Edmund Arthur Gliddon (1847–76)
  m. Mary Frances Humphreys
- Julia Gliddon b. 1843
- Edward Christopher Gliddon (1841–1905)
  m. Maria Martha Matilda Feltus
- Henry John Gliddon (1839–1917)
  m. Mary Nally in 1868
- Marianne Gliddon b. 1837

Swinburne Percy (1816–27)
- Ruby b. 1843
- Harriet
- Ruth
- Marianne

Mary Florimel (1813–49)
m. John Gliddon

John Horatio (1812–46)
m. Harriet Lapham
- Beatrice Mary b. 1853
  m. William Bright Morris
- Bryan Courthope (1852–75)
- Kathleen Sarah (1848–1920)
- Edith Anastasia (1846–65)
- Ellen Katherine b. 1844
- Egerton Webbe b. 1842
- Anastasia (1840–4)
- Walter (1838–1917)
  m. Annette Baumer
- Margaret Anne b. 1836
  m. Godfrey Giovanni Laurence

Thornton (1810–73)
m. Katherine Gliddon

FAMILY TREE

BIBLIOGRAPHY

Editions cited are those consulted by the author. For a full bibliography of Leigh Hunt's published works, see the Chronology.

BOOKS

Ackroyd, Peter: *Dickens* (London: Sinclair-Stevenson, 1990)

Allingham, William: *A Diary*, ed. H. Allingham and D. Radford (London: Macmillan, 1907)

—— *Letters to William Allingham* , ed. H. Allingham and E. Baumer Williams (London: Longmans, Green, 1911)

Ashton, Rosemary: *Thomas and Jane Carlyle: Portrait of a Marriage* (London: Chatto & Windus, 2001)

—— *G.H. Lewes: A Life* (Oxford: Clarendon Press, 1991)

Aspinall, A. (ed.): *Three Early Nineteenth Century Diaries* (London: Williams & Norgate, 1952)

Auden, W.H., and Pearson, Norman Holmes (eds.): *The Portable Romantic Poets* (New York: Penguin, 1977)

Austin, C.: *Fields of the Atlantic Monthly* (San Marino, California: Huntington Library, 1953)

Barzun, Jacques (ed.): *The Selected Letters of Lord Byron* (New York: Grosset & Dunlap, 1953)

Bate, Walter Jackson: *The Stylistic Development of Keats* (London: Routledge & Kegan Paul, 1945; reissued, 1958)

Bateson, F.W.: *Wordsworth: A Re-Interpretation* (London: Longmans, 1954)

Bay, J. Christian: *The Leigh Hunt Collection of Luther Albertus Brewer* (Cedar Rapids, Iowa: privately printed for the Torch Press, 1933)

Beers, Henry A.: *A History of English Romanticism in the Nineteenth Century* (London: Kegan Paul, Trench, Trübner, 1902)

Bernbaum, Ernst, et al. (eds.): *The English Romantic Poets: A Review of Research* (New York: MLA, 1950)

Blainey, Ann: *Immortal Boy: A Portrait of Leigh Hunt* (New York: St Martin's, 1985)

—— *The Farthing Poet: A Biography of Richard Hengist Horne, 1802–84* (London: Longmans, 1968)

Bloom, Harold, and Munich, Adrienne (eds): *Robert Browning: A Collection of Critical Essays* (New York: Prentice-Hall, 1979)

Blunden, Edmund: *Charles Lamb* (London: Longmans, Green, 1954)

—— *Leigh Hunt: A Biography* (London: Cobden-Sanderson, 1930; Hamden, Conn.: Archon, 1970)

—— *Leigh Hunt's 'Examiner' Examined* (London: Cobden-Sanderson, 1928)

—— *Shelley* (Oxford University Press, 1965)

—— et al. (eds.) *The Christ's Hospital Book* (London: Hamish Hamilton, 1953)

Brack, Jr., O.M., and Stefanson, D.H.: *A Catalogue of the Leigh Hunt Manuscripts in the University of Iowa Libraries* (Iowa: Friends of the University of Iowa Libraries, 1973)

Brewer, Luther A.: *Leigh Hunt and Charles Dickens* (Cedar Rapids, Iowa: privately printed for the Torch Press, 1930)

—— *Leaves from a Leigh Hunt Notebook* (Cedar Rapids, Iowa: privately printed for the Torch Press, 1932)

—— *My Leigh Hunt Library, Collected and Described by Luther A. Brewer* (New York: Burt Franklin, 1970)

—— *My Leigh Hunt Library: The Holograph Letters* (University of Iowa, 1938)

—— *Notes from a Leigh Hunt Note-Book* (Cedar Rapids, Iowa: privately printed for the Torch Press, 1932)

—— *Some Letters from My Leigh Hunt Portfolios* (Cedar Rapids, Iowa: privately printed for the Torch Press, 1929)

—— *Stevenson's Perfect Virtues* (Cedar Rapids, Iowa: privately printed for the Torch Press, 1922)

Brougham, (Lord) Henry: *Life and Times*, 3 vols. (Edinburgh: Blackwood, 1871)

Brown, Charles Armitage: *The Letters of Charles Armitage Brown*, ed. J. Stillinger (Harvard, 1966)

Burton, Sarah: *A Double Life: A Biography of Charles and Mary Lamb* (London: Viking, 2003)

Butler, Marilyn: *Romantics, Rebels and Reactionaries* (Oxford University Press, 1981)

Buxton, John: *Byron and Shelley: The History of a Friendship* (London: Macmillan, 1968)

Cameron, Kenneth Neill (ed.): *The Esdaile Notebook: A Volume of Early Poems by*

Percy Bysshe Shelley (New York: Knopf, 1964)

—— *Shelley and his Circle 1773–1882*, vols. 1–4 (Harvard University Press, vols. 1–2, 1961; vols. 3–4, 1970)

—— *Romantic Rebels: Essays on Shelley and his Circle* (Harvard University Press, 1973)

Carlyle, Thomas: *Reminiscences*, ed. James A. Froude (New York: Scribner's, 1881)

—— *Reminiscences*, ed. Charles Eliot Norton (London: Macmillan, 1887)

Cheney, David R. (ed.): *The Correspondence of Leigh Hunt and Charles Ollier in the Winter of 1853* (Sheen Common, UK: The Keats-Shelley Memorial Association, 1976)

—— *Musical Evenings, or Selections, Vocal and Instrumental* (Columbia: University of Missouri Press, 1964)

Collins, A.S.: *The Profession of Letters* (New York: E.P. Dutton, 1929)

Coote, Colin: *John Keats* (London: Hodder & Stoughton, 1995)

Cowden Clarke, Charles and Mary: *Recollections of Writers* (London: Sampson Low, Marston, Searle & Rivington, 1878)

Cox, Jeffrey: *Poetry and Politics in the Cockney School* (Cambridge: Cambridge University Press, 1998)

Crane, David: *Lord Byron's Jackal: A Life of Edward John Trelawny* (London: HarperCollins, 1998)

Cronin, Richard: *The Politics of Romantic Poetry* (London: Macmillan, 2000)

David, Saul: *Prince of Pleasure: The Prince of Wales and the Making of the Regency* (London: Little, Brown, 1998)

De Quincey, Thomas: *Essays* (London: Ward, Lock, n.d.)

—— *Reminiscences of the English Lake Poets* (London: Dent, 1907)

Dibley, David Jesson (ed.): *Leigh Hunt: Selected Writings* (Manchester: Carcanet Press, 1990)

Dickens, Charles: *Bleak House* (1853; New York: Norton, 1977)

—— *Letters*, vol. 1, ed. M. House and G. Storey (Oxford: Clarendon Press, 1965)

Dowden, Edward: *The French Revolution and English Literature* (New York: Scribner's, 1897)

Drinkwater, John: *The Pilgrim of Eternity: Byron – A Conflict* (London: Hodder & Stoughton; New York: Geo. H. Doran, 1925)

Dunlap, Rhodes (ed.): *Hunt on Eight Sonnets of Dante* (Iowa City: University of Iowa School of Journalism, 1965)

Eberle-Sinatra, Michael: *Leigh Hunt and the London Literary Scene* (London: Routledge, 2005)

Edgecombe, Rodney Stenning: *Leigh Hunt and the Poetry of Fancy* (Madison:

Farleigh Dickinson University Press, 1994)

Elwin, Malcolm (ed.): *The Autobiography and Journals of Benjamin Robert Haydon* (London: Macdonald, 1950)

Fenner, Theodore: *Leigh Hunt and Opera Criticism* (University of Kansas Press, 1972)

Fields, James T.: *Yesterday with Authors* (Boston: Houghton Mifflin, 1887)

—— *Biographical Notes and Personal Sketches with unpublished fragments and tributes from Men and Women of Letters* (Boston: Houghton Mifflin, 1881)

Fields, Mrs James T.: *A Shelf of Old Books* (New York: Scribner's, 1895)

Finlayson, Iain: *Browning – A Private Life* (London: HarperCollins, 2004)

Fogle, Stephen F.: *Leigh Hunt's Autobiography: The Earliest Sketches* (Gainesville: University of Florida Press, 1959)

Foot, Paul: *Red Shelley* (London: Bookmarks, 1984)

Forster, John: *The Life of Charles Dickens*, 3 vols. (London: Chapman & Hall, 1872–4)

Froude, James Anthony (ed.): *Thomas Carlyle: A History of the First Forty Years of His Life 1795–1835*, 2 vols. (London: Longmans, Green & Co., 1882)

—— (ed.) *Thomas Carlyle: A History of His Life in London*, 2 vols. (London: Longmans, Green & Co., 1884)

Gates, Eleanor M. (ed.): *Leigh Hunt: A Life in Letters* (Essex, Conn.: Falls River, 1999)

Gates, Payson G.: *William Hazlitt and Leigh Hunt: The Continuing Dialogue*, ed. Eleanor M. Gates (Essex, Conn.: Falls River, 2000)

Gilfillan, George: *Modern Literature and Literary Men* (New York: Appleton, 1850; 3rd edn, 1857)

Gill, Stephen: *William Wordsworth: A Life* (Oxford University Press, 1989)

Gittings, Robert: *John Keats* (Boston: Little, Brown, 1968)

Graham, Walter: *English Literary Periodicals* (New York: Nelson, 1930)

Green, David Bonnell, and Wilson, Edwin Graves (eds.): *Keats, Shelley, Byron, Hunt and Their Circles: A Bibliography 1950–1962* (Lincoln: University of Nebraska Press, 1964)

Greenblatt, Stephen, and Gunn, Giles (eds.): *Redrawing the Boundaries: The Transformation of English and American Literary Studies* (New York: Modern Language Association of America, 1992)

Gross, John: *The Rise and Fall of the Man of Letters* (London: Weidenfeld & Nicolson, 1969)

Grundy, Francis H., *Pictures of the Past* (London, 1879)

Gunn, Peter (ed.): *Byron: Selected Letters and Journals* (London: Penguin, 1984)

Hall, S.C. (ed.): *The Book of Gems (The Modern Poets and Artists of Great Britain)* (London: Whitaker, 1838)

—— *A Book of Memories of Great Men and Women of the Age* (London: J.S. Virtue, 1877)

—— *Retrospect of a Long Life* (London: Bentley, 1883)

Hannay, James, *Characters and Criticisms* (Edinburgh: William Nimmo, 1865)

Hare, Augustus J.C.: *The Story of My Life*, 6 vols. (London: George Allen, 1896)

Harper, Henry H.: *Byron's Malach Hamoves* (Boston: privately printed, 1918)

Hartley, Robert A. (ed.): *Keats, Shelley, Byron, Hunt and Their Circles: A Bibliography 1962–1974* (Lincoln: University of Nebraska Press, 1978)

Hawkins, Desmond: *Shelley's First Love* (London: Kyle Cathie, 1992)

Hawthorne, Nathaniel: *Our Old Home* (Boston, Houghton Mifflin, 1891)

Haydon, F.W (ed.).: *B.R. Haydon: Correspondence and Table-Talk*, 2 vols. (London: Chatto & Windus, 1876)

Hazlitt, William: *Complete Works*, 21 vols. (London: J.M. Dent, 1930–4)

—— *Essays* (London: Harrap, 1920)

—— (ed.) *The Round Table 1817* (Oxford: Woodstock, 1991)

—— *The Spirit of the Age* (London: Everyman, 1951)

Hazlitt, William Carew: *Memoirs of William Hazlitt, with Portions of his Correspondence*, 2 vols. (London: R. Bentley, 1867)

Holmes, Richard: *Coleridge: Early Visions, 1772–1804* (New York: Pantheon, 1989)

—— *Coleridge: Darker Reflections, 1804–1834* (New York: Random House, 1999)

—— *Shelley: The Pursuit* (London: Quartet, 1976)

Horne, R. H. (ed.): *A New Spirit of the Age*, 2 vols. (London: Smith, Elder, 1844)

Hough, Robert L. (ed.), *Literary Criticism of Edgar Allan Poe* (Lincoln: University of Nebraska Press, 1965)

Houtchens, Lawrence H. and Carolyn W.: *Leigh Hunt's Dramatic Criticism* (New York: Columbia University Press, 1949)

—— *Leigh Hunt's Literary Criticism* (New York: Columbia University Press, 1956)

—— *The English Romantic Poets and Essayists* (London: University of London Press; republished New York: New York University Press for the Modern Language Association of America, 1957)

—— *Leigh Hunt's Political and Occasional Essays* (New York: Columbia University Press, 1962)

Hughes-Hallett, Penelope: *The Immortal Dinner* (London: Viking, 2000)

Hunt, F. Knight: *A History of Newspapers and of the Liberty of the Press* , 2 vols. (London: David Bogue, 1850)

Hunt, Leigh: *Autobiography*, 2 vols. in one (New York: Harper & Bros, 1850)
—— *The Autobiography of Leigh Hunt*, ed. J.E. Morpurgo (London: Cresset Press, 1949)
—— *Beaumont and Fletcher* (ed. with S. Adams Lee) 2nd edn, (London: Henry G. Bohn, 1862)
—— *A Book for a Chimney Corner* (London: Chatto & Windus, 1887)
—— *A Book for a Corner* (*Works*, vol. iii) (New York: Derby & Jackson, 1859)
—— *The Book of the Sonnet* (Boston: Roberts Bros, 1867)
—— *Captain Sword and Captain Pen*, ed. Rhodes Dunlop (Iowa City: Friends of the Iowa University Libraries, 1984)
—— (ed.), *Classic Tales, Serious and Lively*, 5 vols. (London: J. Hunt & C. Reynell, 1806–7)
—— *Coaches and Coaching* (New York: James Pott, n.d.)
—— *The Companion* (London: Hunt & Clarke, 1828, reprinted New York: AMS Press, 1967)
—— *The Correspondence of Leigh Hunt, Edited by his Eldest Son Hunt*, 2 vols. (London: Smith, Elder, 1862)
—— *Critical Essays on the Performers of the London Theatres* (London: John Hunt, 1807)
—— *A Day By the Fire, & Other Papers* (Boston: Roberts Brothers, 1870)
—— *The Dramatic Works of Wycherley, Congreve, Vanburgh and Farquhar with Biographical and Critical Notes* (London: Edward Moxon, 1849)
—— *Essays*, ed. R. Brimley Johnson (London: Dent, 1891)
—— *Essays*, ed. Arthur Symons (London: Walter Scott, 1888)
—— (ed.) *The Examiner 1808–1822*, 15 vols. (London: Pickering & Chatto, 1996–8)
—— *Imagination and Fancy, or Selections from the English Poets* (London: Smith, Elder, 1846)
—— *The Indicator and The Companion, Essays and Miscellanies selected from* (*Works*, vol. iv) (New York: Derby & Jackson, 1859)
—— *The Indicator: A Miscellany for the Fields and the Fireside* (2 vols. in one) (New York: Wiley & Putnam, 1845)
—— *A Jar of Honey from Mount Hybla* (London: Smith, Elder, 1858)
—— *The Liberal: Verse and Prose from the South No. 1* (London: John Hunt, 1822; reprinted by the University of Salzburg, 1978)
—— *London Journal*, 2 vols., 1834–5 (New York: AMS Press, 1967)
—— *Lord Byron and Some of his Contemporaries, with Recollections of The Author's Life and of His Visit to Italy* (London: Henry Colburn, 1828, 2nd edn.)
—— *Men, Women and Books*, 2 vols. (London: Smith, Elder, 1847)
—— *The Months: Descriptive of the Successive Beauties of the Year* (London: Ivor

Nicholson & Watson, 1936)

—— *Musical Evenings, or Selections Vocal and Instrumental*, ed. David Cheney (Columbia: University of Missouri Press, 1964)

—— *The Old Court Suburb* (London: Hurst & Blackett, 1855)

—— *On Eight Sonnets of Dante* (Iowa City: University of Iowa School of Journalism, 1965)

—— *Romances of Real Life* (London: Hamilton, Adams, 1888)

—— *Selections from the English Poets* (*Works*, vol. ii) (New York: Derby & Jackson, 1859)

—— *Shakespeare's Songs & Sonnets* (Boston: Houghton, Mifflin, 1882)

—— *Stories in Verse* (London: Routledge, 1885)

—— *Table Talk, to which are added Imaginary Conversations of Pope and Swift* (London: Smith, Elder, 1902)

—— *Tales and Adventures* (New York: Simpkin, 1927)

—— *The Old Lady and the Maid-Servant* (London: Dent, 1929)

—— *The Religion of the Heart* (London: Chapman, 1853)

—— *The Palfrey* (London: How & Parsons, 1842)

—— *The Poetical Works of Leigh Hunt* (London: Edward Moxon, 1862)

—— *The Seer, or, Common-places Refreshed* (2 vols.) (Boston: Roberts, 1864)

—— *The Story of Rimini and Other Poems* (Boston: Ticknor, 1844)

—— *The Town: Its Memorable Characters and Events* (London: Smith, Elder, 1870)

—— *What is Poetry?*, ed. Albert S. Cook (Boston: Ginn & Co, 1893)

—— *The Wishing-Cap Papers* (Boston: Lee and Shepard, 1873)

—— *Wit and Humour, Selected from the English Poets* (London: Smith, Elder, 1846)

—— *The Works of Leigh Hunt*, vol. iii: *Selections from English Authors* (Philadelphia: Willis P. Hazard, 1854)

Selected periodical publications – uncollected

—— 'Memoir of James Henry Leigh Hunt written by himself, *Monthly Mirror*, 7 (April 1810), pp. 243–8

—— 'The Works of Henry Howard, Earl of Surrey, and of Sir Thomas Wyatt the Elder', ed. George Frederick Nott, *Edinburgh Review*, 27 (December 1816), pp. 390–422

—— 'The Family Journal', *New Monthly Magazine and Literary Journal*, January 1825, pp. 17–28; February 1825, pp. 166–76; March 1825, pp. 276–82; April 1825, pp. 353–69, 419–23; May 1825, pp. 457–66; June 1825, pp. 548–55; July 1825, pp. 41–5; September 1825, pp. 199–206; October 1825, pp. 323–32; November 1825, pp. 429–31; December 1825, pp. 514–18

—— 'The Wishing Cap', *Tait's Edinburgh Magazine*, January 1833, pp.

435–42; March 1833, pp. 689–93; April 1833, pp. 141–8; June 1833, pp. 275–80; July 1833, pp. 417–21; September 1833, pp. 695–701

—— 'Lady Mary Wortley Montagu, Letters and Works, edited by Lord Wharncliffe', *London and Westminster Review*, 37 (April 1837), pp. 130–64

—— 'Memoirs of the Colman Family, by R.B. Peake', *Edinburgh Review*, 73 (July 1841), pp. 389–424

—— 'The Life, Journal and Correspondence of Samuel Pepys, Esq. by the Rev. John Smith', *Edinburgh Review*, 74 (October 1841), pp. 105–25

—— 'Madame Sévigné and her Contemporaries', *Edinburgh Review*, 76 (October 1842), pp. 203–36

—— 'George Selwyn and his Contemporaries, by John H. Jesse,' *Edinburgh Review*, 80 (July 1844), pp. 1–42

Ireland, Alexander: *List of the Writings of William Hazlitt and Leigh Hunt, Chronologically Arranged* (New York: Burt Franklin, 1970 (facsimile edition originally published in 1868))

Jack, Ian: *English Literature 1815–1832* (Oxford: Clarendon Press, 1963)

—— *Keats and the Mirror of Art* (Oxford: Clarendon Press, 1967)

Johnson, Edgar: *Charles Dickens* (London: Allen Lane, 1952; rev. edn, 1977)

Johnson, R. Brimley: *Leigh Hunt* (1896; reprinted New York: Haskell House, 1970)

—— (ed.) *Leigh Hunt: How Friendship Made History and Extended the Bounds of Human Freedom and Thought* (London: Ingpen & Grant, 1928)

—— (ed.) *Prefaces by Leigh Hunt* (Chicago: Walter M. Hill, 1927)

Jones, Frederick L. (ed.): *Maria Gisborne and Edward E. Williams, Shelley's Friends: Their Letters* (University of Oklahoma Press, 1951)

Jones, John: *The Egotistical Sublime: A History of Wordsworth's Imagination* (London: Chatto & Windus, 1960)

—— *John Keats's Dream of Truth* (London: Chatto & Windus, 1969)

Jones, Stanley: *William Hazlitt: A Life – From Winterslow to Frith Street* (Oxford: Clarendon Press, 1989)

Kaplan, Fred: *Dickens* (London: Hodder & Stoughton, 1988)

Keats, John: *Keats's Poetical Work*, ed. H.W. Garrod (Oxford: Clarendon Press, 1958)

Kendall, Kenneth E.: *Leigh Hunt's Reflector* (The Hague/Paris: Mouton, 1971)

Kent, Charles (ed.): *Leigh Hunt as Poet and Essayist* (London: Frederick Warne, 1889)

Knight, William (ed.): *Tales by Leigh Hunt, Now First Collected* (London: W. Paterson, 1891)

Lamb, Charles: *Prose & Poetry*, ed. George Gordon (Oxford: Clarendon Press, 1921)

—— *Essays*, ed. Rosalind Vallance and John Hampden (London: Folio Society, 1963)

Landré, Louis: *Leigh Hunt: Contribution à l'histoire du Romantisme anglais*, 2 vols. (Paris: Les Belles Lettres, 1935–6)

Langford, John Alfred: *Prison Books and their Authors* (London: William Tegg, 1861)

Law, Marie Hamilton: *The English Familiar Essay in the Early Nineteenth Century* (New York: Russell & Russell, 1965)

Linton, W.J.: *Memories* (London: Lawrence and Bullen, 1895)

Locker-Lampson, Frederick: *My Confidences* (London: Nelson, 1896)

Logan, James V., Jordan, John E., and Frye, Northrop (eds.): *Some British Romantics: A Collection of Essays* (Ohio State University Press, 1966)

Lucas, E.V. (ed.): *The Letters of Charles Lamb*, 3 vols. (London: Dent/Methuen, 1935)

Lulofs, Timothy J., and Ostrom, Hans (eds.): *Leigh Hunt: A Reference Guide* (Boston: G.K. Hall, 1985)

Macaulay, Thomas Babington: *Letters of Thomas Babington Macaulay*, 6 vols., ed. Thomas Pinney (Cambridge: Cambridge University Press, 1976)

Macready, W.C.: *Macready's Reminiscences, and Selections from His Diaries and Letters*, ed. Sir Frederick Pollock, Bart., 2 vols. (London: Macmillan, 1876)

Mahoney, Charles: *Romantics and Renegades: The Poetics of Political Reaction* (London: Palgrave Macmillan, 2002)

Marshall, William H.: *Byron, Shelley and The Liberal* (Philadelphia: University of Pennsylvania Press, 1960)

McCown, Robert (ed.): *The Life and Times of Leigh Hunt: Papers Delivered at a Symposium at the University of Iowa, April 13, 1984 commemorating the 200th anniversary of Leigh Hunt's birth* (Iowa City: Friends of the Iowa University Libraries, 1985)

McGann, Jerome J.: *Romantic Ideology* (Chicago: University of Chicago Press, 1983)

Mellow, James R.: *Nathaniel Hawthorne in His Times* (Baltimore: Johns Hopkins University Press, 1980)

Merriam, Harold G.: *Edward Moxon, Publisher of Poets* (New York: Columbia University Press, 1939)

Miller, Barnette: *Leigh Hunt's Relations with Byron, Shelley and Keats* (New York: Columbia University Press, 1910)

Mineka, Francis: *The Dissidence of Dissent: The Monthly Repository 1806–38* (Chapel Hill: University of North Carolina Press, 1944)

Mitchell, Alexander: *A Bibliography of the Writings of Leigh Hunt* (London:

The Bookman's Journal, 1930–1)

Milford, H.S. (ed.): *The Poetical Works of Leigh Hunt* (London and New York: Oxford University Press, 1923)

Mizukoshi, Ayumi: *Keats, Hunt and the Aesthetics of Pleasure* (London and New York: Palgrave Macmillan, 2001)

Moir, D.M.: *Sketches of the poetical literature of the past half-century* (Edinburgh: William Blackwood, 1856)

Monkhouse, Cosmo: *Life of Leigh Hunt* (London: Walter Scott, 1893)

Moore, Doris Langley: *The Late Lord Byron* (Philadelphia and New York: Lippincott, 1961)

Moore, Thomas: *The Letters and Journals of Lord Byron, with Notices of his Life* (London: John Murray, 1-vol. edn., 1908)

Morley, Edith J. (ed.): *Henry Crabb Robinson on Books and their Writers*, 3 vols. (London: Dent, 1938)

Morrison, Robert and Eberle-Sinatra, Michael (gen. eds.): *The Selected Writings of Leigh Hunt*, 6 vols. (London: Pickering and Chatto, 2003) (*Periodical Essays 1805–14*, eds. Greg Kucich and Jeffrey N. Cox; *Periodical Essays 1815–21*, eds. Greg Kucich and Jeffrey N. Cox; *Periodical Essays 1822–38*, ed. Robert Morrison; *Later Literary Essays 1844–67*, ed. Charles Mahoney; *Poetical Works 1801–21*, ed. John Strachan; *Poetical Works 1822–59*, ed. John Strachan)

Motion, Andrew: *Keats* (London: Faber & Faber, 1997)

Mumford Jones, Howard: *The Harp That Once – A Chronicle of the Life of Thomas Moore* (New York: Henry Holt, 1937)

Munby, A.N.L. (ed.): *Letters to Leigh Hunt from his son Vincent, with some replies* (Cambridge: Cloanthus Press, 1934)

Norman, Sylva: *Flight of the Skylark* (University of Oklahoma Press, 1954)

Norton, Charles Eliot (ed.): *Two Note Books of Thomas Carlyle* (London: The Grolier Club, 1898)

Ollier, Edmund (ed.): *Essays by Leigh Hunt* (London: Chatto & Windus, 1890)

O'Neill, Michael: *Literature of the Romantic Period: A Bibliographical Guide* (Oxford: Clarendon Press, 1998)

Paulin, Tom: *The Day-Star of Liberty: William Hazlitt's Radical Style* (London: Faber & Faber, 1998)

Pickering, Leslie P.: *Lord Byron, Leigh Hunt and The Liberal* (London: Drane's, 1925)

Powell, Thomas: *The Living Authors of England* (New York, 1849)

Priestley, J.B. (ed.): *Essayists Past and Present: a Selection of English Essayists* (London: Herbert Jenkins, 1925)

Procter, Bryan Waller (Barry Cornwall): *An Autobiographical Fragment and*

Biographical Notes (etc) (London: Bell, 1877)

Prothero, Rowland E. (ed.), *The Works of Lord Byron: Letters and Journals*, 6 vols. (London: Murray, 1898–1901)

Quennell, Peter: *Byron in Italy* (London: Collins, 1941)

Reiman, Donald H. (ed.): *Shelley and his Circle 1773–1882* vols. 5–10 (Cambridge: Harvard University Press, vols. 5–6, 1973; vols. 7–8, 1986; vols. 9–10, ed. with Doucet Devin Fischer, 2002)

—— (ed.) *The Romantics Reviewed: Contemporary Reviews of British Romantic Writers*, 3 vols. (London and New York: Garland Publishing, 1972)

Ricks, Christopher: *Keats and Embarrassment* (Oxford University Press, 1973)

Roe, Nicholas: *John Keats and the Culture of Dissent* (Oxford: Clarendon Press, 1997)

—— ed. *Leigh Hunt: Life, Poetics, Politics* (London: Routledge, 2003)

Russell, Richard: *Leigh Hunt and Some of His Contemporaries* (Bridport: C.J. Creed, 1984)

—— *The Wider Family of Leigh Hunt* (privately published, 1989)

Sadler, Thomas (ed.): *Diary, Reminiscences and Correspondence of Henry Crabb Robinson*, 3 vols. (London: Macmillan, 1869)

Saintsbury, George: *A Short History of English Literature* (New York: Macmillan, 1898)

—— *Historical Manual of English Prosody* (London: Macmillan, 1923)

—— *A History of English Prose Rhythm* (Bloomington: Indiana University Press, 1965)

Sanders, Charles Richard: *Carlyle's Friendships and Other Studies* (Durham, N.C.: Duke University Press, 1977)

Scott, William Bell: *Autobiographical Notes of the Life of William Bell Scott*, 2 vols. (London: Osgood, McIlvaine & Co, 1892)

Scott, W.S. (ed.): *New Shelley Letters* (London: Bodley Head, 1948)

Seymour, Miranda: *Mary Shelley* (London: John Murray, 2000)

Shelley, Percy Bysshe: *The Complete Poetical Works*, ed. Thomas Hutchinson (Oxford University Press, 1905)

Smith, F.B.: *Radical Artisan: William James Linton, 1812–97* (Manchester: Manchester University Press, 1973)

Spark, Muriel: *Mary Shelley* (New York: Meridian, 1987)

Stillinger, Jack (ed.): *The Letters of Charles Armitage Brown* (Harvard, 1966)

Stout, George Dumas: *Leigh Hunt's Money Troubles: Some New Light* (St Louis: Washington University Studies, vol. xii, Humanistic Series, No. 2, pp. 221–32, 1925)

—— *The Political History of Leigh Hunt's Examiner* (St Louis: Washington University Studies, Language and Literature, No. 19, 1949)

Symons, Arthur (ed.): *The Essays of Leigh Hunt* (New York: Dutton, 1890)

Tatchell, Molly: *Leigh Hunt and His Family in Hammersmith* (London: Hammersmith Local History Group, 1969)

Thompson, E.P.: *The Making of the English Working Class* (London: Gollancz, 1964)

Thompson, James R.: *Leigh Hunt* (Boston: Twayne, 1977)

Trams, A. Francis: *More Marginalia: Based on Leigh Hunt's Copy of Henry E. Napier's 'Florentine History' 1846* (Cedar Rapids, Iowa: Torch Press, 1931)

Trelawny, Edward John: *Adventures of a Younger Son*, 2 vols. (London: G. Bell and Sons, 1914)

—— *Records of Shelley, Byron and the Author*, 2 vols. (London: Pickering, 1878)

—— *Recollections of the Last Days of Shelley and Byron* (London: Edward Moxon, 1858)

Whipple, A.B.C.: *The Fatal Gift of Beauty: A Dramatic Recreation of the Tempestuous Final Years of Byron and Shelley* (New York: Harper & Row, 1964)

White, Newman Ivey: *Portrait of Shelley* (New York: Knopf, 1968)

Winbolt, S.E.: *The Poetry and Prose of Coleridge, Lamb and Leigh Hunt* (The Christ's Hospital Anthology) (London: W.J. Bryce, 1920)

Wise, J. Thomas (ed.): *Letters from Percy Bysshe Shelley to J.H. Leigh Hunt*, 2 vols. (London: privately printed, 1894)

Wu, Duncan: *Romanticism: An Anthology*, (Oxford: Blackwell, 1998, 2nd edn.)

ARTICLES

Allentuck, Marcia: 'Leigh Hunt and Shelley: A New Letter': *Keats–Shelley Journal*, 33 (1984), p. 50

Altick, Richard D.: 'Harold Skimpole Revisited', *The Life and Times of Leigh Hunt: Papers Delivered at a Symposium at the University of Iowa April 13, 1984 commemorating the 200th anniversary of Leigh Hunt's birth* (Iowa City: Friends of the Iowa University Libraries, 1985) pp. 1–15

Bayley, John: 'Keats and Reality', *Proceedings of the British Academy*, XLVII (London: Oxford University Press, 1962), pp. 98–105

Blainey, Ann: 'The Courtship of Marianne Hunt', *Books at Iowa* 23 (November 1975)

Brack, Jr., O.M.: 'Lord Byron, Leigh Hunt and *The Liberal*: Some New Evidence', *Books at Iowa* 4 (April 1996)

Cox, Jeffrey: 'Leigh Hunt's Cockney School: The Lakers' "Other"' –

Romanticism on the Net, 14 (May 1999)

Crompton, Louis: 'Satire and Symbolism in Bleak House', _Nineteenth-Century Fiction_, vol. 12, no. 4 (March 1958), pp. 284–303

Dart, Gregory: 'Cockneyism', _London Review of Books_, vol. 25, no. 24, 18 December 2003

Dickens, Charles: 'Leigh Hunt: A Remonstrance', _All The Year Round_, 24 December 1859, pp. 206–8

Diedrick, Charles: 'Charles Dickens's Journalistic Career', _Dictionary of Literary Biography_, vol. 55

Fielding, K.J.: 'Leigh Hunt and Skimpole – Another Remonstrance', _The Dickensian_, vol. lxiv (January 1973), pp. 5–9

Fogle, Stephen F.: 'Leigh Hunt and the End of Romantic Criticism', in _Some British Romantics: A Collection of Essays_, ed. James V. Logan, John E. Jordan and Northop Frye (Ohio State University Press, 1966), pp. 119–39

—— 'Skimpole Once More', _Nineteenth-Century Fiction_, vol. 7, no 1, pp. 1–18

Garnett, Mark: '"One that loved his fellow-men": The Politics of Leigh Hunt', _The Charles Lamb Journal_ 97 (1997), pp. 2–8

Gates, Eleanor M.: 'Leigh Hunt, Lord Byron and Mary Shelley: The Long Goodbye', _Keats–Shelley Journal_, 35 (1986), pp. 149–67

Grovier, Kelly: 'An imprisoned wit', _Times Literary Supplement_, no. 5266, 5 March 2004

Harling, Philip: 'Leigh Hunt's _Examiner_ and the language of patriotism', _English Historical Review_, November 1996, vol. 111, no. 444, p. 1159

Hill, T.W.: 'Hunt–Skimpole', _The Dickensian_, vol. xli (June and September 1945), pp. 114–20, 180–4

Hunt, Thornton: 'A Man of Letters of the Last Generation', _Cornhill Magazine_, January 1860, reprinted in the _Cornhill Magazine_ (London: Smith & Elder, 1860), vol. I, pp. 85–95

Janowitz, Annie: Review of Nicholas Roe, _John Keats and the Culture of Dissent_ in _Romantic Circles_ (1998)

Kaier, Anne: 'John Hamilton Reynolds: Four New Letters': _Keats–Shelley Journal_, 30 (1981), pp. 182–90

Kucich, Greg: 'Leigh Hunt and the Insolent Politics of Cockney Coteries', _Romanticism on the Net_, 14 (May 1999)

Laplace-Sinatra, Michael: '"A Natural Piety": Hunt's Religion of the Heart', http://fido.bfriars.ox.ac.uk/allen/hunt.htm

Mahoney, Charles: Review of _The Examiner 1808–12_ (Pickering & Chatto, 1996) in _The Wordsworth Circle_, 28.4 (1997)

—— Review of _The Examiner 1813–17_ (Pickering & Chatto, 1997) in

Romantic Circles: Reviews (1998): http://www.rc.umd.edu/reviews/examiner.html

—— Review of *The Examiner 1818–22* (Pickering & Chatto, 1998) in *Romantic Circles: Reviews* (2002): http://www.rc.umd.edu/reviews/examiner2.html

Mizukoshi, Ayumi: 'The Cockney Politics of Gender – The Cases of Hunt and Keats', *Romanticism on the Net*, 14 (May 1999)

O'Neill, Michael: Review of *The Examiner 1808–1822* (Deguchi, 5 vols.) in *Times Literary Supplement*, 8 October 1999

Robinson, Charles E.: 'The Shelleys to Leigh Hunt: A New Letter of 5 April 1821', *Keats–Shelley Review*, 31 (1980), pp. 52–6

—— 'Shelley to the Editor of the Morning Chronicle: A Second New Letter of 5 April 1821', *Keats–Shelley Review*, 32 (1981), pp. 55–8

Roe, Nicholas: 'The Hunt Era': Review of Jeffrey N. Cox, *Poetry and Politics in the Cockney School* and Yasuo Deguchi, *The Examiner, 1818–22* in *Romanticism on the Net*, 14 (May 1999)

Sanders, Charles: 'The Correspondence and Friendship of Thomas Carlyle and Leigh Hunt', *Bulletin of the John Rylands Library*, 45 (March 1963), pp. 439–85, and 46 (September 1963), pp. 179–216

Scrivener, Michael: 'Romanticism and the Law – The Discourse of Treason, Sedition and Blasphemy in British Political Trials, 1794–1820', Romantic Circles Praxis Series, n.d.

Smith, Walter C.: 'Reminiscences of Carlyle and Leigh Hunt', *Good Words*, XXIII (1882)

Stam, David H.: '"A Glutton for Books", Leigh Hunt and the London Library, 1844–46', *Biblion* (Bulletin of the New York Public Library), vol. 6, no. 2, spring 1998, pp. 149–89

Thorpe, Clarence DeWitt: 'Leigh Hunt as Man of Letters', in *Leigh Hunt's Literary Criticism*, ed. Lawrence and Carolyn Houtchens (New York: Columbia University Press, 1956), pp. 3–73

Wheatley, Kim: 'The *Blackwood's* Attacks on Leigh Hunt', *Nineteenth-Century Literature*, vol. 47, no. 1 (June 1992), pp. 1–31

Wu, Duncan: 'Leigh Hunt's "Cockney" Aesthetics', *Keats–Shelley Review*, 10 (1996), pp. 77–97

—— Review of *The Examiner 1808–1822* (Deguchi, 5 vols.), *The Charles Lamb Bulletin* (October 1999), pp. 180–2

NOTES

Publication details not given below may be found in the Bibliography. Many direct quotations from Hunt come from his *Autobiography* (1850), as detailed in the first such reference for each chapter, unless otherwise specified. The following abbreviations are used:

AES: *Leigh Hunt's Autobiography: The Earliest Sketches* (ed. Fogle, 1959)

Auto: *The Autobiography of Leigh Hunt* (ed. Morpurgo, 1949). References to a two-volume work denote Hunt's original 1850 edition.

BLH: Edmund Blunden, *Leigh Hunt* (1930)

CLH: *The Correspondence of Leigh Hunt* (ed. Thornton Hunt, 2 vols., 1862)

CHP: Carl H. Pforzheimer Collection, New York Public Library

CRW: Charles Cowden Clarke, *Recollections of Writers* (1878)

HAJ: *The Autobiography and Journals of Benjamin Robert Haydon* (ed. Elwin, 1950)

LAB: Luther A. Brewer: *My Leigh Hunt Library: The Holograph Letters* (1938)

LHL: *Leigh Hunt: A Life in Letters* (ed. Gates, 1999)

LJB: *Letters and Journals of Lord Byron* (one-volume references are to Moore (1908); multi-volume references to Prothero (1898–1901))

LPP: *Leigh Hunt: Life, Poetics, Politics* (ed. Roe, 2003)

MTH: Molly Tatchell, *Leigh Hunt and His Family in Hammersmith* (1969)

SC: *Shelley and his Circle, 1773–1882* (ed. variously Cameron, Reiman and Fischer, 10 vols., 1961–2002).

SLH: *The Selected Writings of Leigh Hunt* (ed. Morrison and Eberle-Sinatra, 6 vols., 2003).

THC: Thornton Hunt: 'A Man of Letters of the Last Generation', *Cornhill Magazine*, January 1860

Epigraph (p. viii)

Zachary Leader (ed.), *The Letters of Kingsley Amis* (New York: Talk Miramax Books, 2002), p. 242.

Prologue

'unmistakably, one of the leading writers of his age': SLH, General Introduction, vol. I, p. xii.

'growing awareness of the significant contribution': Dart, pp. 19–20.

'embodied the spirit of his age': Kelly Grovier, pp. 3–4.

'our spiritual grandfather': Anne Oliver Bell and Andrew McNeillie (eds.), *The Diary of Virginia Woolf* (5 vols., London: Hogarth Press, 1977–84), vol. II, p. 130.

'William Blake first': LPP, Introduction, p. 1.

'The position of Leigh Hunt in our literature': Arthur Symons (ed.), *Essays by Leigh Hunt* (1888), Introduction, p. xiii.

'anything resembling' a collected edition of his work: SLH, vol. I, pp. xi–xii.

'alone among the leading writers of his age': Edmund Gosse, 'Leigh Hunt', *More Books on the Table* (London: Heinemann, 1923), p. 297.

a 'complete and uniform issue': George Saintsbury, 'Leigh Hunt', *The Collected Essays and Papers of George Saintsbury* (4 vols., London: J.M. Dent, 1923–4), vol. II, pp. 159–60.

'a careful life of Leigh Hunt': BLH, p. xi.

1: *'Fit for nothing but an author'*

'London's foremost necropolis': brochure published by Friends of Kensal Green Cemetery, www.kensalgreen.co.uk

'almost the first place in a history of prosody': George Saintsbury, *A History of English Prosody* (3 vols., London: Macmillan, 1910, 2nd edition, 1923), vol. III, p. 94

'no rival in the history of English criticism': Jack (1963), p. 323.

'our spiritual grandfather': *The Diary of Virginia Woolf*, vol. II, p. 130, quoted in Roe, 'Leigh Hunt: Interviews and Recollections, 1832–1921', LPP, pp. 214–32.

'foul, atrocious and malignant' libel: *The King v. John and Leigh Hunt: A Report of the Trial for a Libel on the Prince Regent* (London: Printed and sold by M. Jones, 1812) and *The Prince of Wales v. the Examiner: a Full Report of the Trial of John and Leigh Hunt* (London: Printed by and for John Hunt, 1812).

'The first room I have any recollection of': Auto, p. 14. All subsequent Hunt
    quotations in this chapter come from Auto, Chapters I–V, unless otherwise
    specified.
'black eyes, and his mouth': Procter, pp. 195–6.
'against her father's pleasure': THC, p. 85.
'a man rather under than above the middle stature': ibid., pp. 85–6.
'unimaginative' . . . 'anxious, speculative' temperament: ibid., p. 86.
read 'eloquently and critically': ibid., p. 86.
'It is with pleasure I inform you': LAB, pp. 2–3.
'humbly beseech your Worships': BLH, pp. 9–10. See also Blunden et al.
    (eds.).
'a fool for refining': THC, p. 88–9.
the 'inestimable advantage': Coleridge, Biographia Literaria, I, Works (7 vols.,
    New York: Harper, 1884, ed. W.G.T. Shedd), vol. III, pp. 146–7.
'full of puns and jokes': Burton, p. 78.
'a newly refurbished boarding house': Housey! (Christ's Hospital Newsletter),
    Autumn 2003, p. 5.
'At the age of fifteen' . . . 'long semi-monastic confinement': THC, pp.
    85–6.
'A man is but his parents . . . drawn out': Auto, p. 54.
'little of a Hunt' . . . 'remarkably straight and upright', etc.: ibid., pp. 87–8.
'proofs of poetic genius': SC 37, vol. I, pp. 275–6.

2: 'Needled & threaded out of my heart'

'You will perceive, Sir': LAB, pp. 3–4.
'Men grow in England': Auto, p. 114. All subsequent Hunt quotations in
    this chapter come from Auto, Chapters V–VIII, unless otherwise speci-
    fied.
'fair' . . . 'enchanting' . . . 'His severest trial': THC, p. 86. For Hunt's early
    loves, see also Auto, pp. 92–100.
'allowed to be beautiful': AES, pp. 46–7.
'To someone shy and vulnerable': Blainey (1975), p. 2.
'He undertook to rate me': quoted ibid.
'Beware, my dearest, dearest Marian': Hunt to Marian, 4 September 1806,
    LAB, p. 26.
'Do me the favour': Hunt to Marian, 26 April 1803, ibid., p. 20.
'you might have come down': Hunt to Marian, 1 August 1803, ibid., p. 10.
'The lover [Hunt] could not be content': CLH, vol. I, pp. 6–7, quoted in SC
    78, vol. I, p. 419.

'Dearest girl, refuse not': Hunt to Marian, 10 February 1804, quoted in
Blainey (1985), pp. 27–8.

'I am afraid it is all over': Hunt to Anne Kent, 10 February 1804, LAB, p. 12.

'vicious oetheopy', etc.: Hunt, *Critical Essays on the Performers of the London
Theatres* (1807), reprinted from the *News*, 9 November 1806, pp. 621–2.

'Nothing seemed to escape his eye or ear': Houtchens (1949), p. vii.

more than six hundred: SLH, vol. I, p. 25.

'opened the way for theatrical criticism by Coleridge, Hazlitt and Lamb':
LPP, p. xii.

'made actors wince': THC, p. 86.

'the greatest dramatic critic': quoted in BLH, p. 43.

'*A crowded house*': the *News*, II, 25 May 1806, pp. 430–1, reprinted as an
Appendix in Hunt, *Critical Essays on the Performers of the London Theatres*
(1807), pp. 17–21.

'Sweet-natured, homely Robert': Blainey (1985), p. 32.

'Now cannot you sit down': Hunt to Marian, February 1806, CLH, vol. I,
pp. 22–3.

'Your last letter is so good': Hunt to Marian, 22 July 1807, LAB, p. 31.

'I requested, with a manner that shewed my confidence': Hunt to Marian, 27
July 1807, SC 78, vol. I, pp. 417–18.

'You need not be jealous': Hunt to Marian, 22 July 1807, LAB, p. 31.

'those luxurious fellows, the Turks': Hunt to the Hunters, 12 July 1807, SC
77, vol. I, p. 414.

'I hope to God': Hunt to Marian, 18 October 1808, LAB, p. 36.

'Thereafter' . . . 'the vicissitudes of his life': THC, p. 86.

'I am not exactly agitated, but': Hunt to Marianne, 12 June 1809, SC 103,
vol. II, pp. 553–4.

3: *'The Prince on St Patrick's Day'*

'As noble a specimen': HAJ, pp. 126–7.

'I have never seen in anyone else': P.G. Patmore, quoted in BLH, p. 300.

'one of the most lamentable instances': *Examiner*, no. 2, 10 January 1808.

'England has ever sacrificed': *Examiner*, no. 4, 24 January 1808.

'A reform in parliament': *Examiner*, no. 44, 30 October 1808.

'noted for promotion' . . . 'a perfect Falstaff', etc.: *Examiner*, no. 43, 23
October 1808.

'The subject of Ireland' . . . 'What a crowd of blessings': *Examiner*, no. 92,
1 October 1809.

'Never, surely, was anything more calculated': *Morning Post*, 2 October 1809.

'particularly revolting' . . . 'His soldiers', etc.: *Examiner*, no. 140, 2 September 1810.

'excite the disaffection of the soldiery': *Report of the Proceedings on an Information filed ex-officio by His Majesty's Attorney General against John and Leigh Hunt* (Stamford, England: Printed and Published by and for John Drakard, 1811).

'Permit me, although a stranger': Shelley to Hunt, 2 March 1811, CLH, vol. I, p. 52.

'a yea and nay man': Auto, p. 265. All subsequent Hunt quotations in this chapter come from Auto, Chapters IX–XIII, unless otherwise specified.

'opened to my mind': Shelley to Godwin, 10 January 1812, quoted in Auto, p. 487 n8.

'He is a man of cultivated mind': Shelley to Hogg, 8 May 1811, Shelley, *Works*, vol. VIII, p. 81.

'all subjects relative to Wit, Morals and a true Refinement': Prospectus, p. viii.

'Reform of periodical writing': Hunt, *Reflector*, January 1811.

'found literature, poetry especially' . . . Leigh Hunt found the 'mild' Hayley: THC, pp. 91, 93.

'transformed the 18th Century magazine essay': see Saintsbury (1898), pp. 700–1.

'the ancestry of the magazine article': Kenneth Neill Cameron, 'Leigh Hunt', in Cameron (1973), p. 159.

'the weekly of the Radical intelligentsia': E.P. Thompson, p. 741

'the special sweetness' . . . 'strong yet delicately cut': Hughes-Hallett, p. 76.

'Friendship' . . . 'was a romantic passion with me': AES, p. xii; Auto, p. 83.

'inbred' . . . 'a loose grouping of minds': Burton, p. 5.

'What I would not give': Hunt, 'Wishing Cap No. II, A Walk in Covent Garden', *Examiner*, no. 844 (4 April 1824), pp. 210–11, republished in *The Wishing-Cap Papers* (1873), pp. 27–8.

'How often did we cut': Hazlitt, 'On the Conversation of Authors', *London Magazine*, September 1820, pp. 250–62; *Works*, vol. XII, pp. 36–9.

'very temperate and pleasant': LHL, p. 46.

'in his droll and extravagant way': Henry Crabb Robinson, Diary, 17 January 1812, in Sadler (ed.), vol. I, p. 370.

nine articles in the first issue, etc.: Kendall, p. 24.

'old, mad, blind, despised': Shelley, *Sonnet: England in 1819*, line 1.

'his follies and his vices': *Examiner*, no. 177, 19 May 1811.

'a native imbecility': *Examiner*, no. 179, 2 June 1811.

'among the high political men': Bentham, quoted in Stout, p. 5.

'I was at Mrs R's' . . . 'I referred him', etc.: *Examiner*, no. 219, 8 March 1812.

'threw caution to the winds' . . . 'raving in a madhouse': Burton, pp. 266–7.

'coughed down': THC, p. 91.

'Glory of the People', etc.: *Morning Post*, 17 March 1812.

'What person' . . . 'corpulent gentleman of fifty', etc.: *Examiner*, no. 221, 22 March 1812.

'Everything is a libel': Henry Crabb Robinson, Diary, 16 March 1812, Sadler (ed.), vol. I, pp. 375–6.

'The rest of this week': *Examiner*, no. 222, 29 March 1812.

'Do your worst!': *Examiner*, no. 226, 26 April 1812.

'in expectation' . . . 'When the names of the special jurors': *The King v. John and Leigh Hunt: A Report of the Trial for a Libel on the Prince Regent* (London: Printed and sold by M. Jones, 1812) and *The Prince of Wales V. the Examiner: a Full Report of the Trial of John and Leigh Hunt* (London: Printed by and for John Hunt, 1812)

'I feel somewhat anxious about the verdict': Brougham, vol. II, p. 72.

'Sir, you have most unaccountably': *Examiner*, no. 257, 29 November 1812.

'My disorder has been a bilious one': LJB, p. 120.

'I have made the requisite summaries': Hunt to John Hunt, 14 July 1812, Pierpont Morgan Library, New York; LHL, p. 21; SC, 214, vol. III, p. 99.

'The roles in their relationship had reversed': Blainey (1985), p. 57.

'Do not be alarmed': Hunt to Marianne, September 1812, LAB, p. 57.

'There is a green about it': Hunt to Brougham, 17 September 1812, CLH, vol. I, p. 61.

4: 'The wit in the dungeon'

'a libel tending to traduce and vilify the Prince of Wales' et seq.: *The King v. John and Leigh Hunt: A Report of the Trial for a Libel on the Prince Regent* (London: Printed and sold by M. Jones, 1812) and *The Prince of Wales V. the Examiner: a Full Report of the Trial of John and Leigh Hunt* (London: Printed by and for John Hunt, 1812)

'Knowing that what it is very proper': Auto, p. 235. All subsequent Hunt quotations in this chapter come from Auto, Chapters XIII–XV, unless otherwise specified.

'walked out and in furiously': HAJ, p. 183.

'Hunt gets his living': ibid., p. 147.

Leigh Hunt 'behaved nobly': ibid., pp. 159, 127.

'I am quite aware': Hunt to John Hunt, 14 July 1812, LAB, p. 89.

'remarkably clever' . . . 'his black bushy hair', etc.: ibid., pp. 142–3.

'Full of his fun': ibid., p. 102.

'a great pleasure': ibid., p. 183.

a 'scandalous and defamatory' libel, etc.: *The King v. John and Leigh Hunt*.

'Why separate two persons': *Examiner*, no. 267, 7 February 1813.

'I am almost envious': Marianne to Hunt, 26 April 1813, LAB, p. 61.

'cut off from all other': *Examiner*, no. 268, 14 February 1813.

'there was no other such room': Lamb, quoted in Auto, p. 243.

'Pray do not repress': Hunt to Marianne, 22 May 1813, LAB, p. 75.

'luxurious comforts' . . . 'But now to my letter': LJB, p. 183.

'pointed the way': BLH, p. 77.

'misanthropy': Marshall p. 2 n6.

'a thing whose greatest value': LJB, vol. III, p. 225.

'the most easy and discoursing manner': BLH, p. 77.

'if not agreeable': LJB, p. 183.

'there dropped in': ibid., pp. 183–4.

'not . . . conferring the least obligation': Hunt to Marianne, 25 May 1813, CLH, vol. I, p. 88.

'Hunt is an extraordinary character': Byron, Journal, 1 December 1813, LJB, p. 209.

'the rapid succession of adventure': ibid., pp. 209–10.

'It is my wish that our acquaintance': ibid., II, 296–7.

'to break the set cadence': THC, p. 93.

'a kind of prison salon of Whigs and reformers': SC 226, vol. III, p. 141n.

'the pride of a fellow-rebel': HAJ, p. xviii.

'I used to visit him': ibid., p. 186.

'an enormous debt of loyalty': Burton, pp. 267–8.

'Then the lantern, the laugh': Blunden, *Lamb*, pp. 64–5

'My father so entirely sympathized': CRW, p. 17.

'a pleasure that rendered the day': ibid., p. 190.

'Dear Sir, I shall be truly happy': ibid., p. 191.

'Extraordinary mind!': HAJ, pp. 200–1.

'He needed her more than she needed him': Blainey (1985), p. 68.

'very handsome note': Byron to Hunt, 9 February 1814, LJB, vol. III, pp. 27–8.

'the principal poetic vision of Napoleonic Europe': BLH, p. 83.

'In our admiration of its abundant beauties': ibid., pp. 84–5n.

'one foot in the aristocratic': Cox, p. 126.

'Pray tell me': Hunt to Thornton Hunt, 20 April 1813, CLH, vol. I, p. 84.

advising Cowden Clarke on Mozart's finest arias: for Hunt's list (omitted from the version of this letter at CRW, pp. 192–3), see Barnard, 'Hunt and Charles Cowden Clarke', LPP, pp. 40, 55 n18.

5: 'A new school of poetry'

'The whole business of life': Auto, p. 250. All subsequent Hunt quotations in this chapter come from Auto, Chapters XIV–XVII, unless otherwise specified.

'an universal and decent philosophy': Hunt, preface to the first bound annual edition of the *Examiner* (1808).

'a merger between political analysis' . . . 'If the political scene': SLH, vol. I, pp. xxxvii, lii.

'Addison to Hazlitt's Steele': Payson G. Gates (ed. Eleanor M. Gates), p. 39.

'convivial intellectual adventure': SLH, vol. II, p. 5.

'took the lead in identifying the beauties': LPP, p. 5.

'whatever is going forward': THC, p. 87.

'may have been ironic': Nikolaus Pevsner and Bridget Cherry, *The Buildings of England – London 4: North* (London: Penguin Books, 1998), p. 234.

'common life with tragedy': *Examiner*, no. 374, 26 February 1815.

'a tasteful sensibility': F.W. Hawkins, *The Life of Edmund Kean* (2 vols., London: Tinsley Bros, 1869), vol. I, pp. 315–16.

'Leigh Hunt has written': Byron to Moore, 1 November 1815, LJB, p. 289.

'You will be pleased to hear': Hunt to Brougham, 26 September 1815, LHL, p. 67.

'the safest thing': Byron to Murray, 4 November 1815, LJB, p. 289.

'You and Leigh Hunt have quarreled': Byron to Murray, 9 April 1817, LJB, p. 350.

'Leigh Hunt's poem is a devilish good one': Byron to Moore, 29 February 1816, LJB, p. 293.

'gem of great grace': *Edinburgh Review*, XXVI (June 1816), p. 477.

'I thought, and think very highly': Byron to Moore, 17 April 1817, LJB, p. 351.

'With respect to Hunt's poem': Moore to Byron, undated, LJB, p. 293n.

'I have read the story of Rimini': Hazlitt to Hunt, 15 February 1816, published by P.P. Howe, 'New Hazlitt Letters', *London Mercury*, vol. VII, no. 41, March 1932. Hazlitt's phrase *'This will do'* is an in-joke, referring to Francis Jeffrey's notorious review of Wordsworth's *Excursion* (1814), which began: 'This will never do.'

'tears with smiles': Hazlitt, 'Hunt's Story of Rimini', *Edinburgh Review*, no. LII (June 1816), p. 477. Hazlitt's authorship of this review is disputed; his original article was so heavily edited by Francis Jeffrey that it is often excluded from the Hazlitt canon and attributed to Jeffrey.

'present my remembrances': Byron to Moore, 31 March 1817, LJB, p. 347.

'I wish I could send you' . . . 'particularly flattered': Moore to his mother,
    3 March 1814, LJB, I, p. 309.

a 'refined Bacchanalian' poet: *Examiner*, no. 456, 22 September 1816.

'I had much rather Hunt': LJB, II, 255.

'You . . . are always right in *politics*': Moore to Hunt, LJB, pp. 471–2.

'We never, in so few lines': John Wilson Croker, 'On Leigh Hunt', *Quarterly Review*, no. XIV (January 1816), p. 481.

Clarke leapt to Hunt's defence: see Barnard, 'Hunt and Charles Cowden Clarke', LPP, pp. 43–5, amid previously unpublished letters from Hunt to Clarke.

'his face jaundiced with bile': *Examiner*, no. 434, 21 April 1816.

'When party feeling ran high': Thomas Medwin, *Conversations of Lord Byron* (London, 1824), pp. 402–3.

''Twill be an era in my existence': CRW, p. 133.

'revelled . . . in the liberty-loving': ibid., p. 16.

'the promise of which': Hunt, *Lord Byron*, vol. I, pp. 409–10.

'We became intimate': ibid., p. 247.

'dark and vivid': Dorothy Hewlett, *Adonais* (1938), p. 64, quoted in Motion, pp. 114–15.

'thickly from a central parting' . . . 'brilliant, reflecting, gay, and kind': THC, p. 188.

'unhesitating and prompt admiration': CRW, p. 132.

'a familiar of the household': ibid., p. 133.

'sympathised with the lowest commonplace': Motion, p. 116.

'ardent grappling with nature' . . . 'very striking and original thinker': Hunt, 'Young Poets', *Examiner*, no. 466 (1 December 1816), pp. 761–2.

'seeking to comfort Harriet': Seymour, p. 175.

'Leigh Hunt has been with me all day': Shelley to Mary, 16 December 1816, Works, IX, pp. 211–13.

'one of the most severe emotional crises of his life': Holmes, *Shelley*, p. 352.

'One more gentle, honourable': Shelley, quoted in Morpurgo, Introduction to Auto, p. x.

£1400, to 'extricate' him from a debt: SC 454, vol. V, p. 482.

'He was so kind as to listen': Shelley to Byron, 17 January 1817, *Works*, vol. IX, p. 219.

sat 'silent and still': Hunt, *Lord Byron*, vol. I, p. 449n.

'common stock in trouble as well as joy': Hunt to Shelleys, 10 July 1821, CLH, vol. I, p. 164.

'a new generation of poets': Motion, p. 108.

'This sealed his fate': ibid., p. 130.

'Very glad I am': Keats to Cowden Clarke, 31 October 1816, HAJ, p. 295n.

'prematurity of intellect and poetical power': ibid., p. 295.

'intoxicated . . . with an excess of enthusiasm': Severn, quoted in Motion, p. 117.

'sweet, small baritone voice': CRW, p. 16.

'Nature had gifted him': THC, pp. 88–9

'Damn him': Procter, p. 197.

'He dashed from Hunt to his lawyers': Gittings, p. 110.

'He was fond of being the idol': HAJ, p. 143.

'Terrible battle this, Haydon': ibid., p. 249.

'As to that detestable religion': ibid., p. 298.

'Accidentally meeting him': ibid., p. 312.

Both 'may have felt the necessary luxury': Gittings, p. 116.

'in a kind of obstinate self-justification' . . . 'even weaker': ibid., p. 116.

Keats's 'instinct' . . . 'written himself down': ibid., p. 116.

'There's Hunt infatuated': Keats to Benjamin Bailey, 8 October 1817, *Letters of John Keats 1814–1821* (ed. H.E. Rollins, 2 vols., 1958), vol. I, p. 169.

'What has become of Junkets': Hunt to Clarke, 1 July 1817; Barnard, 'Hunt and Charles Cowden Clarke', LPP, p. 49.

trying to raise money to keep Hunt afloat: SC 404, vol. V, pp. 227–8.

the huge sum of £1400: SC 454, vol. VI, p. 482.

'I walk out quite a buck again': Letter to Shelleys, 21–4 April 1818, SC 474, vol. VI, p. 554.

6: The 'Cockney' School

'Cockney school' attacks: 'Z' (John Gibson Lockhart), 'On the Cockney School of Poetry, No. 1', *Blackwood's Edinburgh Magazine*, vol. II, no. VII, October 1817, pp. 38–41. The complete series is reprinted in Reiman, *Romantics Reviewed* (1972), Part C, I, p. 138ff; II, p. 524ff; II, p. 627ff.

'Hunt far more compelling': Kim Wheatley, 'The *Blackwood's* Attacks on Leigh Hunt', *Nineteenth-Century Literature*, vol. 47, no. 1 (1992), p. 6.

'who, is in love with Hunt' . . . 'smuggering fondness': W.B. Pope (ed.), *Invisible Friends, The Correspondence of Elizabeth Barrett Browning and Benjamin Robert Haydon*, 1842–1845, p. 16 and Pope, ed., *Diary of B.R. Haydon*, II, 83 and 136–7, quoted in Payson G. Gates (ed. Eleanor M. Gates), pp. 59–60 and 243–4, 66n.

'vulgar descriptions, silly paradoxes': *Quarterly Review*, vol. XVII, no. XXXIII (April 1817), p. 155.

a 'copyist of Mr Hunt': ibid., vol. XIX, no. XXXVII (April 1818), pp. 204–5.

'live and die unhonoured': ibid., XVIII (January 1818), pp. 324–5. For a full discussion of Hunt's dealings with Gifford, see Wheatley, 'Leigh Hunt, William Gifford and the *Quarterly Review*', LPP, pp. 180–97.

'I made no answer to Gifford myself': Hunt to Shelley, 12 November 1818, SC 504, vol. VI, p. 740.

'indifferent to the *politics*': Hunt to Archibald Constable, 19 August 1816, LHL, p. 76.

'a visionary company' . . . 'This gathering of writers': Cox, pp. 5, 11.

'It is a great pity that people': Keats to Haydon, 14 March 1818, H.B. Forman (ed.), *The Letters of John Keats* (New York, 1935), p. 118.

'I have no doubt that he will appear': Barnard, 'Hunt and Charles Cowden Clarke', LPP, p. 49.

'Selfdeluder' . . . 'a great Poet': ibid., pp. 51–2.

The 'immortal dinner': Hughes-Hallett, pp. 72–3.

'to understand why': SC 579, vol. VII, p. 85.

'reducing poetry to a parlour-game': Gittings, p. 111.

'the best of the three' . . . 'a poor effort': ibid., pp. 189–90.

'full of the most sickening stuff you can imagine': Keats to his brother George, 17 December 1818, *Letters,* II, quoted in SC 504, vol. VI, p. 742.

'I have been very busy': Hunt to Clarke, December 1818, CRW, p. 200 (date supplied by Barnard, LLP, pp. 49–50).

oblivious to Keats's growing reaction against him: SC 504, vol. VII, p. 742.

'Hunt had given Keats a great deal': Jack (1967), p. 22.

'would probably never have been reviewed': Wheatley, p. 5.

'fast by the ribs': Hunt, *Examiner*, no. 584, 7 March 1819.

'little cage': Hunt, 'Farewell to John Keats', *Indicator*, 20 September 1820, no. L, p. 400.

'his eyes swimming with tears': Hunt, 'On the Suburbs of Genoa and the Country about London', *Literary Examiner*, no. VIII (23 August 1823) p. 117; see also *The Wishing-Cap Papers* (1873), p. 239.

a disgruntled servant of the Hunts: Maria Gisborne, Journal, 20 August 1820; Frederick L. Jones (ed.), pp. 44–5.

'patience at my lunes': Keats to Hunt, 13 August 1820, *Letters of John Keats 1814–1821* (ed. H.E. Rollins, 2 vols., 1958), vol. II, p. 316.

behaved 'very kindly to me': Keats to Charles Kent, 14 August 1820, *Letters*, vol. II, pp. 316–17, 321, quoted in SC 814, vol. X, p. 696.

'almost wholly benign': Bayley, pp. 98–105.

'Hunt has been here with me': Shelley to Byron, 9 July 1817, *Works*, vol. IX, p. 233.

'I cannot doubt that': Shelley to Hunt, 8 December 1816, *Works*, vol. IX, p. 210.

'When shall I see you again?' . . . 'I confess that. . .': SC 469, vol. VI, pp. 523–6.

'taught [him] something': SC 469, vol. VI, p. 530.

'By far the most interesting': Wu (1998), p. 620.

'Of all the ineffable Centaurs': Byron to Moore, 1 June 1818, LJB, II, p. 177.

'a very disgusting woman' . . . 'He, though a man I very much dislike' . . . 'Hunt imitated Hazlitt capitally': Morley (ed.), vol. I, p. 221.

'walking Encyclopaedia': CRW, p. 26.

'I see a good deal': Hunt to Mary Shelley, 25–7 July 1819, CLH, vol. I, p. 134.

'Hunt never gave dinners': Procter, p. 196.

as 'pleasant' a member: Hunt to Mary Shelley, 9 March 1819, CLH, vol. I, p. 128.

'Well, dear & illustrious vagabonds': SC 474, vol. VI, pp. 553–6.

'So Shelley has been hanging his head' . . . 'A letter from you': Hunt to Shelley, SC 504, vol. VI, pp. 739–40.

a better start in life: BLH, p. 139.

'He was a fine little fellow': SC 529, vol. VI, pp. 839–40.

'four or five hundred pounds': Shelley, Works, vol. X, pp. 10–11.

'ruin' him . . . 'what in the interval': Peacock to Shelley, December 1818, Works, vol. X, p. 19.

'doubts and difficulties': Hunt to Mary Shelley, 8 March 1819, SC 517, vol. VI, pp. 790–4.

'we would try to muster up': Shelley to Hunt, 27 September 1819, Works, vol. X, p. 86.

'Chaucer, as well as Milton': Hunt to Shelley, 20 September 1819, CLH, vol. I, p. 148.

'This is the commencement': Examiner, no. 575, 3 January 1819.

'the annus mirabilis': SLH, II, 173, quoting 'the phrasing on the book jacket' of James Chandler's England in 1819 (Chicago, 1998).

'You do not tell me': Shelley to Hunt, 14–18 November 1819, Letters, vol. II, no. 530, p. 151.

'Men in the Brazen Masks': Examiner, no. 608, 22 August 1819.

'this flaming robe of verse': Hunt, Preface to The Masque of Anarchy (1832), p. 5.

'Hunt was in England publishing': Paul Foot, p. 221.

a 'private room': Indicator, no. I (20 October 1819), p. 9.

'Lucrezia Borgia was hardly worse' . . . 'How you delight me': Hunt to Shelley, 23 August 1820, SC 814, vol. X, pp. 689–94.

'for they liked it enough': Auto, p. 281. All subsequent Hunt quotations in this chapter come from Auto, Chapters XVI–XVII, unless otherwise specified.

'to love everything': Sadler (ed.), vol. I, p. 255.

'We are writing': Hunt, Indicator, no. XXVI (5 April 1820), p. 202.

'I would come to you instantly' . . . 'beautiful impossibility': Hunt to Shelley, 28 August 1821, CLH, vol. I p. 167.

'irritable beyond anything': Marianne Hunt to Mary Shelley, 24–6 January 1821, quoted in Marshall, p. 19 n78.

'a hard bout of it this time': Hunt to Shelley, 1 March 1821, CLH, vol. I, p. 161.

'I consented at last with the less scruple': Shelley to Hunt, 1 March 1821, CLH, vol. I, p. 162.

'Leigh Hunt is a good man': Byron to Moore, 1 June 1818, LJB, pp. 379–80.

'these regions mild' . . . 'should come out and go shares': Shelley to Hunt, 26 August 1821, Shelley, Works, vol. X, pp. 318–19.

He 'absolutely refused': Holmes, Shelley, p. 716.

'a newspaper – nothing more nor less': Byron to Moore, 25 December 1820, LJB, vol. V, p. 143.

'That ever the time should come': Hunt to Shelley, 7 September 1821,

'We are coming': Hunt to Shelley, 21 September 1821, CLH, vol. I, pp. 172–3.

7: 'I never beheld him more'

'if he had recommended a balloon': Auto, p. 289. All subsequent Hunt quotations in this chapter come from Auto, Chapters XVII–XIX, unless otherwise specified.

'anxiously and daily': Mary Shelley to Maria Gisborne, 21 December 1821, Mary Shelley, Letters (2 vols., ed. Frederick L. Jones, University of Oklahoma Press, 1944), vol. I, p. 153.

'I was not sure whether. . .': Hunt to Byron, 27 January 1822, unpublished letter in the Berg Collection, New York Public Library.

'within 30 or 40': Shelley, Works, vol. X, p. 349.

'As it has come to this' . . . 'annoys me on more than one account': Shelley to Byron, 15 February 1822 (presumably, though dated 1823 by Moore, LJB, p. 573).

'with tolerable willingness': Shelley to Hunt, 2 March 1822, Works, vol. X, p. 361.

a total of £550: Marshall, p. 35.

'Be assured that there is no such coalition': Byron to Moore, 24 January 1822, LJB, p. 553.

'on his way to you': Moore to Byron (undated, c. January 1822), LJB, p. 553 fn.

'I have not the smallest influence': Shelley to Smith, 11 April 1822, *Works*, vol. X, pp. 377–8.

he had 'pledged' himself: Thomas Medwin quoted in Moore, LJB, p. 553 fn.

'connection with these people': James Kennedy, *Conversations with Lord Byron and Others* (Philadelphia, 1833), p. 135.

'a publication set up for': LJB, VI, p. 213.

'in time to have interceded': Shelley to Mary, 10 August 1821, *Works*, vol. X, p. 304.

'I would have written by Hunt': Hogg to Shelley, 29 January 1822, quoted in Marshall, p. 36 n39.

'the evils of your remaining in England': Shelley to Hunt, 25 January 1822, *Works*, vol. X, p. 349.

'To Leigh Hunt, Esq., In admiration. . .': Reproduced by kind permission of Richard Russell, Esq.

'It was at 2 o'clock': 'Letters from Abroad, Letter II – Genoa', *The Liberal*, I, p. 270.

'faculty of eliciting': Shelley to Hunt, 24 June 1822, *Works*, vol. X, p. 408.

'Between ourselves, I greatly fear': Shelley to Smith, 29 June 1822, *Works*, vol. X, p. 410.

'a gentleman in dress and address' . . . 'that and something more': Trelawny (1858), pp. 106–7.

'The most rural of these gentlemen': Byron to Murray from Ravenna, 5 March 1821 ('Observations upon "Observations" – A Second Letter to John Murray Esq on the Rev. W.L. Bowles's Strictures on the Life and Writings of Poets'), LJB, p. 711.

'You and [Francis, Lord] Jeffrey, and Leigh Hunt': Byron to Sir Walter Scott, from Pisa, 12 January 1822, LJB, p. 547.

'rushed into my father's arms' . . . a grand change had come over': Thornton Hunt, 'Shelley, By One Who Knew Him', *Atlantic Monthly*, Boston, vol. xi (February 1863), p. 190.

'Lord B's reception of Mrs H': Trelawny (1858), pp. 111–12.

'Lord B . . . has it in his power': Hunt to the Shelleys, 21 September 1821, CLH, vol. I, p. 172.

'Lord Byron must of course': Shelley to his wife Mary, 4 July 1822, *Works*, vol. X, 413.

'Shelley found Byron so irritable' . . . 'I have been kept day after day': Trelawny (1858), p. 109.

'I have consigned a letter': Byron to Murray, from Pisa, 8 July 1822, LJB, p. 563.

'Leigh Hunt is here': Byron to Moore, to Moore, Pisa 12 July 1882, LJB, p. 563.

'Utopian delight': BLH, p. 173.

'or you are lost' . . . 'as if in anger': Holmes, *Shelley*, pp. 729 and n56, 789.

'Is that a human body?' . . . 'The heat from the sun': Trelawny (1858), p. 134.

'a black place': Hunt, *Lord Byron*, vol. I, p. 18.

'What can fill up the place': Hunt to Vincent and Mary Novello, 9 September 1822, CRW, p. 217.

8: *'The wren and the eagle'*

'under the influence of gin and water': Auto, p. 331. All subsequent Hunt quotations in this chapter come from Auto, Chapters XIX–XX, unless otherwise specified.

'Both men had suffered seriously': Quennell, pp. 245–6.

'Was it for this': ibid., p. 249.

'not a single subject': Trelawny, *Records* (1878), I, p. 75.

'Leigh Hunt is sweating articles': Byron to Moore, from Pisa, 27 August 1822, LJB, p. 565.

'I see somebody represents': Byron to Murray, from Genoa, 23 September 1822, LJB, p. 570.

'I saw the waves foaming': Hunt to Bessy Kent, October 1822, CLH, vol. I, p. 191.

'What can I say of my present life?': Mary Shelley to Clare Clairmont, 20 December 1822, *The Life and Letters of Mary Wollstonecraft Shelley* (ed. Mrs Julian Marshall, London: Bentley, 1889), p. 55.

'I have a particular dislike': Byron to Murray, 6 October 1822, LJB, vol. VI, pp. 119–20.

'I am afraid the journal' . . . 'I believe the Hunt brothers to be honest men': Byron to Murray, 9 October 1822, LJB, p. 569.

'seldom just and never generous': Trelawny to Claire Clairmont, 27 November 1869, H.B. Forman (ed.), *Letters of E.J. Trelawny* (Oxford: Frowde, 1910), p. 222.

'Bitter indeed': Hunt, *Lord Byron*, vol. I, p. 18.

'I must trouble you': undated letter quoted in Nicolson, Harold, Byron: *The Last Journey, April 1823–April 1824* (London: Constable, 1948), p. 29

'Sympathy' . . . 'would probably have drawn': Hunt, *Lord Byron*, vol. I, p. 82.

'What a pity it is': Marianne Hunt, *Unpublished Diary of Mrs Leigh Hunt, Pisa, September 18, 1822 – Genoa, October 24, 1822* (London: Macmillan, reprinted from the *Bulletin and Review of the Keats–Shelley Memorial, Rome*, edited by Sir Rennell Rodd and H. Nelson Gayn, no. 2, p. 6.

'a great schoolboy': see also J.R. Lowell to F.C. Norton, 11 August 1855, C.E. Norton (ed.), *Letters of James Russell Lowell* New York, 2 vols., 1894), vol. I, pp. 237–8.

'one of the most uncompromisingly British matrons': Marchesa Iris Origo, *The Last Attachment* (London, 1949), p. 320.

'If Lord Byron appeared': Guiccioli, *Vie de Byron*, p. 1532 (Origo, p. 32), quoted in Marshall, p. 60 n55.

'Can anything be more absurd': Marianne Hunt, *Unpublished Diary of Mrs Leigh Hunt*, p. 7.

'I was very hungry': quoted in Rhodes Dunlap (ed.), Introduction to Hunt's *Captain Sword and Captain Pen*, p. xi.

'sick and weary to death' . . . 'Hunt is a bore': Theodore Hook, *John Bull*, no. 98 (27 October 1822), p. 781.

'thinking to find it full of notes': Theodore Hook (anonymously), 'The Cockney's Letter', ibid., no. 146 (28 September 1823), p. 309.

'If you have . . . purposely kept back': Byron to Murray, 22 October 1822, LJB, vol. VI, p. 127.

'My original motives': Byron to Murray, 25 October 1822, LJB, vol. VI, pp. 156–7.

'Murray . . . seems to stick at nothing': Byron to Mary Shelley, 14 October 1822, first published in O.M. Brack, Jr.: 'Lord Byron, Leigh Hunt and *The Liberal*: Some New Evidence', *Books at Iowa* 4 (April 1996).

My 'wife and six small': Hunt to Byron, 11 November 1822, LAB, p. 122.

'He is but too likely': Hunt to Henry Hunt, late November 1822, Pierpont Morgan Library, New York (V8c/MA 987).

'Of Hunt I see little': Byron to Moore, from Genoa, 20 February 1823, LJB, p. 572.

his 'unworthy' association with Hunt: LJB, pp. 572–3.

'the signal for the bloodhounds': Alexander Kilgour, *Anecdotes of Lord Byron from Authentic Sources, with Remarks Illustrative of his Connection with the Principal Literary Characters of the Present Day* (London, 1825), p. 47.

'You have perhaps heard of a journal', etc.: 'Letter from London', *Blackwood's Edinburgh Magazine*, XI (1822), pp. 237, 331, 363, 460, 463, 740–1.

'Byron, Shelley, Moore, Leigh Hunt': Wordsworth to Walter Savage Landor, 20 April 1822, Ernest de Selincourt (ed.), *The Letters of William and Dorothy Wordsworth. The Later Years* (3 vols., London, 1939), vol. I, p. 69.

'set of writers for the purpose': John Watkins, *Memoirs, Historical and Critical, of the Life and Writings of the Rt Hon Lord Byron, with Anecdotes of Some of his Contemporaries* (London, 1822), pp. 408–14.

'dart[ing] backwards and forwards': Hazlitt, 'On Jealousy and Spleen of

Party', *Works*, vol. XII, p. 378.

'Dear Lord Byron': Hunt to Byron from Albaro, 7 April 1823, quoted in BLH, pp. 183–4.

'With regard to my connection': Hunt to Byron, 8 April 1823, ibid., p. 184.

'I waited in vain for these arrangements' . . . 'In the meantime Hunt is all kindness': Mary Shelley to Jane Williams, July 1823, *The Life and Letters of Mary Wollstonecraft Shelley* (1889), pp. 80–1.

9: *'A hen under a penthouse'*

'Just as I find a companion': Mary Shelley to Jane Williams, July 1823, *The Life and Letters of Mary Wollstonecraft Shelley* (ed. Mrs Julian Marshall, London: Bentley, 1889), p. 82.

'strange enough': Auto, p. 368. All subsequent Hunt quotations in this chapter come from Auto, Chapters XX–XXII, unless otherwise specified.

'You rose early' . . . 'There are no gentlemen's seats': Mary Shelley to Hunt, 26 and 28 July 1823, *The Life and Letters of Mary Wollstonecraft Shelley* (1889), pp. 89–91. 'At Palazzi', p. 91, appears to be a misreading for Mary's anti-Byron joke 'or palazzi'.

more than fourteen hundred editorial contributions: SLH, vol. I. p. xxx.

'Cockney classicism' . . . 'Hunt is more fascinated': Wheatley, LPP, pp. 181, 195 n7.

'these kindlier days of criticism': Auto, vol. II, p. 99.

'Unable to perceive the smell of flowers': THC, p. 89.

Thornton Hunt deleted in purple ink: see SC 801, vol. X, p. 639.

'I have not forgotten Monday night': deleted by Thornton Hunt from Leigh Hunt to Bessy Kent, 2 July 1822, CLH, vol. I, p. 185. Letter no. 86 in CHP.

wishing he could 'send you': deleted by Thornton Hunt from Leigh Hunt to Bessy Kent, 7 November 1822, CLH, vol. I, p. 198. Letter no. 89 in CHP.

'Take a pat, madam': deleted by Thornton Hunt from Leigh Hunt to Bessy Kent, 20 December 1822, CLH, vol. I, p. 198. Letter no. 91 in CHP.

'touch up my portrait for you': deleted by Thornton Hunt from Keigh Hunt to Bessy Kent, 22 May 1823, CLH, vol. I, p. 206. Letter no. 94 in CHP.

'Why cannot I run underground': Letter no. 96 in CHP.

'I think the trees' . . . 'I give you then tenderest of embraces': deleted by Thornton Hunt from Leigh Hunt to Bessy Kent, March 1824, from Florence, CLH, vol. I, p. 213. Letter no. 181 in CHP.

'saturated blackguard': Mary Novello to Hunt, 27 July 1823, quoted in BLH, p. 196.

'Yes, now Hunt is there': Mary Shelley to Hunt, 9 September 1823, *The Life and Letters of Mary Wollstonecraft Shelley* (1889), p. 96.

'Accident introduced me': Lamb, *London Magazine*, October 1823.

'We had bay': Mary Novello to Hunt, 19 October 1823, CLH, vol. I, pp. 209–10.

'Tell me when are you coming?': Hunt to Bessy Kent, 2 June 1824, CLH, vol. I, p. 221.

'a sense of the wonders': Michael Laplace-Sinatra, '"A Natural Piety": Hunt's Religion of the Heart', http://fido.bfriars.ox.ac.uk/allen/hunt.htm

'not prepared to deny' . . . 'for an unusual length of time': BLH, p. 217.

'the *Liberal* volumes' . . . 'You will perceive from the accounts': John Hunt to Hunt, 19 September 1823, British Museum MS.ADD 38108, f. 308.

'in consideration of your former exertions' . . . 'your brother . . . manifested': Novello to Hunt, 15 December 1823, quoted in BLH, pp. 204–5.

'solitary as my nature is' . . . 'the death of Lord B.': John Hunt to Hunt, June 1824, ibid., pp. 205–6.

'the most perplexing papers': Brown, 17 November 1824, ibid., p. 206.

'dull as a hen': Hazlitt reported by F.W. Haydon (ed.), vol. II, p. 98.

'a good deal of truth in it': W. Carew Hazlitt, vol. II, p. 304.

'no books except mine': *Literary Examiner*, no. 1 (5 July 1823), p. 1.

'There are persons who': Hazlitt, in P.P. Howe (ed.), *The Complete Works of William Hazlitt* (21 vols., London: J.M. Dent, 1930–4), vol. VIII, p. 69.

'I have no quarrel with you': Hazlitt to Hunt, 21 April 1821, HM 20600, Henry E. Huntington Library, San Marino, California.

'I have always said': Hunt to Hazlitt, 23 April 1821, P.P. Howe, *Life of William Hazlitt* (London: Hamish Hamilton, 1947), pp. 323–5.

'He improves upon acquaintance': Hazlitt, 'Mr Moore – Mr Leigh Hunt', *The Spirit of the Age*, in P.P. Howe (ed.), *Complete Works*, vol. XI, p. 176.

'The dinner of the family': Brown (ed. Stillinger), *The Letters of Charles Armitage Brown*, p. 212.

'If you please, I will print': John Hunt to Hunt, BLH, pp. 219–20.

'I shall set him down' . . . 'Mud – mud is our object': ibid., p. 220.

10: *'A poetical Tinkerdom'*

'against expecting London': Mary Novello to Hunt, 19 December 1824. British Library Add. Ms 38108, quoted in LPP, p. 8.

'bosky bourns' . . . 'clouds of dust': Auto, p. 412. All subsequent Hunt quotations in this chapter come from Auto, Chapters XXIII–XXIV, unless otherwise specified.

'at odds with the thrusting commercial and imperial spirit of the times': Nicholas Roe, 'Leigh Hunt's Track of Radiance', LPP, p. 8.

'He didn't know what to do with it': George Smith, *Recollections of a Long and Busy Life*, unpublished MS in National Library of Scotland, pp. 9–10.

'He had no grasp of things material': THC, p. 90.

'Pleasant were the walks and talks': Mary Cowden Clarke, CRW, pp. 48–9.

'He is the only poet': Hazlitt (ed. Carew W. Hazlitt), *The Spirit of the Age* (New York: Bell, 1894), pp. 330–1.

'Each of them understood the others': see Procter, pp. 195–201.

'Have you seen the caricature': Procter to Hunt, 27 July 1826, quoted in BLH, p. 224.

'The familiar love between British botany and verse': BLH, p. 225.

'I shall be bound to pay you': Mary Shelley to Hunt, 30 October 1826, *The Life and Letters of Mary Wollstonecraft Shelley* (ed. Mrs Julian Marshall, London: Bentley, 1889), pp. 151–2.

'That house was to have become the property': Hunt, *New Monthly*, March 1825.

'Frustration must be retrospective': BLH, p. 228.

'Have you read Leigh Hunt's last hit': Haydon, quoted in BLH, p. 228.

passed on Hazlitt's testimony: Haydon, letter to Mary Russell Mitford, 10 November 1825; F.W. Haydon (ed.), vol. II, pp. 96–9.

'Sorry I am to write so much': ibid., vol. I, p. 111.

'The False Lion and the Real Puppy': unpublished in Hunt's lifetime; published in full in *The Novello Cowden Clarke Collection* (Brotherton Library, University of Leeds, 1955), pp. 15–16.

'the poor boy' . . . 'the over-sensitive soul' . . . 'embedded': Gittings, p. 4.

'It is unlikely' . . . 'that Hunt's rendering': BLH, pp. 234–5.

'Warped by the author's self-pity': Quennell, p. 255.

'cannot hide his weakness': Morpurgo, Introduction to Auto, p. viii.

'the miserable book': *Quarterly Review*, no. LXXIV, March 1828, p. 403.

an 'underbred' book: Locker-Lampson, p. 295.

'two hours . . . the other night': Hunt to Lord Holland, 3 March 1817, SC 387, vol. V, p. 118.

'The name of Lord Holland': Hunt to Lord Holland, 3 March 1817, SC 387, vol. V, p. 118.

'The family connexions of Mr Shelley': Hunt, *Lord Byron*, vol. I, p. 178.

'was not' . . . an ideological reformer': SC 500, vol. VI, p. 702.

'a "taint" in it' . . . 'free sentiment': Hunt, *Lord Byron*, vol. I, pp. 57–8, 168–9.

'It is painful to think': LJB, p. 184.

'decent to revenge upon the dead' et seq.: LJB, pp. 573–5.

'a good man' . . . 'martyr', etc.: Byron to Moore, 1 June 1818, LJB, pp. 379–80.

'the whole of this caustic': LJB, p. 380n.

'I am so much annoyed': Moore, Shelley to Byron, 15 February 1822, LJB, p. 573.

'The records and opinions': Payson G. Gates (ed. Eleanor M. Gates), *William Hazlitt and Leigh Hunt: The Continuing Dialogue*, p. 134.

'went so far as to say': Robinson, Diary, 28 September 1832, Sadler (ed.), vol. III, p. 13.

'Perhaps I err': BLH, p. 229.

'Sometimes music poured in': Hunt, 'Dreams on the Borders of the Land of Poetry', Harrison Ainsworth's *Keepsake* (1828), quoted in BLH, p. 229.

'his unlucky quarto was redeemed': ibid., p. 236.

Keats will 'be known hereafter': Hunt, *Lord Byron*, vol. I, pp. 442–3.

'I am at once the sickliest': Hunt, *Athenæum*, no. 3143 (25 March 1893), pp. 377–8, reprinted in R. Brimley Johnson (1896), pp. 136–42.

'My education was in one respect remarkable': Hunt to [Lord] Francis Jeffrey, 14 March 1833, Pforzheimer Collection, New York Public Library.

'great privation': Marianne to Brougham, 19 November 1830, LHL, p. 200.

'the same as ever': Betty T. Bennett (ed.), *The Letters of Mary Wollstencraft Shelley* (3 vols., Baltimore: Johns Hopkins University Press, 1980–8), vol. II, p. 131.

'What hope in it!': 'The Politician', *Chat of the Week*, 7 August 1830, New Series I, pp. 221–3.

'cheerful sentimentalism': SLH, vol. III, p. xiv.

'the sunny side of everything': Morley (ed.), vol. I, p. 255.

'This book aided Spenser': LH quoted in THC, p. 95.

'like that of a violinist parting with his instrument': Miller, p. 7.

'Leigh Hunt's sons, now young men': Mary Shelley, quoted in MTH, p. 58.

'My hand-in-hand companion': Hunt to G.J. De Wilde, 3 January 1838, CLH, vol. I, p. 304.

'sort of literary historical essay – a species of unconcealed forgery, after the manner of a more critical and cultivated Pepys': Thornton Hunt, THC, p. 93.

'Leigh Hunt's self-importance': A. Aspinall (ed.), p. 278.

'my sense of your great merits': John Stuart Mill, *Collected Works*, vol. XII, p. 359; see also Stanley Jones, p. 241, and Paulin, p. 51.

'a pleasant, innocent, ingenious man': Carlyle, Journal, 17 March 1832, Norton (ed.), p. 257.

'Leigh Hunt writes "wishing caps": Froude (ed.) (1882), vol. I, p. 264.

'continued abuse': ibid., vol. II, p. 29.

'Literary *men!*': Carlyle, Journal, 28 January 1832, ibid., pp. 250–1.

'There looks through him': Carlyle, quoted in MTH, p. 58.

'an experiment which I should hardly think': Hunt to Carlyle, 28 May 1833, Sanders, p. 112.

'We make an exception of him': Thomas Carlyle to Jack Carlyle, 28 October 1834, Carlyle, *Letters*, vol. VII, p. 327.

'a delightful house' . . . "fish" Chelsea': Thomas and Jane Carlyle to Jack Carlyle, 25 February 1834, ibid., p. 104.

their 'indescribable, dreamlike household': Carlyle, Journal, 24 May 1834, Froude (ed.) (1882), vol. II, p. 426.

'The Frau Hunt lay drowsing': Carlyle to his wife Jane, 17 May 1834, Carlyle, *Letters*, vol. VII, pp. 152–3.

'Let Hunt say what he will': Froude (1882), vol. II, p. 427.

'Hunt's household . . . Nondescript!': Carlyle, Journal, 24 May 1834, Froude (ed.) (1882), vol. II, p. 426.

'hugger-mugger, *un*thrift, and sordid collapse': Carlyle, Journal, 22 June 1866, vol. I, p. 175.

'continually sending round notes': ibid., II, p. 435.

'Hunt is always ready': Carlyle to Alexander Carlyle, 27 June 1834, ibid., II, p. 439.

'almost nightly': Carlyle, Journal, 4 June 1834, Norton (ed.) (1887), vol. I, p. 104.

'His house excels': Carlyle to Alexander Carlyle, 27 June 1834, ibid., vol. II, pp. 439–40.

'Dark complexion': Carlyle, Journal, 22 June 1866, ibid., vol. I, p. 175.

'His theory of life and mine': Carlyle to John Carlyle, 22 July 1834, ibid., vol. II, pp. 441–2.

'Hunt is limited': Carlyle, Journal, 26 July 1834,. ibid., vol. II, p. 444.

'What? . . . is it a portrait?' . . . 'And so . . . having no patience': Jane Carlyle to Margaret Carlyle, 1 September 1834, Carlyle, *Letters*, vol. VII, pp. 287–8.

'Mrs Hunt I shall soon be quite terminated with': Jane Carlyle to Margaret Carlyle, 21 November 1834, ibid., pp. 338.

'consolation': Jones (ed.), *Letters of Mary Shelley*, vol. II, p. 4, and *Letters of Mary Wollstonecraft Shelley* (ed. Bennett), vol. II, pp. 51–2, quoted in Payson G. Gates, p. 330 n176.

'Acid-tongued': Sanders, p. 94.

'sang, talked like a pen-gun': Jane Carlyle to Thomas Carlyle, 12 October 1835, Carlyle, *Letters*, vol. VIII, pp. 222, 224–5.

'chivalrous, polite, affectionate': Carlyle, *Journal*, 22 June 1866, Norton (ed.) (1887), vol. I, p. 174.

'animation . . . a "dangerous" man among women': THC, p. 89.

'Nelly' . . . 'jaundiced': original MS in the Carl H. Pforzheimer Collection, now housed in the New York Public Library.

'pray pronounce the word' . . . 'owing to the lesser animal spirits', etc.: Hunt, 'Pope, in some lights in which he is not usually regarded', *Men, Women and Books* (1847), II, pp. 35–6.

11: *'A sort of literary Robin Hood'*

'We have a kindness': Thomas Macaulay, *Edinburgh Review*, January 1841.

'I commence this journal': Marianne Hunt, 'A Letter and Fragment of a Diary', *Keats–Shelley Memorial Bulletin*, no. X, 1959.

'The inevitable dictates of daily life': Thornton Hunt, 'A View of Leigh Hunt's Intimate Circle', from an unpublished work entitled *Proserpina*, quoted in BLH, p. 359.

'I am sent to Coventry!': Marianne Hunt, 'A Letter and Fragment of a Diary', *Keats–Shelley Memorial Bulletin*, no. X, 1959.

'mismanaging, unthrifty wife': quoted in BLH, p. 258.

'the reverse of handsome': Thornton Hunt, quoted in MTH, p. 42.

'a well-intended but ill-advised treatment': Auto, p. 545. All subsequent Hunt quotations in this chapter come from Auto, Chapters XXIV–XXV, unless otherwise specified.

'surprising that she should have survived': MTH, p. 44.

'Fate joined [Leigh Hunt]': Thornton Hunt, op. cit., quoted in BLH, p, 358.

'After breakfasting with a friend': Linton, p. 116.

'What man . . . has praised him': Hunt to Forster, quoted in BLH, p. 261.

'Notwithstanding his abilities': R. Dunlap (ed.), *Captain Sword and Captain Pen*, pp. 75–81.

'imperceptibly, almost like a flower' . . . 'done no better': Blainey (1968), pp. 68–9.

'but with the select of the earth': Merriam, p. 29.

one who had 'long assisted': Blainey (1968), p. 72.

'A genuine young poet': Hunt to William Tait, n.d. (1832), LAB, p. 135.

'our best living poet': Hunt to S.C. Hall, 27 May 1837, quoted in Payson G. Gates (ed. Eleanor M. Gates), p. 172.

'The stream, or brooklet of poetry': Hunt to Talfourd, 5 August 1836, LHL, pp. 283–4.

among his 'favourite' works: CLH, vol. II, p. 56.

'the best poem I ever wrote': Hunt to Hall, 27 May 1837, LHL, p. 299.

'one of the most amiable': Blainey (1968), pp. 72–3.

'in all seriousness' . . . 'heard him discourse': Horne, quoted in BLH, p. 274.

'bad health, incipient old age': Carlyle, *Letters*, vol. VIII, p. 309.

'Mrs Hunt I never saw but once': William Bell Scott, quoted in BLH, p. 276.

'smarmy German manner': John Hollander, 'Robert Browning: The Music of Music', in Bloom and Munich (eds.), pp. 106–11.

his 'child-like' nature: Finlayson, p. 116

'The link of evidence is here lost': Hunt, *Tait's Edinburgh Magazine*, January 1833; reproduced in full, BLH Appendix 3, pp. 368–73.

his 'Cameronian rigour': Ashton (2001), p. 195.

'sweet and dignified': Allingham, 28 June 1871, Allingham (1907), p. 204.

'There is frequently a noble homeliness': Hunt, *Examiner*, 12 May 1839.

'an early recognition': Ashton (2001), p. 205.

'no longer *friendly*': Carlyle, Journal, 15 May 1838, Froude (ed.) (1884), vol. I. p. 145.

'Mr Hannay knew Carlyle very well': Hare, vol. V, p. 384.

'the only person, I believe': ibid., p. 384.

'homely manliness': Blainey (1968), p. 85.

'repelled' . . . 'Scotch, Presbyterian, who knows what': Carlyle, Journal, 22 June 1866, Norton (ed.) (1887), vol. I, p. 174.

'happily . . . I have next to nothing to do with Hunt': Carlyle, Journal, 15 May 1838, Froude (ed.), vol. I, p. 145.

'joined us about nine o'clock': John Hunter's diary for 4 March 1839, quoted in Smith, pp. 99–100.

'No! Force must be met by force': Linton, pp. 44–5.

'melodious as a bird on a bough': Carlyle, Journal, 22 June 1866, Norton (ed.) (1887), vol. I, p. 174.

'sweet influences of which the heavens': BLH, p. 257.

'Man, it's a sad sight': Horne (ed.), vol. II, pp. 279–80.

'wonderfully different in the street': Allingham, 11 July 1847, Allingham (1907), p. 38.

'If I ever have any doubts': Allingham, 21 August 1849, ibid., p. 55.

'several of the great men of the time': Allingham (1911), p. 1n.

'I was shown into the study': Allingham, 27 June 1847, Allingham (1907), pp. 35–6.

'I hate Dante': Allingham, 2 July 1847, ibid., p. 37.

'I was informed that the poet was at home': Coventry Patmore to Sir Edmund Gosse, quoted in BLH, p. 288.

'obliged to return': ibid., p. 275.

'Carlyle, Craik and I arose': Hunter, quoted in BLH, p. 278–9.

'seemed to hold my destinies': Macready, Journal, 29 January 1845, J.C.
   Trewin (ed.), *The Journal of William Charles Macready, 1832–1851* (London:
   Longmans, 1967), p. 121.

'Now, Hunt . . . if you will change': Madame Vestris, quoted in BLH, p. 279.

'I wish I could be in London': Horne (ed.), vol. II, p. 280.

'hearty, grey and a veteran', etc.: Haydon, Journal, 5 February 1840; HAJ,
   p. 575.

'Do tell me how you felt': Blanchard to Hunt, quoted in BLH, p. 281.

'It was really an exciting scene' . . . 'The success sufficed to inspire': G.H.
   Lewes, ibid., p. 282.

'too refined and purely beautiful': Linton, p. 38.

'The success sufficed to inspire': G.H. Lewes, quoted in BLH, p. 282.

asking Mary Shelley whether it would displease Hunt: LJB, pp. 742–3.

leaving Moore with a £6000 debt: Mumford Jones, pp. 206–8.

begging him finally to forget their quarrel over Byron: Mumford Jones, pp.
   313–14, quoted in SC 500, vol. VI, p. 703.

'when the lovely organ strain': Hunt, note end Act II, *A Legend of Florence*.

'Glanced over the paper': Macready, Diary, 24 November 1840, vol. II, p. 166.

12: *'A track of radiance'*

'I heard the other day': Macaulay to Hunt, 27 March 1841, *Letters of Thomas
   Babington Macaulay* (ed. Pinney), III, p. 369.

'ties up their independence': *Examiner*, 1815, quoted in Hughes-Hallett, p. 259.

'It is easy to say to a man' . . . 'A man can only do as he can': Auto, p. 437.
   All subsequent Hunt quotations in this chapter come from Auto, Chapters
   XXV–XXVI, unless otherwise specified.

'The period between 1844 and 1859': Charles W. Mahoney, Introduction to
   SLH, vol. IV, p. xiii.

'Should you ever meet with it': Hunt to Allingham, 27 September 1844,
   Letters to William Allingham, p. 5.

'It will . . . be a companion': Elizabeth Barrett to R.H. Horne, 3 December
   1844; Horne, 'Portraits and Memoirs', *Macmillan's Magazine*, no. 22
   (September 1870), p. 364.

'Ere long there will be a change': Mary Shelley to Hunt, 20 April 1844,
   Letters of Mary Shelley, Jones (ed.), vol. II, p. 218.

'I have just read of poor Haydon!': Hunt to Forster, 11–12 August 1846,
   CLH, vol. II, p. 89.

'In religious feeling': Horne (ed.), p. 318, in 'William Wordsworth and

Leigh Hunt', pp. 307–32.

'*the* Companion': Gilfillan, 'Leigh Hunt', *Modern Literature and Literary Men* (1850), p. 660.

'He had been in low water': BLH, p. 293.

'a most welcome and gratefully acknowledged compensation': THC, p. 94.

'seemed much amused': Haydon, Journal, 13 October 1832; HAJ, p. 502.

'not so much of a Maecenas': Macaulay to Hunt, 6 March 1841, *Letters*, vol. III, p. 365.

'I am sorry and ashamed': Maculay to Hunt, 27 March 1841, ibid., vol. III, p. 368.

'distress and gratitude': Macaulay to Macvey Napier, 30 March 1841, ibid., vol. III, p.

'I'm afraid I have no good news for you': Macaulay to Hunt, late August 1841, ibid., vol. III, 387.

'Hunt had outlived his generation': Morpurgo, Introduction to Auto, p. viii.

'the most constant and enthusiastic' . . . 'an easy, colloquial air': Blainey (1968), pp. 114–15.

'You may imagine': Hunt to Ainsworth, 12 December 1843, LHL, p. 417.

'Permit me to thank you': Margaret Smith (ed.) *The Letters of Charlotte Brontë*, (2 vols., Oxford: Clarendon Press, 1995–2000), vol. I, p. 586.

'I took up Leigh Hunt's book': Charlotte Brontë to W.S. Williams, 16 April 1849, ibid., vol. II, p. 202.

'illuminated the fog and smoke of London': *The Town*, 1848, quoted in BLH, p. 299.

'Hunt charmed him': Alexander Ireland, quoted in BLH, p. 324n.

'I guess indeed': ibid., p. 300.

'Hunt, with his "singing robes" about him': ibid., pp. 302–3.

'He saw everything through books': THC, p. 95.

'the dignity and poetry of the autobiographer': BLH, p. 303.

'honesty and eloquence' . . . 'habit of denouncing': Ashton, p. 309.

'by far the best book of the autobiographic kind': Carlyle to Hunt, 17 June 1850, *The Collected Letters of Thomas and Jane Welsh Carlyle*, ed. Charles Richard Sanders (Durham, N.C.: Duke University Press, 1970–), vol. XXV, pp. 97–8.

'right to be placed upon the same shelf': Kent (ed.), p. xi.

'I do not like to have received so much pleasure': Duke of Devonshire to Hunt, 15 June 1850, CLH, vol. II, pp. 137–8.

'brave and tender-hearted Leigh Hunt': Horne, quoted in Blainey (1968), p. 74.

'if one discounted' . . . 'a great and good man': Elizabeth Barrett Browning to her sister Henrietta, 7 July 1850, quoted in Finlayson, p. 297.

'I think he has been wronged by many': Elizabeth Barrett Browning to Mary
   Russell Mitford, 25 July 1841. Philip Kelley, Ronald Hudson and Scott
   Lewis (eds.): *The Brownings' Correspondence* (13 vols., Winfield, Kansas:
   Wedgestone Press, 1984–95), vol. V, p. 89.

'particular reasons for wishing to give his opinion': Hunt, *Leigh Hunt's Journal*,
   no. 1, 7 December 1850.

'I hope dear old Leigh Hunt': Thackeray to Allingham, 29–30 November
   1850, Gordon N. Ray (ed.), *The Letters and Private Papers of William
   Makepeace Thackeray* (4 vols., London: OUP, 1945), vol. II, p. 711.

'the best of all Leigh Hunt's children': Grundy, *Pictures of the Past*, quoted in
   MTH, p. 2.

Hunt's 'favourite' child: ibid.

'always too brilliantly discursive': Morpurgo, Introduction to Auto, p. xiv.

'the Signor of merit': Ashton, p. 324.

A self-styled 'glutton for books': Stam, pp. 149–89.

'Wherever one looks': Roe, 'Leigh Hunt's Track of Radiance', LPP, p. 1.

publisher of 'free-thinking' books: see Ashton, p. 324.

13: 'A perfect child'

'tell Leigh Hunt': Dickens to Forster, 11 December 1837, Madeline House
   and Graham Storey (eds.), *The Letters of Charles Dickens*, vol. I, 1820–39
   (Oxford: Oxford University Press, 1965), pp. 340–1.

'What a face is his': Forster, vol. II, p. 84.

'compare Hunt's writings on Christmas': BLH, p. 278n.

'Knowing fellow, is he not?': Dickens to John Macrone, March 1836, *Letters*,
   vol. I, p. 137.

'You are an old stager': Dickens to Hunt, 13 July 1838, ibid., p. 414.

'If ever a man of genius': Hunt, review of *Oliver Twist* in *Literary Examiner*, 24
   November 1838, pp. 740–1.

'Your books': Hunt to Dickens, 13 July 1838, *Letters*, vol. I, p. 686.

the 'excellent object': Dickens to R.H. Horne, (October–November) 1839,
   ibid., vol. VII (addenda), p. 808.

'only my own folks': Dickens to J.P. Harley, 7 February 1839, ibid., vol. I, p.
   506.

'treading on each others' heels': Dickens to Hunt, 12 May 1840, Madeline
   House and Graham Storey (eds.), *Letters*, vol. II, 1840–41 (Oxford:
   Oxford University Press, 1969), pp. 66–7, 66 n2.

'great esteem and regard': Dickens to the Committee of the Western

Literary Institution, 10 July 1840, ibid., pp. 98–9.

'I fancied there was the slightest possible peculiarity': Dickens to Hunt, 10 July 1840, ibid., p. 99.

'what Leigh Hunt would call': Dickens to Forster, 22 January 1841, ibid., p. 190.

citing Hunt's name: Dickens to the editors of four American newspapers, 27 April 1842, M. House, G. Storey and Kathleen Tillotson (eds.), *The Letters of Charles Dickens*, vol. III, 1842–3 (Oxford: Oxford University Press, 1974), pp. 212–13, 215n.

'when that leg of mutton': Dickens to Hunt, 19 July 1842, ibid., p. 273.

if 'a small one': Dickens to Hunt, 20 December 1842, ibid., p. 398 and n.

'poor, noble, honourable' Hunt: Forster, *Life of Dickens*, vol. III, p. 413 (dates corrected in Kathleen Tillotson (ed.), *The Letters of Charles Dickens*, vol. IV, 1844–6 (Oxford: Oxford University Press, 1977), p. 581 n2).

'Leigh Hunt called': Macaulay, *Journal*, vol. II, p. 354, quoted in Richmond Croom Beatty, *Macaulay: Victorian Liberal* (1971, orig. Norman, Okla.: 1938), p. 332.

'I made a present of it': AES, pp. 21–2.

'No man . . . was more generous': BLH, p. 347.

'He was incapable of feeling': R.H. Horne, quoted in BLH, p. 348.

'A friend came forward' etc.: HAJ, pp. 126, 191, 198, 235.

'No,' Hunt replied: Hunt to Trelawny, 14 July 1823, LAB, p. 148.

'You must not think ill of me': Hunt to G.J. de Wilde, CLH, vol. II, p. 61.

'No-one who knows and cherishes you': Dickens to Hunt, 24 May 1844, *Letters*, vol. IV, p. 131 and n3.

'worthy' . . . 'lustre': Auto, p. 268n. All subsequent Hunt quotations in this chapter come from Auto, Chapter XXVI, unless otherwise specified.

'I was not glad': Dickens to Hunt, 7 January 1846, *Letters*, vol. IV, p. 467.

'I don't know what I should have done': Dickens to Forster, 5 July 1846, ibid., p. 581 and n1.

'confirmed me in adopting literature': J.A. Davies, 'Leigh Hunt and John Forster', *Review of English Studies*, 1968, N.S. xix, 25–40, quoted in Graham Storey and K.J. Fielding (eds.), *The Letters of Charles Dickens*, vol. V, 1847–9 (Oxford: Oxford University Press, 1981), p. 77 n3.

'one of the most genial': Circular sent to the Friends of Leigh Hunt about Performances for his Benefit, June 1847. Copy in British Museum (Dexter Collection). *Letters*, vol. V, pp. 692–3.

'For the private information of the committee': Dickens to Charles Rawlins, 26 June 1847, *Letters*, vol. V, p. 101.

'A pleasant fellow, very busy now': Allingham, 27 June 1847, Allingham

(1907), pp. 35–7.

'*particularly disagreeable*': Macready, *Journal*, 29 January 1845, J.C. Trewin (ed.), *The Journal of William Charles Macready, 1832–1851* (London: Longmans, 1967), p. 242.

'Hunt is a *bore*': ibid., p. 222.

'made a profound impression': BLH, p. 298.

'Even in his hottest warfare' . . . 'If my friend Jerrold': BLH, p. 305.

'I cannot, of course, speak decisively': Dickens to Mrs Tagart, 13 June 1848, *Letters*, vol. V, pp. 337–8.

'If I could think of the kindest word': Dickens to Hunt, 26 November 1848, ibid., p. 447.

'Am I a beast': Dickens to Charles Knight, 4 September 1850, Graham Storey and Kathleen Tillotson (eds.), *The Letters of Charles Dickens*, vol. VI, 1850–2 (Oxford: Oxford University Press, 1988), p. 163 and n3.

'a child . . . I don't mean literally', etc.: Charles Dickens, *Bleak House*, ed. George Ford and Sylvère Monod (Norton, 1977), p. 64.

'In the affairs of the world': Byron to Murray, from Genoa, 9 October 1822, LJB, vol. VI, pp. 122–5.

'a little bright creature': *Bleak House*, p. 66.

'a mere child in the world': ibid., p. 65.

'I envy you your power', ibid., p. 67.

'the overweening assumptions' etc.: ibid., p. 86.

'Last Friday I was sitting down to dinner': CLH, vol. I, p. 269.

'Hunt's philosophy of money obligations': Forster, vol. III, p. 6, quoting Dickens, 'Leigh Hunt: A Remonstrance', *All The Year Round*, 24 December 1859, pp. 206–8.

'Browne has done Skimpole': Dickens to Forster, 9 March 1852, *Letters*, vol. VI, p. 623 and n7.

'You will see from the enclosed': Dickens to Forster, 17 March 1852, ibid., p. 628.

'I have again gone over': Dickens to Forster, 18 March 1852, ibid., p. 628.

'pained and perplexed': British Museum, Additional MS 38542. Reprinted by Luther A. Brewer in *Joys and Sorrows of a Book Collector* (Iowa, 1928) and *Leigh Hunt and Charles Dickens* (Iowa, 1930), pp. 29–30.

'Separate in your own mind': Dickens to Hunt, early November 1854, Graham Storey and Kathleen Tillotson (eds.), *The Letters of Charles Dickens*, vol. VII, 1853–1855 (Oxford: Oxford University Press, 1993), p. 460.

'Skimpole. I must not forget Skimpole': Dickens to the Hon. Mrs Richard Watson, 21 September 1853, ibid., p. 154.

'sickly large wife. . .' etc.: Carlyle to Alexander Carlyle, 27 June 1834, ibid., vol. II, pp. 439–40.

'I never in my whole life': Carlyle to his brother Jack, ibid., vol. VII, p. 327.

drinking some 'fragrant' coffee: *Bleak House*, pp. 523–4.

'He inculcated the study': THC, p. 89.

'had once been a beauty': *Bleak House*, p. 526.

'Look at the enclosed': Dickens to W.H. Wills, 17 July 1853, *Letters*, vol. VII, pp. 114–15, 115 n1.

'very poor. Page 591, first column': Dickens to W.H. Wills, 5 August 1853, ibid., p. 125 and n12.

'All good things, as well as all bad': Hunt, *The Old Court Suburb* (1855), vol. I, p. 75.

'O Heaven, Hunt's not lounging': Dickens to W.H. Wills, 7 August 1853, *Letters*, vol. VII, p. 128 and n4.

'the Incarnation of Selfishness': *Bleak House*, p. 729.

'spoiled child of the public': Auto, p. 39.

'I was sincerely congratulating myself' . . . 'What could it be?': Hunt, Additional MS 38542, British Museum, reprinted by Luther A. Brewer in *Joys and Sorrows of a Book Collector* (Iowa, 1928) and *Leigh Hunt and Charles Dickens* (Iowa, 1930), pp. 31–3.

'want of consideration': Forster, vol. III, p. 26.

'At Dickens's own house': Wilkie Collins, quoted in Brewer, *Leigh Hunt and Charles Dickens* (Iowa, 1930), p. 26.

'to have a little conversation with you': Hunt to Dickens, 8 November 1854, *Letters*, vol. VII, p. 465 n2.

'No, I won't come and take tea with you': Dickens to Hunt, 13 November 1854, ibid., p. 465.

'no less a person than Leigh Hunt': Dickens to Wills, 27 November 1854, ibid., p. 473.

'many remembrances' of Hunt: Dickens to Forster, 24 October 1859, Graham Storey and Kathleen Tillotson (eds.), *The Letters of Charles Dickens*, vol. VIII, 1856–58 (Oxford: Oxford University Press, 1995), p. 141.

'to shake your hand speedily': Dickens to Hunt, 31 January 1855, ibid., vol. VII, p. 518.

'I have been so constantly engaged': Dickens to Hunt, 4 May 1855, ibid., p. 608.

'but I hope you will not now think': Dickens to Hunt, 28 June 1855, ibid., p. 660.

'I don't know when I have talked so much': Dickens to Hunt, 6 July 1855, ibid., p. 668 and n3.

'Your letter has moved me': Dickens to Hunt, Dickens to Hunt, 11 June 1858, ibid., vol. VIII, p. 582.

'Believe me, I have not forgotten that matter': Dickens to Hunt, 23 June 1859, G. Storey (ed.), *The Letters of Charles Dickens*, vol. IX, 1859–61 (Oxford: Oxford University Press, 1998), p. 83.

'I little thought I should never see': Dickens to Thornton Hunt, 31 August 1859, ibid., p. 114.

'What I told Hunt': Dickens to Forster, 24 October 1859, ibid., p. 141 and n4.

'necessity of something being done': J.W. Dalby to Thornton Hunt, 19 October 1859, quoted in BLH, p. 317.

'one who knew Leigh Hunt well' . . . 'Above all other things': Dickens, 'Leigh Hunt: A Remonstrance', *All The Year Round*, 24 December 1859, pp. 206–8.

'An odd declaration by Dickens': Macaulay, quoted in T.W. Hill, 'Hunt – Skimpole', *The Dickensian*, vol. XLI, part 3, no. 275, 1 June 1945, p. 183.

'only helps to prove the rashness': A.W. Ward, *Dickens* (London: Macmillan, 1882), p. 120.

'nothing remained to Dickens': Forster, vol. II, p. 125.

'I wish I could think': Algernon Charles Swinburne, *The Swinburne Letters*, vol. VI, p. 161 (quoted in LPP, pp. 227–8).

'Nothing, least of all its verisimilitude': Sir Arthur Quiller-Couch, *Charles Dickens and other Victorians* (Cambridge: Cambridge University Press, 1925), p. 91.

'The name of Leigh Hunt has drifted': Stephen Leacock, *Charles Dickens* (New York: Doubleday, 1936), p. 164.

'bad taste is one of the diagnostics of genius': Hesketh Pearson, *Dickens: His Character, Comedy and Career* (New York: Harpers, 1949), p. 182.

'the irresponsible artist': Kaplan, pp. 315–16.

'Of course, only a semiliterate': Martin Amis, *Experience* (New York: Talk Miramax Books, 2000), p. 226.

'Everyone in writing': Dickens to Hunt, early November 1854, *Letters*, vol. VII, p. 460.

14: *'One that loves his fellow-men'*

Molly Tatchell, Leigh Hunt and His Family in Hammersmith (London: Hammersmith Local History Group, 1969) is the locus classicus on Hunt's final years, beyond Auto, Chapters XXV and XXVI ('Life Drawing Towards Its Close'), pp. 437–63.

'Reckoning that his family': Thornton Hunt, CLH, vol. II, p. 164.

'a corresponding saving in rent': MTH, p. 2.

'an intemperate woman' . . . 'In my opinion': Dr George Bird to Walter
    Leigh Hunt (Hunt's grandson), 27 June 1899, published in the Nation, 22
    May 1909, p. 75.

'stout, genial, motherly woman': Linton, pp. 46–7.

'a grievous trial': MTH, p. 5.

'morbid dread': Thornton Hunt, CLH, vol. II, p. 164.

'Alas . . . to be at Craigcrook': Hunt to John Hunter, 25 September 1855,
    CLH, vol. II, p. 228.

'Mrs Hunt [is] so helpless': quoted in MTH, p. 46.

'I have been in the midst': Hunt to Ollier, British Museum, Add. MS. 33,515.

'her rheumatism has never': Hunt to William Wetmore Story, Bulletin and
    Review of the Keats-Shelley, Memorial Rome, no. 2 (1913), pp. 78–92.

'should guard the hands': Southwood Smith, quoted in BLH, p. 327.

other reasons for Hunt to choose Hammersmith: MTH, pp. 3–4.

'one of the most dangerous coquettes': Grundy, Pictures of the Past, quoted in
    MTH, p. 47.

'The air can scarcely have been salubrious': MTH, p. 5.

'a little bowed, a little disheartened': BLH, p. 321.

'I own that I am disposed to say grace': Lamb, 'Grace Before Meat', quoted
    in BLH, p. 321.

'the object of this book' . . . 'The point for reflection': Hunt, preface to The
    Religion of the Heart, pp. xv and xx.

'natural piety' . . . 'not that all should think alike': ibid., pp. xviii, xii–xiii.

'like an old lady': BLH, p. 322.

'Ah, dear Hazlitt and Lamb': Hunt, The Dramatic Works of Wycherley, Congreve,
    Vanbrugh, and Farquhar with Biographical and Critical Notes, pp.
    lxxxviii–lxxxix.

'glistened with interest and enthusiasm': George Jacob Holyoake to Hunt, 25
    November 1854, LAB, p. 355.

'a very plain and shabby little house' . . . 'a beautiful and venerable old
    man', etc.: Hawthorne, pp. 459–69.

'gone to live a long way off': CLH, vol. II, p. 218.

'truly brilliant in conversation': Edward L. Pierce, Memoir and Letters of
    Charles Sumner (Boston, 1877), vol. II, p. 47.

'When he looked out of his dingy old windows': James T. Fields, Barry
    Cornwall and Some of his Friends (1876), quoted in MTH, p. 11.

'By a curious effect': Hunt to Ollier, 4 July 1855, CLH, vol. II, p. 203.

'I have just got a "railway wrapper"': Hunt to Ollier, 29 November 1853,

Cheney (ed.) (1976), p. 13.

'a cup of tea': William Bell Scott, quoted in MTH, p. 25.

'He would "take a fancy'. . . 'eating and praising 3 eggs': Grundy, quoted in MTH, p. 26.

'Physicians proclaim it': Hunt to Ollier, 31 December 1853, CLH, vol. II, p. 196.

'[Hunt] complained that there were two drawbacks': Carlyle to Lord Ashburton, 30 September 1854, MS Acc. 1138 National Library of Scotland, quoted in Ashton, p. 359.

'almost pathetic'. . . 'kind and pitying': Carlyle, Journal, 22 June 1866, (ed. Norton) (1877), vol. I, p. 175.

'romantic' and 'foreign-looking': Lady Ritchie, quoted in MTH, p. 31n.

'tall, dark, grizzled, bright-eyed': Locker-Lampson, pp. 294–5.

'Well, winter is now gone'. . . 'including certain powers of cross-country cabs', etc.: see Cheney (ed.) (1976).

'a book of stories'. . . 'a pure-hearted man'. . . 'there are fewer to speak ill': Dickens, 'By Rail to Parnassus', Household Words, vol. XI, no. 273 (Saturday 23 June 1855), pp. 477–80.

'Lilliputian bit of a house': Hunt to Charles Kent, 9 June 1858, LAB, p. 383.

'something of value'. . . 'declined receiving the money': J.A.V. Chapple and Arthur Pollard (eds.), The Letters of Elizabeth Gaskell (Manchester: Manchester University Press, 1966), pp. 596–7. See also W.W. Story's letter to Thornton Hunt, 24 March 1861, LAB, pp. 346–7.

'an old man with snowy hair'. . . 'He was then living in a small house': Mrs James T. Fields, pp. 10–11, 14–15, 28–9.

'a poet not remarkably strong': BLH, p. 326.

'she with a cough': Hunt to Ollier, 2 December 1856, CLH, vol. II, p. 206.

'three or four sums': Procter to Hunt, 16 May 1858, quoted in BLH, pp. 329–30.

'Lee was hospitalised for dementia', etc.: see SLH, vol. IV, pp. 291–2.

'Finished my third regular reading', etc.: quoted in BLH, pp. 344–5.

'The world became a duodecimo': ibid., p. 344.

'what the young ladies': Hunt to Procter, 19 December 1857, CLH, vol. II, p. 248.

'the history of it'. . . 'very acceptable': Sir Percy Shelley Bt to Hunt, 1858, quoted in BLH, pp. 331–2.

'I knew Keats himself': 'English Poetry versus Cardinal Wiseman', Fraser's, December 1859.

'Great men of advanced and unworldly natures': Hunt, The Occasional No XV, 'A Word or Two Respecting the "Shelley Memorials"', Spectator, 13

August 1859, pp. 834–5.

'He sat surrounded by his books': Thornton Hunt, CLH, vol. II, p. 164.

'There is a trellis on two sides': ibid., p. 228.

'Good children, and a great relief': ibid., p. 240.

'presided over by a nimble-fingered little nymph': Locker-Lamson, pp. 295–6.

'mercurial qualities': James T. Fields (1887), p. 383, and Mrs James T. Fields, p. 20.

'I shall not soon forget': James T. Fields to Hawthorne, 23 February 1863; Austin, *Fields of the Atlantic Monthly*, p. 226.

'the not very attractive suburbanity of Hammersmith': Hunt to Charles Kent, August 1859; Kent (ed.), Introduction, p. xliii.

'little articles I have written': Hunt to Lady Shelley, 19 August 1859, CLH, vol. II, p. 294.

'your bright countenance': Hunt to Lady Shelley, 24 August 1859, ibid., pp. 312–13.

'The sense of beauty and gentleness': Thornton Hunt, Postscript to 2nd edition of Auto, 1860, p. 452.

'We have real open fields': Hunt to Procter, August 1859, quoted in MTH, p. 52.

'before long': Hunt to Jacintha Hunt from Putney, 20 August 1859, CLH, vol. II, p. 312.

'I may chance, some quiet day': Hunt, *Literary Examiner*, no. II, 12 July 1823, p. 22.

'uttering inquiries and messages of affection': THC, p. 87.

'So gentle was the final approach': Thornton Hunt, Postscript to Auto, 1860 edition, p. 452.

'simply exhaustion': ibid.

EPILOGUE

'The world grows empty': Clarke, 'On Hearing of Leigh Hunt's Death', CRW, pp. 271–2.

'What a treasure': Hunt, 'My Books', *Literary Examiner*, no. II (12 July 1823) p. 22.

'Some people will be surprised': *West London Observer*, Saturday 3 September, 1859, quoted in MTH, p. 85.

'His silence': Forster to Thornton Hunt, 17 November 1859, LAB, p. 249.

'Poor poet!' . . . 'People said that': Locker-Lampson, pp. 297–8.

'Leigh Hunt belonged essentially': THC, pp. 85–95.

'Those are poems of a decisive character': BLH, p. 339.

'no sufficiently strong objection': Dickens to Thornton Hunt, 5 August 1861, letter shown by Luther A. Brewer to Blunden, BLH, p. 340n.

'locked up in Florence' . . . 'full of intimate talk': Browning to Isa Blagden, 18 June 1862, quoted in Finlayson, p. 514.

'monkey-face': W.J. Linton, quoted in MTH, p. 68.

'Have been agitated and distressed' . . . 'There is something ludicrous': Anna T. Kitchell, *George Lewes and George Eliot* (London, 1933), quoted in MTH, p. 70.

'He was . . . a gentleman and a scholar': Thornton Hunt, 'A View of Leigh Hunt's Intimate Circle', from Proserpina, unpublished, quoted in BLH, p. 358.

'so sunny a nature': Forster, vol. III, p. 6n.

'qualities which make a man of genius': Edmund Ollier, Introduction to *Essays by Leigh Hunt* (1890), pp. xxx–xxxi.

'a fine kind of man: Allingham, 7 February 1868, Allingham (1907), p. 172.

'what a fine thing . . . to abolish Hell': Allingham, 30 June 1873, ibid., p. 226.

'Why did you put such books': Allingham, 3 November 1888, ibid., pp. 381–2.

'likely to be honoured with more love from posterity': Horne, vol. I, p. 319.

'his idealizing faculty': BLH, pp. 341–2.

'somewhat too plump' . . . 'when circumstance seemed to stretch': ibid., p. 342.

'Had there been no Elia . . . Hunt lived a Romantic': Morpurgo, Introduction to Auto, pp. xiii–xviii.

'many admirable qualities': Quennell, p. 232.

'both famous and infamous': James R. Thompson, pp. 18–19.

'the last survivor of a race of giants': Blainey (1985), p. 191.

'grossly underrated': Edgecombe, pp. 9–13.

'in the love and camaraderie of the Hunt circle': Cox, p. 225.

'one of the most energetic': Wu (1998), p. 620.

'Wherever one looks' . . . 'the domestic, suburban milieu': LPP, pp. 1 and xii.

'editor, reviewer, critic', etc. . . . 'a far more important and compelling figure': SLH, General Introduction, vol. I, p. xix.

INDEX

Leigh Hunt is referred to as LH. Works by authors other than LH are credited in brackets after the title.